Adoption in America

Adoption in America

HISTORICAL PERSPECTIVES

Edited by E. Wayne Carp

THE UNIVERSITY OF MICHIGAN PRESS

Ann Arbor

2005   2004   2003   2002   4   3   2   1

A CIP catalog record for this book is available from the British Library.

Library of Congress Cataloging-in-Publication Data

Adoption in America : historical perspectives / edited by E. Wayne
    Carp.
        p.   cm.
    Includes index.
    ISBN 0-472-10999-5 (Cloth : alk. paper)
    1. Adoption—United States—History.   I. Carp, E. Wayne, 1946–

HV875.55 .A3642   2002
362.73'4'0973—dc21   2002009737

ACKNOWLEDGMENTS: *Grateful acknowledgment is made to the
following publishers and journals for permission to reprint this material:*

The essay, "What's Love Got to Do with It," is derived from "Artificial
Families: The Politics of Adoption," chapter 6 in *Friends of the Family:
The English Home and Its Guardians, 1850–1940,* by George K.
Behlmer, copyright 1998 by the Board of Trustees of the Leland
Stanford Junior University. Material from *Friends of the Family* is used
here with the permission of the publishers, Stanford University Press.

Parts of the introduction are derived from *Family Matters: Secrecy and
Disclosure in the History of Adoption,* by E. Wayne Carp, copyright 1998
by the President and Fellows of Harvard University, and reprinted with
permission of Harvard University Press.

Contents

Introduction

A Historical Overview of American Adoption

E. Wayne Carp

Adoption touches almost every conceivable aspect of American society and culture. Adoption commands our attention because of the enormous number of people who have a direct, intimate connection to it—some experts put the number as high as six out of every ten Americans.[1] Others estimate that about one million children in the United States live with adoptive parents and that 2 to 4 percent of American families include an adopted child.[2] According to incomplete 1992 estimates, a total of 126,951 domestic adoptions occurred, 53,525 of them (42 percent) kinship or stepparent adoptions.[3] Because of the dearth of healthy white infants for adoption, 18,477 adoptions in 2000 were intercountry adoptions, with slightly more than half of those children coming from Russia and China.[4] In short, adoption is a ubiquitous social institution in American society, creating invisible relationships with biological and adoptive kin that touch far more people than we imagine.

Any social organization that touches so many lives in such a profound way is bound to be complicated. Modern adoption is no exception. That is why it is so important to have a historical perspective on this significant social and legal institution. Newspapers, television news shows, and magazines frequently carry stories about various facets of adoption. Numerous online chat rooms and listservs focus on issues related to the subject. There is a reason for this prominence of adoption. While raising any family is inherently stressful, adoption is filled with additional tensions that are unique to the adoptive relationship. From the moment they decide they wish to adopt a child, couples begin to confront a series of challenges. First comes the problem of state regulation. A host of state laws govern every aspect of legal adoptions: who may adopt, who may be adopted, the persons who must consent to the adoption, the form the adoption petition must take, the notice of investigation and formal hearing of the adoption petition, the effect of the adoption decree, the procedure for appeal, the confidential nature of the hearings and records in adoption proceedings, the issuance of new birth certificates, and adoption subsidy payments.[5] Second, since World War II, the entire edifice of modern adoption has been enveloped in secrecy. Records of adoption proceedings are confidential, closed both to the public and to all the parties involved in the adoption: birth parents, adoptees, and adoptive parents. Third, in a nation that sanctifies blood kinship, adoptive families and adoptees are stigmatized because of their lack of biological relationship.

With the onset of World War II, a revolution began in the world of adoption that only a historical perspective can explain. A few examples will illustrate this point. In reaction to the stigmatization, rationalization, and secrecy associated with adoption, the adoptee search movement emerged and began to demand the opening of adoption records. Opposing these adoptees, some birth mothers argued that they were promised secrecy when they relinquished their children for adoption and that abrogating that promise constituted an invasion of privacy.[6] Since World War II, intercountry adoptions have increased tremendously, but critics have denounced such adoptions as a shameful admission of a nation's inability to care for its own people, exploitative of its poorest class, destructive of children's cultural and ethnic heritage, and riven by baby-selling scandals.[7] Since the mid–nineteenth century, formal adoption—the legal termination of the birth parents' (traditionally defined as a heterosexual couple) parental rights and the taking into the home of a child—has been the way Americans have created substitute families. But nontraditional families are becoming more common. Thirty percent of adoptive parents are single mothers,[8] and gay and lesbian couples are increasingly winning the legal right to become adoptive parents.[9] And as an outgrowth of in vitro fertilization technology, researchers have developed "embryo adoption," where an infertile couple can adopt a donated frozen embryo, bringing into question the very meaning of the institution of adoption. The embryo is implanted into the uterus of the adopting mother, who then gestates and gives birth to the baby. Embryo adoption obviates the need for legal adoption because many state laws maintain that a woman who gives birth to a child is the biological parent.[10] The growth of assisted reproductive technologies, along with almost every aspect of modern adoption—whether the state's intervention into the family or removal of children from their country of origin—raises profound emotional and ethical considerations that only the history of adoption can begin to illuminate.

In light of the potential richness of the topic, it is surprising that there have been no comprehensive histories of adoption in the United States and that scholars generally have neglected the topic.[11] This lacuna results in part from the fact that the primary sources necessary for writing such a history—adoption case records—have been sealed by tradition and state law. For professional historians, this has been an almost insurmountable barrier: no sources, no history.[12] Consequently, one of the primary purposes of this book is to draw attention to the topic of adoption and demonstrate its richness and complexity as a subject for research. A second purpose is to showcase innovative scholarship on the topic of adoption. The book also seeks to lay an empirical foundation of historical knowledge for future studies. Finally, the history of adoption is an orphan, ignored and neglected in the major fields of family and childhood history. These essays are offered as the beginning of a self-contained subfield of history—a declaration of independence, if you will—that will shed light on the main currents of American social history and public policy such as definitions of family, children's rights, and the growth and effect of state intervention in individual and family life.

Throughout American history, adoption—generally viewed as an inferior type of kinship relation—has been shaped by the nation's waxing and waning attachment to biological kinship and by demographic trends, consequences of primitive legal and environmental circumstances during the seventeenth and eighteenth centuries; of disease, civil war, industrialization, urbanization, and immigration in the nineteenth century; and of the Great Depression, World War II, and changes in sexual mores during the twentieth century. These upheavals in American history have resulted in the growth of child-centered state and federal laws governing adoption, the standardization and professionalization of adoption practices, the increasing trend away from strict matching criteria, the broadening definition of "adoptable" children, and the emergence of protest movements against sealed adoption records.

Although colonial Americans derived their culture and laws from England, they departed from English practices in the area of adoption. English common law did not recognize adoption. English legal opposition to adoption stemmed from a desire to protect the property rights of blood relatives in cases of inheritance, a moral dislike of illegitimacy, and the availability of other quasi-adoptive devices such as apprenticeship and voluntary transfers. Consequently, England did not enact its first adoption statute until 1926.[13] In contrast, what is noteworthy about the history of adoption in America is that at its inception, colonists were less preoccupied with the primacy of biological kinship, practicing adoption on a limited scale and frequently placing children out as apprentices in what would today be called foster care. The fluid boundaries between consanguine and nonconsanguine families in colonial America led in some cases to the informal adoption of children, particularly in Puritan Massachusetts and Dutch New York.[14]

Adoption became more common in the early nineteenth century. Historian Susan L. Porter's essay, "A Good Home: Indenture and Adoption in Nineteenth-Century Orphanages," focuses on four private nonsectarian Protestant orphan asylums between 1800 and 1820 and discovers that the female managers "embraced adoption as one means of solving their difficulties with the indenture system." But adoption did not emerge as the preferred system of child care in the early nineteenth century because elite families with whom the children were placed often treated them as servants rather than family members. This experience led the female managers to favor blood relatives when considering child placement. Porter also sheds light on the demographics of adopted children and adoptive parents. She finds that few of the children were very young and that most parents were middle class rather than wealthy, did not have biological children, and generally preferred girls. Most significantly, Porter finds that rather than the happy, successful adoption outcomes often portrayed by those favoring adoption, 20 percent of adopted children had negative family experiences. Asylum managers' experience with adoption led them to conclude that it "could never replace the natural home." Like early-twentieth-century professional social workers, these nineteenth-century orphan managers came to view adoption in casework terms. The best solution for the orphanage was to place the child with blood relatives, but when that was not possible, adoption was considered.

In the mid–nineteenth century, the number of formal legal adoptions increased, though it is impossible to know precisely by how much. Many of these adoptions were enacted by state legislatures by means of private bills passed at the request of parents who desired name changes for their children. In Massachusetts between 1781 and 1851, the General Court enacted 101 private name-change acts, a dramatic rise from the 4 that took place during the previous century.[15]

The increased incidence of private legislation legalizing informal adoptions reflected profound changes occurring in U.S. society, especially in the North. By the mid–nineteenth century, large-scale immigration, urbanization, and the advent of the factory system and wage labor had led colonial America's compact, stable, agricultural communities to give way to crowded, sprawling, coastal cities. One effect of these wrenching economic and social transformations was that urban and rural poverty became major problems. Consequently, humanitarian and religious child welfare reformers all over the United States turned to large-scale institutions such as public almshouses and private orphanages to reduce the expense of poor relief and, with utopian expectations, to reform, rehabilitate, and educate paupers.[16] The adoption of children increased slightly with the founding of these institutions. In the first forty-five years of its existence, for example, the Boston Female Asylum adopted out 4.9 percent of its children.[17]

In the decades that followed, child welfare reformers severely criticized almshouses and orphanages for their expensiveness, rigid routines, harsh discipline, and failure to produce independent and hardworking children. Influenced by the child-development theories of John Locke and Horace Bushnell, these reformers extolled "God's orphanage"—the family—over the institution's artificial environment and attributed to the family the ability to produce at little expense sociable, independent, and industrious citizens.[18] The most influential institution in the new movement toward home placement was the New York's Children's Aid Society (CAS), founded in 1853 by the Reverend Charles Loring Brace, a transplanted New Englander and graduate of Yale Divinity School. During the following forty years, the CAS placed out eighty-four thousand eastern children on "orphan trains" in the western states of Michigan, Ohio, Indiana, Iowa, Missouri, and Kansas. Some of these children were adopted, though exact numbers are unknown.[19]

The large-scale placing-out movement inaugurated by the widely imitated CAS had enormous consequences for the history of adoption. The origins of America's first adoption laws can be traced to the increase in the number of middle-class farmers desiring to legalize the addition of children to their families.[20] By the mid–nineteenth century, state legislatures began enacting the first general adoption statutes, designed to ease the legislative burden caused by private adoption acts and to clarify inheritance rights. These general adoption statutes, first passed in Mississippi in 1846 and Texas in 1850 (both states that had once been subject to France or Spain), were influenced by the civil law tradition embodied in the Napoleonic Code. However, these statutes merely provided a legal procedure "to authenticate and make a public record of private adoption agreements," analogous to recording a deed for a piece of land.[21]

In addition to adoption by deed, state legislatures began to enact a second type of general adoption statute. Lawmakers were influenced by profound changes in domestic-relations law, particularly regarding child custody law. Postrevolutionary republican sentiment of equality toward the family coupled with judicial discretion destroyed traditional paternalistic custody rules, grounded in Anglo-American law, that granted fathers an almost unlimited right to their minor legitimate children. Increasingly, the primacy of paternal custody rights was undermined by a judicial disposition to view women with a special capacity for moral and religious leadership and child rearing.[22] This resulted in one of the two most important elements in the development of the modern law of child custody, the introduction of maternal-paternal equality.[23] The second important doctrinal development was the codification by the 1840s of the "best interests of the child" standard, which state judges increasingly used to settle custody disputes. Four principles were associated with this child welfare doctrine. The first stipulated that children of "tender age" or delicate health ought to be placed in the woman's custody.[24] Second, older boys should be placed in the care of the father.[25] Third, the court should respect the child's formed attachments and ties of affection. Fourth, the court should be guided by the child's wishes if he or she were capable of exercising a "reasonable discretion."[26]

The new ideas about child custody were embedded in the most important of these new general adoption statutes, "An Act to Provide for the Adoption of

Children," passed in 1851 by the Massachusetts legislature. This statute, a milestone in the history of adoption, reflected Americans' new conceptions of childhood and parenthood by emphasizing the welfare of the child and establishing the principle (if not the practice) that judges were to determine whether prospective adoptive parents were "fit and proper." In addition, the act severed the legal bonds between biological parents and their children, thus freeing the child from all legal obligations to their parents of origin.[27] The Massachusetts Adoption Act, as it was commonly called, marked a watershed in the history of the American family and society. Instead of defining the parent-child relationship exclusively in terms of blood kinship, it was now legally possible to create a family by assuming the responsibility and emotional outlook of a biological parent.[28] Pennsylvania, which in 1853 became the second state to enact such a child-centered adoption law, mandated that "the courts were to be satisfied that the 'welfare of such child will be promoted by such an adoption.'"[29] In the next quarter century, the Massachusetts Adoption Act came to be regarded as a model, and twenty-four states enacted similar laws.[30]

The increase in the number of adopted children was reflected in children's novels and stories. Examining thirty adoption narratives written between 1850 and 1887, Carol S. Singley, a professor of English, notes in her essay, "Building a Nation, Building a Family: Adoption in Nineteenth-Century American Children's Literature," that the early ones were dominated by a sentimental Christian emphasis on salvation, charity, and moral action, whereas later adoption fiction increasingly emphasized market relations and money. In this later period, fictional adoptive parents believed that blood ties were stronger than the artificial ones created by adoption.

The stigma of adoption in both American society and fiction was echoed in Great Britain. Unlike the United States, where adoption had been legal since the mid–nineteenth century, English common law prohibited adoption until 1926. In "What's Love Got to Do with It? 'Adoption' in Victorian and Edwardian England," historian George K. Behlmer shows, however, that England increasingly practiced de facto adoption. Victorian England began to demand legalization because adoption was increasingly linked to disreputable practices. Adoption was associated both with the criminal treatment of illegitimate children ("baby farming," the payment of money to foster parents to care for children born out of wedlock) and with the selling of children to childless couples through newspaper advertisements. In addition, in a system of ad hoc adoption without the legal termination of parental rights, adoptive parents had no security against birth parents demanding the return of their children. With growing public and private anxiety over adoption practices, World War I orphans and illegitimate war babies acted as catalysts for the passage of the Children's Act of 1926, which legalized adoption in England.

Reform of Victorian England's adoption practices coincided with the height of adoption reform in the United States. The CAS also played an instrumental, though unintended, role in these changes. Brace's reckless child-placing system (a primary feature of which was the breakup of intact biological families), coupled with America's high infant-mortality rate (a product of unsanitary conditions in crowded cities and lack of medical knowledge), helped to initiate a Progressive Era (1900–1917) child welfare reform movement that featured the growth of sectarian child welfare institutions, the professionalization of social workers, the standardization of adoption procedures, and an expanded state role in regulating adoptions. The implementation of this movement's goals—keeping families of origin together, ensuring biological parents' consent to the severing of kinship ties, thorough investigation of adoptive parents and homes before placement, and preventing third-party or independent adoptions (the practice by which doctors and lawyers placed children for adoption)—became the raison d'être of professional social workers.[31]

Paula F. Pfeffer's essay, "A Historical Comparison of Catholic and Jewish Adoption Practices in Chicago, 1833–1933," demonstrates that in the late nineteenth century, the city's Catholic and Jewish leaders were alarmed at Brace's tactic of placing their children in Protestant homes, which meant that Catholic and Jewish children would be raised in an alien faith. Like their Protestant counterparts, both denominations argued internally about whether placing children in institutions or in families represented the best solution to the problem of dependent children. In 1882 Catholics responded by founding St. Vincent's Infant Asylum for orphans and pregnant unmarried women, and in 1907 Jewish leaders founded the Jewish Home Finding Society of Chicago. Although Catholics tended to favor institutions more than did Jews, as the twentieth century wore on, these communities came to embrace similar practices—professionalization of staff, increasing emphasis on adoption, and reliance on government funding.

Although Progressive Era Catholic leaders were slow to embrace adoption as a solution to dependent children, the period constituted a second milestone in the history of adoption because the subject first became prominent in popular discussion. In "Rescue a Child and Save the Nation: The Social Construction of Adoption in the *Delineator*, 1907–1911," Julie Berebitsky discusses how a popular women's magazine, the *Delineator*, ran its very successful Child-Rescue Campaign, which popularized adoption and expanded the definition of adoptive motherhood. The *Delineator* series, which ran from 1907 to 1911, elevated motherhood by emphasizing the power of "mother love" to overcome a child's hereditary deficits and urged readers to fulfill their civic duty by adopting children. In its literary conventions, the *Delineator* series differed from other adoptive novels and stories in that the endings to the *Delineator* stories were not always happy. Although the Child-Rescue Campaign resulted in numerous adoptions, Progressive reformers were more interested in advancing the cause of children in general than in appealing only to prospective adoptive mothers. As a result, the *Delineator* began to shift its focus from adoption to national issues such as mothers' pensions.

During the early twentieth century, child welfare reformers began to lobby state legislatures. With respect to adoption, one of the most important legislative results was the 1917 Children's Code of Minnesota, which became the model for state laws over the next two decades. Minnesota became the first state to require an investigation to determine whether a proposed adoptive home was suitable for a child. The state's Board of Control was responsible for examining adoption petitions and offering written advice to the court in all adoption cases. The statute also provided for children to have six-month probationary residence periods in adopting parents' homes. Moreover, the law closed adoption records to public inspection, although those directly involved in the adoption—adopted persons, adoptive parents, and birth parents—could access the record. This point is important because of the common belief that throughout the history of American adoption, state laws denied triad members access to their adoption records.[32] Child welfare reformers hailed Minnesota's Children's Code as a model law.[33] For the next two decades, adoption reformers concentrated their efforts on lobbying state legislatures to provide everyone involved in the process with certain safeguards—consent decrees, social investigations, probation periods, and confidential records.[34]

Three other important reforms in adoption practice and law mark the Progressive Era as a watershed in the history of adoption. Child welfare advocates persuaded many states to remove the word *illegitimate* from birth certificates and devised the amended birth certificate to shield children from the opprobrium surrounding their adoptions. In 1933, two enterprising registrars of vital statistics in Illinois, Henry B. Hemenway and Sheldon L. Howard, proposed that when an adopted child's name was changed, the clerk of the court would forward the adoption decree to the state registrar of vital statistics, who would "make a new record of the birth in the new name, and with the name or names of the adopting parent or parents." Like other adoption records, the amended and original birth certificates were to be sealed from the public but not from members of the adoption triad and the courts.[35] Child welfare reformers also successfully argued that children should not be separated from their families of origin for light and transient reasons. As early as 1900, breaking up families had become practically taboo, at least in theory, and family preservation had become a fundamental principle among all child savers. Professional social workers made it a point of pride to rarely recommend that children be adopted. This ideal would remain axiomatic among professional social workers until after World War II.[36]

Progressive Era social workers institutionalized their reform efforts in universities and national organizations, both public and private. Graduate schools of social service administration were established at a number of institutions of higher learning, including the University of Chicago, thereby helping to professionalize social workers.[37] The U.S. Children's Bureau was established in 1912 and quickly became the leading institution for providing the public with information about adoption. Through World War II, the bureau was instrumental in setting standards for adoption agencies and guiding state legislatures, social workers, researchers, and the public on every aspect of adoption. In 1921 the private, nonprofit Child Welfare League of America (CWLA) was founded. It would become increasingly important in setting adoption standards for both public and private agencies.[38]

Acting as a counterweight to the reform of adoption practices, however, was Americans' cultural definition of kinship as based on blood, which stigmatized adoption as socially unacceptable. Social workers had to overcome widespread popular prejudice against adoption to convince would-be adopters that taking a child into the home was not abnormal. During the late nineteenth and early twentieth centuries, a broad segment of the American public believed that adoption was an unnatural action that created ersatz or second-rate families. The language used underscored the inferior nature of adoption: in popular discourse, adoptive parents were always juxtaposed with "natural" or "normal" ones.[39] Discriminatory laws reinforced the notion that the adoptive relationship was inherently flawed. In inheritance cases, for example, jurists regularly ruled that adoption violated the legal principal of consanguinity, or blood ties. Thus, adopted children did not in practice have the same inheritance rights as birth children. In other cases dealing with disputed custody over adopted children, both courts and legislatures favored birth parents' appeals to restore guardianship of their children.[40]

Medical science contributed to popular cultural prejudices against adopting a child by coupling the stigma of illegitimacy with adoption. The post-1910 rise of the eugenics movement and psychometric testing led adopted children to be linked to inherited mental defects. Studies such as Henry H. Goddard's *The Kallikak Family* claimed to demonstrate children's tendency to inherit their parents' social pathology, particularly criminality and feeblemindedness. Using the Yerkes-Bridges modification of the Binet-Simon intelligence test, psychologists and social workers uncovered a strong connection between unmarried mothers and the purported hereditary trait of feeblemindedness. It was but a small conceptual step to include adopted children in the equation. The purported link between feebleminded unwed mothers and their illegitimate children cast a pall over all adoptions, and even popular magazines warned adoptive parents against the risk of "bad heredity." Adopted children were thus doubly burdened: they were assumed to be illegitimate and thus tainted medically, and they were adopted and consequently lacked the all-important blood link to their adoptive parents.[41]

Using the case records of the Washington Children's Home Society (WCHS), historian Patricia S. Hart's essay, "A Nation's Need for Adoption and Competing Realities: The Washington Children's Home Society, 1895–1915," discusses the general strategy that WCHS adoption workers employed during the Progressive Era to combat popular prejudice and negative medical opinion. They argued that environmental circumstances, such as placement in families and Christian love, were more important than heredity. In addition, adoption was inexpensive, saving the state the costs of supporting dependent children in institutions. Adoption benefited the state in other ways as well, preventing these potential criminals from becoming a permanent underclass. WCHS case records reveal, however, that the experience of adoption triad members, especially birth mothers and adoptive parents, does not fit Michael Foucault's theory of sexuality or social workers' expectations. Overwhelmingly, children admitted to the WCHS were neither criminals nor the offspring of foreigners. Birth mothers relinquished their children as a result of poverty, divorce, nonsupport, or abuse. Children were admitted to the WCHS because of "poverty, death of a parent, dislocation, deteriorating adult relationships, or serious neglect or physical abuse." Neither civic ideals nor infertility motivated adoptive parents. Rather, they sought to adopt children for reasons ranging from love and companionship to family resemblance and gender. But despite these efforts, cultural and medical stigmas made many potential adoptive parents extremely wary of adopting a child.

Historian and policy analyst Brian Paul Gill's "Adoption Agencies and the Search for the Ideal Family, 1918–1965" reveals another important method that twentieth-century adoption agencies employed to provide for the best interests of the child and make adoption respectable and culturally acceptable. Agencies attempted to match the physical, ethnic, racial, religious, and intellectual characteristics of prospective adoptive parents and children, thereby creating units that resembled biological families. One consequence of this policy of matching was that disabled children were automatically excluded from adoption. Adoption workers also began to probe the inner lives of would-be adoptive parents in an effort to discover which ones were psychologically healthy. Gill believes that adoption workers' pursuit of this aesthetic ideal of the family "was perhaps the most ambitious program of social engineering (in its perfectionism, if not its scale) seen in twentieth-century America."

Soon after the onset of the Great Depression in 1929, unprecedented levels of adult unemployment, homelessness, hunger, and misery provided additional impetus for legislation applying to children, as local governments and private agencies were unable to cope with massive suffering and unemployment. President Franklin Roosevelt's Federal Emergency Relief Act (1933) and the Social Security Act (1935) provided much-needed federal funding for child welfare services. The resulting influx of federal financial support strengthened and expanded existing adoption programs while creating new state welfare departments where none had existed previously. By the end of 1937, forty-four states had enacted new adoption laws or revised old ones, many of them providing for a social investigation by the state welfare department or a licensed children's agency before the court hearing and a trial period for children in prospective adoptive homes.[42]

In the late 1930s, the CWLA began to address the issue of adoption standards as a result of member societies' complaints about the practices of commercial adoption agencies and maternity homes. Such notorious adoption mills as the Cradle Society, the Willows, and the Veil Maternity Home accepted payment when adoptive parents received children, ignored commonly accepted social work practices, and provided inadequate safeguards for everyone directly involved in the adoption. CWLA member agencies were also concerned about the large number of independent adoptions made by physicians.[43] In the 1940s, the Children's Bureau estimated that slightly more than half of U.S. adoptions occurred outside the purview of licensed agencies. Professional social workers increasingly believed that the lack of a proper social investigation often led to tragedy. As one agency executive wrote, "Only last year we had an unfortunate experience when a physician in good standing insisted on placing a baby with one of his patients who was unmarried, in her 40's and psychopathic, having been committed to the State Institution some years previous."[44]

Responding to the widespread deviations from sound adoption casework principles and increasing number of independent adoptions, the CWLA in 1938 published its first set of adoption standards, which fit on a single page. The standards were grouped into safeguards for children, for adoptive parents, and for the state. The first safeguard for the child could also be considered one for the biological parents: the child was not to be unnecessarily deprived of kinship ties. Professional social workers still considered maintaining the family of origin to be the most desirable course of action regarding children threatened by dependency. The second and third safeguards for the child revolved around the adoptive parents' motivation and suitability for the adoption. The adopters must desire the child "for the purpose of completing an otherwise incomplete family group," have "a good home and good family life . . . and be well adjusted to each other," and promise to love, support, and educate the child. Adoptive parents should expect that a reputable child-placing institution would keep their identities from the biological parents, physically and mentally match the child in accord with the adoptive parents' expectations, and complete the adoption proceedings "without unnecessary publicity." Finally, the state should require "for its own sake and the child's protection" that there be a trial period of residence before the adoption was finalized and that the child's birth records be revised to prevent "unnecessary embarrassment in case of illegitimacy." The standards recommended that for "good advice and best results," both natural and adoptive families should consult a "well-established children's organization."[45] The CWLA's adoption standards presented member agencies with a model of desirable practices to which child-placing organizations should aspire. Failure to conform to CWLA standards resulted in suspension from the league.[46]

In the decade before World War II, both the Children's Bureau's increasing attention to adoption and the CWLA's formulation of adoption standards were symptomatic of the beginning of far-reaching changes in adoption policy and practice. E. Wayne Carp and Anna Leon-Guerrero's "When in Doubt, Count: World War II as a Watershed in the History of Adoption" argues that World War II constituted a third watershed in the history of adoption. Using WCHS case records from 1895 to 1973, the authors show that adoption was transformed by a series of external circumstances—wartime necessity, economic changes, new ideas in social work, postwar affluence, an increase in the number of children available for adoption, repudiation of the standard of the "unadoptable" child, more liberal attitudes on race, and strong demand by childless couples for adopted children. The changes of the war years affected birth parents' age, education, occupation, and marital status; adopted children's age and birth status; and adoptive parents' child preferences and motivations for adopting.

The initial sign that the old order was changing was the decline during the 1920s and 1930s of the eugenic stigma surrounding adopted children, as studies demonstrated the successful social adjustment of adoptions, medical experts repudiated eugenic "science," and adoption agencies and the popular media assured adoptive parents that the dangers of adoption had been largely obviated by scientific advances. The second sign that adoption practices were changing was social workers' and state bureaucrats' gradual postwar move toward shrouding adoption in secrecy. They acted for many reasons, including desires to defend the adoptive process, to protect the privacy of unwed mothers, to increase the workers' influence and power, and to bolster the professionalization of social work by treating clients with psychoanalytic theory. As a result, secrecy became pervasive after World War II, preventing those directly involved in adoption from gaining access to information about their lives.[47]

After 1940, demographic changes, such as an increase in the number and availability of adoptable children, accelerated the change in adoption practices. In addition to the continued high numbers of homes broken by death, divorce, and desertion, the number of children born out of wedlock grew drastically. With social bonds loosened by wartime, illegitimacy rates began to soar, especially among nonwhites, continuing their upward flight for the next forty years.

The "demand" by childless couples for infants during the Cold War was an additional factor leading to radical changes in traditional adoption practices. Beginning in the mid-1940s and reaching its peak in the late 1950s, the baby boom era's dramatic rise in marriages and births was largely responsible for the increased demand for children to adopt and resulted in adoption agencies being inundated with requests for children. Parenthood became a patriotic necessity. The media romanticized babies, glorified motherhood, and identified fatherhood with masculinity and good citizenship. According to historian Elaine Tyler May, this celebratory pronatal mood "marginalized the childless in unprecedented ways." Uncomfortable at being childless and the subject of public opprobrium, an unprecedented number of these childless couples sought to adopt as one solution to their "shame" of infertility.[48] Adoption agencies were inundated with requests for children. Contributing to the unprecedented numbers of childless couples applying to adopt children were new medical treatments—semen examination, test tubal patency, and endometrial biopsies—that permitted physicians to diagnose physical sterility more easily and accurately early in marriage. Consequently, adoption overwhelmingly became a service for infertile couples.[49]

These factors, combined with wartime prosperity, produced a remarkable increase in the number of applications to adopt a child. Between 1937 and 1945, adoptions had increased threefold, from about 16,000 to 50,000 annually. A decade later, the number of adoptions had nearly doubled again, to 93,000, and by 1965 it climbed to 142,000, of which one-third to half were adoptions by relatives.[50] In less than thirty years, the number of adoptions had grown nearly ninefold. Overwhelmed by the number of applications and constricted by inflexible rules, adoption agencies aroused much ill will and resentment among childless couples.[51]

These problems led the CWLA to hold national adoption workshops and conferences in 1948 and 1951.[52] The organization discovered that while social welfare in general was retreating from social reform and caseworkers were being criticized for complacency toward the poor, individual child welfare agencies were reforming traditional adoption practices.[53] No single factor can account for all the changes that occurred at the local level in different parts of the country. While pressure from would-be adoptive parents challenged social workers to alter their policies, adoption agencies were also affected by such larger factors as deep humanitarianism (spawned by revulsion at World War II atrocities and by Allied propaganda espousing the cause of democracy and attacking illiberal regimes) and demographic shifts resulting from the migration of more than one million African Americans from the South to northern and western cities (which liberalized race relations).[54] Taken as a whole, these changes were the beginning of the fourth watershed in the history of adoption.

Nowhere were these changes in the zeitgeist more noticeable than in agencies' definition of the "adoptable" child. Before World War II, social workers refused to accept children with physical and mental handicaps in the belief that adoptive parents desired only "perfect" children. In the postwar era, social workers began to abandon the idea of the unadoptable child and broadened the definition of adoptability to include "any child . . . who needs a family and who can develop in it, and for whom a family can be found that can accept the child with its physical or mental capacities."[55] With the enlarged definition of adoptability, social workers for the first time initiated serious efforts to place disabled, minority, older, and foreign-born children.

With the CWLA taking the lead, minorities, especially dependent African-American children, soon felt the effects of the profession's expanded definition of adoptability. The war years represented a turning point in opening up America's child welfare system to the idea of placing black children for adoption. Progress was slow: for example, Philadelphia and Cleveland maintained inadequate segregated child welfare institutions and failed to provide adoption services for African-American children. But in 1939 the New York State Charities Aid Association for the first time extended adoption services to African-American children, placing eighteen to twenty children each year during World War II.[56] Additional factors paving the way for the expansion of adoption services to African Americans included black militancy against continuing wartime segregation and discrimination, a sharp increase in the number of nonwhite out-of-wedlock births, and federal and state action and court rulings in favor of equal rights.[57] In 1948, *Child Welfare*, the premier journal for professional social workers, reported, "We find over the country a growing conviction, translated in practice, that the color of a child's skin, the texture of his hair, or the slant of his eyes in no way affects his basic needs or the relation of his welfare to that of the total community."[58] Years before *Brown v. Board of Education* (1954) and more than a decade before the civil rights movement, many of the nation's adoption agencies began placing an increasing number of African-American children.[59]

The end of World War II also witnessed the first phase of an upsurge of intercountry adoptions. Between 1946 and 1953, American citizens and organizations such as International Social Services, American Branch, brought to the United States for adoption 5,814 foreign-born orphans and abandoned children, many from war-torn Greece, Germany, and Japan. What researchers Howard Altstein and Rita J. Simon label the second phase of intercountry adoptions began between the end of the Korean War in 1953 and 1962. In this period, "for the first time in history, relatively large numbers of Western couples, mostly in the United States, were adopting children who were racially and culturally different from themselves." Asia (primarily the Republic of Korea) was the origin of almost one-third of the fifteen thousand children adopted during this period and 65 percent of the thirty-two thousand foreign-born children adopted by American citizens between 1966 and 1976. Consequently, Korean children became the largest group of foreign adoptees within the United States, and the country became the world's leading receiver of foreign children.[60]

From the 1970s to the 1990s, unanticipated racial, sexual, constitutional, and demographic changes in American society deepened the fourth watershed in the history of adoption and began the fifth, which was marked by open adoption and the adoption rights movement. One trend that continued with renewed energy was the placement of special-needs children, especially African Americans, in adoptive homes. In 1967, the CWLA created the Adoption Resource Exchange of North America, an independent national clearinghouse for hard-to-place children that annually helped agencies find homes for almost two hundred physically, emotionally, or mentally disabled children.[61] By 1969, public and private adoption agencies' concerted efforts to find homes for minority children resulted in more than 19,000 children being placed. Of the 171,000 children adopted that year, 14,000 (8 percent) were African American.[62] These programs still left tens of thousands of older, minority, and physically and mentally disabled children needing placement.

The social work profession responded in a number of ways to increase special-needs adoptions.[63] In their vigorous recruitment efforts, agencies were surprised to discover that white families occasionally would request black infants for adoption or would agree to adopt black babies when asked to do so by caseworkers. By 1965, transracial adoption had become the "little revolution," as agencies all over the nation increasingly placed black babies with white families.[64] Four years later, the CWLA revised its *Standards* to reflect the new practice, unequivocally stating that "racial background in itself should not determine the selection of the home for a child" and recommending that "agencies should be ready to help families who wish to adopt children of another race."[65] In 1971, transracial adoptions reached their peak, with 468 agencies reporting 2,574 such placements.[66]

While professional adoption workers went far in overhauling inflexible practices and liberalizing the definition of adoptability, the tumultuous events of the 1960s overtook such efforts in ways of which such professionals did not always approve. Essentially liberal in its political and social beliefs, the social work profession did not anticipate that 1960s radicalism would substantively affect adoption policies or practices. Officials and caseworkers were caught by surprise when dissidents from both within and without the profession began to challenge some of its basic tenets in the early 1970s. The first manifestation of discontent emerged in 1972, when black social workers, influenced by the black power movement and its emphasis on racial separatism, revolutionary violence, and black nationalism, began denouncing transracial adoption as cultural genocide.[67] The National Association of Black Social Workers' case against transracial adoptions was remarkably effective. In 1972, transracial adoptions fell 39 percent, to 1,569, and three years later, only 831 transracial adoptions occurred.[68] In the following years, transracial adoptions declined steeply, as child welfare workers preferred to keep African-American children in foster care rather than place them with white families despite evidence that demonstrated the success of transracial adoptions.[69] Concern over social workers' discriminatory practices prompted Congress to enact the Howard M. Metzenbaum Multiethnic Placement Act of 1994, which prohibited adoption agencies from denying any person the opportunity to become an adoptive parent based solely on the person's race, color, or national origin.[70]

Social workers also failed to foresee the radical decline in the availability for adoption of healthy white infants, which resulted in some of the most important changes in adoption policy. A number of factors were responsible, including the 1960s sexual revolution, access to birth control, the Supreme Court's legalization of abortion in *Roe v. Wade* (1973), and unwed mothers' increasing unwillingness to relinquish their babies for adoption. As a result of these profound cultural, social, legal, and demographic changes in American society, the number of adoptions declined substantially. Nonrelative adoptions in the United States fell from a record high of 89,200 in 1970 to 47,700 in 1975. The number rose slightly, to 50,720 in 1982, and remained at about this level for the rest of the decade.[71] By 1975, some adoption agencies began to stop taking requests for healthy, white infants. Social workers often informed prospective adopters that they would likely wait three to five years for such a child.[72]

A second consequence of the 1970s demographic decline was the redefinition of the population of adoptable children, making it more inclusive and less concerned with matching children's physical, mental, racial, and religious characteristics with those of parents. The adoptable population increasingly comprised older children, members of minority groups, and special-needs children. In the 1990s, drug-exposed infants, children with AIDS, and infants born HIV positive were added to the special-needs category. About one hundred thousand of these children who were unable to find adoptive homes or were not legally free for adoption became fixtures in foster care, where they were shunted from one caretaker to another. This situation prompted Congress to pass the Adoption Assistance and Child Welfare Act of 1980, one of the first federal laws ever to address the problems of adopted children. Congress's landmark legislation mandated that child welfare agencies provide preplacement preventive services, take steps to reunify children with their biological parents, and periodically review cases of children in long-term foster care. "Permanency planning" legislation, as it was soon called, sought to place children in stable homes, either by returning them to their families of origin or by placing them in adoptive homes. The Adoption Assistance and Child Welfare Act also encouraged the states to develop adoption-subsidy programs for special-needs adoption, with the national government reimbursing the states 50 percent of the subsidy. By 1993 the federal government was distributing an estimated one hundred million dollars to forty states.[73]

In 1997, a bipartisan Congress enacted the Adoption and Safe Families Act (ASFA), which amended the Adoption Assistance and Child Welfare Act of 1980. The ASFA was a response to a crisis in America's system of foster care and adoption. In the wake of a 1996 congressional hearing, lawmakers viewed the original legislation as a failure as a result of the doubling of the number of children in foster care to approximately 500,000 and the failure of its original aim to shift these foster children into adoptive homes. Another goal of the ASFA was to prevent children from being returned to unsafe homes. Like the legislation of 1980, the ASFA allocated federal funds to the states as an incentive to promote adoptions. The law represented a major shift in federal policy away from family reunification and preservation toward efforts to create new adoptive families for the children.[74]

A third consequence of the dearth of white, U.S.-born infants was an increase in intercountry adoptions, with the main source of children shifting from Korea in the 1950s to Latin America in the 1970s and 1980s and more recently to Russia, Romania, and China. Intercountry adoptions in 2000 constituted 14.5 percent of U.S. adoptions, or 18,477. Although intercountry adoptions are popular among private agencies and prospective parents, numerous critics denounce such adoptions for failing to protect the rights of birth parents, encouraging trafficking in children for financial gain, and resulting in cultural genocide.[75] As a result of such objections, the United States has recently signed the Hague Convention, which regulates intercountry adoptions by placing adoption agencies under international scrutiny.[76]

A fourth consequence of the decline in adoptable infants was open adoption, a major and controversial innovation. In an effort to encourage birth mothers to relinquish their babies, case workers began experimenting with allowing pregnant women to decide who would parent their children. The result was open adoption, where the identities of birth and adoptive parents were exchanged and ongoing contact between the parties was encouraged. By the mid-1980s, open adoption had evolved into a continuum of interactions between birth mothers and adoptive parents, ranging from annual updates on children's welfare to active involvement by both parties in raising the child. Open adoptions have become increasing popular, commanding center stage in adoption practice.[77] In the two years following placement, an estimated 55 percent of adoptive families in California during 1988–89 had contact with their children's birth families.[78]

Ideological warfare has marked the debut of open adoption. Such proponents of open adoption as Reuben Pannor and Annette Baran have argued that adoptees have had psychological problems caused by traditional, closed adoptions, where birth and adoptive parents' identities were kept secret from each other. These adoption rights proponents advocate an end to all closed adoptions.[79] Opponents of open adoption have argued that there is no way to know its effects on children, making them guinea pigs in a social experiment for ideological reasons. Others have argued that continued contact with birth parents could disrupt children's relationships with their adoptive parents and make it difficult for adolescents to form cohesive identities.[80] Recent research suggests that only a small percentage of open adoptions feature both families in constant contact and that open adoption consequently does not appear to cause much disruption to children's healthy psychological development.[81]

The birth of the adoption rights movement accompanied the 1970s decline in the availability of white infants, the revolution in adoption practices, and the upsurge in minority, special-needs, transracial, and open adoptions. Though the movement's roots lay in the 1950s, when twice-adopted former social worker Jean M. Paton began her lifelong crusade to provide adopted persons with a voice and a cause, adoption rights did not become a major social issue until two decades later. The movement's most vocal and visible leader, Florence Fisher, a New York City homemaker, spent twenty years searching for and finally finding her birth mother and then founded the Adoptees' Liberty Movement Association (ALMA) in 1971. Along with aiding adult adoptees who were searching for members of their original families, ALMA's principal goals were "to abolish the existing practice of 'sealed records'" and to secure the "opening of records to any adopted person *over eighteen* who wants, for any reason, to see them." With the popular reception of *The Search for Anna Fisher* (1973), a book recounting the dramatic story of her success in reuniting with her birth family, Fisher became the movement's undisputed leader and the head of the nation's largest and most influential adoption search group. ALMA's example sparked the creation of hundreds of other such groups across the United States, Canada, and the United Kingdom. By 1978, the multiplicity of adoptee search groups led to the formation of a national umbrella organization, the American Adoption Congress.[82]

Adoption rights activists, who are primarily adult adoptees and birth mothers, contend that they are entitled to identifying information in the adoption record. They have pursued their agenda—repealing laws that sealed adoption records—through court challenges, reform of state legislation, and state initiatives.[83] The results have been mixed. States have tried to accommodate the potentially clashing rights of birth parents, some of whom have been promised confidentiality, and of adopted adults who want unrestricted access to the information in their records. Consequently, by the mid-1990s seventeen states permitted court-appointed intermediaries to read adoption files, locate birth parents, and inquire whether they were interested in meeting children relinquished for adoption. Moreover, nineteen states have established formal mutual-consent adoption registries, where both birth parents and adoptees can register their names: when both parties register, they are informed of the match and a meeting is arranged. Another six states have authorized the release of identifying information with the consent of both the adopted person and the birth mother, without a formal registry.[84] Momentum appears recently to have shifted, favoring adoptees' access to records. Oregon, Tennessee, Delaware, and Alabama have joined Kansas and Alaska in permitting adopted persons access to their original birth certificates, and the CWLA's 2000 adoption standards advise member agencies "to support efforts to ensure that adults who were adopted have direct access to identifying information about themselves and their birth mothers."[85]

Professor Barbara Melosh's essay, "Adoption Stories: Autobiographical Narrative and the Politics of Identity," reveals the differences among adoption triad members in coming to grips with the institution of adoption during an era when many are demanding the right to access their records and search for their biological kin. Melosh finds that adoptive parents' accounts applaud the postwar consensus that celebrated adoption as a positive form of substitute family formation. Still, many of their accounts are tinged with self-doubt and sadness as they recount their struggles with the losses of infertility, the formation of a substitute identity of parenting not based in biology, and, often, the search for a child. Recent counternarratives to the postwar adoptive parent success story stress that love is not enough and that adoptive families are not permanent or exclusive. In a similar vein, most of the autobiographies by adopted persons lament the loss of the birth mother and the implementation of adoption secrecy. These accounts often seem to be constructed to further the agenda of the adoption reform movement by providing details about the search's difficulties and the eventual triumphal reunion with the birth mother. Similarly, birth mothers' memoirs often denounce traditional adoption practices for inflicting lasting wounds that include unresolved guilt and grief and intense longing to reclaim relinquished children. Paradoxically, by portraying themselves as powerless victims of circumstances, birth mothers contradict their extraordinary strength in writing these accounts, searching for their children, and participating in the adoption rights movement. And unlike those of adoptive parents, accounts by adopted persons and birth mothers actively involved in the adoption reform movement repudiate this postwar consensus by reclaiming the blood ties that adoption supposedly erased.

American adoption practices have changed radically over the past two and a half centuries. Originally an informal, spontaneous occurrence comparable to apprenticeship, adoption has become a formalized legal institution governed by statute in fifty separate state jurisdictions with increasing federal involvement. During the past century, social workers have become professionalized, and the U.S. Children's Bureau and the CWLA have developed uniform standards for regulating adoptions. Since World War II, adoption has changed from an elitist institution that restricted the children available to a practice that includes foreign, minority, older, physically and mentally disabled, and HIV-positive children. Moreover, the past fifty years have seen a movement away from secrecy to an embrace of open adoption and legislative mechanisms for uniting adopted adults with their biological parents. More recently, the Internet has played an important role in facilitating adoptions and reunions between adopted and biological family members. In spite of all these changes, however, the United States has retained a pervasive cultural bias toward blood ties, and many people still view adoption as a second-rate form of kinship. These trends—federal statutes; special-needs, transracial, and intercountry adoptions; openness in the adoption process; conflict over the opening of adoption records; and the stigma of adoptive kinship—show no signs of abating and will remain powerful factors in future controversies affecting adoption in the United States.

NOTES

1. In a survey of 1,554 Americans, 6 out of 10 respondents had personal experience with adoption, meaning that they, a family member, or a close friend was adopted, had adopted a child, or had placed a child for adoption (Evan B. Donaldson Adoption Institute, *Benchmark Adoption Survey: Report on the Findings* [New York: Donaldson Institute, 1997]).

2. Kathy S. Stolley, "Statistics on Adoption in the United States," *Future of Children* 3 (spring 1993): 34–36.

3. Victor Eugene Flango and Carol R. Flango, "How Many Children Were Adopted in 1992," *Child Welfare* 74 (Sept.–Oct. 1995): 1018–32. Unless otherwise indicated, the term *adoption* in this essay refers to unrelated adoptions.

4. U.S. State Department. "Numbers of Immigrant Visas Issued to Orphans Coming to U.S. FY2000." <http://travel.state.gov/orphan_numbers.html> (Feb. 8, 2002).

5. Joan H. Hollinger, "Introduction to Adoption Law and Practice," in *Adoption Law and Practice*, ed. Hollinger et al. (New York: Matthew Bender, 1992), 1:8–15.

6. E. Wayne Carp, *Family Matters: Secrecy and Disclosure in the History of Adoption* (Cambridge: Harvard University Press, 1998).

7. Elizabeth Bartholet, "International Adoption: Overview," in *Adoption Law and Practice*, ed. Hollinger et al. 2:33–35; Kenneth J. Hermann Jr. and Barbara Kasper, "International Adoption: The Exploitation of Women and Children," *Affilia* 7 (spring 1992): 45–58.

8. Stolley, "Statistics," 37.

9. Eight states and the District of Columbia explicitly permit adoption by homosexuals, while only three states, Mississippi, New Hampshire, and Florida, explicitly deny homosexuals the ability to adopt (Karla J. Starr, "Adoption by Homosexuals: A Look at Differing State Court Opinions," *Arizona Law Review* 40 (1998): 1497–98; Gina Holland, "Mississippi Bans Gay Adoptions," May 3, 2000, <http://abcnews.go.com/sections/us/DailyNews/adoptionban...503.html> (Feb. 21, 2002); see also Robert Horowitz and Hiromi Maruyama, "Legal Issues," in *Issues in Gay and Lesbian Adoption*, ed. Ann

Sullivan [Washington, D.C.: CWLA, 1995], 13). For a brief overview of the difficulties facing gay and lesbian prospective adoptive parents in the United States, see Jeffrey G. Gibson, "Lesbian and Gay Adoptive Parents: The Legal Battle," *Human Rights* 26 (spring 1999): 7–12. However, the influential American Academy of Pediatrics has recently come out in support of legislation and legal efforts to provide the possibility for homosexuals or same-sex couples to adopt children (American Academy of Pediatrics, "Coparent or Second-Parent Adoption by Same-Sex Parents," *Pediatrics* 109, no. 3 [Feb. 2002]: 339–40.

10. Susan Lewis Cooper and Ellen Sarasohn Glazer, *Choosing Assisted Reproduction: Social, Emotional, and Ethical Considerations* (Indianapolis: Perspectives Press, 1998), chap. 9.

11. The only existing comprehensive history of American adoption focuses on the issue of secrecy and disclosure in adoption history. See Carp, *Family Matters*.

12. The few pioneering articles that have been written about adoption have avoided the evidentiary problem by writing legal histories of adoption based primarily on state statutes and case law. See, for example, Stephen B. Presser, "The Historical Background of the American Law of Adoption," *Journal of Family Law* 11 (1971–72): 443–516; Jamil S. Zainaldin, "The Emergence of a Modern American Family Law: Child Custody, Adoption, and the Courts, 1796–1851," *Northwestern University Law Review* 73 (1979): 1038–89; Joseph Ben-Or, "The Law of Adoption in the United States: Its Massachusetts Origins and the Statute of 1851," *New England Historical and Genealogical Register* 130 (1976): 259–73. They are limited to the eighteenth and nineteenth centuries and have little to say about twentieth-century adoption or about how adoption practices actually worked or how they affected members of the adoption triad—birth parents, adopted persons, and adoptive parents. For an exception to this statement, see Jamil S. Zainaldin and Peter L. Tyor, "Asylum and Society: An Approach to Industrial Change," *Journal of Social History* 13 (fall 1979): 23–48.

Recent publications, dissertations, and research in progress in history, literature, law, sociology, and anthropology suggest that this state of affairs is passing. See, for example Carp, *Family Matters;* E. Wayne Carp, "Orphanages vs. Adoption: The Triumph of Biological Kinship, 1800–1933," in *With Us Always: A History of Private Charity and Public Welfare,* Donald T. Critchlow and Charles H. Parker, eds. (Rowman & Littlefield, 1998): 123–44; E. Wayne Carp, *Bastard Nation: Discovering Family Origins Through the Democratic Process* (Lawrence: University Press of Kansas, forthcoming 2003); Ellen Herman, "Families Made by Science: Arnold Gesell and the Technologies of Modern Child Adoption," *Isis* 92, no. 4 (Dec. 2001): 684–715; Ellen Herman, "Child Adoption in a Therapeutic Culture," *Society* 39 (Jan./Feb. 2002): 11–18; Marianne Novy, ed., *Imagining Adoption: Essays on Literature and Culture* (Ann Arbor: University of Michigan Press, 2001); Elizabeth J. Samuels, "The Idea of Adoption: An Inquiry into the History of Adult Adoptee Access to Birth Records," *Rutgers Law Review* 53 (2001): 367–455; Julie Berebitsky, *Like Our Very Own: Adoption and the Changing Culture of Motherhood, 1851–1950* (Lawrence: University Press of Kansas, 2000); Julie Berebitsky, "'To Raise as Your Own': The Growth of Legal Adoption in Washington," *Washington History* 6 (spring–summer 1994): 5–26, 105–7; Katarina Wegar, *Adoption, Identity, and Kinship: The Debate Over Sealed Birth Records* (New Haven and London: Yale University Press, 1997); Judith S. Modell, *Kinship with Strangers: Adoption and Interpretations of Kinship in American Culture* (Berkeley: University of California Press, 1994); Barbara Melosh,

Strangers and Kin: The American Way of Adoption (Cambridge: Harvard University, 2002); Naomi Cahn and Joan Heifetz Hollinger, eds., *Family Ties: An Adoption Reader* (2003): Brian Paul Gill, "The Jurisprudence of Good Parenting: The Selection of Adoptive Parents, 1894–1964" (Ph.D. diss., University of California at Berkeley, 1997); Jill R. Deans, "'Divide the Child in Two': Adoption and the Rhetoric of Legitimacy in Twentieth-Century American Literature" (Ph.D. diss., University of Massachusetts, 1998); Patricia Hart, "A Home for Every Child, a Child for Every Home: Relinquishment and Adoption at the Washington Children's Home Society, 1896–1915" (Ph.D. diss., Washington State University, 1997); Janine M. Baer, "History and Consequences of Sealing Adoption Records" (master's thesis, San Francisco State University, 1995). Additional evidence that adoption studies are beginning to generate substantial interdisciplinary scholarly attention is the founding in 1997 of *Adoption Quarterly* and the 1998 establishment of the Evan B. Donaldson Adoption Institute.

13. George K. Behlmer, *Friends of the Family: The English Home and its Guardians* (Stanford, Calif.: Stanford University Press, 1998), chap. 6; Michael Grossberg, *Governing the Hearth: Law and the Family in Nineteenth-Century America* (Chapel Hill: University of North Carolina Press, 1985), 268–69; C. M. A. McCauliff, "The First English Adoption Law and Its American Precursors," *Seton Hall Law Review* 16 (1986): 656–77.

14. John Demos, *A Little Commonwealth: Family Life in Plymouth Colony* (New York: Oxford University Press, 1970), 89; Ben-Or, "Law," 260, 265; Yasuhide Kawashima, "Adoption in Early America," *Journal of Family Law* 20 (1981–82): 677–96.

15. Ben-Or, "Law," 270. For a concise statement of how adoption went from a private agreement to a legal institution, see Edward A. Hoyt with Michael Sherman, "Adoption and the Law in Vermont, 1804–1863: An Introductory Essay," *Vermont History* 64 (summer 1996): 159–73.

16. David M. Rothman, *The Discovery of the Asylum: Social Order and Disorder in the New Republic* (Boston: Little, Brown, 1971); William I. Trattner, *From Poor Law to Welfare State: A History of Social Welfare in America*, 5th ed. (New York: Free Press, 1994), chap. 4.

17. Susan Lynne Porter, "The Benevolent Asylum—Image and Reality: The Care and Training of Female Orphans in Boston" (Ph.D. diss., Boston University, 1984), 198.

18. Bernard Wishy, *The Child and the Republic: The Dawn of Modern American Child Nurture* (Philadelphia: University of Pennsylvania Press, 1967), chaps. 2–3; Susan Tiffin, *In Whose Best Interest? Child Welfare Reform in the Progressive Era* (Westport, Conn.: Greenwood Press, 1982), chaps. 3–4.

19. Marilyn Irvin Holt, *The Orphan Trains: Placing out in America* (Lincoln: University of Nebraska Press, 1992), chaps. 2–3; Miriam Z. Langsam, *Children West: A History of the Placing-Out System of the New York Children's Aid Society, 1853–1890* (Madison: State Historical Society of Wisconsin, 1964).

20. Presser, "Historical Background," 480–89.

21. Helen L. Witmer et al., *Independent Adoptions: A Follow-up Study* (New York: Russell Sage Foundation, 1963), 30; Grossberg, *Governing the Hearth*, 271. As early as 1808, Louisiana's legal code contained an adoption statute, but it was abolished in 1825 (Grossberg, *Governing the Hearth*, 270).

22. Grossberg, *Governing the Hearth*, chap. 7, esp. 234–38.

23. Zainaldin, "Emergence," 1070–72.

24. According to Zainaldin, "'Tender age' usually means infancy through eleventh or twelfth birthday" ("Emergence," 1072 n.151). He provides no source for this statement.

25. Zainaldin states, "This grouping usually included boys 11 years and older" (ibid., 1073 n.154). Again, he provides no source for this statement.

26. Ibid., 1073–74.

27. *Acts and Resolves Passed by the General Court of Massachusetts*, 1851, chap. 324; Zainaldin, "Emergence," 1084–85.

28. Zainaldin, "Emergence," 1042–43, 1085.

29. Grossberg, *Governing the Hearth*, 272.

30. Witmer et al., *Independent Adoptions*, 30–31.

31. Carp, *Family Matters*, 14–25.

32. Ibid., chap. 2.

33. Gioh-Fang Dju Ma, *One Hundred Years of Public Services for Children in Minnesota* (Chicago: University of Chicago Press, 1948).

34. Carp, *Family Matters*, 21–25.

35. Sheldon L. Howard and Henry B. Hemenway, "Birth Records of Illegitimates and of Adopted Children," *American Journal of Public Health* 21 (June 1931): 644–47.

36. E. Wayne Carp, "Professional Social Workers, Adoption, and the Problem of Illegitimacy, 1915–1945," *Journal of Policy History* 6 (1994): 161–84.

37. Robyn Muncy, *Creating a Female Dominion in American Reform, 1890–1935* (New York: Oxford University Press, 1991), chap. 2.

38. Carp, *Family Matters*, 22–28. There are several excellent studies of the U.S. Children's Bureau, though none recognize the important role it played in formulating national adoption policies and practices. See, for example, Kriste Lindenmeyer, *"A Right to Childhood": The U.S. Children's Bureau and Child Welfare, 1912–1946* (Urbana: University of Illinois Press, 1997). A scholarly study of the CWLA is desperately needed.

39. R. L. Jenkins, "On Adopting a Baby: Rules for Prospective Adoptive Parents," *Hygeia* 13 (Dec. 1935): 1068.

40. Peter Romanofsky, "Early History of Adoption Practices, 1870–1930" (Ph.D. diss., University of Missouri at Columbia, 1969), 67–69.

41. Henry H. Goddard, *The Kallikak Family: A Study in the Heredity of Feeblemindedness* (New York: Macmillan, 1912); Hamilton Cravens, *The Triumph of Evolution: American Scientists and the Heredity-Environment Controversy, 1900–1941* (Philadelphia: University of Pennsylvania Press, 1978), 47–48. For psychometric testing, see Michael M. Sokal, ed., *Psychological Testing and American Society, 1890–1930* (New Brunswick, N.J.: Rutgers University Press, 1987). The belief that unwed mothers were feebleminded was widespread. See Carp, "Professional Social Workers," 172, n.77; Ada Elliot Sheffield, "Program of the Committee on Illegitimacy—Committee Report," in *Proceedings of the Forty-Sixth Annual National Conference of Social Work . . . 1919* (Chicago: Rogers & Hall Co., 1920), 78; "Our Adopted Baby," *Woman's Home Companion* 43 (Apr. 1916): 5.

42. Michael B. Katz, *In the Shadow of the Poorhouse: A Social History of Welfare in America* (New York: Basic Books, 1986), 213; Linda Gordon, *Pitied but Not Entitled: Single Mothers and the History of Welfare* (New York: Basic Books, 1994), 185–90; Carl A. Heisterman, "A Summary of Legislation on Adoption," *Social Service Review* 9 (June 1935): 269–77.

43. Carp, *Family Matters,* 26.

44. Mary Ruth Colby, *Problems and Procedures in Adoption* (Washington, D.C.: U.S. Government Printing Office, 1941), 21; "Regarding Adoptions," CWLA *Special Bulletin* (Mar. 1937), CWLA Records, suppl., box 41, "Special Bulletins" folder, Social Welfare History Archives, University of Minnesota, Minneapolis.

45. "Minimum Safeguards in Adoption," Nov. 5, 1938, CWLA Records, box 15, folder 5.

46. Zitha R. Turitz, "Development and Use of National Standards for Child Welfare Services," *Child Welfare* 46 (1967): 246–48. In 1948, for example, the CWLA suspended the Tennessee Children's Home Society from membership for its failure to adhere to the league's adoption standards (Linda Tollett Austin, *Babies for Sale: The Tennessee Children's Home Adoption Scandal* [Westport, Conn.: Praeger, 1993], 50).

47. Carp, *Family Matters,* chap. 4.

48. Elaine Tyler May, *Barren in the Promised Land: Childless Americans and the Pursuit of Happiness* (New York: Basic Books, 1995), 127–40, 156.

49. Richard Frank, "What the Adoption Worker Should Know about Infertility," *Child Welfare* 35 (Feb. 1956): 1–5.

50. Sophie van Senden Theis, "Adoption," in *Social Work Year Book,* vol. 4 (New York: Russell Sage Foundation, 1937), 23; I. Evelyn Smith, "Adoption," in *Social Work Year Book,* vol. 4 (New York: Russell Sage Foundation, 1947), 9, 24; Stolley, "Statistics on Adoption in the United States," 28.

51. Carp, *Family Matters,* 29–31.

52. Michael Schapiro, *A Study of Adoption Practice* (New York: CWLA, 1956) 1:10.

53. Trattner, *From Poor Law to Welfare State,* 308–10.

54. Neil A. Wynn, "The Impact of the Second World War on the American Negro," *Journal of Contemporary History* 6 (1971): 42–53.

55. CWLA, *Report on Adoption Practices, Policies, and Problems* (New York: CWLA, 1949), 21.

56. CWLA, *Child Care Facilities for Dependent and Neglected Negro Children in Three Cities: New York City, Philadelphia, Cleveland* (New York: CWLA, 1945), 55.

57. Andrew Billingsly and Jeanne M. Giovannoni, *Children of the Storm: Black Children and American Child Welfare* (New York: Harcourt, Brace, Jovanovich, 1972), 27–38, 72–73; Harvard Sitkoff, *A New Deal for Blacks: The Emergence of Civil Rights as a National Issue,* rev. ed. (New York: Hill and Wang, 1993), 11–18.

58. "Special Problem of the Negro Child," *Child Welfare* 27 (1948): 5.

59. Annie Lee Sandusky et al., *Families for Black Children: The Search for Adoptive Parents,* vol. 2, *Programs and Projects* (Washington, D.C.: U.S. Government Printing Office, 1972); Patricia Collmeyer, "From 'Operation Brown Baby' to 'Opportunity': The Placement of Children of Color at the Boys and Girls Aid Society of Oregon," *Child Welfare* 74 (Jan.–Feb. 1995): 242–63.

60. Howard Altstein and Rita James Simon, introduction to *Intercountry Adoption: A Multinational Perspective,* ed. Altstein and Simon (New York: Praeger, 1990), 3.

61. CWLA, *Adoption Resource Exchange of North America* (New York: CWLA, 1968). The phrase *special needs* was first used to refer to handicapped children in 1958. See Helen Fradkin, "Adoptive Parents for Children with Special Needs," *Child Welfare* 37 (Jan. 1958): 1–6.

62. U.S. Department of Health, Education, and Welfare, National Center for Social

Statistics, *Adoptions in 1969*, supp. to *Child Welfare Statistics—1969* (Washington, D.C.: U.S. Government Printing Office, 1969).

63. Fradkin, "Adoptive Parents," 1–6.

64. Harriet Fricke, "Interracial Adoption: The Little Revolution," *Social Welfare* 10 (July 1965): 92–97; Bernice Q. Madison and Michael Schapiro, "Black Adoption—Issues and Policies: Review of the Literature," *Social Service Review* 47 (1973): 531–60.

65. CWLA, *Standards for Adoption Service*, rev. ed. (New York: CWLA, 1968), 34.

66. Opportunity: A Division of the Boys and Girls Aid Society of Oregon, "Survey of Adoption of Black Children," typescript (Portland, Ore., 1972). In 1968, there were 733 transracial adoptions nationwide (Opportunity, "Survey").

67. Allen J. Matusow, *The Unraveling of America: A History of Liberalism in the 1960s* (New York: Harper and Row, 1984); Harvard Sitkoff, *The Struggle for Black Equality, 1954–1992*, rev. ed. (New York: Hill and Wang, 1993), chap. 7; Joyce A. Ladner, *Mixed Families: Adopting across Racial Boundaries* (New York: Anchor Press, 1977), 98–99. For the best history of the arguments against transracial adoption, see Rita J. Simon and Howard Altstein, *Adoption across Borders: Serving the Children in Transracial and Intercountry Adoptions* (Lanham, Md.: Rowman and Littlefield, 2000), chap. 3.

68. Howard Altstein and Rita James Simon, "Transracial Adoption: An Examination of an American Phenomenon," *Journal of Social Welfare* 4 (winter 1977): 65.

69. The results of Simon and Altstein's twenty-year study of transracial adoptees and their families are summarized in Rita J. Simon, Howard Altstein, and Marygold Melli, *The Case for Transracial Adoption* (Lanham, Md.: American University Press, 1994). See also Rita J. Simon, "Adoption and the Race Factor: How Important Is It?" *Sociological Inquiry* 68 (1998): 274–79; Simon and Altstein, *Adoption across Borders*, chap. 4.

70. Richard P. Barth, "Adoption," *Encyclopedia of Social Work*, 19th ed. (Washington, D.C.: National Association of Social Workers, 1995), 1:52.

71. National Committee for Adoption, *Adoption Factbook* (Washington, D.C.: National Committee for Adoption, 1985), 14.

72. Alfred Kadushin, *Child Welfare Services*, 3d ed. (New York: Macmillan, 1980), 470.

73. Richard P. Barth, "A Decade Later: Outcomes of Permanency Planning," in *The Adoption Assistance and Child Welfare Act of 1980 (Public Law 96-272): The First Ten Years* (St. Paul, Minn.: North American Council on Adoptable Children, 1990); Barth, "Adoption," 51–52.

74. Naomi R. Cahn, "Children's Interest in a Familial Context: Poverty, Foster Care, and Adoption," *Ohio State Law Journal* 60 (1999): 1189–90; Stephanie Jill Gendell, "In Search of Permanency: A Reflection on the First 3 Years of the Adoption and Safe Families Act Implementation," *Family Court Review* 39, no. 1 (Jan. 2001): 25. See also Martin Guggenheim, "The Foster Care Dilemma and What to Do About It: Is the Problem that Too Many Children Are Not Being Adopted Out of Foster Care or that Too Many Children Are Entering Foster Care?" *University of Pennsylvania Journal of Constitutional Law* 2, no. 1 (1999): 141–49; Elizabeth Bartholet, *Nobody's Children: Abuse and Neglect, Foster Drift, and the Adoption Alternative* (Boston: Beacon Press, 1999). It is too early to say whether the Adoption and Safe Families Act of 1997 is a success. For a cautiously optimistic view, see Gendell, "In Search," 32–35. For a more critical view, see Robert Gordon, "Drifting Through Byzantium: The Promise and Failure of the Adoption and Safe Families Act of 1997," *Minnesota Law Review* 83 (1999): 637–701.

75. Tamar Lewin, "New Families Redraw Racial Boundaries," *New York Times*, Oct. 27, 1998, A1, A18.

76. The official name of the treaty is the Hague Convention on Protection of Children and Cooperation in Respect of Intercountry Adoption (Treaty Doc. 10551) (Miles A. Pomper, "Adoption Treaty Approved by Senate Panel," *Congressional Quarterly Weekly* 4 [Apr. 4, 2000]: 915–16).

77. Ruth G. McRoy, Harold D. Grotevant, Kerry L. White, *Openness in Adoption: New Practices, New Issues* (New York: Praeger, 1988); Carp, *Family Matters*, chap. 7.

78. Barth, "Adoption," 55.

79. Reuben Pannor and Annette Baran, "Open Adoption as Standard Practice," *Child Welfare* 63 (1984): 245–50.

80. Carp, *Family Matters*, 214–15.

81. Barth, "Adoption," 55. For cautiously optimistic views of open adoption, see Harriet E. Gross, "Open Adoption: A Research-Based Literature Review and New Data," *Child Welfare* 72 (May–June 1993): 269–84; Harriet E. Gross, "Variants of Open Adoptions: The Early Years," *Marriage and Family Review* 25 (1997): 19–42.

82. Carp, *Family Matters*, chap. 5.

83. Ibid., chap. 6.

84. Joan H. Hollinger, "Aftermath of Adoption: Legal and Social Consequences," in *Adoption Law and Practice*, 1995 supp., ed. Hollinger et al. (New York: Matthew Bender, 1995), 2:51, app. 13-A.

85. Sam Howe Verhovek, "Oregon Adoptees Granted Access to Birth Records," *New York Times*, May 31, 2000, A16; Alvin Benn, "State Opens Birth Records," *Montgomery Advertiser*, Aug. 2, 2000, 1A; CWLA, *Standards of Excellence for Adoption Services*, rev. ed. (Washington, D.C.: CWLA, 2000), 89.

A Good Home

Indenture and Adoption in
Nineteenth-Century Orphanages

Susan L. Porter

Adoption in the nineteenth century occurred at the nexus of new attitudes about the family, women's roles, childhood, and class. Today, adoption is generally seen as a means by which middle-class infertile couples can establish families by relieving young unmarried women of their unwanted babies, and the ideal adoptee is a newborn. But two hundred years ago, Americans, who had no tradition of adopting nonrelatives, were reluctant to admit babies from different class and ethnic backgrounds into their homes. Infant mortality, especially among bottle-fed babies, was very high and illegitimacy was seen as a "blood taint." However, as families in this period became increasingly conceptualized as emotional rather than economic units, and as a developing ideology of separate spheres named women as the guardians of the home, motherhood took on new importance and status. Thus, although adoption was considered perilous, middle-class families began to express interest in taking in children to raise as their own.[1]

Unrelated children could commonly be found as apprentices or indentured servants in nineteenth-century households. In the colonial period, children of all classes generally spent a number of years in homes other than their own learning the skills that would make them productive members of a family economy. But, after the American Revolution, the U.S. economy diversified, and middle-class couples, at least in urban centers on the eastern seaboard, began to conceive of their children more as objects of devotion and sentimental attachment than as potential labor. Working-class children, however, still spent much of their youths in other people's homes, working as domestic servants or trade apprentices. Indenture remained common because poor and working-class parents needed to provide their children with occupational skills and reduce household expenses at a time when economic changes were making it more difficult for working-class families to survive. Adoption, therefore, may have been

27

understood more as an offshoot of indenture (an economic and conditional contract based on the exchange of labor) rather than as a legal arrangement based on mutual sentiment.[2]

Massachusetts passed the country's first adoption law in 1851. This watershed event has led legal historians, for example, to frame the history of adoption in terms of the development of family law and the interests of the state. As these scholars observe, the legal practice of adoption became customary in countries that adopted Roman law, but, in the United States, which followed English jurisprudence, American common law prohibited adoption, emphasizing the inviolability of (legitimate) blood claims. Adoption issues reached the courts in regard to dynastic issues about inheritance and the preservation of family names in families that had money and estates but lacked legitimate offspring, even though adoption was undoubtedly more common as a way of providing for the orphaned offspring of relatives and other close connections. In these cases, however, policies were established primarily through legislation.[3]

Social welfare historians have regarded adoption, like other child welfare issues, from the perspective of its relationship to apprenticeship and other forms of indentured labor, the traditional means of handling children whose parents were unable to care for them. Orphaned children without estates were also informally adopted by relatives and close connections when possible, but families on the margins of survival often could not afford to permanently provide for extra children. Like legal historians, social welfare historians have framed their concerns in terms of the interests of the state and the elite classes that maintain it. In this formulation, adoption was either a means of moving children from unhealthy environments into families that would train them to be productive citizens of the modern state or a means of providing innocent victims of misfortune with the advantages of middle-class family life and a secure future.[4]

Most recently, women's and family historians have begun to study adoption from the perspective of sentiment, marking legal issues and the interests of the state as secondary. As motherhood became increasingly valued in the nineteenth century, these scholars argue, families became willing to go to ever greater lengths to fill their "empty cradles." As a result, poor or illegitimate children whose parents could not maintain them now had the opportunity to grow up in a complete family where they would be loved and provided for.[5]

All of these perspectives are based on the assumption that as childhood came to be seen as a particular stage of life, public child welfare policies and case law came to be dominated by the perceived best interests of the child rather than those of adults. Thus, for example, children were for the first time removed from the family or a family replacement into institutional or other settings that meant to improve on rather than replicate the family structure. Boarding schools, academies, and orphan asylums came to be seen as places where the future stakeholders of a new republic based on independence rather than deference and class hierarchy would acquire the book learning and habits of industry and order they needed to function as virtuous citizens. Because the United States was seen as rich in resources and scarce in labor, all young men and women were believed to have the capacity to succeed if they could learn to function in socially productive ways. The fact that poverty continued to exist in American society could be explained only by defects in character that were generally seen as environmental rather than inherited.

Thus, institutions were designed to remove children from unfit families or disrupted households and place them in environments where they could learn moral and occupational skills. Middle-class and elite policymakers had a bifurcated social vision: children belonged in good families, but poor families were by definition defective, even when their heads were "deserving" men and women whose suffering was brought on by tragedy rather than incapacity or deviant behavior. Consequently, children were placed in institutions that would serve as home and school and then indentured into families during adolescence to learn the skills and moral lessons that would lead to success in life.[6]

In this essay, I will suggest that integrating institutions—in this case, orphanages—into the adoption triad reveals a new perspective on nineteenth-century adoption in a transitional phase. The managers of private, nonsectarian Protestant orphan asylums established by women between 1800 and 1820 were primarily concerned about the welfare of the children who became their wards and used whatever options they had to further that welfare as they perceived it. As early as the 1820s, adoption was one of those options. Managers embraced adoption as one means of solving their difficulties with the indenture system.

However, because the managers found that adoptive parents did not make as clear a distinction between indenture and adoption, in the end they decided that adoption was not the panacea for which they had hoped. In addition, they were not convinced that adoption was a better alternative to returning children to their relations when possible. Many mothers, fathers, and other relatives who relinquished their children to institutions did not see themselves as permanently giving up their parental roles. Most chose to place their children in orphan asylums as part of their own survival strategies, expecting to maintain contact with their offspring at the orphanages, after indenture, and into adulthood. When able, these parents asked to have their children returned to them for indenture. Although asylum managers were at first reluctant to comply with such requests, eventually they recognized that returning children to blood relatives was the best placement alternative because they were the parties most invested in the children's welfare.

The managers of orphan asylums saw their work as promoting rather than rejecting a family model. In the first two decades of the 1800s, the women who ran asylums believed that they were encouraging better futures for the children by indenturing them in families like their own. By the 1830s, difficulties with indenture and a burgeoning domestic ideology led asylum managers to try a variety of means of reestablishing homes for their inmates, including returning them to their relations when feasible and allowing increasing numbers to be adopted by middle-class couples who wished to raise children as their own. Thus, institutions came to use adoption as one alternative to an indenture system that the managers saw as problematic.

American women established more than a dozen orphan asylums between 1800 and 1820. While their objectives were almost identical, they served somewhat different clienteles. The Boston Female Asylum (founded in 1800) and the Female Orphan Society of Norfolk, Virginia (1804), took in girls who had lost one or both parents; the Orphan Asylum of the City of New York (1806) and the Philadelphia Orphan Society (1815) admitted boys and girls who were full orphans. The Washington City Orphan Asylum (1815) was designed for half-orphaned and orphaned girls but began to admit both sexes in 1828. Despite these variations, however, these institutions were more alike than different.[7]

Their founders created these associations out of sympathy for dependent children and their determination that vulnerable young children should grow up independent and self-reliant. The Boston Female Asylum (BFA), the first such institution, was created when Hannah Stillman, the wife of Boston's most prominent Baptist minister, heard about a poor young girl who had been seduced and then read a newspaper report about a female humane society in Baltimore. Stillman began to think of ways to protect young girls and decided that an orphan asylum that would serve as home and school would be most effective because "a good education is one of the best barriers for the security and defence of assailed virtue." Asylums in New York and Philadelphia were established after epidemics. Because the early officers needed to demonstrate that women could be efficient managers, they were careful to balance their compassion with prudence, but they held firm to their belief that asylums should be well-ordered families rather than rigid institutions. The managers attempted to hire matrons and teachers who would provide love and warmth as well as the training and education required for the orphans' future success, and the highest compliment an employee could receive was that she performed her role "with the fidelity of a mother."[8]

Still, orphanage managers worried that the children did not receive enough personal attention and loving care. The managers attempted to fill such gaps by taking children home for holidays and on outings with their families or by assigning each board member personal responsibility for a few children. Managers felt confident that the children's experience in the asylums was positive, especially as the institutions gained confidence and status in their communities from their work and the new moral authority women were achieving as mothers.[9]

Early orphan asylums were designed to protect young boys and girls from the evils of a public poor law system that apprenticed even very young impoverished children through work contracts designed for older children. While indenture was the traditional means of providing children with artisan skills, contracts offered few protections against neglect and abuse and provided virtually no guarantees that the children would be educated above and beyond their trade provisions, many of which were minimal for girls and irrelevant for younger apprentices. The orphanages generally admitted children who were under ten and educated them in the institution until they reached the traditional apprenticeship age (eleven to fourteen), when they were indentured to families in the usual manner. The orphanages retained the idea of apprenticeship because boys needed to learn trades and because the managers believed that adolescent children should be part of families where they would have "the advantages of a permanent home, thorough instruction in all necessary things and the power of making friends who may be of incalculable benefit to them through life." Orphanage managers hoped to protect young children from becoming "hewers of wood and drawers of water" and expected that the children would be treated well in their receiving families.[10]

Asylum founders saw themselves as providing long-term solutions to the problem of children who were too young to be a financial help to either their families of origin or their families of indenture; in fact, most children stayed in the institutions for several years. One of the founders' primary tasks was to create a stable environment for the children, a physical setting in which the children could devote themselves to educational achievement and character development. Another goal was to find secure placements when the children were ready to leave. Both tasks turned out to be more complicated than anticipated.

At the beginning of the applicant interview process, the founders saw both the children and their relatives as the blameless victims of misfortune and were sympathetic rather than judgmental. But conflicts quickly arose with particularly difficult, interfering, or untruthful relatives. In the first month of the BFA's existence, for example, the managers discovered that the facts of a case had been misrepresented. Hannah Fovell, the third child admitted, had been described as being in a "most wretched forlorn situation, deprived of *Parental* protection by Death in one of the authors of her being and cruelly abandoned by the other— Thrown into a Negro Flat and exposed to the vilest precepts and examples Imagination could paint." Two weeks later the managers discovered that the child's aunt had invented most of the story. Hannah's mother had left the child in her aunt's care for a few months while pursuing a job in western Massachusetts. Hannah's mother had sent money for her support and was planning to claim her in three months. The aunt had placed Hannah in the asylum when more funds failed to appear, but when payment was received, the aunt decided to reclaim the girl. The managers let her go, ordering the matron to deliver her "with the cloaths she had on when put under her protection." The managers could have insisted that the aunt pay the child's board for her time at the BFA, but they did not. Sixteen months later, Hannah's mother, again penniless and out of work successfully requested her readmission. The managers' sympathy for the child clearly outweighed their difficulties with her relatives.[11]

Some observers believed that the ladies were too kind, even naive, and admonished them "carefully to guard against impositions. Experience has already taught the necessity of this as such impositions have been attempted." The managers of the first women's organization in Boston, as concerned for their own reputations as the welfare of their wards, took this advice seriously and began to pass rules to protect themselves. By October 1803 the BFA managers had voted to limit the visits of relatives who were late in returning children and to check the veracity of applicants' stories. The tone of these new policies revealed a distrust of the children's relations as well as an increased focus on the value of the managers' work as advocates for children in need of protection from evil influences. The disadvantages of exposure to intemperate or immoral relatives seemed more compelling than the maintenance of familial ties.[12]

A parallel trend applied in relation to indenture, especially at institutions that admitted half-orphans. At first, a number of children were returned to parents or other relatives who had remarried or otherwise recovered their ability to maintain an older and potentially productive child (nine of sixty-five [13.8 percent] BFA placements before 1815). However, the managers became more disgruntled with birth families and became less likely to return children to them (only five of eighty-five [5.9 percent] BFA placements between 1816 and 1825).[13]

The apprenticeship experience was particularly important for children who had spent several years in an institution. As the Philadelphia managers commented in 1834, "a child reared within the bounds of such an institution, is more liable to imposition, more open to temptations, than one of the same age who has been abroad, observing the ways of men; but may they not likewise be more free from the taint of vicious example?" Thus they "implore[d] those to whom they are transferred at the age of 12 years—to blend the character of parent with that of master towards these orphan children." The managers hoped that the children would be regarded more as family members than as unpaid workers. Orphanage officials believed that girls in particular, because they did not learn artisan skills, should be placed in homes where they would have the best advantages—well-educated mistresses and masters, financial comforts, and useful connections.[14]

Managers looked for these homes among their peers and tried to be accommodating to friends and neighbors believed to be as sympathetic and motherly as the managers themselves. When, in 1802, Hannah Smith requested that she "might take Betsy Durril at an earlier period than the time of her regular dismission," the managers voted "that Mrs. Smith be permitted to take Betsy Durril as soon as she wishes." It would have been hard to refuse this favor to the wife of the man who had just collected and donated nine thousand dollars for the BFA building fund.[15]

The managers' faith in their peers and focus on "advantages" meant that relatives who requested that children be returned to them for the apprenticeship period were at a disadvantage. This became clear as early as 1806 in a BFA debate over Mary Barron, a child admitted in 1802. Mary's mother had remarried and had for more than a year requested that her daughter be bound out to her. She had "lost her other children" and felt that she was now "competent to the maintenance of this daughter." When the time came for Mary's indenture, the managers discussed this plea and that of Susannah Nye Freeman, "a lady who had long preferred her solicitation for the first girl. The claim of parental feelings obtained its due influence in the decision; which was operated with the utmost tenderness, candor and resolution." In the end, however, the officials voted to bind Mary to Freeman.[16]

Eventually, however, the officers' duty to advocate for their wards forced them to question this stance after children who were bound to the managers' friends and peers were treated poorly. The conflict between the managers' duties and their class identity could be painful. In 1803 Hannah Fovell, the child whose aunt had lied about her background, was indentured to Elizabeth Sumner, the widow of former governor Increase Sumner. Finding the girl "troublesome," Sumner tried to return her to the BFA three years later. The officers informed Sumner that they could make no exceptions, even for her, to the rule that children were bound "without warranty" and told her to do "with her that which she should judge to be most advantageous to the child and convenient to herself." Sumner then transferred Hannah to a Mrs. Schellebeck, from whom she suffered "very cruel treatment." Hannah ran away, finding protection in the Caswell family. After a year, the Schellebecks demanded her return and "she was yielded very unwillingly by her kind protectress, from whom she parted with extreme reluctance." Sometime later, Hannah absconded again. At this point the board felt obliged to intervene in an area in "which motives of delicacy had long prevented their enquiring into minutely." The child was found and "restored to the Asylum" while the managers sought a legal opinion about whether they could legally bind her out to someone new. After a favorable decision, Hannah was returned to the Caswells with a formal indenture. Under the influence of kindness, a manager later commented, Hannah Fovell became "a good and useful girl."[17]

Hannah Fovell's case exemplifies the managers' developing distrust of the wealthy women who took children in as apprentices. Hard experience taught the managers that neither birth parents nor surrogate families could always be relied on to take proper care of the orphans. As the Philadelphia officers lamented in 1829, "the Board consider the duties of the Binding Committee the most arduous, and most liable to disappointment. . . . The waywardness of children may frequently require discipline and habitual strictness, but can afford no apology for cruelty or total neglect; nor should those who assume the responsibility of masters and protectors to orphan children, use them otherwise than mercifully and justly."[18]

The managers' frustration over placements led them to rethink their attitude toward the orphans' relatives. In 1822 the BFA managers decided to send Margaret Cuddy to live with her father, William, who had remarried a "worthy woman" and "by industry and frugality . . . obtained the means of establishing a home for their family, into which it is their wish to receive one of his two children. These children have been preserved from want and vice; and will be restored, prepared to be a comfort and assistance, to a father who will, it is believed, discharge with faithfulness his parental duty toward them." The managers' decision in this case was based on moral as well as financial considerations. Because Cuddy had demonstrated virtue and perseverance, he deserved to have his daughter returned to him. By 1825 the board was willing to tell a relative that if the situation were "equally advantageous," "her claim of relationship would give her a preference." This policy was exercised several times during the next few months when children were bound to relations who offered "eligible" places.[19]

Over time, more and more orphans were returned to relatives perceived as financially secure and morally responsible. As a result, by the 1840s, almost half of the BFA orphans were indentured to family members (see table 1). In 1850 the Washington City Orphan Asylum (WCOA) reported that four of the seven children who left that year went to relatives, two were adopted, and only one was bound to a family.[20]

The asylum managers had come to recognize that placement in an elite family could not guarantee a child's security or happiness when the relationship was contractual rather than emotional. The managers had found that mis-

TABLE 1.   BFA Orphans Indentured to Relatives

Year Indentured	Number	Total Cohort	Percentage of Cohort
1802–15	9	65	13.8%
1816–25	5	85	5.9
1826–37	26	107	24.3
1838–45	37	85	43.5
1846–55	77	131	58.8
1856–65	61	151	40.4
1867–75	48	108	44.4

tresses often sought to "procure the most service at the least price. . . . In the idea of the servant they lose sight of the child, the one needing all the instruction and forbearing and restraint which childhood always required. . . .You take a child . . . in punishing her faults consider how you would endeavor to correct those of your own children." Increasingly believing that children could thrive only in environments where they felt ties based on sentiment and loyalty, the managers returned orphans to their relatives when this option was viable.[21]

However, although asylum managers wished every orphan to experience both economic security and a loving home, the majority of the children could not return to their families of origin. Thus, in the 1820s, when asylum managers began to be approached by families who wished to adopt children to bring up as their own, the officials saw these placements as ideal opportunities (see table 2). The first such BFA adoption took place in 1822, when the managers discovered that a four-year-old child who had been in the asylum for a year did not "come within the number of those for whom this charity was designed." The problem of her disposition was solved when Josiah Bradlee, a wealthy Dorchester merchant, and his second wife, Joanna Frothingham Bradlee, sister to two BFA board members, offered to adopt the girl.[22]

Such informal adoptions often took place outside the formal structure of the asylum, and many may have gone unrecorded. In June 1824, for example, the BFA managers noted that a child whose admission application had been discussed in April had been "adopted by a friend." Some friends may even have asked asylum officers to look out for potential adoptees. In 1832 Rebecca Gratz, the longtime secretary of the Philadelphia Orphan Society (POS), wrote to her sister-in-law that she had "promised our friend Mrs. Furness to apply for a little girl out of the asylum for her—well there is a good little girl I have kept my eye on and she is ready for a place." Many children who were considered too young to be in orphanages may also have found homes through the managers' acquaintances. An infant placed at board by the WCOA managers in January 1841, for example, was never admitted because the child was adopted in April by "Mrs. Darnell who engaged to accept it as her own."[23]

TABLE 2.   BFA Orphans Adopted

Year Adopted	Number	Total Cohort	Percentage of Cohort
1816–25	3	85	3.5
1826–37	6	107	5.6
1838–45	16	85	18.9
1846–55	6	131	4.6
1856–65	12	151	7.9
1866–75	4	108	3.7
	47	667	7.0

Many other adoptions undoubtedly occurred as part of the process of placing children when households dissolved. Relatives or family friends often took in children who were sickly or were for other reasons unlikely to do well in an orphanage. In 1836, a grandmother adopted Amelia Smith's older brother, Hosea, for example, while she was placed in the POS because he was "more delicate than Amelia and therefore an object of greater interest." Mr. and Mrs. John Staniford of East Cambridge, Massachusetts, had adopted Mary Ann Collier's sister in 1831, when she was placed in the BFA. Two years later the Stanifords asked to take Mary Ann as well. As the managers noted, "They have no children of their own and have now the means as well as the disposition to act as parents." In addition, relatives and family friends who had formed a connection with the orphans before they entered the institution sometimes later asked to adopt them. Ten BFA orphans between 1822 and 1875 were adopted through such connections: five by aunts, one by a grandmother, and four others by those who "though not related had always shown the interest of a parent."[24]

These situations may have been common, but they were not the ones asylum managers publicized. The classic asylum adoption story is represented by an 1838 New York case. Susan Brown, "a very attractive little orphan girl, aged about two years," had lost both parents. As the Orphan Asylum Society of the City of New York managers reported, "we had many offers for her adoption." They were pleased that

> the infant immediately took to Mr. and Mrs. G., called them mother and father and accompanied them to their home most cheerfully. Mr. G., after keeping her a week, upon calling for the indenture said he would not give her up for $1,000. He presented the Society with a donation of $50 and requested for the future to be considered a subscriber for $25 per annum. He also pledged himself to educate her in the best manner, to give her all the advantages that money could procure, that in case misfortune should arise she might be able to educate others and retain a respectable station in life, still considering her his own child.[25]

At least in theory, adoption would solve the conflict between empathy and opportunity that the managers continually faced in their attempts to protect their wards. The adopted child would be treated and educated like a member of the family. The child's physical and emotional needs would be served, and her parents would consider themselves amply repaid by the pleasure of having a complete family. The managers would be rewarded (even monetarily, as in this case) for making everyone happy. In this sentimental image, the managers were matchmakers between needy young children and childless middle-class couples; the children were, like Susan Brown, young, appealing, and usually female. The expectation was that the child and her new mother and father would live happily and prosperously ever after.

But asylum adoptions were only part of a larger trend, as children became a valued emotional commodity in a culture that revered the family. In 1842 an adoption agency opened in Boston. Eunice and Anstrice Fellows, two unmarried middle-aged, spinster sisters, ran the organization from their large house on Tremont Street and published a monthly newsletter, the *Orphans' Advocate and Social Monitor.* They hired agents who traveled throughout the northeast, matching children and homes to "infuse joy and quiet and happiness into social life." The service was free; interested families were told only that they must treat the children "as equal members of the family circle." If the sisters' account can be believed, they were extremely successful: between 1842 and 1856 they claimed to have placed between three and five hundred children per year, more than any institution. Requests came from as far away as Washington, D.C.; and one third of the placements between 1843 and 1854 occurred outside Massachusetts.[26]

These children, like the children adopted from asylums, were legally bound through an indenture contract at least until 1851, when the Massachusetts adoption law was enacted, and probably later. As Joseph Ben-Or has pointed out, this law may have been a response to the geometrically increasing numbers of private acts submitted to the Massachusetts legislature to legally change the names of adopted children. Although comparative statistics on orphanage adoptions do show higher rates of adoption from the BFA (the POS recorded only five adoptions and the WCOA only recorded three for children admitted before 1841, much lower numbers than the BFA's nineteen), it is clear that families across the United States had begun to express interest in adopting children who were unrelated or even illegitimate.[27]

In this period, however, the meanings of adoption, whether legal or through indenture, are complex. Although the sentimental representation of the adoption story emphasizing the heartwarming match between the childless couple and the adorable toddler appealed to both the Fellows sisters and asylum managers, it is not clear that most people who adopted children either fit this pattern or shared these expectations. An analysis of the data for fifty-six children adopted from the BFA, the POS, and the WCOA demonstrates that while asylum managers prayed that orphans would be adopted by "persons who ... will supply, as far as may be the places of their natural protectors," real adoption stories rarely match this idealized image.[28]

First, few of the children were adopted very young. Only about a quarter (fourteen of the fifty-three children for whom age is known) were adopted before they were six years old, and another quarter (thirteen children) were adopted at the usual time of indenture. Thus, the typical child left the asylum at the age of seven or eight, too old to be an adorable toddler but old enough to have a known character, young enough to benefit from a middle-class education but not too young to be helpful in the household.[29]

Second, it is not at all clear that most of the adoptive families were childless couples. In the fifteen cases for which information about offspring is available, seven had living birth children. In addition, three children were taken by single women "to be brought up as a sister" and a number of others may have been adopted by widows.[30]

Third, not all the adopted children went to wealthy homes. Although the couples who adopted children not connected to them by blood or friendship were able to offer significant economic and social advantages, the three children adopted by family friends and five taken by relatives went to homes that were economically quite similar to those of the orphans' parents. Harriet Morton, for example, was adopted from the BFA in 1840 at the age of seven by Mr. and Mrs. Benjamin Hawes, an older couple (he was sixty-nine and she was fifty-two) with grown children (a carpenter and an apothecary), who "took care of her in infancy." Louisa Smith went to live in Beverly with her aunt and uncle, a sea captain, as an adopted child in 1843, when she was almost twelve. At eighteen, she went to work as a cook at the asylum. Two months later, she left to stay with another mariner relative, and later that year, she became a servant in the home of a wealthy Boston trader. Adoption may have provided Smith with emotional security, but it certainly did not save her from having to support herself.[31]

Finally, only a minority of the adoptions led to the outcomes the managers envisioned. The success stories were proudly recorded. Catherine Reed, for example, adopted from the BFA by Dr. and Mrs. John Nelson of Lexington in 1835 at the age of twelve, was later described as "a good and dutiful child. Her moral character is without a blemish and she is readily admitted into the best society." At age twenty-one Reed married a clerk who was related to her adoptive mother and had at least two children of her own. Likewise, Susan Dimond, adopted in 1839, was described by her adoptive mother as "a very superior girl." After training to become a teacher, she married a missionary and went with him to England. As the BFA managers effused, "the little girl who was once a street-beggar has now become the wife of a most deserving young man and has gone with him to live among those to whom she will find many opportunities of repaying the good which was once done to her."[32]

Others achieved emotional attachment but not upward mobility. Mary Ann Collier, for example, stayed with the Staniford family even after Mrs. Staniford died in 1840 and lived in Cambridge for many years thereafter. She married John Fraser, a Cambridge carpenter, in 1844 and had at least three children. While Mary Ann was probably financially secure, her adoption did not move her into a different class.[33]

Although the orphans described here achieved the managers' goals of emotional family ties, eleven of the fifty-five adopted children (20 percent) who survived to the age of eighteen had negative experiences with their new families. These figures demonstrate a side of the adoption experience rarely discussed in literature on the subject. Five orphans, including two of the three adopted by single women, were transferred to new homes during their minorities because they, the asylum managers, or their adoptive parents were dissatisfied, and six others, like Louisa Smith, are known to have left as soon as they turned eighteen. At least one was abused. Adoption did not necessarily imply a permanent commitment on the part of the adoptive parents or a guarantee for the child's future security.[34]

Because the legal document for all placements was an indenture contract, the managers retained the same responsibility for adopted children as for the rest of their wards' welfare and attempted to oversee all placements. The managers understood that adoptions could be as problematic as regular placements. When the BFA managers reported in 1849 that Sally Ann Frye had "served her apprenticeship acceptably and is capable of supporting herself well," they could have been describing any indentured orphan. They may have been disappointed that Frye's adoption did not lead to a long-term attachment, but they were not surprised.[35]

Asylum officials' experience with Samuel Coves, a prospective adoptive father, may shed light on their discretion. In 1839 Coves expressed interest in adopting Lucinda Nash, aged three and a half, from the BFA. The Coveses, who had "lost their own children," were cautious about this endeavor. Before officially approaching the managers, Coves had gone to talk to Lucinda's uncle, her nearest available relative (Lucinda's father was at sea) and gained his permission to pursue the adoption. In his official request, Coves wrote, "I will be bound for her support and education, provided I can have the legal custody of the child free from all interference of the father or other relations." The Coveses were equally reserved about their emotional commitment to the child:

> The intention of Mrs. Coves and myself, is to give her the same maintenance and education that we would give to our own daughter, and generally to look upon her as far as we are able as upon our own child. What we can do for her will depend much on her character and disposition, but we are so favorably impressed by the child that we doubt not but that we shall be amply repaid for giving her a home as long as she shall need it. It is for you to decide what will be best for the child, and I can only add, should you place her under our care, we shall feel a deep responsibility for her welfare.[36]

This letter reveals the conditional nature of adoption as it evolved from indenture, a contractual arrangement based on economic mutual self-interest, into a legal contract based on sentiment. The key words here are "to look at her as far as we are able as upon our own child." Families were used to taking in children as servants or apprentices and sometimes developed close personal attachments to them. When this happened, the families remained the children's patrons throughout life and even occasionally left them legacies. However, although close, these were generally not relationships between equals. Patronage was not parentage. In an environment with no tradition of nonblood adoptions, adoptive parents may have questioned their ability to develop truly parental attachments. Even indenture, a contract based on obligations, could have seemed onerous when an adolescent child was sick, unruly, or unproductive. Adoption implied permanent emotional as well as economic responsibilities and adoptive parents must have sometimes questioned the balance between their desire to have heirs and the extent of their duty. As the statistics demonstrate, some adoptive children were like their indentured peers: they had mixed experiences in their apprenticeship home and were transferred elsewhere or stayed until their contracts expired, when they moved on.

In this case, as in others, the asylum managers banked on sentiment and allowed the Coveses to adopt Lucinda Nash. The risk in this case was probably justified: although I could find no information about Lucinda's later movements, her name was eventually changed to Coves. But other children were less lucky, and once again the asylum managers found no easy answers to their placement predicament.[37]

The mixed attitudes toward adoption also are clear in the placement patterns of the children matched through the *Orphans' Advocate*. Children and families not matched by agents (probably about one-fifth of the total placements) were listed in the monthly newsletters. An analysis of these listings indicates that, at least at first, prospective adoptive families did not see as great a distinction between indenture and adoption as the Fellows sisters would have liked. The listings of children who needed homes contained mostly young children. Most of these children were young and male, with median ages of six in 1843; seven in 1847; five in 1851; and three in 1855 (see table 3). But families wanted children, and girls in particular, who were an age to be helpful in the household. In the 1840s, only slightly more than a quarter of the families willing to take children were interested in adoption, and they overwhelmingly preferred older children. More than five out of six families wanted girls (see table 4).

The Fellows sisters were well aware of these facts and repeatedly admonished their readers to adopt infants, boys as well as girls. As one 1846 piece argued, "Would you adopt a child that shall love you as your own? Take an infant. Would you have one whom you shall love as your own? Take an infant. Would you do good by taking another's child? Let it be an infant. Indeed, for all purposes of usefulness, pleasure, or benefit to yourselves and others, take an infant." In 1848 the sisters declaimed, "If we were to become a helpless orphan child, we should not like to become a boy. . . . It is almost as great a misfortune to be born a poor boy, and lose father and mother, as with deformed and crooked limbs." In 1849, they reflected that "when we first entered upon these labors, it seemed to be taken for granted that nobody was going to adopt a babe. . . . We cannot see why all persons, adopting a child, should not prefer one that would know no other parents, and one whom they could bring up from the first, according to their own ideas of what is proper."[38]

However, while the articles the Fellowses published relentlessly promoted infant adoption and emotional family bonds, the data demonstrate that infant adoption was a hard sell. Although the sisters succeeded over time in convincing families to adopt younger children (the median age of children requested declined from eleven in 1843 to three in 1854), even in 1854 only slightly over one-quarter (twenty-six of ninety-nine, or 26.3 percent) of the families expressed interest in taking infants. Boys remained difficult to place: even in 1854, seven of every ten families requested girls (see table 4). When the Fellowses reminded their readers in 1855 to "Remember that *young children* need homes as well as older ones," they delineated the boundaries of the market. Adding that "this class of children are those that more particularly impose their claims upon community. Would that all orphan boys had found friends before they became suitable inmates of the States Prisons," the sisters not only revealed their belief in the family as guardian of the interests of the state but also delineated the cultural concerns about boys, those less desirable "little curly-headed rogues in jackets and trowsers."[39]

Believing that "the family relation, divinely ordained, is the only medium for imparting proper education and direction to the young mind," Eunice and Anstrice Fellows opposed even the temporary placement of children in institutions and, to some extent, saw them as competitors. While the Fellowses

TABLE 3.   *Orphans' Advocate*—Children Needing Homes

	1843	1847	1851	1855	Totals
Under 1	11 (12.8%)	34 (10.9%)	88 (25.5)	72 (32.3%)	205 (21.2%)
1–5 yrs	22 (25.6)	75 (24.1)	99 (28.7)	76 (34.1)	272 (28.2)
6–9 yrs	34 (39.5)	86 (27.7)	84 (24.3)	59 (26.5)	263 (27.3)
10+ yrs	19 (22.1)	116 (37.3)	74 (21.4)	16 (7.2)	225 (23.3)
Totals	86	311	345	223	968
Median age					
All	6 yrs	7 yrs	5 yrs	3 yrs	6 yrs
Girls	6	7	5	4	5
Boys	7	8	5	3	6
Boys (%)	71.3	57.3	58.9	57.0	59.1

TABLE 4. Orphans' Advocate—Homes for Children, 1843–54

	1843		1847		1851		1854		Totals	
	Girls	Boys	Girls	Boys	Girls	Boys	Girls	Boys	Girls	Boys
All Listings										
Under 1	0 (0%)	0 (0%)	6 (1.6%)	4 (7.0%)	16 (7.2%)	5 (7.9%)	17 (14.5%)	14 (28.0%)	41 (4.8%)	23 (12.3%)
1–5	7 (5.2)	2 (11.8)	28 (7.2)	9 (15.8)	58 (26.1)	16 (25.4)	64 (54.7)	25 (50.0)	157 (18.3)	52 (27.8)
6–9	22 (16.7)	1 (5.9)	52 (13.4)	3 (5.3)	84 (37.8)	4 (6.3)	30 (25.6)	5 (10.0)	188 (21.9)	13 (7.0)
10+	101 (76.5)	14 (82.4)	301 (77.8)	41 (71.9)	64 (28.8)	38 (60.1)	6 (5.1)	6 (12.0)	472 (55.0)	99 (52.9)
Totals	132	17	387	57	222	63	117	50	858	187
(% Boys)	11.8%		13.2%		22.4%		30.2%		18.2%	
Median age (yrs)	11	12	11	12	8	10	3	2	10	10
Adoptions only										
Median age (yrs)	7.5	3	9	3	8	5.5	3	2	7	3
% of Total	26.1%	11.1%	27.8%	35.6%	97.3%	68.8%	100%	100%	55.3%	61.5%

admired the charitable impulse behind such institutions, they felt that orphanages were expensive and unnatural. The sisters were also suspicious of
the managers' desire to follow the welfare of the children after placement. It
was a point of pride for the Fellowses to trust adoptive families to care prop-
erly for children. As the *Orphans' Advocate* commented in 1848, "according to
our experience in this matter, there is no method so good as to content our-
selves with bringing together the benevolent seeker after a needy child, and
the friends of the little one, and to assume no other than advisory responsibility beyond that. . . . There is such a thing as *doing too much,* as well as too
little." The Fellowses were enraged when they found a prospective home for a
sibling pair they had met in a Philadelphia asylum, but the managers refused
to release the children because the officials "could not entrust them so far
away among strangers!" As the Fellowses argued,

> if the children come here to be adopted, they are at once the happy chil-
> dren of prosperous, kind, and worthy people. If they stay in the institu-
> tion till the age of twelve or fourteen years, they will probably be bound
> out, the girl to service, and the boy to a trade, to lead lives very different
> from what would in the other case be their lot. We put it to the con-
> science of any intelligent parent, which of the two destinations he would
> prefer for his children, if called to leave them orphans.[40]

The sisters' concern for the upward mobility of orphans in many ways reflected that of their opponents in this matter. But the interchange also reveals
the complicated understandings of adoption in this period. The Fellowses and
the orphanage managers shared the goal of representing the best interests of the
children they served, but their differing attitudes were shaped by their divergent
experiences. While neither orphanage officials nor the Fellows sisters expected
to be their wards' only advocates, the managers saw themselves as acting in loco
parentis after the children were placed. The Fellows sisters, like the agents of the
New York Children's Aid Society and other such organizations, trusted in a self-
regulating community: "neighbors," they argued, "are quite as ready to interfere
in behalf of an adopted, as of an own child."[41]

Both groups understood that adopted children, like indentured ones, remained part of a larger community that could include their relatives. Adoptions
were not closed, as they would be in the twentieth century: when children were
adopted, their relatives were consulted and were expected to know the children's whereabouts. While the level of contact between those relatives and the
child varied with the preferences of the adoptive family and the age of the child,
the expectation was that the children would know that they had been adopted.
The *Orphans' Advocate* repeatedly cited examples in which "the mother saw
him often, and was received with kindness whenever she visited him." It also

approvingly reported an 1848 Philadelphia court case in which the judge ruled that while a four-year-old should stay with her adoptive parents because they could provide for her better than her mother, the mother "could visit her child whenever she pleased," to which the adoptive mother, who deeply commisserated her situation, readily assented.[42]

The relations between adoptive and birth families were often open but may also have been strained. The Philadelphia case was brought to court because the mother wished to regain custody of her child. Samuel Coves was determined to make his adoption of Lucinda Nash contingent on a guarantee of noninterference from her relatives. Children who were adopted young would have fewer memories of their previous families, a fact that may have made such adoptions particularly appealing to those responsible for such matches.

As Jamil Zainaldin and Peter Tyor argue in their study of Boston's Temporary Home for the Destitute, founded in 1847, the market for adoptable children grew rapidly in Boston in the 1850s and '60s. In this short-term asylum, younger children became the most marketable commodity (see table 5). The percentage of children adopted from the Temporary Home increased steadily between the 1840s and the 1880s. The institution began to "concentrate more exclusively on meeting the needs of the childless population" and in 1871 opened a "Baby Department" to handle requests for "superficially intelligent, appealing, white, healthy youngsters." Between 1860 and 1880 the average age of adopted children decreased from 4.1 to 1.3, while the mean age of those returned to parents or friends increased from 6.5 to 7.1. Still, as in the BFA and other orphan asylums, in every cohort more children were returned to their relatives than were adopted, and until the 1880s, significantly more were indentured than were adopted.[43]

Asylum managers who saw their institutions as schools rather than as temporary shelters were defensive about the *Orphans' Advocate* and the increasing numbers of institutions, such as the Temporary Home and the Children's Aid Society, that sent children into homes at young ages. In 1857, when a philan-

TABLE 5.   Placements—Temporary Home for the Destitute

Years	Adoptions		Placed Out		Returned to Parents or Friends		Totals
1846–55	39	(18.6%)	101	(48.1%)	70	(33.3%)	210
1856–65	103	(21.4)	183	(38.0)	195	(40.5)	481
1866–77	244	(23.6)	415	(40.1)	376	(36.3)	1,035
1878–88	388	(30.8)	184	(14.6)	688	(54.6)	1,260

Note: Calculated from Zainaldin and Tyor "Asylum and Society," table 1, p. 27. Zainaldin and Tyor use estimated figures for some categories in some years; this chart includes only years for which figures are complete: 1849, 1851, 1860, 1865, 1870, 1871, 1875, 1876, 1880, 1881, 1882, 1883, 1885, 1888.

thropist wrote that "Orphan Asylums [are] evils only to be maintained to prevent greater evils and . . . the time will come for more Christian methods of doing good," the BFA managers responded angrily, arguing that "we doubt whether a better behaved set of children will be found anywhere. Nor do we think that under the care of our Matron they suffer any lack of fondness and care; indeed we venture to assert that they meet with more tenderness here than in most families in which they are placed." The managers were not referring only to indenture. As they remarked, "we believe that often, when children of a younger age are taken to be adopted, the adoption is only another name for service." Their experience had led them to distrust the motives of people who stated their wish to bring children up as their own but did not treat their wards as full family members.[44]

The BFA managers' response and the emphasis on infant adoptions may have been two sides of the same coin. Adoptive parents must have worried about their ability to bond with the children of strangers and may have had more success with helpless and appealing infants who had not yet revealed their personalities or expressed their wills. This concern may have also fueled the preference for female children, who were perceived as more dependent, compliant, and malleable. As one *Orphans' Advocate* article stated, boys were "sturdy oaks," while girls "twine[d] themselves like the ivy round every fibre of your hearts."[45]

In addition, adoption could never replace the natural family. Like the Temporary Home, the BFA responded to the Victorian reverence for the family by encouraging the reestablishment of family homes when possible (see table 1). Social welfare historians, including Zainaldin and Tyor, have argued that this trend reflected a social control agenda because "even inadequate parents must be encouraged to 'bear rather than escape' their responsibility." But the orphanage managers' perspective had less to do with social control than with distrust of their peers and the recognition that children needed to be members of families. As the BFA managers noted with satisfaction after Elizabeth Bull left her adoptive home to live with her brother, "she bears a very respectable character, and is a member of Dr. Codman's church." Whether Bull remained with her adoptive family or reconnected with her family of origin was less relevant than the character effected through the formative influence of a good home.[46]

From the perspective of the welfare of the child, then, asylum managers did not see adoption as a panacea. Having determined that adolescent children should live in homes rather than institutions, managers never outright rejected adoption, just as they continued to indenture approximately half the children throughout the century, well after apprenticeship had become virtually obsolete. If the asylum programs were successful in teaching the children moral rectitude, basic skills, and self-reliance, then the orphans could be offered various futures with mistresses, relatives, or adoptive families that might lead not only to independence but also to personal happiness.

The managers maintained the family ideal as they searched for placements. Because officials saw themselves as "moral mothers," they perceived the children as blameless victims in need of sympathy and protection as well as education; as prosperous but dependent women, the managers recognized their wards' need for economic security. After years of coping with the daily operations and frustrations of the social work experience, they developed a professional stance that judged individuals rather than classes. Thus, orphanage managers continued to experiment with a variety of placements, depending on the current options at their disposal and the particular pool of children and relatives. But because these women believed that the asylum could approximate the family and that they and the matrons could serve as surrogate mothers, the managers remained convinced that orphanages served children better than temporary institutions or adoption agencies. Orphan asylums would prepare children for life by educating them carefully and finding them good homes—not just any homes.

NOTES

1. For overviews, see Stephen Mintz and Susan Kellogg, *Domestic Revolutions: A Social History of Family Life* (New York: Free Press, 1988), chap. 3; Stephanie Coontz, *The Social Origins of Private Life* (New York: Verso Press, 1988), chaps. 4–6. On wet nursing, see Janet Golden, *A Social History of Wet Nursing in America: From Breast to Bottle* (New York: Cambridge University Press, 1996).

2. On indenture, see Mintz and Kellogg, *Domestic Revolutions,* 32–36; Robert F. Seybolt, *Apprenticeship and Apprenticeship Education in Colonial New England and New York* (New York: Columbia University Press, 1917); Bruce Laurie, *Artisans into Workers: Labor in Nineteenth-Century America* (New York: Noonday Press, 1989), chap. 1.

3. Stephen B. Presser, "The Historical Background of the American Law of Adoption," *Journal of Family Law* 11 (1976): 443–516; Jamil S. Zainaldin, "The Emergence of a Modern American Family Law: Child Custody, Adoption, and the Courts, 1796–1851," *Northwestern University Law Review* 73 (1979): 1038–89; Joseph Ben-Or, "The Law of Adoption in the United States: Its Massachusetts Origins and the Statute of 1851," *New England Historical and Genealogical Register* 130 (Oct. 1976): 259–72.

4. LeRoy Ashby, *Endangered Children: Dependency, Neglect, and Abuse in American History* (New York: Twayne, 1997); Walter I. Trattner, *From Poor Law to Welfare State: A History of Social Welfare in America,* 5th ed. (New York: Free Press, 1995); David J. Rothman, *The Discovery of the Asylum: Social Order and Disorder in the New Republic,* rev. ed. (Boston: Little, Brown, 1990); Thomas Haskell, "Capitalism and the Origins of the Humanitarian Sensibility," *American Historical Review* 90 (1985): 339–61, 547–66; E. Wayne Carp, "Orphanages vs. Adoption: The Triumph of Biological Kinship, 1800–1933," in *With Us Always: A History of Private Charity and Public Welfare,* ed. Donald T. Critchlow and Charles H. Parker (Lanham, Md.: Rowman and Littlefield, 1998), 123–44.

5. Margaret S. Marsh and Wanda Ronner, *The Empty Cradle: Infertility in America*

from Colonial Times to the Present (Baltimore: Johns Hopkins University Press, 1996); Elaine Tyler May, *Barren in the Promised Land: Childless Americans and the Pursuit of Happiness* (New York: Basic Books, 1995), 37–42.

6. Ashby, *Endangered Children*, 18–28; Priscilla Ferguson Clement, *Welfare and the Poor in the Nineteenth-Century City: Philadelphia* (Rutherford, N.J.: Fairleigh Dickinson University Press, 1985), 199–222.

7. BFA Record Books, 1800–1866, including minutes, correspondence and annual reports, in Papers of the BFA, Massachusetts State Library, Boston; Records of the Female Orphan Society of Norfolk, Virginia, Manuscript Department, University of Virginia, Charlottesville; Mrs. Jonathan Odell, Mrs. Woolsey Rogers, Mrs. John G. Smedburg, and Miss Janet T. Sherman, eds., *Origin and History of the Orphan Asylum Society in the City of New York* (New York: Bonnell, Silver and Co., 1896); Papers of the POS, Historical Society of Pennsylvania, Philadelphia; Records of the Hillcrest Children's Center (formerly the WCOA), Manuscript Division, Library of Congress.

8. *J. Russell's Gazette*, Dec. 9, 1799; BFA annual report, 1844; see also annual reports for 1851, 1854, and 1855.

9. Lawrence A. Cremin, *American Education: The National Experience, 1783–1876* (New York: Harper and Row, 1980), 63–67. See also Bernard Wishy, *The Child and the Republic: The Dawn of Modern American Child Nurture* (Philadelphia: University of Pennsylvania Press, 1968); Anne Louise Kuhn, *The Mother's Role in Childhood Education: New England Concepts, 1830–1860* (New Haven: Yale University Press, 1947).

10. BFA annual report, 1841. Most children were apprenticed from almshouses as quickly as a place could be found for them. Lawrence W. Towner's study of children apprenticed by the Boston Overseers of the poor includes infants; the median age of the children indentured was between eight and nine. See Towner, "The Indentures of Boston's Poor Apprentices, 1734–1805," *Transactions* (Colonial Society of Massachusetts) 43 (1962): 417–68.

11. BFA minutes, Dec. 1800, Apr. 1802.

12. BFA minutes, July 1801, Oct. 1803; letter from Reverend Samuel West, BFA minutes, Aug. 1801.

13. Statistics collected from data in Admissions Registers, which generally listed birth date, dates of admission and departure, and the name and residence of the person to whom the child was released. Sometimes they included the parents' names and occupations and other comments. BFA Admissions Register, BFA Collection, Archives, University of Massachusetts, Boston: POS Admissions Register, Papers of the POS, Historical Society of Pennsylvania; WCOA Admissions Register, Records of the Hillcreast Children's Center, Manuscript Division, Library of Congress. Many fewer children were returned to relatives from the POS, perhaps because extended families were less likely to ask for children to live with them than were parents. Only eight of the children admitted before 1825 (6.6 percent), were bound out to relations.

14. POS, *Nineteenth Annual Report of the Philadelphia Orphan Society* (Philadelphia: Lydia R. Bailey, 1834), 5.

15. BFA minutes, May 1802. The first orphans were indentured young, at about 8.5 years, approximately the same age as girls from the almshouse. The median age for almshouse indentures in the period 1791–1805 was 6.9 for males and 7.8 for females. Over the period 1791–1805, the difference between the ages at which boys and girls were indentured grew (Towner, "Indentures of Boston's Poor Apprentices," table of

indentures). The number of girls indentured decreased during the period 1791–1805, while the total for boys remained relatively constant. Either fewer girls were being sent to the almshouse, or fewer were being successfully dispatched to families (BFA minutes, May 1802). Businessmen faced the same issue in this period as they moved from family partnerships to large corporate entities (see Peter Dobkin Hall, "Family Structure and Class Consolidation among the Boston Brahmins," [Ph.D. diss., State University of New York at Stony Brook, 1973], 105–11.

16. BFA minutes, Jan. 1806, Feb. 1806. Susannah Nye Freeman was a subscriber with close ties to many of the managers, who, like her, came from mercantile families and were married to merchants (BFA minutes, May 1805, Jan. 1806).

17. BFA minutes, Sept. 1803, Nov. 1808; [Abigail Frothingham Wales], *Reminiscences of the Boston Female Asylum* (Boston: Eastburn's Press, 1844), 47.

18. *Fourteenth Annual Report of the Philadelphia Orphan Society* (Philadelphia: Lydia R. Bailey, 1829), 4–5.

19. BFA minutes, Mar. 1822. The children were indentured, not simply released, as a check on their relatives (BFA minutes, May 1825). In July, Harriet Dorr was bound to her sister and brother-in-law, a mason. In October, Matilda Blanck was indentured to her mother. In November, Charlotte and Mary Louisa Fay were apprenticed to their aunt, "a very respectable woman." One other request was denied (BFA minutes, July 1825, Oct. 1825, Nov. 1825).

20. WCOA annual report, 1850, in WCOA minutes. Although this shift was most dramatic in institutions that admitted half-orphans, it was clear in all the orphanages. The POS, which admitted only "true" orphans, placed with relatives only 15 of the 215 children (7.0 percent) admitted before 1835 and 8 of the 56 children (14.3 percent) admitted between 1835 and 1840. Figures do not include girls kept to work in the asylum and boys transferred to Girard College.

21. BFA annual report, 1841.

22. BFA minutes, Sept. 1820, Apr. 1822. The child was probably illegitimate.

23. BFA minutes, June 1824; David Philipson, ed., *Letters of Rebecca Gratz* (Philadelphia: Jewish Publication Society of America, 1929), 145; WCOA minutes, Jan. 1841, Apr. 1841. The POS refused to let the child be adopted because Mrs. Furness was a Unitarian. Gratz, a Jew, was outraged by this vote.

24. POS minutes, June 1836; BFA minutes, Dec. 1831, Dec. 1833, June 1834. Amelia Smith was five years old; Hosea was six and a half. The children had been sent to their grandmother in Philadelphia after their parents died in New York. The Colliers, British immigrants, had eight children, one an infant, when the father deserted the mother.

25. Orphan Asylum Society of the City of New York, "Thirty-Second Annual Report" (1838), in Odell et al., *Orphan Asylum Society of the City of New York Annual Reports,* 207–8.

26. *Orphans' Advocate and Social Monitor* 5, no. 11 (Nov. 1846). Anstrice (1800–1875) and Eunice C. (1802–1883) Fellows came from a large farm family in Ipswich, Massachusetts. After they stopped publishing *The Orphan's Advocate* in 1857, they moved to Chelsea, just outside Boston, and eventually back to the north shore. The out-of-state requests for children numbered 349, or 32.9 percent of 1,060 listings offering "Homes for Children" in the sample. These figures are based on a sample representing listings from every fourth year between 1843 and 1855, the years for which complete runs of *The Orphans' Advocate* are extant. Issues of the newsletter can be found in collections at the Simmons College Archives, Boston, the Widener Library, Harvard

University, Cambridge, Mass., and the American Antiquarian Society, Worcester, Mass. The sample includes all listings of "Homes for Children" and "Children Needing Homes" on the last page of each issue. The newsletter stopped listing the locations of homes available in Oct. 1852 and dropped the entire category in Jan. 1855.

27. There were 186 such requests from 1842 to 1851, 67 from 1832 to 1841, and 34 from 1822 to 1831 (calculated from Ben-Or, "Law," app., 270–72). The three asylums mentioned were all approximately the same size in the periods when the adoptions took place. The Washington and Philadelphia orphanages may have privately placed children on a regular basis without admitting them; in addition, it is clear that both institutions did eventually place children in adopted families on a more regular basis. The WCOA's 1850 annual report remarked that two of the seven children who left the institution (which held forty-seven children in 1850) were adopted. The annual reports for the Orphan Asylum Society of New York also indicate some adoptions in the 1830s. The 1836 annual report, looking back at three decades of history, stated, "Some few have been adopted in families of the first respectability" ("Thirty-First Annual Report," in Odell et al., *Annual Reports,* 191).

28. WCOA annual report, 1850.

29. Ages calculated from data in Asylum Registers. See note 13. This figure remained constant. Even among the last group of children adopted between 1863 and 1867, the median age was seven, and the children's ages ranged from three to twelve.

30. Data calculated from asylum minutes, genealogical research and birth, marriage, and death records in the BFA Collection, Papers of the POS, and Records of the Hillcrest Children's Center.

31. BFA minutes, Mar. 1840, Oct. 1843, Dec. 1849; U.S. Census, 1850, Schedule 1 (Population). Most of the unrelated adoptive fathers were engaged in mercantile or professional occupations; those whose wealth could be determined owned property valued between two thousand and five hundred thousand dollars (BFA minutes, July 1836, Mar. 1840). Most of these data come from a study of orphans admitted to the various asylums between 1800 and 1840. While I did analyze Boston adoptions up to 1877 in comparison to other BFA placements, I did not attempt to trace these adoptive families in public records or to find follow-up reports for the children admitted after 1840 anywhere but in the asylum registers. I found data on wealth for only eight families.

32. Letter from Mrs. John Nelson, BFA minutes, Dec. 1841; U.S. Census, 1850. In at least two cases, courts legally changed the adoptive children's names as a measure of the family's commitment. Two of the Boston girls became teachers, entering a genteel profession that would not have been as available to them as indentured servants. By the 1820s, teaching had become a common occupation for young, unmarried middle-class women (Richard M. Bernard and Maris A. Vinovskis, "The Female School Teacher in Antebellum Massachusetts," *Journal of Social History* 10 [1977]: 332–45; Carl F. Kaestle and Maris Vinovskis, *Education and Social Change in Nineteenth-Century Massachusetts* [Cambridge: Cambridge University Press, 1980]).

33. See Records of Births, Marriages, and Deaths, Massachusetts Department of Vital Statistics.

34. Ann Hopkins had been adopted in 1834 by Patrick Hopkins (no relation), "a labouring man" in Charlestown with no children of his own who had supported Ann after her mother died. Two years later he sent her to work for another woman, "destitute and with evident marks of neglect and ill treatment." Recognizing that Ann "had been unfortunately placed," the BFA managers used this opportunity to cancel the indentures

and send her to another home in Pittsfield, out of the "reach of those who have abused their trust." Another child was also transferred due to the death of the adoptive father and "other circumstances connected with the case," language often used to describe abuse (BFA minutes, June 1823, June 1834, Mar. 1836, Apr. 1836, July 1844). This is a small sample, and I have no follow-up information for thirty-seven of the fifty-five adopted children who survived to the age of eighteen.

35. BFA minutes, Dec. 1849. If Frye had been welcomed into the family, she would not have needed to support herself: her adoptive father was a Springfield merchant.

36. Letter from Samuel Coves, in BFA minutes, Dec. 1839.

37. The pattern of BFA adoptions makes this clear (see table 2). As more families expressed interest in adopting children, the numbers increased; almost a fifth of the children placed between 1838 and 1845 were adopted. Yet only six children (4.6 percent) were adopted during the next decade. There was another spate of interest in the mid-1860s; ten of the sixteen children adopted between 1865 and 1875 were placed between 1863 and 1867.

38. *Orphans' Advocate and Social Monitor* 5, no. 11 (Nov. 1846): 85; *Orphans' Advocate and Social Monitor* 7, no. 11 (Nov. 1848): 85; *Orphans' Advocate and Social Monitor* 8, no. 1 (Jan. 1849): 4.

39. *Orphans' Advocate and Social Monitor* 14, no. 11 (Nov. 1855): 58; *Orphans' Advocate and Social Monitor* 7, no. 12 (Dec. 1848): 91. On concerns about "boy culture," see E. Anthony Rotundo, *American Manhood: Transformations in Masculinity from the Revolution to the Modern Era* (New York: Basic Books, 1993), chaps. 2–3.

40. *Orphans' Advocate and Social Monitor* 7, no. 9 (Sept. 1848): 69. After visiting Philadelphia, they commented in relation to the POS, "what it does, it does well" (*Orphans' Advocate and Social Monitor* 7, no. 7 [July 1848]: 52. The Fellows sisters were particularly chagrined that the BFA, "with its rich benefactors and large endowments, receives no more destitute children in a whole half century than we direct to good and happy homes, where the blessings of the family distill like the evening dew, in the space of a single year; and yet for the more than eight years we have toiled in this work, we have received less pecuniary aid from the public that has been bestowed on this Institution would amount to for a single month" (*Orphans' Advocate and Social Monitor* 9, no. 6 [June 1850]: 44). On investigation and follow-up, see *Orphans' Advocate and Social Monitor* 7, no. 4 (Apr. 1848): 29; *Orphans' Advocate and Social Monitor* 7, no. 9 (Sept. 1848): 68, 69.

41. *Orphans' Advocate and Social Monitor* 7, no. 6 (June 1848): 42.

42. *Orphans' Advocate and Social Monitor* 7, no. 6 (June 1848): 42. *Philadelphia Daily News*, June 12, 1848, quoted in *Orphans' Advocate* 7, no. 7 (July 1848): 54.

43. Jamil S. Zainaldin and Peter L. Tyor, "Asylum and Society: An Approach to Industrial Change," *Journal of Social History* 13 (1979): 23–48.

44. BFA annual report, 1857.

45. *Orphans' Advocate and Social Monitor* 7, no. 12 (Dec. 1848): 91.

46. BF minutes, May 1833. In the 1837–45 cohort, when 19 percent of the children were adopted, 43.5 percent of those children were placed with blood relations; in the next decade, when adoptions declined to 3.8 percent, 58.8 percent of adopted children went to relatives. Thereafter, the percentage remained consistent, with slightly more than four of every ten children returning to their families of origin (Zainaldin and Tyor, "Asylum and Society," 31).

Building a Nation, Building a Family
Adoption in Nineteenth-Century American Children's Literature

Carol J. Singley

Although orphans and orphanhood are frequently discussed in studies of nineteenth-century American fiction, few critics have turned their attention specifically to the subject of adoption.[1] This omission is striking both because adoption is a logical outcome of orphanhood and because adoption occurs frequently in American literature and culture. Indeed, adoption plots shape such now classic nineteenth-century novels as Susan Warner's *The Wide, Wide World* and Mark Twain's *The Adventures of Huckleberry Finn*. Adoption is also a familiar event in American society, affecting, according to one source, more than 10 percent of the population.[2] Nineteenth-century literature written expressly for children offers a unique lens through which to view the complexities of adoption. Written to instruct as well as entertain readers, this literature highlights issues of concern not only to parents and families but also to society as a whole. Americans took special interest in children, sometimes ascribing qualities to them that were perceived in the young republic. In the more than thirty children's novels and stories, written between 1850 and 1887, that I examine in this essay, the experiences of adoption reveal a range of American attitudes toward self and family. These narratives even serve as a microcosm of the society and nation as a whole.

Adoption as Trope

An analysis of adoption extends our understanding of nineteenth-century American literary and cultural practices as well as of the premises underlying those practices. A focus on adoption as a distinct narrative form provides an opportunity to study the structure of stories, particularly the bildungsroman (novel of development), of which the adoption narrative is but a subset. For example, plots involving orphans yield a multitude of narrative possibilities, since separation from home and family frees the character for adventures that are impossible for a child living securely at home. Adoption narratives may include various subplots and extended plots, as orphans struggle first to find a home and then to accept a new family's behaviors and values and as adoptive families cope with the challenges of assimilating new, young members. In some stories, adoptions are meant to be temporary or may even fail because of conflicts—over a child's fit with the new family or because of circumstances that impede successful bonding. In rare instances, the narratives do not involve family ties at all.[3] However, in contrast to orphanhood, adoption constitutes narrative closure, or resolution. Adoption stories typically end with a child being taken in by a new family and with the acknowledgment—legal and otherwise—of the finality of this domestic arrangement.

Adoption generally resonates positively—that is, it is preferable to institutionalized care, indenturing, or foster care, and it benefits both children and parents. Most adoptees eagerly look forward to joining their new families. For example, in a story about two homeless children, adoption is "good news" that "gladden[s] the hearts of the little orphans."[4] In another narrative, a boy who was once passed over for adoption gratefully acknowledges his new home, saying, "the old life was . . . a hard bitter reality from which you saved me."[5] When asked if she would be glad to be adopted, the heroine of another tale responds, "Glad? . . . It's just next to having God for my father."[6] Adoption also benefits adults by curing loneliness, providing an outlet for parental affection, and encouraging acts of Christian charity. In most stories, the care and expense of adopting a child are amply rewarded when the child helps with household chores, obeys the parents' wishes, and matures into a virtuous, responsible adult. As one woman muses about her prospective adoptive daughter, "I should so love to dress her and teach her and have her always near me. . . . I could learn her to dust the things and feed the canaries—and soon she could run errands. I don't believe she'd be so much care after all."[7] In another story, a woman responds to her physician's reminder that "God gives us our homes make somebody happy in" by adopting an orphan otherwise destined to remain in an asylum.[8]

Adoption narratives share structural characteristics. They look forward and backward, simultaneously engaging issues of origins and new beginnings, and thus invite consideration of the past as well as the present and future. Adoption is by nature intercultural and interfamilial, even if it involves members of the same kinship group.[9] It involves a disruption of genealogy and a grafting of new lineage onto the child's present one. Inevitably, this realignment raises questions of identity for both child and family. Because adoption entails separation from birth parents as well as connection with new families or parents, it is by definition paradoxical, involving both loss and gain. In every successful adoption, the child leaves one domestic and social setting for another, absorbing the rules, values, and customs of the new home. Adoption thus presents an opportunity—even a laboratory—for the study of cultural and biological differences, including those of class, race, ethnicity, and geography. For example, adoption may entail changes in socioeconomic status: the adoptive family is usually more affluent than the birth family, although not always. Adoption may also involve differences of ethnicity or race as well as physical relocation (whether minor shifts in region or major changes in citizenship). Finally, because adoption involves both birthright and circumstance—both nature and nurture—it challenges readers to rethink such presumably stable categories as mother, father, child, and family. At the heart of every adoption narrative, then, are questions of inherited and constructed identity.

The distinctive features of adoption narratives make them potent signifiers of national as well as familial issues. Indeed, even the word *adoption* is highly metaphoric. Whereas *adoption* refers to the act of taking a child into one's own family through legal means and raising that child as one's own, it also suggests many related concepts. *To adopt* may mean to take and follow a course of action by choice or assent, as in adopting a constitution. It may mean to take up and make one's own, as in adopting an idea, or to take on or assume, as in adopting a certain view. And it may refer to the choice of a standard, such as in adopting a textbook or policy.[10] In American literature in particular, *adoption* is a richly allusive term that describes not only a reconfiguration of family ties but also a complex network of attitudes and behaviors toward larger issues of independence and affiliation.

Indeed, with its focus on origins, broken lineage, and fresh beginnings, adoption serves as a powerful trope for the story of the United States itself. The nation was founded, after all, on Puritan settlers' separation from their "birth parent," England. This disaffiliation, formalized with the signing of the Declaration of Independence and the adoption of the U.S. Constitution, began a process of national self-definition that continues today. Since achieving political autonomy, the United States has stood in ambiguous and often ambivalent relationship to its parent nation (and to Europe generally). Americans' conflicting desires to emulate the Old World and to develop a distinctive identity have fueled debate over appropriate balances of separation, independence, and interdependence. Americans have, furthermore, frequently identified themselves as children, perceived their children's literature as uniquely descriptive and supportive of the national character, and represented the republic in language used to describe the family.[11]

In children's fiction published between 1850 and 1887, we can trace a development of attitudes and practices surrounding adoption. The stories provide sentimental accounts of children saved from homelessness, help young readers learn patience and obedience, encourage Christian charity, and portray America as a beneficent adoptive home. The majority of this literature was written by white, middle-class authors for a similarly white, middle-class readership. Although a few gifted authors create complex settings, characters, and plots, the majority of these novels and stories lack originality and literary merit. However, because the literature is by definition popular, it tells us a good deal about everyday nineteenth-century views of children and families—or at least about what adults thought children should know about themselves and their families. These adoption fictions engage complex views about the ties of blood and affection, the roles of nature and nurture, and the tensions between autonomy and affiliation.

Most of this literature is religious in tone and content; some of it was published by the American Sunday-School Union or other religious and philanthropic organizations. Indeed, many tales are blatantly moralistic—even propagandistic—in keeping with the didactic nature of most children's literature at this time.[12] In the extreme, adoption serves as little more than a vehicle for authors to impart lessons to their readers. It is not surprising that religious values figure so prominently in juvenile fiction of the mid– to late nineteenth century, since religion remained a potent force in American culture throughout the century and beyond. What is surprising, however, is the extent to which adoption literature engages not only sentimentalized, Christian codes of conduct associated with this period but also the forms and doctrines of religious faith that preceded the period. Indeed, nineteenth-century adoption literature owes significant debts to seventeenth-century Calvinism.

At the same time, adoption fiction of this period records ongoing tensions between spiritual and secular notions of worth. At midcentury, a shift in emphasis from religious to economic values was evident in many aspects of American life. By the end of the Civil War, the market rivaled the Bible as a source of authority, and economic doctrines competed with Christian ones as driving forces of human activity. Whereas adoption narratives of the 1850s reflect a primarily Christian emphasis on salvation, charity, and moral action, adoption fiction published later demonstrates an increasing emphasis on money, with corresponding representations of children as objects of possession and display.

These religious and economic influences were intersected, in turn, by those of gender, class, and locale. First, virtually all of these adoption stories encode the ideology of separate spheres for men and women, which, as scholars have noted, shaped and even regulated daily life in the mid–nineteenth century.[13] Views of women as spiritualized repositories of pious feeling and domestic harmony and of men as adventure-seeking bastions of reason and right action translated into corresponding behavioral expectations for adoptees, birth parents, and adoptive parents. Indeed, gender distinctions in some tales are so marked as to shape even basic elements of plot, with different endings for boys and girls. Second, in stories of this period, adoption implies moral, social, and economic mobility; almost always, it is a step up for the adoptee. Poverty, while not explicitly equated with sin, often connotes moral degradation. The child's adoption is represented either as a rescue from these deplorable circumstances or as a reward for exemplary Christian behavior and adherence to Anglo-European, middle-class values. Finally, adoption narratives reveal the U.S. preoccupation with its geography and demography. For example, reflecting the nation's romance with its agrarian roots, adoption narratives often associate the country with positive values and the city with negative ones. In some adoption stories, authors' choices of settings reflect their readers' anxiety about the growth of urban areas, influx of immigrants, and ethnic assaults on Anglo-European hegemony. In other narratives, particularly those involving male protagonists, the American West beckons as seductively as the most welcoming of eastern homes.

Faith and Family

All of these adoption narratives are grounded in Christian doctrine and teachings. The authors make liberal use of biblical quotations in epigraphs and throughout the text, interrupt narrative discourse to sermonize on various points, and use the circumstances surrounding adoption to preach about Christian values and behavior. It is common, for example, to find allusions to Moses, an adopted child who was reluctantly relinquished by his birth mother and miraculously restored to her care, and David, as a child forsaken by his mother and father but adopted by God. Christ frequently appears as an edifying model and inspiration. For example, the opening phrase of the Lord's Prayer, "Our Father," may be enlisted to comfort parentless children, as is the beatitude "Blessed are the poor in spirit." Biblical scripture may be used to motivate and reassure adoptive parents, who are asked to "love thy neighbor as thyself," "be kindly toward one another," and emulate Christ, who loved the poor. Authors of adoption fiction freely make moral judgments. They often portray birth parents in black-and-white terms, either as morally reprobate and neglectful of their children—often because of drunkenness—or as loving but financially unable to provide for their children. These authors frequently link children and adoptive parents in narratives of salvation in which one becomes a catalyst for the other's spiritual conversion.

These Christian lessons, with their emphasis on selfless charity, are based in nineteenth-century sentimental ideology, but they also derive from earlier, Calvinist forms of Christianity.[14] Adoption fiction of the period exhibits this debt in several ways. As scholars have noted, Calvinism has exerted tremendous influence on American culture and literature through the nineteenth and twentieth centuries.[15] Calvinism survives not only in the Protestant emphasis on original sin, limited election, and irresistible grace but also in a preoccupation with self-improvement and duty to others that shapes basic relationships in the family and society. The didactic quality of nineteenth-century adoption literature reflects a nation whose early religion prohibited art for its own sake. The Puritans, wary of representations that might rival God's creation, approved only of edifying forms of writing, such as diaries and journals, or of literature that explicitly reinforced Calvinist doctrine, such as sermons. Following in this tradition, adoption fictions sometimes appear as little more than contexts or excuses for religious preaching.

To Calvinist theology we can also trace conflicting American notions of the individual and the community. Puritan ministers, for example, urged congregations to develop independent relationships with God while also preaching the responsibilities of membership in a privileged church community. This ambivalence toward affiliation goes to the heart of adoption, in which parents take in virtual strangers and children separate from family members and reestablish intimate ties with others. Calvinism also left a legacy of moral exactitude. Nineteenth-century writers often portray characters as either good or evil and represent the suffering that leads to adoption as instructive—as a test of faith or a measure of God's grace. Authors soften Calvinism's hard edges but retain its emphasis on spiritual worthiness, self-examination, and requisite salvation.

One novel in particular, Maria J. B. Browne's *Laura Huntley* (1850), demonstrates the peculiar combination of seventeenth- and nineteenth-century sensibilities common to literature of this period. Laura is adopted in infancy by the Huntleys, whose children have died. Nothing is known about Laura's birth parents, but the narrator implies their bad moral character by describing them as animals rather than humans:

> Laura Huntley's parents were probably very degraded, vicious people, without the fear of God before their eyes, who did not want the care and trouble of a poor little helpless infant; so she was wrapped in a miserable old filthy blanket, and laid behind a pile of rubbish near a wharf, where some decayed buildings had lately been torn away. There she lay in her helplessness, unconscious of the inhuman treatment she had received from her natural protectors—more inhuman than the most savage beast was every guilty of . . . exposed in all human probability by her own mother![16]

The narrator's comment that abandonment is common in "heathen lands, rather than in a Christian city"[17] implies that Laura's parents are immigrants. In keeping with a nineteenth-century ideology that equated nurturing children with femininity, the narrator singles out the mother for blame and makes no mention of Laura's father. The adoptive parents, in contrast, represent middle-class, Anglo-European, Christian virtues. Only through their guidance, the narrator suggests, can Laura have a better life.

Although orphans are usually portrayed as innocent victims of their parents' death or abandonment, they were also thought to inherit their parents' errant tendencies. This labeling of the adoptive child as a "bad seed" alludes not only to scientific theories of inherited characteristics but also to Calvinist belief in original sin. Adoption in these cases functions as a moral corrective—or even an act of salvation—for which the child is expected to be grateful. In *Laura Huntley,* only through self-discipline, commitment to Christian principles, and obedience to her parents' wishes can Laura become an accepted member of the family.

Mrs. Huntley is a representative nineteenth-century sentimental mother, with good intentions and caring actions, who "determined . . . to adopt the little foundling, and bring her up as if she had been their own daughter." Regardless of how much they care for Laura, however, the adoptive parents do not attempt to hide the fact that she is adopted. Nor do they pretend that their love for her is the same as for their biological children. In contrast to twentieth-century adoption narratives in which adoption is secret—for example, William Faulkner's *Light in August*—nineteenth-century fictions make frequent use of terms such as *adopted daughter* and *foster parents.* The Huntleys "loved [Laura] *almost* as well as they could have done if she had been truly their own" and anticipate that she will reciprocate these feelings. They expect her "to act the part of a dutiful and faithful daughter, and to return the love and kindness which had rescued her from such a deplorable destiny, and procured for her a heritage of so much blessedness."[18]

Laura does not measure up to her new parents' expectations, however. By age thirteen, she has become "selfish, wayward, and full of concealment." She breaks a glass and claims that the servants broke it: "first deceit, and then falsehood!" laments the narrator.[19] The narrator does not say that Laura is bad because she is adopted—all children, not just Laura, require guidance and discipline. Nevertheless, Laura serves as a special example to young readers, who must learn obedience and self-restraint. Her adoptive status heightens her vulnerability to parental authority. Unlike biological children, she has a tenuous, temporary place in the household and must earn her right to keep it. Indeed, when Laura's indulgent mother despairs of correcting her behavior, her adoptive father threatens "to send her to the work-house—to service anywhere." This threat is effective because Laura has nowhere else to go, and a home with an adoptive family is infinitely better than an asylum or indentured service. Mrs. Huntley "mildly and tenderly" intercedes on Laura's behalf, making arguments that reinforce parental responsibility toward children and the importance of a loving, nurturing environment:

[I]f they sent Laura away from them, at least, until every effort in her behalf proved unavailing, she might become worse and worse, and grow up into an abandoned and ruined woman. Wrong as her conduct had been, it was still their duty to be forbearing.[20]

Mr. Huntley, however, favors a sterner, more Calvinist approach. Laura is required to apologize publicly for her misdeeds and is expelled from school until she changes her behavior. The narrator reports that Laura "*did improve* under her severe discipline . . . and now she gives promise of becoming a virtuous and respectable woman," but he cautions that such "reformations are always of an uncertain character, until the heart is regenerated by the Holy Spirit."[21]

While very much in the tradition of nineteenth-century sentimentality, *Laura Huntley* also evokes a 1711 sermon by Calvinist minister Cotton Mather on the occasion of the deaths of John and Abigail Foster, which left two children orphaned. In a sixty-eight page pamphlet entitled *Orphanotrophium; or, Orphans Well-Provided For,* Mather outlines God's plan for orphans and humans' responsibility for compliance with that plan. Mather's sermon subtitled "The Orphans Patrimony," begins with an epigraph from Psalms 27.10, the same biblical verse that prefaces *Laura Huntley:* "When my father and mother forsake me, then the Lord will take me up" (see fig. 1).[22] In an extended commentary on the biblical text of David, Mather commends his sermon both to the bereaved children and to parents, who might through God's will be called on to forsake their children:

Behold here, A Legacy for Orphans, to befriend their Temporal Interests, and their Eternal too. Some Children that were made Orphans, caused me to Prepare it; and it may be more Parents, who See themselves Likely to leave Orphans, will Dispense it. Some will, it may be, leave it with other Tokens of their Love and Care, unto Such as these, for whom it is intended as a Monitor and a Comforter.[23]

Mather next tackles the painful question of parents' premature death and asks how orphaned children might come to see themselves as not "Forsaken," since they, "above any in the World, have cause to make this prayer incessantly, O Great God, Leave me not!" However, rather than indulge in self-pity or anger over their loss, Mather implores his congregants to view orphanhood as an opportunity for renewed faith and prayer: "No Singular Affliction befals them, without Some excellent Fruits of Righteousness brought forth unto the Church of God." Just as the songs of David were produced by adversity, so too, orphans might embrace their lot as "Happy Troubles."[24]

Mather thus represents orphanhood as a kind of fortunate fall. He reassures the congregation that although earthly parents forsake their children, God the Father will never forsake them. He thereby establishes adoption as a charitable act of salvation that replicates God's actions. Indeed, he urges

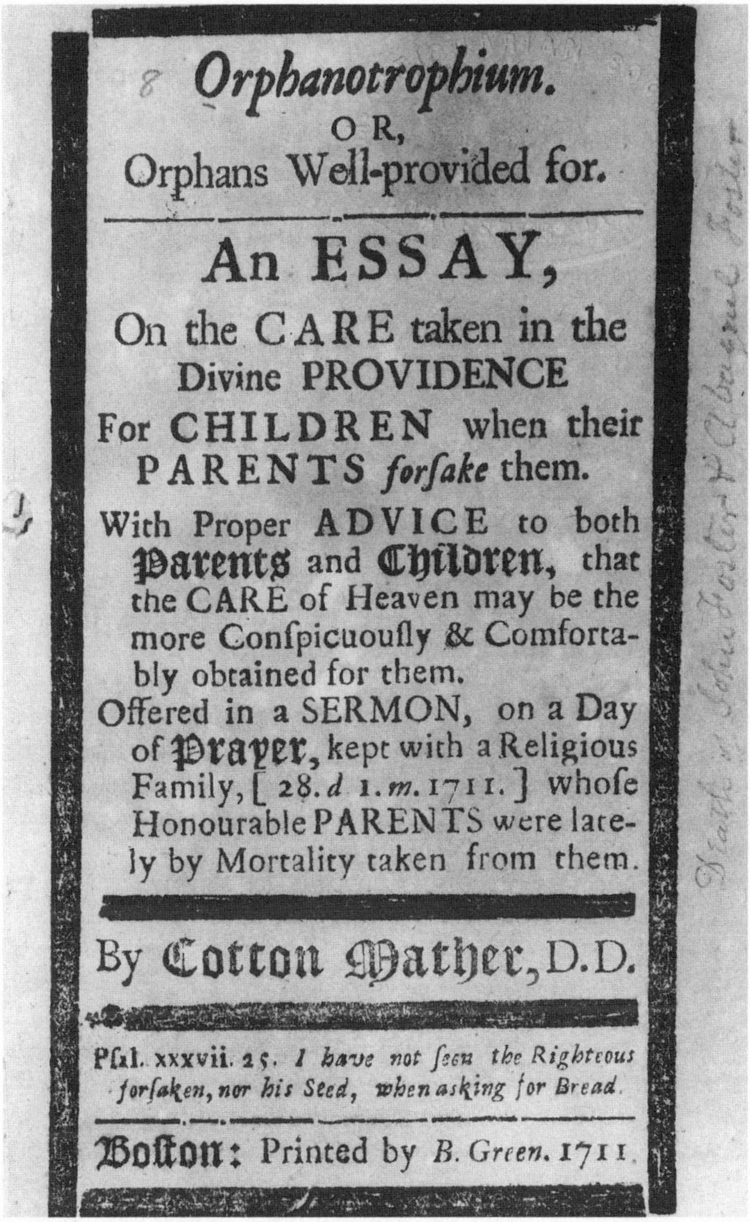

8 *Orphanotrophium.*
O R,
Orphans Well-provided for.

An ESSAY,

On the CARE taken in the
Divine PROVIDENCE
For CHILDREN when their
PARENTS *forfake* them.
With Proper ADVICE to both
𝕻𝖆𝖗𝖊𝖓𝖙𝖘 and 𝕮𝖍𝖎𝖑𝖉𝖗𝖊𝖓, that
the CARE of Heaven may be the
more Confpicuoufly & Comforta-
bly obtained for them.
Offered in a SERMON, on a Day
of 𝕻𝖗𝖆𝖞𝖊𝖗, kept with a Religious
Family, [28. *d* 1. *m.* 1711.] whofe
Honourable PARENTS were late-
ly by Mortality taken from them.

By 𝕮𝖔𝖙𝖙𝖔𝖓 𝕸𝖆𝖙𝖍𝖊𝖗, D.D.

Pfal. xxxvii. 25. *I have not feen the Righteous
forfaken, nor his Seed, when asking for Bread.*

𝕭𝖔𝖋𝖙𝖔𝖓: Printed by *B. Green*. 1711

Fig. 1. Cotton Mather, *Orphanotrophium; or, Orphans Well-Provided For* (1711). (Courtesy of the American Antiquarian Society.)

orphans to see that the "Lord will make a better Provision for me, than ever my Parents could." Orphanhood thus becomes a natural state of affairs; being mortal, parents must die—and frequently before their children—and thus "make room for the children." Although Mather acknowledges that there is no greater passion than parents' love for their children, he directs his audience to a greater love, that of the heavenly Father, of whom earthly fathers are but approximations. Fatherless children, then, are fortunate beings who can more easily and heartily turn their attention toward God. All children, but orphans in particular, are "the Foster-children of Providence."[25]

Mather's *Orphanotrophium* creates a public context for discussing adoption and treats the subject with a degree of candor and pride, not shame, that continues through the nineteenth century. Because the affliction of orphanhood, according to Mather's Calvinism, is actually a privilege that brings one closer to the ultimate desire, "Adoption by God,"[26] it is a subject that can be addressed openly rather than secretly. His explanation of orphanhood as inevitable and divinely willed also guides adult behavior in narratives such as *Laura Huntley*, in which the birth parents' death or abandonment is a condition of the plot. Parents who anguish over the possibility of dying and deserting their children must turn their fear into prayerful willingness to commit the children to God's care. Parents must accept other adults as interim caretakers of their children, as foster parents into whose hearts God puts the desire "to Foster them, & Furnish them, & Cherish them." And parents must view orphanhood and adoption as pathways to salvation. Given the state of fallen humanity, suffering and death are not only inevitable but desirable, for they inspire faith in God as the ultimate redeemer: when the parents are "laid Asleep . . . the Orphans are Savingly Awakened, & brought home unto God their Saviour."[27]

Mather also informs children of their Christian obligations. Finding themselves in a world in which "Iniquity abounds and the Love of many waxes cold," orphans must pray to God to "take them up."[28] Most importantly, they must be "Dutiful unto their Parents" to earn divine favor. Children achieve heaven only by obeying their heavenly father and their earthly parents, whether birth or adoptive. The injunction that children yield their wills to their parents'—prevalent in Puritan times and common throughout the nineteenth century—pertains especially to adoptive children, whom Mather presents as examples for others. Further, orphaned children, because they do suffer, evoke the image of Christ: "Orphans . . . You may with a Filial Familiarity, make your Approaches unto God; your dear Jesus has led you the way." Mather's invocation of Christ suggests that the more dire their circumstances, the greater the opportunity for orphans to commend themselves to God: orphans can "take more Satisfaction in the Great God their Father, than ever they took in their Parents."[29] This image of Christ also extends to foster or adoptive parents, who emulate Christ's loving sacrifice and God's providential care when they take in bereft and needy children.

Mather's points in *Orphanotrophium* are reiterated in *Laura Huntley*. For example, the fact that Laura's birth parents have forsaken her signifies not only their mortality but their original sin—that is, their inability to accomplish good for their child, however well intentioned they might be. Their abandonment is a regrettable but inevitable state of affairs. Indeed, describing Laura's orphanhood, the narrator evokes Adam and Eve's fall from the Garden of Eden:

> Think a moment, of being cast off in your early childhood from your mother's bosom, and your father's care, and of being dependent for your daily food . . . on the cold and stinted charity of the world—of resigning your soft white pillow for a restless bed on a board or the cold pavement—your clean nice clothing for a scanty covering of rags—your lovely home with all its refinements, and all its comforts—the home that seems to you as happy as a Paradise; to be a houseless and homeless wanderer.[30]

The Huntleys become agents of God's will, although, like Laura's birth parents, they do not possess power to create good by themselves. They happen "to be walking by" and hear an infant's cry. The narrator attributes their rescue of Laura not to them but to God, interjecting, "ought I not rather to say God directed them." In language similar to that of Mather's sermon and the biblical text of David on which it is based, the narrator explains that it is God "who feathers the soft breast . . . of the little helpless bird in the wild depths of its native forest. . . . He saw the deserted child, when she was forsaken of father and mother, and he provided for her."[31]

The Huntleys must nurture, guide, and discipline Laura so that she will follow a Christian path. When she misbehaves, they respond in two ways: with feminine gentleness, associated with nineteenth-century sentimentality, and with masculine firmness, reminiscent of seventeenth-century Calvinism. Laura's mother, representing the softer approach, attempts to reform Laura through gentle persuasion and positive example, but it is her father's sternness, drawn from patriarchal Calvinism, that accomplishes their goal. Mr. Huntley's threat to punish Laura by putting her out to service may be no less terrifying to a helpless child than the threat of hell would have been to a Puritan believer in Mather's congregation. And Laura's public confession of her wrongs, her resolve to offend no more, and her "promise of becoming a virtuous and respectable woman,"[32] all of which earn her a place in her adoptive parents' home, parallels the Calvinist sinner's conversion to faith and hope for eternal residence with God. It would be exaggeration to say that adoption narratives such as *Laura Huntley* are merely nineteenth-century forms of seventeenth-century conversion narratives. Nevertheless, we should not underestimate the importance of spiritual transformation in adoption fiction of this period. In these stories, adoption becomes the mechanism whereby nonbelievers are brought to faith and believers strive to emulate God's benevolence and generosity.

If *Laura Huntley* exemplifies Mather's plea for parents and children to prepare for the inevitability of death and possible need for adoption, another novel, Sarah S. Baker's *Bound Out; or, Abby at the Farm* (1868), recounts events when no such provisions are made. This novel of spiritual transformation focuses not on the child's reform and acceptance of Christian principles but on the adoptive parents' conversion to faith. In his sermon, Mather advises both birth and adoptive parents to lay up a "Good Stock" for their children in the form of wealth (obtained honestly in service to God), prayers, and plans for their children after their parents' death.[33] The heroine in *Bound Out*, however, finds herself without such Christian provisions. Young Abby becomes responsible for her adoptive parents' spiritual transformation, and through her steadfast piety and good works, the adults in her new household convert to Christian faith.

The narrative opens with Abby living in an orphan asylum. When a farm family needs extra help, they select her as their indentured servant. Mournfully leaving her "kind matron" at the asylum, Abby joins a rude, irreligious household where she is fed and sheltered but not loved. Abby's faith and her Christlike ability to turn the other cheek sustain her during this period of neglect. However friendless and tempted toward bitterness she may be, she "had been taught to look to the 'God of the fatherless' as her Guide and her Comforter, and she was trying to be truly his child." Her quiet suffering—she even faints from an infection she tells no one about—works wonders on her adoptive family. She brings order to the household, ends the distribution of whiskey to the farmhands, and by her example persuades family members to read the Bible. Abby's reward is her adoption: her reformed parents eventually embrace her as their own daughter. The narrator concludes, in language linking the domestic and the spiritual, that Abby "had but loved and lived as a Christian; and others had been led by her to seek the better way—and she had made for herself an affectionate family circle, where she was henceforth to find a real home."[34] The novel's frontispiece illustration, a pastoral scene in which two children stand securely next to their parents and gaze at the town church, underlines the interrelatedness of nature, religion, and adoption in literature of this period. Adoption restores a natural domestic harmony, fulfills the Christian mandate to serve others, and replicates God's acts of salvation (see fig. 2).

Moral and National Opportunities

Many novels of this period combine judgments of character with moral commentaries on the state of society in general. For example, *The Three Darlings: or, The Children of Adoption*, published in 1854 by the Female Guardian Society,

Fig. 2. Frontispiece, "October," from Sarah S. Baker, *Bound-Out; or, Abby at the Farm* (1868). (Courtesy of the American Antiquarian Society.)

cautions women against the proliferation of vice found in American cities and expresses fear of immigrants, especially Irish Catholics. Mary Farrall, ill and poverty stricken, struggles to raise her three daughters in a dirty immigrant neighborhood. The author suggests that her troubles began with an impetuous marriage, made against her parents' wishes, to a "reckless Irish youth" who brought her to America and became a drunkard. In contrast to Mary, who suffers and eventually dies as a result of her transgression, the childless adoptive mother, Mrs. Darlington, presumably of English and Protestant background, marries a "pious and enterprising young man," also presumably English and Protestant.[35] The Darlingtons offer the children a comfortable, Christian home. The author thus presents adoption as a positive alternative to the unstable environment that immigrant families of non-English ethnicity provide.

In a sense, then, adoption serves to accomplish social reform. Such is the case in *Blind Nellie's Boy* (1867) by Timothy Shay Arthur, the author of popular temperance literature. In his novel, Christian teachings facilitate personal development and socially relevant, moral action. When a woman sees the older of two hungry, destitute boys offer a bite of apple to the younger one, she feels compelled to help. By responding to God's message to "take those who are dear and save them from the evil that would devour their souls,"[36] she saves the boys from homelessness. She also battles social ills such as poverty and racism. For example, she struggles not to let her good deeds inflate her pride—"I had fallen into the error of thinking myself a little better than my neighbors, because of what I had done." And she fights bigotry in a fellow church member who labels the boys "young Arabs" and claims that nurture cannot correct nature. The neighbor's prejudice reflects a widespread fear that immigrant populations—in this case, the Irish—would destroy American society:

> Do you know anything about the blood of these children? Who and what were their parents? Vicious, and of a low grade of intellect, no doubt. You are a very indiscreet, or a very courageous and hopeful woman. But, if you don't repent of your romantic charity before ten years have flown, I'm no prophet. The tooth of ingratitude bites very sharply, you know. . . .
>
> They are low Irish, of course. Have you thought about their influence on your children? No amount of washing can make a pig a clean animal.[37]

Acting on the principle that we are all God's children, the narrator treats the orphaned boys as kindly as she treats her biological children. When one adopted boy falls ill, she nurses him, exposing her biological son to the disease. Even after her biological child dies of this disease, the woman finds that her "heart still had joy in giving." The couple's devotion is amply repaid when the boys grow up, establish successful careers, and thank their adoptive parents for raising them. The narrator acknowledges such rewards when her other biological children and husband subsequently die and she remarks, "but for the poor homeless lads I found in the market-place, I would be alone, unloved, and in poverty."[38]

Blind Nellie's Boy is exceptional among literature of this type because it probes the psychology of its narrator, who is unusually reflective about the meanings of Christian charity. Initially motivated by the book of Genesis and God's call to love unconditionally all the beings he created, the narrator resolves to think of her adopted son as "one of God's children, precious to Him as those who are borne of my bone and flesh of my flesh. . . . I will do my duty by him as I would by one of my own." However, she soon conducts a soul-searching inquiry into the nature of her love for her adopted and biological children and finds that she truly loves her adopted boys as much as the biological ones. This discovery not only transforms her abstract sense of moral obligation into personal passion and commitment but contradicts the popular wisdom of her day, which stressed the biological aspects of motherhood:

> According to all theory, there was a difference in the quality or degree of love that a mother bore for her own child, and that felt by her for the child born of another woman. Nature, it is said, has, in motherhood, its mysterious but unerring instincts; some holding that, thereby, a mother may know her own child though there be no external signs of recognition. I had accepted these ideas as self-evident. But now I was at fault. This waif . . . had crept into my heart, and made for himself a place there as sacred and as abiding as that held by any of my own children. I could find no difference in the quality of my love.[39]

Going against these "instincts" of "nature," the narrator shows that maternal roles are socially constructed, not innate. Indeed, *Blind Nellie's Boy* suggests that nurture is more important than nature, a view central to social reform movements in which this and other novels of the period participate.

Most literature of this period details the circumstances of orphanhood to make specific moral and social points. In a few stories, however, this information is withheld until the story's conclusion, creating narrative suspense and the potential for reunification with a birth parent. These stories reveal a fascination with noble origins, as found in European fairy tales, rather than an interest in fresh beginnings, as typifies American literature. For example, in a rather sensationalized 1871 tale, *Fleda's Childhood,* by Aunt Hattie (Harriet Newell Woods Baker), a girl's origins remain a mystery until the end of the story, when it is disclosed that she was first stolen and then abandoned by a servant after her mother died.[40] Although Fleda continues to live with her adoptive family after her origins become known, her status is significantly enhanced by the discovery that she has aristocratic blood.

In some narratives, this European interest in the recovery of lost, noble ancestry combines with a more American emphasis on moral conscience and right action. For example, in a small conduct book entitled *The Lighthouse* (1863?), a young girl, the sole survivor of a shipwreck, is adopted by a childless, elderly couple who keep a lighthouse. The moral nature of the story is set out by the narrator, who draws an analogy between the maritime beacon and divine light. Lighthouses "are built to warn the seamen of rocks and dangers, and to direct them to a safe harbor. Christians are to live holy lives, which will direct wanderers from the dreary paths of sin into the peaceful ways of godliness."[41] The girl embodies Christian virtues similar to those of Abby in *Bound Out.* Her singularly courageous and faithful tending of the light during a storm is rewarded when she saves the ship on which her father is sailing. In this fairy-tale ending, the father, daughter, and elderly couple sail together to England, living as one blended family of child and birth and adoptive parents.

In another novel, Sarah S. Baker's 1860 *Coming to the Light,* a girl named Fidgety Skeert is similarly orphaned in a shipwreck, taken to an orphan asylum, and put into service with a Christian family. The adoptive mother is initially reluctant to take in a child while she still mourns the death of two biological children. Indeed, her doctor's distinction between sheltering and actually adopting—"Psha, I did not say anything about adoption. . . . Get an orphan. Do what you can for her. . . . Bring her up like a Christian"[42]—opens the narrative to the possibility that Fidgety will not stay with her adoptive family. However, the parents gradually come to love her, and Fidgety similarly feels great affection growing for her adoptive family.[43] She gradually endears herself to her adoptive mother by responding to lessons and exhibiting a talent in music. The mystery of Fidgety's origins is solved when she is discovered to have come from a wealthy English family. She then sails to England to stay with her ill grandfather, but when he dies and she inherits his estate, she returns to the United States and her adoptive family.

The authors of both *The Lighthouse* and *Coming to the Light* place tremendous responsibility on children. These writers' emphasis on obedience, self-reflection, and independence—all legacies of American Puritanism—distinguishes these stories from their English counterparts.[44] *The Lighthouse* and *Coming to the Light* also reflect a common theme in adoption literature, the adoptee's fantasy of noble birth, made possible when origins are unknown. But these works also tell a highly American story of radical separation from England, the birth nation, and of ambivalent desire for return. Both novels respond to Americans' anxiety toward their past and future by incorporating into the endings aspects of the old and new. These stories suggest an American fantasy in which ties to England are simultaneously retained and renounced. For example, in the idyllic conclusion of *The Lighthouse,* the birth father, adoptive parents, and child all improbably return to England as one harmoniously blended, cross-generational family. In *Coming to the Light,* Fidgety—evocative of Nathaniel Hawthorne's Pearl in *The Scarlet Letter*—sails to England to claim her legacy. But she is freed from Old World ties when this sickly patriarch dies. She is then able to return to her rightful home in America, enriched by English genealogy but otherwise independent of it.[45]

Gendered Narratives

As these examples demonstrate, adoption fiction of the mid– to late nineteenth century is overwhelmingly feminine—that is, female protagonists vastly outnumber male protagonists,[46] and as Anne MacLeod notes, most of these didactic fictions were authored either by women or by clergymen.[47] This gender specificity invites us to examine adoption literature as itself a gendered form of narrative. Indeed, adoption plots featuring boys and girls are noticeably divergent, especially in their endings. Whereas stories about boys and girls may both begin with sentimental, moralistic portrayals of birth parents' abandonment or death and the protagonists of both sexes may encounter trial or failed adoptions, virtually all stories involving girls end in successful adoption. Such is not the case in stories involving boys.

Virtually all the tales with female protagonists follow the structural pattern of *Bound Out.* In this story, a combination of sound Christian and domestic practices leads to Abby's happy, permanent installation in a family. However, an adoption story about a young boy, *Little Bob True* (1858?), features a different ending. This 250-page novel opens as sentimentally as any in this period, with a tearful, 30-page description of Bob's mother's death.[48] However, from an early point, Bob thinks about how he can make his own way in the world. Even on the sorrowful trip to a neighbors' house, where he first finds refuge, Bob exhibits interest in people and events around him. He experiences a succession of temporary placements with families and single men who provide him with confidence and skills that he later uses to make his fortune. By the end of the novel, having worked as a miner and canal boat driver, Bob is heading West on horseback, assisted—but not adopted—by a former male schoolteacher (see fig. 3).

In another story, *My Teacher's Gem* (1863?), a boy develops a mutually beneficial relationship with a man, but the alliance falls short of adoption. After Joe's mother dies of complications at Joe's birth and his father dies of alcoholism, he manages on his own until one evening he meets a drunken gentleman on the street. Joe inspires the man to renounce his profligate ways; in return, the man provides Joe with a good home, schooling, and an apprenticeship. This patron—he is never referred to as "father"—tells Joe that "you and I are alike." Even though the man is the boy's senior, the relationship is more a partnership than an adoption. The narrator states that "the principal thing was this: Joe was useful to the gentleman, and the gentleman was useful

Fig. 3. Frontispiece, "The Driver Boy," from *Little Bob True, the Driver Boy* (1858). (Courtesy of the American Antiquarian Society.)

to Joe."⁴⁹ Another tale, *Orphan Willie,* the title story in the collection, dispenses with the male guardian figure altogether, allowing the male protagonist to pursue his own interests. After Willie's mother dies and his guardian uncle becomes destitute, Willie, who has a strong desire for "roving," sets out by himself with "no fear for the future." Equipped with only a song and a guitar, he plans to travel the country and become "a pioneer among the minstrels of America."⁵⁰

In stories with one male protagonist, such as *Little Bob True, My Teacher's Gem,* and *Orphan Willie,* the main character may benefit from the help of a teacher or sponsor but is not integrated into a household. Girls, in contrast, are almost always taken into their new families' homes. These gender differences are consistent with the nineteenth-century separate-spheres ideology, in which men's and women's lives were viewed as different and complementary. Women were expected to value the solace and security of home, men the freedom and adventure found outside the home. Authors of juvenile fiction, reflecting cultural values of their day, often portray females seeking affiliation through adoption and males resisting such affiliation. These gender distinctions hold in fiction aimed at adults as well as at children. For example, Maria Susanna Cummins's *The Lamplighter* and Nathaniel Hawthorne's "My Kinsman, Major Molineux" follow this pattern.⁵¹ In Cummins's sentimental novel, the heroine finds comfort in a number of loving homes before finally reuniting with her presumed dead father. In Hawthorne's story, a young man seeking lodging with an uncle is instead helped by a stranger who prepares the boy to make his own way in the world. In an interesting variation on this pattern, however, a few juvenile adoption narratives about two brothers or a pair of male friends end in successful adoption. Consciously or unconsciously, authors of these stories may have considered the pairs of boys to constitute a domestic society and therefore concluded the stories as they would narratives about girls, with adoptions into traditional homes. In stories about individual boys, however, authors generally avoid adoption. Even series titles reinforce the ideology of separate spheres. *Fleda's Childhood,* a story of female adoption, was published in the "Happy Home Series. For Girls," but *Little Bob True,* a story of male adoption, appears in a series with the more general title, "Series for Youth."

The gendering of adoption narrative may also be seen in relation to the developing republic. At a time when the United States was intent on demonstrating its political and economic independence, adoption, which connotes dependence, was associated with feminine rather than masculine values. Self-reliance, autonomy, and the ability to survive on one's own became the hallmark of the American success story, especially the male success story. Adoption stories broadly reflect these social realities for the two sexes. Females seek the shelter and protection of adoption because through it they are identified with home and domesticity, but males resist these familial attachments because the measure of their worth is their ability to succeed in the outside world. At the end of *Little Bob True,* it is significant that Bob is heading not homeward but westward into the frontier, a typically masculine American domain of adventure and opportunity.

Adoption and the Market

As powerful as gender typing was in the nineteenth century, it was often mediated by a more powerful influence, that of the market. Indeed, many stories demonstrate the struggle to keep Christian virtues alive in a capitalistic society that increasingly emphasized wealth, appearance, and status. Such a tension is evident in *The Three Darlings* (1854), discussed earlier, which depicts poverty as a virtue. The narrator states the novel's purpose to serve as a guidebook for readers who question, "What good can *we* do? We have no money, we have no influence."[52] Mrs. Darling, herself poor, takes in three destitute children who help earn their way by stringing beads. The children even manage to make gifts for more impoverished children still at the orphan asylum and thereby meet their obligations to family and society. In this story, as in *Laura Huntley,* the children are expected to return their parents' efforts with devotion, obedience, and labor: "We are not your parents, but . . . you owe to us the duty of a child," announces the adoptive mother.[53]

In fiction published after the Civil War, however, we see shifts in emphasis from religious to economic values and corresponding shifts in representations of adoptees—both male and female—as acquired objects. In a certain sense, children were always commodified, since they enjoyed few legal protections and fell under adult control. However, even the most sentimental texts cannot ignore the importance of money. For example, Julia A. Mathews's *Nettie's Mission* (1869), in which a kind minister and his wife adopt an orphaned girl, employs the language of possession and purchase. The clergyman describes the protagonist as having "*belonged* to some of those people on the shore" and tells a store clerk that he plans on "taking her home for a pet for my wife."[54] In some narratives, an adoptee's physical attractiveness increases her appeal. In *The Lighthouse,* the elderly couple who adopt the young girl are drawn to her for decorative reasons: "she looked so bright and beautiful in their homely room."[55] Although one can well imagine the pleasure that children, especially orphans, might derive from envisioning themselves so favored, one wonders whether the couple might have rejected a less attractive child.

As the United States became more industrialized, self-serving values associated with a market economy competed in adoption fiction with Christian mandates to subordinate self-interest to needs of others. These opposing values are apparent in *Coming to the Light,* in which the adoptive mother who still mourns the death of her biological children inspects children at an orphanage as if she were shopping for a new possession. In a concession to Christian charity, the woman decides on Fidgety, the least attractive child, but the matron of the asylum judges children on their appearance, recommending one with Anglo-European features: Mary Jane is "the prettiest, sweetest-tempered child we've ever had; she's got the whitest skin and the blackest eyes. . . . [I]f she was dressed like a lady's child, she'd be a perfect picture."[56]

Even the most overtly religious texts reveal their engagement in commercialized culture. For example, the narrator of Aunt Fanny's *One Big Pop-Gun* (1866) announces the need to teach children selflessness and quotes from Matthew and Luke about loving one's neighbor as oneself. But this tale for middle- and upper-class children, in which a girl's father dies in the Civil War and her mother becomes too ill and poor to raise her, valorizes the same materialism against which it preaches. The opening scene in *One Big Pop-Gun* evokes Darwinian theories of survival of the fittest as well as bourgeois capitalism. Two starving brothers compete with swans for a piece of cake that a wealthy boy throws into a lake. The boy, grandson of a rich gentleman, is selfish and demanding until he learns through contact with the poor boys that there is a nobler spirit of giving. Howard eventually shares his toys, hands over the larger share of his apple to another child, and uses the twenty dollars his grandfather gives him to host a party for orphaned, poor, and lame children. The author evokes Christ's sympathy for the poor to criticize the inhumane social conditions that have led to the boys' mother's death:

> On the wretched bed, unwatched, uncared for, covered with a ragged sheet, lay the earthly remains of the poor young creature, whose body had been starved, and whose heart had been broken. She had tried to find bread for herself and her children among her fellow-creatures, and had tried in vain; for she had sought help from those who had savagely shut out from their hearts and consciences the Sermon on the Mount— who had fattened and grown rich on the sales of work wrung out of the hunger and desperation of thousands of women such as this one.[57]

But even as the author rails against the evils of capitalism, her text feeds the reader's appetite for manufactured goods. For example, she describes in detail the many shops where Howard buys suits of clothing, toys, books, and candy that he gives to children who are objects of his charity. And neither Howard nor his grandfather is so moved by the plight of impoverished children that they adopt any; instead, the two orphaned boys are taken in by a policeman and his wife.

In three post–Civil War narratives, adoptees appear as little more than commodities. In "The Little Orphan," in *True Friendships. A Book for Girls* (1868–1874?), a child is rescued from her "gloomy" home and from her "dying mother, who was a widow, and destitute of every comfort," by a kind woman who cannot keep the child because the woman has a large family and no money.[58] The girl must live in an orphan asylum until a wealthy gentleman adopts her, not as a mission of charity but as a playmate for his biological daughter. Indulging his daughter's desire for an orphan instead of a horse for Christmas, the father hopes that she will learn responsibility. Instead, Helen treats Katy as a plaything, torturing her by "curling her hair, and dressing and undressing her" and becoming petulant and abusive when Katy does not comply. The servant, following Helen's lead, also taunts Katy and locks her in a closet. When the father returns after a three-month trip, Helen is "radiant with exercise and the pleasure of meeting her father again," but Katy is a wild and "sad little figure." To punish Helen, not to help Katy, the father sends Katy to live with a widowed aunt in the country. Four years later, when Katy has acquired refined manners, she is taken back into the family and finally treated as Helen's sister and equal.[59]

A similar treatment of the adoptee as acquired merchandise occurs in *Fleda's Childhood*, in which a woman whose children are dead descends imperiously on orphanages, looking for someone to adopt. She makes a shopping list of demands: "I want a girl. She must be an orphan, or certainly without relatives to interfere with her; and she must be so young as never to know another mother beside myself. . . . I should not wish to take one who was not perfectly healthy."[60] When she finds Fleda, "who seemed like her own," she is ecstatic, treating the girl as a prize who, when displayed against other children, "seldom lost in the comparison." The woman evokes Christian principles but does so only in service of her own desire. She represents God as a sort of sales clerk accommodating an order, telling her husband, "pray for me that I may be grateful to my Father in heaven for sending me to that Asylum before any other lady found her. I love to think He kept her there for me; and that He will help me to train her for heaven."[61] Although Fleda seems spoiled at first, eventually the couple feels "*richly repaid* for the care and *expense* they had *bestowed* on Fleda."[62] The language registers the parents' both moral and economic interests, suggesting that they have made a good investment.

In a story of adoption by "Pansy" (Isabella Macdonald Alden), "The Esselstynes; Or, Alphonso and Marguerite," published in *Mother's Boys and Girls* (1887), religion becomes completely self-justifying. When the affluent Mrs. Esselstyne sees two orphaned children she wishes to adopt, she declares confidently, "God has sent them," and takes them home. She waits in her well-appointed drawing room while the servants bathe and dress the children (see fig. 4). Then, displaying them as if they were expensive dolls, she changes their names and takes them shopping for lavish sets of clothes. The numerous illustrations in this short story underline the text's reliance on materiality and appearance as well as the transformative power of nurture over nature. Explicit

Fig. 4. "Here is a picture of Mrs. Esselstyne, waiting in her sitting-room, for the children to be brought to her," from Pansy [Isabella Macdonald Alden], "The Esselstynes; or, Alphonso and Marguerite," in *Mother's Boys and Girls* (1887). (Courtesy of the American Antiquarian Society.)

references to class emphasize the differences that separate the little charges from their adopting family—"Here is a picture of the little girl, as she looked when Jane [the servant] saw her out of the window. She was begging a penny of Miss Helena St. Marks, who was passing by" (see fig. 5). The name *Marks*, which denotes a currency, underlines money's role in the narrative. Both the illustrations and commentary emphasize the contrasting conditions of the children before and after their adoption—"Here is a picture of Alphonso as he looked after he was dressed. . . . he is at the window with Mrs. Esselstyne's sister" (see fig. 6).[63] The children have no voice in this text, existing merely to demonstrate the purchasing power of their adoptive family. Emphasizing appearance and money, these nineteenth-century descriptions prefigure conditions in the twentieth century, with lawyers and agencies setting high fees for adoption placements and selective middle-class families seeking healthy, white children who will easily adapt to their new families' customs and values.

Adoption narratives from 1850 to 1887 provide valuable insights into American literary practices and cultural values. Sharing structural as well as thematic traits, these popular juvenile fictions constitute a subgenre of the bildungsroman in which adoption constitutes narrative closure, even if only a temporary one. These novels and stories also resonate with issues of the American family, society, and nation. Adoptees, like Americans themselves, wrestle with roots and inherited traditions at the same time that they embark on paths marked by fresh beginnings, resourcefulness, and self-invention. The tension that these characters experience between autonomy and affiliation, between desire for the past and embrace of the future—even their conflicting feelings of displacement and chosenness—all resonate with the qualities we commonly call American.

Indeed, adoption issues reverberate throughout American cultural and literary history. Adoption has resonance for a U.S. society rooted in seventeenth-century Calvinist theology. Believing that earthly existence was but a temporary exile from their true home in heaven, Puritans sought to minimize worldly attachments—including emotional attachments to children—and prayed for eventual adoption by God, their rightful father.[64] Intercultural conflicts immediately challenged the settlers as they clashed with Native Americans over access to and control of the land. We seldom think of these native-white relations in terms of adoption, yet hundreds of captivity narratives from the seventeenth through the nineteenth centuries recount adoptions of white settlers by red-skinned neighbors, and a considerable number of these stories describe settlers who only reluctantly return to their birth families—or do not return at all. Captivity narratives represent some of the earliest examples of American cross-cultural adoptions. Slavery also raises a number of adoption issues. Throughout the nineteenth century, when the United States affirmed and celebrated freedom, it continued to engage in slaveholding and slave trading, a heinous

Fig. 5. "Here is a picture of the little girl as she looked when Jane saw her out of the window. She was begging a penny," from Pansy [Isabella Macdonald Alden], "The Esselstynes; or, Alphonso and Marguerite," in *Mother's Boys and Girls* (1887). (Courtesy of the American Antiquarian Society.)

Fig. 6.   "Here is a picture of Alphonso as he looked after he was dressed. . . . he is at the window with Mrs. Esselstyne's sister," from Pansy [Isabella Macdonald Alden], "The Esselstynes; or, Alphonso and Marguerite," in *Mother's Boys and Girls* (1887). (Courtesy of the American Antiquarian Society.)

form of adoption in which African-American families were systematically separated and sold away from each other. Much literature by nineteenth-century white writers defended these distorted adoptions, yet slave narratives and other kinds of adoption fiction by African-American authors focus our attention not on the formation of adoptive relationships but on escape from slaveholding families and on reunification with birth families.

Nineteenth-century adoption narratives have ideological bases in American religious and economic practices. These tales reflect the sentimental creeds of their day, but they also exhibit debts to a more austere, seventeenth-century Calvinist religion and culture. In the more religious texts, adoption is enacted as Christian salvation; in the more secular ones, it is associated with purchasing power and material display. These narratives mark shifts from church-based to market-based values, with corresponding changes in representations of the child and family. Registering the period's social concerns and frequently employing adoption in the service of reform, the stories generally reinstate hierarchies of gender, class, race, and ethnicity. Adoption tales are paradoxically radical and conservative—that is, they simultaneously rupture and reaffirm bonds of blood, kinship, and community. Juvenile narratives, because they highlight and often simplify these shifting ties of loyalty and affection, make provocative texts for the study of family and social relations in American literature and culture.

NOTES

I gratefully acknowledge the American Antiquarian Society, Worcester, Massachusetts, for a Peterson Fellowship that made research for this essay possible.

1. Jerry Griswold notes that "the American childhood story is almost always the story of an orphan." He discusses adoption as the second of three stages in a child hero's journey to maturity but does not otherwise make adoption the focus of his *Audacious Kids: Coming of Age in America's Classic Children's Books* (New York: Oxford University Press, 1992), 5–11. Nina Baym analyzes plot structures in novels by nineteenth-century American women writers, noting "poor and friendless" orphans who develop a "network of surrogate kin." Like Griswold, Baym views adoption as an intermediary step in the heroine's adventures, focusing on marriage, not adoption, as the concluding narrative event (*Woman's Fiction: A Guide to Novels by and about Women in America, 1820–1870* [Ithaca: Cornell University Press, 1978], 35–38).

2. Christine Adamec and William L. Pierce, *The Encyclopedia of Adoption* (New York: Facts on File, 1991), x.

3. Many nineteenth-century orphanages were founded and supported by religiously affiliated groups. Most, such as the Bethany Orphans' Home, favored placement of children with Christian parents but these orphanages often became children's de facto adoptive homes and families, as the language describing the institutions indicates. At the Bethany Home, for example, inmates "constituted one family" and governance imitated a family model of twelve persons living together, headed by a superintendent,

who, like "the true parent," "stud[ies] and know[s] the individual traits and dispositions of every member of his family." See, for example, Rev. Thomas M. Yundt, *A History of Bethany Orphans' Home of the Reformed Church in the United States, Located at Womelsdorf, Pa.* (Reading, Pa.: Daniel Miller, 1888), 30, 35. However, some institutions, such as the Lutheran-affiliated Orphan's Home in Pittsburgh and the Orphan's Farm School in Zelienople, Pennsylvania, considered themselves permanent facilities for children. Directors of these asylums rejected the practice of "binding out" because, pecuniary temptations frequently resulted in abuse of the children. (*First–Seventh Reports of the Orphan's Home, Pittsburgh, Pa. and the Orphan's Farm School, Zelienople, Butler Co., Pa. with a History of Their Origin, Progress and Present Condition, 1852–1860* [Pittsburgh: W. S. Haven, 1860–66], 19, 20).

   4. Eliza M. French, *The Two Orphans: A Story for Little Children* (New York: Kiggins and Kellogg, 1849–56?), 46.

   5. Carrie L. May, *Brownie Sandford; or, The Recovered Pearl* (Boston: William H. Hill, 1866), 284.

   6. [Julia A. Mathews], *Nettie's Mission* (New York: Robert Carter and Brothers, 1869), 140.

   7. *The Three Darlings: or, The Children of Adoption* (New York: American Female Guardian Society, 1854), 24–25.

   8. Sarah S. Baker [Sarah Schoonmaker], *Coming to the Light; or, The Story of Fidgety Skeert* (New York: Anson D. F. Randolph, 1860), 11.

   9. See Judith Modell, *Kinship with Strangers: Adoption and Interpretations of Kinship in American Culture* (Berkeley: University of California Press, 1994).

   10. *American Heritage Dictionary,* 2d ed. (Boston: Houghton Mifflin, 1982).

   11. See, for example, Griswold, *Audacious Kids,* 13–16, which argues that Americans see their history in terms of child development and invest a sense of national identity in their children's books. In an analysis similar to mine, he identifies a pervasive pattern in American literature as "one of the orphan," but he describes the colonies' break with England not in terms of adoption but as "oedipal rebellion against its parents." In their study of the American Revolution, Edwin G. Burrows and Michael Wallace explore complex relationships between the colonies and its parent nation: "Over and over" Americans and the English "likened the empire to a family . . . in which England enjoyed the rights and duties of parental authority over the colonies while the colonies enjoyed the corresponding rights and duties of children. . . . Such analogues between family and polity . . . lay at the foundation of the English approach to the problems of power and liberty, authority and autonomy" ("The American Revolution: The Ideology and Psychology of National Liberation," *Perspectives in American History* 6 [1972]: 168). Jay Fliegelman similarly describes the revolutionary period in terms of shifting family relations but explicitly mentions adoption: colonists "deserted the English village to find tender parenting and adoption in America" (*Prodigals and Pilgrims: The American Revolution against Patriarchal Authority, 1750–1800* [New York: Cambridge University Press, 1982], 180).

   12. As Anne Scott MacLeod notes, almost all children's fiction until 1850 was didactic, with moral education rather than entertainment its primary goal (*A Moral Tale: Children's Fiction and American Culture, 1820–1860* [Hamden, Conn.: Archon, 1975], 23).

   13. On the ideology of separate spheres, see Nancy F. Cott, *The Bonds of Womanhood: "Woman's Sphere" in New England, 1780–1835* (New Haven: Yale University Press,

1977); Carl N. Degler, *At Odds: Women and the Family in America from the Revolution to the Present* (New York: Oxford University Press, 1980); Mary Kelley, *Private Woman, Public Stage: Literary Domesticity in Nineteenth-Century America* (New York: Oxford University Press, 1984); Anne Firor Scott, *The Southern Lady: From Pedestal to Politics, 1830–1930* (Chicago: University of Chicago Press, 1970).

14. Fliegelman notes a Lockean-based decline in parental authority beginning at the end of the eighteenth century (*Prodigals and Pilgrims*, 12–15). Although a Lockean emphasis on the development of a child's internal governance and the importance of nurture over nature characterizes many nineteenth-century texts, I also find in them a residual Calvinism that includes depravity, strict accountability to higher authority, and public confession and punishment.

15. On Puritanism's influence in American literature, see Aliki Barnstone, Michael Tomasek Manson, and Carol J. Singley, eds., *The Calvinist Roots of the Modern Era* (Hanover, N.H.: University Press of New England, 1997); Sacvan Bercovitch, ed., *The American Jeremiad* (Madison: University of Wisconsin Press, 1978); Sacvan Bercovitch, *The Puritan Origins of the American Self* (New Haven: Yale University Press, 1975); Richard Chase, *The American Novel and Its Tradition* (Garden City, N.Y.: Doubleday, 1957); Emory Elliott, ed., *Puritan Influences in American Literature* (Urbana: University of Illinois Press, 1979); Perry Miller, *The Life of the Mind in America: From the Revolution to the Civil War* (New York: Harcourt, 1965); Ivor Winters, *Maule's Curse: Seven Studies in the History of American Obscurantism* (Norfolk, Conn.: New Directions, 1938).

16. Maria J. B. Browne, *Laura Huntley* (n.p., 1850), 17–18.

17. Ibid., 19.

18. Ibid., 29–30 (emphasis added).

19. Ibid., 33.

20. Ibid., 138.

21. Ibid., 143.

22. Cotton Mather, *Orphanotrophium; Or, Orphans Well-Provided For* (Boston: B. Greene, 1711).

23. Ibid., preface.

24. Ibid., 4–6.

25. Ibid., 9, 12–13, 22.

26. Ibid., 45.

27. Ibid., 22–23.

28. Ibid., 27, 29.

29. Ibid., 29, 49–50, 52.

30. Browne, *Laura Huntley*, 13.

31. Ibid., 19–20.

32. Ibid., 43.

33. Mather, *Orphanotrophium*, 31–35.

34. Sarah S. Baker [Sarah Schoonmaker], *Bound Out; or, Abby at the Farm* (New York: Anson D. F. Randolf, 1868), 3, 6–7, 89.

35. *Three Darlings*, 10.

36. T[imothy]. S[hay]. Arthur, *Blind Nellie's Boy, and Other Stories* (Philadelphia: Perkinpine and Higgins, 1867), 15.

37. Ibid., 18, 20–21.

38. Ibid., 26, 35, 41.

39. Ibid., 6, 36.

40. Aunt Hattie [Mrs. H. N. Baker], *Fleda's Childhood* (Boston: Henry A. Young, 1871?).

41. Asa Bullard, comp., *The Lighthouse. Illustrated* (Boston: Lee and Shepard, 1863?), 17–18.

42. Baker, *Coming to the Light*, 10.

43. In Baker's story, a family's loving practice leads to love itself. See Norman Fiering, who describes the principle that "outward acts can cause inward changes" ("Benjamin Franklin and the Way to Virtue," *American Quarterly* 30 [summer 1978]: 212). See also Fliegelman's discussion of an adoption tale, Jean François Marmontel's "The Errors of a Good Father" (1764), in which a heroine says of her adoptive father, "Natural affection between him and me is become so habitual that it has acquired the force of natural attachment, and the ties of adoption have connected us with the same strength as if they were the bonds of consanguinity." Fliegelman argues that the habit of affection is encouraged by the New World itself, which "creates a bond between child and adopted parent, between immigrant and adopted land as natural as any bond of birth" (*Prodigals and Pilgrims*, 51, 182).

44. Anne Scott MacLeod, "Children's Literature in America from the Puritan Beginnings to 1870," in *Children's Literature: An Illustrated History*, ed. Peter Hunt (New York: Oxford University Press, 1995), 102–3.

45. Although Pearl is not technically orphaned, she is born out of wedlock, abandoned by her birth father, and raised on the outskirts of society by her impugned birth mother. Believing her "of demon origin" and at moral risk with her mother, the Salem magistrates at one point consider placing Pearl with a more reputable family (Nathaniel Hawthorne, *The Scarlet Letter*, 2d ed. Norton critical ed. [New York: Norton, 1978], chap. 7). Hawthorne's historical novel criticizes Puritan repression in the colonies; accordingly, Pearl chooses to return to Europe, where she can enjoy its relative freedoms.

46. For example, in a sampling of twenty-one juvenile fictions in the collection at the American Antiquarian Society—all cataloged under the subject heading "adoption"—thirteen had female protagonists, four had male protagonists, and four had both male and female protagonists.

47. MacLeod, *Moral Tale*, 31.

48. *Little Bob True, the Driver Boy* (Philadelphia: Presbyterian Board of Publication, 1858).

49. Asa Bullard, comp. *My Teacher's Gem* (Boston: Lee & Shepard, 1863?), 43, 47.

50. *Orphan Willie, and Other Stories* (Fitchburg, Mass.: S. C. Shepley, 1847), 32–33.

51. Maria S. Cummins, *The Lamplighter* (1854) (New York: Thomas Y. Crowell, n.d.); Nathaniel Hawthorne, "My Kinsman, Major Molineux" (1832), *Selected Tales and Sketches*, ed. Michael J. Colacurcio (New York: Penguin, 1987): 29–50.

52. *Three Darlings*, preface.

53. Ibid., 97.

54. [Mathews], *Nettie's Mission*, 30–31 (emphasis added).

55. Bullard, comp., *Lighthouse*, 39.

56. Baker, *Coming to the Light*, 23–24.

57. Aunt Fanny, *One Big Pop-Gun* (New York: Sheldon, 1866), 43–44.

58. *True Friendships. A Book for Girls* (Boston: Henry A. Young, 1868–1874?), 90–91.

59. Ibid., 93, 107, 111.

60. Aunt Hattie, *Fleda's Childhood*, 16–19.

61. Ibid., 33–35.

62. Ibid., 89 (emphasis added).

63. Pansy [Isabella Macdonald Alden], "The Esselstynes; or, Alphonso and Marguerite," in *Mother's Boys and Girls* (Boston: D. Lothrop, 1887), n.p.

64. Such belief is demonstrated in the Shorter Catechism, found in *The New England Primer*, where the question, "What is adoption?" is answered: "Adoption is an Act of God's Free Grace, whereby we are received into the Number, and have Right to all the Priviledges of the Sons of God" (Paul Leicester Ford, ed., *The New England Primer: A History of Its Origin and Development with a Reprint of the Unique Copy of the Earliest Known Edition and Many Fac-simile Illustrations and Reproductions* [1897; rpt. with a preface by Lawrence A. Cremin, New York: Teachers College, Columbia University, 1962], n.p.). Fliegelman emphasizes the filial quality of this belief: for Puritans, faith in Christ promised to "transform man's relationship with God from that of servant and master—the primary relationship of the Old Testament—to that of child and parent—the primary relationship of the New Testament" (*Prodigals and Pilgrims*, 173).

What's Love Got to Do with It?

"Adoption" in Victorian and Edwardian England

George K. Behlmer

The problem of regulating English adoption practice proved vexing for politicians and philanthropists alike. Writing in 1887, two American historians gazed enviously across the Atlantic: "In a stable society, like that of England, where distinctions of rank and social position are settled by birth rather than by achievement, the questions connected with the family do not present such complications as in our own American life."[1] Ironically, England's social stability helped to make the issue of adoption so complex. For although legal adoption—the process by which parental rights and responsibilities become fully transferable—was not possible in England until 1926, children had been adopted de facto since time out of mind. Thus, for generations there endured a glaring contradiction between common law and popular practice. During the first quarter of the twentieth century, the exigencies of total war would bring about an end to this anomaly. But it was the anxiety-ridden experience of prewar "adoption" that first created a demand for legalization. The essay that follows will explore some of the painful inflections of a word usually associated with love and compassion.

As England approached its industrial heyday, the term *adoption* increasingly became linked with the criminal treatment of illegitimate children. This dark side of the subject would haunt Victorian social reformers, color the early infant welfare movement, and ultimately complicate the campaign for legalized adoption. Although the story of efforts to protect filius nullius (nobody's child) in England is convoluted,[2] one straightforward fact did much to shape the tale: a combination of legal and moral prejudice had created a hostile climate for unmarried mothers who wished to keep their young children. Aware that the social odds were stacked against such women, the reading public of mid-Victorian England could not ignore those doctors, journalists, and charity workers who began warning about a wholesale "slaughter of the innocents."[3] The preoccupation of polite society with savage instincts, particularly those attributed to the poor, only heightened fears that the disposal of illegitimate off-spring had become a thriving trade by the 1860s.

Short of outright murder, the quickest way for a friendless female to get rid of her child was by paying to have it "adopted." This meant, in practice, find-ing foster parents to take the child in exchange for weekly payments or a lump sum at the time of transfer. Public health activists in the late 1860s discovered that a flourishing trade along these lines was already being conducted through the newspapers. J. B. Curgenven, a general surgeon and honorary secretary of London's reform-minded Harveian Society, and Ernest Hart, an ophthalmic surgeon who served as dean of the St. Mary's Hospital Medical School and from 1866 to 1898 served as editor of the *British Medical Journal,* formed the nucleus of a determined effort to eradicate what they called the "baby farming" business.[4] The scope of baby farming could be inferred, they thought, from the advertisements for "villanously cheap" adoption placed in publications cater-ing to the masses. At least a few reputable London papers also carried such ad-vertisements. It was, for example, a simple matter to insert these notices in the *Daily Telegraph:* "Send a boy of fourteen with three and sixpence and an offer to manage the birth of a baby in concealment, or to dispose of one by adop-tion, and your money will be taken without a word of inquiry, and your little advertisement will appear in due course, to tempt women eager to have done with their children."[5] Under Hart's direction, the *British Medical Journal* set out to show how prevalent baby farming had become. Within a week of offering a five pound premium for full care of a child, the *Journal's* undercover agent re-ceived 333 replies. The visits he subsequently paid to respondents' homes proved "beyond doubt" that many of these women "carried on the business [of adoption] with a deliberate knowledge that the children would die very quickly." No more than a third of those answering the *Journal's* decoy adver-tisements genuinely wanted a child in their lives. Here was a social "gangrene," as the *Times* put it, that had to be cut out.[6]

Despite a well-publicized estimate that about thirty thousand illegitimate children fell into the hands of paid "nurses" each year,[7] it took a more disturb-ing exposé to convince Parliament that baby farming was an ill in need of leg-islative cure. This time the Metropolitan Police became involved. Since no fewer than sixteen infant bodies had been recovered from the streets of Brix-ton during the spring of 1870, police were keenly interested when yet another tiny corpse, this one wrapped in a piece of paper bearing the name "Mrs. Waters," was found among some lumber in the same South London neighbor-hood. Soon thereafter, *Lloyd's Weekly* carried an advertisement that stank of foul play: "*Adoption:* A GOOD home, with a mother's love and care, is offered to any respectable person wishing her Child to be entirely adopted—Premium £5, which sum includes everything. Apply, by letter only, to Mrs. Oliver. Post office. Goar-place, Brixton."[8] Sergeant Relf, the policeman selected to play the part of a reluctant father, met "Mrs. Oliver" at Camberwell Railway Station and followed her home. Once Relf traced the illegitimate child of a seventeen-year-old girl to the same house, he was ready to act. Accompanied by the baby's grandfather, he gained entry to 4 Frederick Terrace, discovering there not one but eleven infants, all grossly neglected.

Evidence gathered about "one of the most horrible . . . stories ever brought to light in a Court of Justice" soon showed that "Mrs. Oliver" was actually Margaret Waters, aged thirty-five. For several years Waters and her husband had prospered in Newfoundland. After his death in 1864, the widow returned to London with three hundred pounds and a plan to start her own collar-sewing business. When this scheme soured, she turned to renting out rooms in her home, and as a landlady, she discovered how eager some women were to part with their babies. So Waters and her sister, Sarah Ellis, twenty-nine, took to feeding their young charges a formula consisting of common lime and water, sometimes spiked with tincture of opium. Receipts found in the house proved that during May–June 1870 alone, the sisters had pawned more than a hundred items of children's clothing. When five of the infants died from the combined effects of starvation and narcotic poisoning, the charges against Waters and Ellis grew to include murder, manslaughter, conspiracy, and obtaining money under false pretenses. Sarah Ellis was lucky to escape with a conviction only on the last charge. Margaret Waters went to the gallows on October 1, 1870.[9]

The alarm over baby farming that arose in the late 1860s endured for a generation. Indeed, the fate of illegitimate infants continued to trouble England even after passage of the sweeping 1908 Children Act. Robert Parr, director of the National Society for the Prevention of Cruelty to Children from 1905 to 1927, kept reminding the public that baby farming was an iceberg phenomenon. To detach its submerged criminal element might require acceptance of radical legal reform, such as William Clarke Hall's plan to make all illegitimate children wards of their local police courts.[10] Until such reform became law, charity workers, Poor Law authorities, and health visitors were urged to comb their areas for those who had already devised new ways to circumvent registration and inspection procedures.[11] This abiding concern with the deceit that sometimes masqueraded as "adoption" survived World War I and would leave its mark on interwar social policy.

Illegitimate infants were not, of course, the only young to be separated from their parents. For example, the children of middle-class families stationed abroad on imperial business often were left with foster parents in England. Rudyard Kipling was one such child, and if Kipling's account of the "House of Desolation" where he spent nearly six miserable years is at all representative, then this custom may have traumatized many otherwise well-off boys and girls.[12] But better known was the use to which both private charities and Poor Law authorities put fostering as a way to simulate "the divine institution of the

family" for abandoned children.[13] To Poor Law children, fostering meant
boarding out in humble homes. Although boarding out had taken root in Scotland as early as 1843,[14] not until 1870 did England's Poor Law Board authorize
guardians to place selected children with foster parents. This liberalization of
policy stemmed largely from the pressure of middle-class women concerned
about the plight of girls in workhouses and the "barracks schools" associated
with them. One can identify less high-minded concerns here as well, the most
evident of which was worry about the future supply of reliable servants. Writing from her Wiltshire home in 1861, Hannah Archer, the wife of a guardian,
warned that a "race" of shameless workhouse girls was unleashing a "torrent of
sin" that threatened not only to pollute other child minds but also to render all
paupers unfit for domestic service. By boarding out the younger workhouse
girls with "trustworthy cottagers" and allowing ladies to supervise them, Archer
believed, guardians might salvage some productive citizens. More immediately
influential were the women who met G. J. Goschen, president of the Poor Law
Board, in early 1870. This deputation was the idea of Miss Preusser, a German-
born activist whose attempts to transplant children from London's East End to
cottages near her Lake District home had run afoul of Poor Law regulations.[15]
Preusser's group argued successfully that guardians should have the option of
sending orphaned and deserted young to foster homes, even when these homes
lay outside local Union boundaries.[16]

Although initially skeptical, Poor Law officials resorted to boarding out with
increasing frequency. As a leading London philanthropist explained in 1883,
"notwithstanding much prejudice and obstruction," the new system was gaining ground not only because it cost less to board out a child than to maintain
it in a workhouse or Poor Law school but also because kindly folk were awak-
ening to the fact that by opening their homes, they could revive boys and girls
so emotionally stunted that some "actually *did not know how to kiss!*"[17] Two administrative reforms helped to popularize boarding out. The Poor Law Acts of
1889 and 1899 effectively permitted guardians to "adopt" certain boys and
girls.[18] By the start of the twentieth century, guardians could assume legal custody over workhouse children under the age of eighteen whose parents had
died, deserted the home, gone to prison for offenses against their young, been
judged morally or mentally unfit, or become permanently disabled while in receipt of Poor Law aid. Where guardians chose to exercise these prerogatives, a
child's parent retained the right of appeal to a police court. But judging from
the fact that in 1908 alone guardians adopted 12,417 such children, these appeals must have been either few in number or singularly ineffective.[19]

A Poor Law adoption did not necessarily end in foster care. And Poor Law
foster care—that is, boarding-out arrangements—affected just 3.7 percent of
all English and Welsh children receiving public relief of some kind in the early
twentieth century.[20] However, guardians began wielding their new power as a

way to reconfigure working-class families. In Edwardian Essex, Poor Law authorities at Braintree used adoption to "break the family tradition" of "viscious habits" that poisoned some rural homes.[21] At about the same time guardians elsewhere started trying to protect abused children through adoption. Prewar evidence drawn from the minute books of Poor Law Unions in the north of England suggests that guardians there most often resorted to adoption where gross "neglect by parents" was at issue: less than 10 percent of the children adopted in Carlisle were either orphans or illegitimate.[22] Curiously, in at least two northern Unions, children who had already been adopted by the guardians were sometimes readopted by local citizens. Darlington's Boarding-Out Committee felt no qualms about allowing respectable folk to tour the workhouse so that they might handpick promising youngsters.[23] In County Durham's Chester-le-Street Union, the Workhouse Visiting Committee permitted one girl, Sarah Thompson, to be readopted twice within a span of fourteen months. Although the minutes are mute as to why young Sarah returned to the workhouse after both placements, she, like Poor Law children in several other localities, may have been exploited as a short-term servant.[24]

The volunteer committees that oversaw such strange placements naturally tended to be middle-class in composition, with "ladies" shouldering much of the visiting work. Ideally at least, "the relationship between the foster-parents and the committee lady . . . becomes one of real friendship, both being deeply interested in the welfare of a little child. If misfortune falls upon the family, the lady is at hand to assist; but if wrong-doing takes place, undesirable lodgers be admitted, . . . it is the duty of the lady to inform the committee, so that they may remove the child to a more desirable home."[25] By 1909, however, it was clear to the Royal Commission on the Poor Laws that children boarded out within a Union's boundaries usually received less attentive supervision than those placed with foster parents living "without" the Union. The reason seemed obvious: whereas within Union boundaries boarding-out committees remained optional and unregulated, outside the Union these bodies were compulsory and, after 1884, the objects of Local Government Board scrutiny. Miss M. H. Mason, who became the board's first inspector of foster children in 1885, was nothing if not earnest about her job: "If the boarding-out system spreads widely," she believed, "only strict rules can save it from degenerating into baby-farming." Thus, Mason gave short shrift to lady visitors whose investigative protocol differed from her own. All too often, she assured a parliamentary committee in 1896, these volunteers failed to check for signs of mistreatment "hidden under tidy clothes" yet tended to be unrealistically demanding about the housekeeping habits of foster mothers.[26]

Very rarely do records offer a glimpse of the Poor Law's boarding-out work through a child's eyes. Still, it is probable that the disorientation that Catherine B. experienced on leaving her Essex workhouse home would have been common. Born in 1890, more than seventy years later, Catherine could recall her earliest memory, —eating "skilly" (a mush made of corn and hot water) at a large workhouse table. She was lame ("my toes were where my heels were") and perhaps as a result became a special favorite of the workhouse matron. But one day when she was four, Catherine found herself in a dogcart heading to a strange place:

> Oh, I was frightened. I hadn't been told a thing, you see. And when I got in [to her new home, in nearby Great Bentley] there was a chair, a little chair in front of the fire and this lady asked me to sit on it. She said, "sit down," and I did and she gave me some biscuits, but I remember I couldn't eat them . . . 'cos I was too upset, couldn't think where I was. And after [the workhouse master and matron] said they were going, I got up to go, thinking I was going back, but I didn't. I had to stop. So I cried, I said, "I don't want to stop here. I want to go back to my other home!" I remember as if it was yesterday. And I was a . . . frail little thing, white face, and they cropped my hair like a boy.

Catherine remained in Great Bentley until she was old enough to earn her keep as a domestic servant.[27] For her, and perhaps for many other wards of the workhouse, resettlement in a new home, whether through boarding out or adoption, did not necessarily lead to a happier life.

Catherine B. might just as easily have spent her first years in one of the many charitable institutions dedicated to saving children classified variously as "friendless," "homeless," or "outcast." Running parallel to the Poor Law's foster care system was a dense if uncoordinated complex of private agencies specializing in virtually the same work. By the end of the nineteenth century, several hundred of these bodies operated throughout England and Wales, although three of them—the Barnardo group, the Children's Home and Orphanage, and the Church of England Waifs and Strays Society—together accounted for as much as half the voluntary effort in this field. Dr. Barnardo's Homes, expanding rapidly from their base in London's East End, was the oldest (1866) and largest of the triumvirate. Thomas John Barnardo, an Irish Protestant zealot whose philanthropic style is best described as martial, proclaimed "the ever-open door" for young outcasts.[28] Barnardo's policy of admitting ragged boys and girls to his homes before investigating their personal circumstances followed naturally from his belief that successful reclamation work often came down to a race against time. "If the children of the slums can be removed from their surroundings early enough, and can be kept sufficiently long under training," he averred, "heredity counts for little, environment counts for everything."[29]

A sense of urgency therefore pervaded Barnardo's work and sometimes drove him to take rash action. Early enemies had lobbed into the Barnardo camp several incendiary charges, the best documented of which centered on his resort to posed photographs of "street arabs."[30] Partly no doubt as a fund-raising ploy but partly also because he deemed divine command superior to human law, Barnardo later confessed to kidnapping in 1885. This confession was shrewdly timed. W. T. Stead, editor of the *Pall Mall Gazette* and a crusader against child prostitution, was then England's most famous prisoner, having been convicted of buying thirteen-year-old Eliza Armstrong as part of a campaign to expose the white slave trade. Not to be outdone, Barnardo revealed that by kidnapping no fewer than forty-seven homeless children, he had elevated "philanthropic abduction" to a "fine art."[31] Although no legal challenges followed this announcement, the combative "doctor" ran out of luck four years later. In 1889, the parents of three children admitted to his homes demanded their return. Subsequent litigation showed that Barnardo had acted irresponsibly, hustling two of these children out of the country in such a way that they could not be traced.[32] Some of Barnardo's well-placed supporters tried to shield him from future legal liability by urging Parliament to limit the rights of parents who had permitted charities to "adopt" their young. The resulting 1891 Custody of Children Act did at least allow courts to prevent the return of children to parents judged unfit. But this was too little too late. Not until the mid-1890s could the Barnardo group once more devote its full attention to the fostering and vocational training of slum children, 4,357 of whom were boarded out by 1906.[33]

Dr. Stephenson's Children's Home and the Church of England Waifs and Strays Society also emerged as leading providers of foster care. As was true of Barnardo's work, the line between fostering and adoption could easily become blurred in these organizations. Thomas Bowman Stephenson, a Methodist minister, had launched his rescue mission on the mean streets of South London in 1869. Although best known during the late-Victorian period as an orphanage, Stephenson's society actually admitted few total orphans. His charges tended rather to be the offspring of widows, deserted wives, and prostitutes, precisely the sort of children who needed saving from the "workhouse system."[34] During their first quarter century the Stephenson institutions helped about half their children to find unskilled employment abroad, principally in Canada, where economic opportunity and a better moral climate appeared to exist.[35] Most of those who remained in England found jobs in domestic service and agriculture. But roughly 2 percent of the Stephenson children are listed in annual reports as "adopted." We are assured that "homes of comfort and happiness" had been located for these fortunate few, although published material sheds no real light on the nature of such adoptions.[36]

The experience of the Church of England Waifs and Strays Society (CEWSS) is more revealing. The CEWSS owed its founding in 1881 to Edward de Montjoie Rudolf, a young civil servant. Like the charities of Barnardo and Stephenson, the Waifs and Strays (as it was popularly known) began work in London, sometimes "hunted" its outcast "quarry" at night inside dustbins and under tarpaulins, and later turned to emigration as one outlet for the children under its care.[37] But whereas the older charities tended to ignore sectarian distinctions, Rudolf from the first ran his agency for the benefit of Anglican young. Moreover, unlike the Barnardo group, which remained the fiefdom of its founder until his death in 1905, the CEWSS adhered closely to a constitution, thereby earning full support—financial as well as spiritual—from the established Church.[38]

Boarding out children in foster homes soon became a key feature of the Waifs and Strays' mission. By 1896 the Society had 2,300 boys and girls on its books, 700 of them in foster homes; and the proportion of CEWSS children boarded out would remain in the range of 20 to 30 percent for several more years.[39] The large majority (69 percent) of children under CEWSS care received no financial support from their relatives. Contributions from Poor Law Unions, other charities, and individuals who sponsored particular boys and girls helped to offset the considerable cost of fostering. But such assistance never fully covered boarding-out bills, with the result that CEWSS administrators were always eager to economize.[40] One way to cut costs was to engineer the adoption of the Society's children. This is not to imply that the Waifs and Strays pounced on every adoption offer it received. Where Nonconformists made offers, Anglican administrators might return children to their parents rather than accept places outside the faith.[41] Nor would CEWSS officials automatically tear a child away from its foster parents, particularly if they made an attractive counteroffer:

> Alice, a child of 3, was boarded out with Mrs. Worley, of Hillingdon [West London]. Her mother dead; father unknown. An offer is made by a lady to adopt her. The foster-parent is in great trouble on hearing this; and one morning presented herself at headquarters with the child, and with tears in her eyes, pleaded that she might keep her. She was quite willing to forego the payment made to her by the Society [five shillings per week] if she could only keep the little one as her own. The child had become most dear to her; she had twined herself around her foster-mother's heart. The request was granted; for who could have refused it?[42]

But for children who had been admitted to CEWSS care as "free cases" or whose sources of outside support had dried up, the prospect of adoption must have been very attractive. Thus, because the mother of John S., an illegitimate child, had disappeared along with her weekly contribution of four shillings, the Society was delighted to adopt him off its account book. Despite having spent three years as a "happy well cared for and loved" foster child, John S. was taken from the only home he knew and given to prospective adopters "on approval."[43]

Quite apart from the baby-farming trade there existed a market for adoption in late-Victorian England, and CEWSS officials were more than willing to supply it. Early in 1887 the society learned that an orphanage in Leominster called the Christian Million Mission had long sought to match homeless children with childless couples.[44] Four years later, an unidentified philanthropist announced that he or she had spent the past two decades arranging adoptions for orphan girls. *Our Waifs and Strays* piously reminded its readers that the CEWSS, too, had become "a middleman or distributor of a most happy and beneficial kind, . . . penetrated with the idea that, wherever there is an orphan or a waif wanting a parent, there is also somewhere a parental heart seeking a child, for the mutual advantage and blessing of both."[45] By the turn of the century England's largest merchandising newspaper, the *Bazaar, Exchange and Mart*, was regularly carrying adoption advertisements. The wording of these notices hinted at the broad range of motivations behind them, from the Staffordshire "lady of position" who wanted a "baby girl, 3 years, orphan, bright, good looking, healthy," to the Surrey woman who frankly sought "an orphan girl as one of the family, for general domestic work." Some advertisers were prepared to pay for the right sort of child, while others wished to be compensated for their kindness. Mrs. Merton from the Isle of Wight, for example, was forty, "without family," and lived in "a pretty seaside home." She wanted a young child of either sex but expected a "premium in accordance with refined upbringings."[46]

CEWSS officers did not need to scour the *Bazaar, Exchange and Mart*.[47] An analysis of nineteen cases involving children born between 1877 and 1909 shows that adoption most commonly took place when the Society's foster parents volunteered to give up their weekly boarding-out fees in return for the right to keep a child.[48] The Society's only detailed information about would-be adopters often came from "ladies" and "gentlemen" who had agreed to sponsor individual children. The case of Edith B., an illegitimate girl born in the Marylebone Union workhouse, suggests how influential these sponsors could be. Since Edith's mother, a servant, had been "a respectable girl before & since her fall," headquarters decided to accept her baby and thereby save the twenty-one-year-old mother from further exposure to the "demoralizing influence of a workhouse." The baby was boarded out with Mrs. Smith of Pelham Street, Mile End, and a Mrs. Billing offered to underwrite this placement. The latter agreed not only to remain responsible for Edith's maintenance but also to collect one shilling per week from her mother. Mrs. Billing subsequently had to persuade a dubious E. de M. Rudolf that this unusual arrangement with an East End foster mother was worth continuing:

I placed [Edith] where she is when we were living very near at Spital-fields. She was a most delicate child & many nurses wd not have under-taken the care of her. Mrs. Smith was a kind & motherly lady on whom I could depend to be kind to the child. She has given her a Mother's love & care & the child is better & stronger now than I ever supposed she could be. I quite agree that Pelham Street is not an ideal boarding out spot—not what wd be called a desirable place—but I think this is more than compensated for by the real love the child has enjoyed & under which she has thrived. I feel I would not remove her merely for the sake of a better neighbourhood.

Thanks to Billing's intervention, Edith remained in her East End foster home. Six years later, the nurturing Mrs. Smith chose to adopt her foster child.[49]

A child's sponsor might also spare CEWSS administrators some of the adoption-related headaches that so pained Dr. Barnardo. Soon after Alice N. was admitted to a receiving home near Brighton in 1902, a Mrs. Desborough agreed to shoulder the expense of maintaining this seven-year-old girl. By late 1906 the Society was poised to send Alice to Canada since she had shown her-self to be intelligent and trustworthy. But because Mrs. Desborough had had the good sense to keep the girl's relatives apprised of her progress, this spon-sor was able to warn headquarters that an elder sister and an uncle objected to Alice's emigration. Soon thereafter, Mrs. Desborough convinced the girl's rel-atives that adoption would now be the best course of action and later warned the prospective adopter that she was taking a risk: "'adoption' has no legal sanction," Mrs. Desborough explained, "and it would not be possible to retain a child in opposition to the claim of a natural guardian, should one appear at any time in the future."[50]

Not every CEWSS child received such close attention from a sponsor, and in some cases no amount of supervision could have anticipated the perils that attended adoption in this era. Lilian W., an illegitimate girl of fourteen, ap-pears to have had no sponsor. Thus, when a Mrs. Edwards of Glamorganshire wrote to the Society asking to adopt a female, there was no one who could vouch for the Welshwoman. Edwards reneged on the adoption after two years because Lilian was once "a bit rude."[51]

The adoption of Hubert B., an eight-year-old orphan boy, failed despite care-ful precautions. Thanks to the interest that the Reverend Badcock of Leeds took in Hubert, the boy was "boarded out free" with Mr. and Mrs. Roberts, genteel friends of the clergyman. Seven months after this de facto adoption, all seemed well. As Rev. Badcock reported to headquarters, "The . . . boy was baptised by me on July 25 [1886]. I have frequent opportunities of seeing the boy in his home & certainly I could desire no more happy position for any boy. Both his 'parents' are devoted to him, but at the same time they treat him very wisely & judiciously. [Hubert] is developing into a fine manly boy both physically and mentally." That Mr. and Mrs. Roberts would soon move to New Jersey gave Rev. Badcock no pause. Three years later, however, trouble arose in the person of Hubert's married sister, who now wanted custody of him. Rev. Badcock was bewildered. Surely the Society had impressed the conditions of this adoption on Hubert's relatives, and by accepting these conditions they had just as surely "yielded up all claims to the child?" Informed that Hubert's relatives could not legally be deprived of his custody, the Reverend urged CEWSS officials to appeal instead to the sister's "sense of gratitude":

> Probably the sister does not realize that the boy is brought up as the only child of a gentleman & lady who are in a good position in America & who *are* giving him a future which is far more promising than any that his relatives can offer him. Then too, the sister cannot realize that after 4 years of love and affection from the adopted parents the boy wd. not at 13 years of age take kindly to a home or friends who had taken him from parents he had learned to love and respect.

But once young Hubert learned of his sister's bid for custody, he could not "settle down at all," so obsessed did he become with seeing his siblings again. By mid-August 1890, Mr. and Mrs. Roberts had sadly accepted that they must give up their son.[52]

The Waifs and Strays worked hard to discourage relatives from disrupting an adoption. To protect adopting parents as well as its own financial interests, the Society began in the late 1890s to use a typed and formidably legalistic "adoption agreement" in these cases. All known relatives were asked to sign the document, which enjoined kinfolk from interfering "in any way with any arrangement that may be made in regard to [an adopted child's] future." In the event that relatives later tried to remove a child from its adoptive home, they would be liable, under this agreement, to reimburse the CEWSS for its "expenses" at a rate of between ten and thirteen pounds per year of care.[53]

How often such coercion served its intended purpose is impossible to know, since the CEWSS did not routinely continue to supervise an adoption, as modern social work aftercare is designed to do. Some of the middle-class men and women who ran the Society's receiving centers clearly believed that poor people could be intimidated. As one Lady Superintendent observed about the adoption agreement that she hoped Kathleen H.'s servant mother would sign in 1915: "*I know it is just paper, but she would not.*"[54] Still, there was no real security for the kind of ad hoc adoption work carried on by the CEWSS and similar children's charities. The cataclysm of world war would soon transform such insecurity into a demand for legal protection.

By the outbreak of war in 1914 both charitable institutions and Poor Law authorities had been arranging adoptions of English children for a generation, despite the legally suspect nature of this work. Adoptions of a less formal sort must have been even more common during these years. In mid-Victorian Lancashire and in East London at the turn of the century, 29 percent of all children could expect to lose one parent and 8 percent both before reaching the age of fifteen.[55] Desertion and judicial separation would have created additional one-parent households. Under these demographic conditions, it seems remarkable that more children did not end up in public or private institutions. A large but unknowable proportion of orphans and children from troubled homes must have been taken in by other families. Unlike nineteenth-century France, where the adoption of orphan young was often arranged through a council of relatives, kinfolk in English working-class districts tended to open their doors spontaneously. Anecdotal evidence suggests that adoption was also undertaken as a neighborly act.[56] A London police court magistrate was "greatly moved" to learn that during the hard winter of 1886–87, four Greenwich children with disabled parents had joined a poor family in the next street.[57] Another patrician student of plebeian culture, Lady Bell, found adoption to be the highest expression of "hospitality" among the ironworkers of Edwardian Middlesborough.[58] Even in Campbell Road, notorious as North London's worst street between the wars, one mother's inability to cope with a sick baby led to its becoming permanently part of a neighbor's brood.[59]

These "articulated notions of community obligation" accounted for many, but not all, working-class adoptions. Some stemmed from the same sense of maternal deprivation that features so prominently in late-twentieth-century discussions of the subject. Childlessness was a source of regret but not "passionate sorrow" for the northern wives whom Elizabeth Roberts interviewed, principally because they had played active and satisfying roles in the rearing of nieces and nephews. But what of poor women without surrogate young? Having suffered seven miscarriages in her thirteen years of marriage, the childless wife of one manual worker explained that she had "consoled myself by adopting an orphan boy, who is the sunshine of my life."[60] Thus, literary representations of adoption as an unnatural act should be treated with caution. "To adopt a child, because children of your own had been denied you," reasoned Nancy in George Eliot's *Silas Marner* (1861), "was to try and choose your lot in spite of Providence." If fatalism remained a defining feature of working-class culture, it did not deter the poor from opening their homes to children who needed them.[61]

All the same, compared to other anglophone nations, England was very slow to grant de facto adoptions full legal security.[62] As early as 1852, one Englishwoman marveled "how easily and frankly children are adopted in the United States, how pleasantly the scheme goes on, and how little of the wormwood of domestic jealousies . . . seems to interfere with it." She concluded that three factors might account for this happy circumstance: America's comparative "abundance of food and . . . unoccupied room"; a high demand for labor; and the absence of primogeniture in U.S. legal codes.[63] By 1900, Michael Grossberg observes, judicial adoption was widely accepted in America and the formation of artificial families had become "routine."[64] Indeed, the routine was such that by 1915 the New York Times Magazine could complain that adoption had evolved int an "exact science," with U.S. children subjected to a battery of medical and mental tests, as well as vetted for "anatomical stigmata," before "any play of the affections" might be considered.[65] Adoption in Progressive Era America was actually far less systematic than this lament implies. The general secretary of the Boston Children's Friend Society warned in 1915, for example, that "numerous" babies offered through local newspapers had come from mothers with mental defects, venereal diseases, or non-white lovers.[66] Even so, American adoption was becoming an increasingly well-regulated practice.

Instead, prior to winning legal recognition in 1926, "adoption" for the English conjured up at least three competing family narratives. Adoption as a gesture of working-class mutuality spoke of hope—hope not only for the needy children taken in but also for the future of a "respectable," self-regulating majority. In stark contrast, adoption as a cynical front for the disposal of unwanted babies testified to the desperate lot of some unmarried mothers. That poverty and social ostracism might override maternal feeling cast doubt on the taxonomy of instinct that helped mainstream English society make sense of human behavior. Third, adoption could signify the gamble that some well-off citizens felt compelled to accept. The greatest risk, they believed, was not that love would fail to flourish in artificial families but rather that working-class kin would one day materialize and, taking advantage of the legal lacunae surrounding adoption, repossess blood relatives. This fear ultimately paved the way for legalization after the Great War.

The war itself served to intensify middle-class concerns about adoption. Nearly three-quarters of a million British soldiers died during World War I; in England and Wales, combat deaths took nearly 7 percent of all males between the ages of fifteen and forty-nine. An estimated 150,000 more citizens, many of them young adults, perished during the lethal influenza outbreak of 1918–19.[67] An alarming number of "war orphans" therefore lost at least one parent during a brief, five-year period. Swelling these ranks were the "war babies," the illegitimate issue of wartime liaisons, whose numbers temporarily reversed a long-term decline in bastardy rates: whereas 4.29 percent of all live births had been illegitimate in 1913, by 1918 the figure stood at 6.26 percent. Not all contemporaries believed that "dead heroes" had fathered these babies or that the "girls" who conceived such children should be praised. Yet never in living memory had there been so many children who needed new homes or so many grieving parents ready to provide them.[68]

As the *Times*'s "personal" columns began to suggest, especially after the start of the Somme offensive in July 1916, more well-off adults were now prepared to overlook eugenic fears about the underclass to bring up others' children as their own. These advertisements often demanded "absolute surrender," however.[69] If the *Spectator* was right that an "epidemic of adoption" had broken out, it was spreading among those who "lived in constant dread" that their new sons and daughters might be "snatched away."[70] Catherine Hartley, the author of two well-received books on woman's nature, typified the sort of middle-class parent for whom adoption entailed terrifying uncertainty. Late in 1917 she implored the home secretary to provide legal relief:

I myself have an adopted son now at a public school, & dearer to me than anyone in the world. [H]e was deserted by his mother under peculiarly painful circumstances in early childhood, but for the last few years I have had terrible trouble, anxiety, & expense as the mother though she had signed a deed giving him up to me, said she wished to have him back. I need not trouble you with further details, which I mention only to show you how earnestly I care. I ask you, in the name of these little ones, to do something to help & protect them.[71]

The legal limbo in which parents such as Hartley lived drove another advocate of reform to declare, "The law has gone so far in the direction of restricting the exercise of parental rights that it might [as] well go a little further" and recognize the validity of these new family configurations. Without law's blessing, genteel adopters would be forced to dodge a child's birth parents by ever more devious means.[72]

Such anxiety would eventually fuel two Home Office investigations into the demand for adopted children. When legalization finally came to England in 1926, some people chose to regard this historic step as "a sacramental ministry of reconstruction," the nation's most poignant effort to heal the wounds of war.[73] More broadly conceived, legalization made possible a new narrative of English family life. Although tinged with anxieties of its own, it was a narrative from which fears about blackmail over the adoption process began to recede. Historians are often surprised to learn how long the gulf between customary adoption and common law endured in England. Still less appreciated—and perhaps more surprising—is the speed with which the dislocations of world war served to harmonize theory and practice.

NOTES

For their perceptive comments on earlier drafts, I wish to thank E. Wayne Carp, Jane Cater, and Ellen Ross.

1. Charles F. Thwing and Mary F. B. Thwing, *The Family: An Historical and Social Study* (Boston, 1887), 164.

2. Older accounts include G. F. McCleary, *The Early History of the Infant Welfare Movement* (London, 1933); Mary Hopkirk, *Nobody Wanted Sam: The Story of the Unwelcomed Child, 1530–1948* (London, 1949); Leslie Housden, *The Prevention of Cruelty to Children* (London: Cape, 1955). More recent analyses appear in George Behlmer, *Child Abuse and Moral Reform in England, 1870–1908* (Stanford, Calif.: Stanford University Press, 1982); Lionel Rose, *The Massacre of the Innocents: Infanticide in Britain 1800–1939* (London: Routledge and Kegan Paul, 1986); Ann R. Higgenbotham, "The Unmarried Mother and Her Child in Victorian London" (Ph.D. diss., Indiana University, 1985).

3. "Infanticide," *Saturday Review* 20 (Aug. 5, 1865): 61.

4. For more on Curgenven, Hart, and the politics of baby farming, see Behlmer, *Child Abuse*, 22–38; George Behlmer, "Ernest Hart and the Social Thrust of Victorian Medicine," *British Medical Journal*, Oct. 3, 1990, 711–13.

5. James Greenwood, *The Seven Curses of London* (Boston, 1869), 24–25; *Pall Mall Gazette*, Jan. 31, 1868.

6. *British Medical Journal*, Jan. 15, 1898, 178–79, May 27, 1871, 563; Select Committee on Protection of Infant Life, Parliamentary Papers (hereafter cited as PP), 1871, QQ. 18–26, 30, 44; *Times* (London), Dec. 14, 1867.

7. J. B. Curgenven, *On Baby-Farming and the Registration of Nurses* (London, 1869), 6, 9. According to official figures, 44,691 English children were born out of wedlock during the year 1869 (Thirty-second Annual Report of the Registrar General, PP, 1871, XV: 28).

8. *Lloyd's Weekly Newspaper*, June 5, 1870.

9. *Times* (London), June 16, 21, July 2, 4, 7, 28, Sept. 24, 1870; *Illustrated Police News*, Oct. 15, 1870.

10. Robert J. Parr, *The Baby Farmer: An Exposition and Appeal* (London, 1909), 27–29, 52–53.

11. *British Medical Journal*, July 16, 1910, 165.

12. Rudyard Kipling, *Something of Myself* (Garden City, N.Y., 1937), 6–19.

13. *Times* (London), Nov. 7, 1874.

14. William Anderson, *Children Rescued from Pauperism; or, The Boarding-out System in Scotland* (Edinburgh, 1871), 98.

15. Louisa Twining, *Recollections of Workhouse Visiting and Management* (London, 1880), 196–99; Florence Davenport-Hill, *Children of the State*, 2d ed. (London, 1889), 183–84.

16. The boarding out of pauper children within Union boundaries was already taking place at Bath (C. W. Grant, *The Advantages of the Boarding out System* [London, (1869)]), 2–3, 33–34.

17. Francis Peek, *Social Wreckage: A Review of the Laws of England as They Affect the Poor*, 3d ed. (London, 1888), 58, 43–44.

18. Even before 1889, Guardians in some Poor Law Unions had encouraged foster parents to "adopt" boarded-out children in the sense of offering them permanent

homes to which they could return at any age (Report from the Select Committee of the House of Lords on Poor Law Relief, PP, 1888, XV, QQ. 3,939–42).

19. Report of the Departmental Committee on the Treatment of Young Offenders, PP, 1927, XII: 116.

20. Royal Commission on the Poor Laws and Relief of Distress, PP, 1909, XVIII, app., 2. As of Jan. 1, 1907, 234,004 persons under sixteen years of age were receiving Poor Law relief in England and Wales. The number of boys and girls boarded out was 8,659.

21. George Cuttle, *The Legacy of the Rural Guardians: A Study of Conditions in Mid-Essex* (Cambridge, 1934), 116.

22. See Cumbria County Record Office: Carlisle Poor Law Union, Register of Children under Control, 1912–55, SPU/Ca/5/11.

23. Darlington Branch Library, Local Studies Department: Darlington Poor Law Union, Minutes of the Boarding-Out Committee (July 8, 1889–Nov. 25, 1897), U/Da 720, entry for Jan. 14, 1892.

24. Durham County Record Office: Chester-le-Street Poor Law Union, Minutes of the Workhouse Visiting Committee, 1913–15, U/CS 27, entries for Jan. 23, July 24, 1913, Mar. 5, 1914. Joseph Brown, president of the Association of Poor Law Unions, testified that workhouse adoption was in "too many instances" a kind of forced labor, with strangers taking away children between the ages of nine and thirteen to use as "little house slaves and nurses" before and after school (Royal Commission on the Poor Laws and Relief of Distress, PP, 1909, XL, QQ. 24,790–92).

25. Henrietta O. Barnett, *Matters That Matter* (London, 1930), 170–71.

26. Royal Commission on the Poor Laws and Relief of Distress, PP, 1909, LXVIII [Lords]: 183–85; *Hospital*, Aug. 31, 1889, 340–41; Report of the Departmental Committee [on] the Maintenance and Education of Children under the Charge of . . . Boards of Guardians, PP, 1896, XLIII, Q. 14,326. The much-publicized death of Dennis O'Neill at the hands of his Shropshire foster parents in 1945 would recall Mason's plea for vigilance. See R. A. Parker, "The Gestation of Reform: The Children Act of 1948," in *Approaches to Welfare*, ed. Philip Bean and Stewart MacPherson (London: Routledge and Kegan Paul, 1983), 203–4.

27. Family Life and Work Experience Archive, Sociology Department, University of Essex: interview 19, "Catherine B."

28. *Night and Day*, Feb.–Mar. 1882, 32–34. Middle-class moralists often denounced "street arabism," pointing out that children swarming in city thoroughfares produced social disorder and bred contempt for authority. See Emma Samuels, "The Adoption of Street Arabs by the State," *Fortnightly Review* 69 (Jan. 1898): 11–18.

29. As quoted in Jean Heywood, *Children in Care: The Development of the Service for the Deprived Child* (London: Routledge and Kegan Paul, 1959), 53–54.

30. Seth Koven offers a shrewd reading of the photographic furor of 1874 in "Dr. Barnardo's 'Artistic Fictions': Photography, Sexuality and the Ragged Child in Victorian London," *Radical History Review* 69 (fall 1997): 25–36.

31. *Night and Day*, Nov. 1885, 149–52. See also T. J. Barnardo, *Worse Than Orphans: How I Stole Two Girls and Fought for a Boy* (London, [1885]). The "Maiden Tribute of Modern Babylon" scandal has received careful attention from Michael Pearson, *The Age of Consent: Victorian Prostitution and Its Enemies* (Newton Abbot: David and Charles, 1972); Deborah Gorham, "The 'Maiden Tribute of Modern Babylon' Re-Visited," *Victorian Studies* 21 (spring 1978): 353–79; Judith Walkowitz, *City of Dreadful Delight:*

Narratives of Sexual Danger in Late-Victorian London (Chicago: University of Chicago Press, 1992).

32. Gillian Wagner, *Barnardo* (London: Weidenfeld and Nicolson, 1979), 218–25. The habeas corpus actions taken against Barnardo in the case of Harry Gossage were perhaps the most celebrated of the doctor's legal woes. For full—and to date unexploited—particulars on this boy's family background, see Warwick County Record Office, Leamington Charity Organisation Society, Case Record Book, CR51/1878, record 890.

33. On efforts to protect the philanthropic "adoption" of children, see Parliamentary Debates, 3d ser. (Lords), 338 (July 16, 1889): 502–14. For the growth of Barnardo's boarding-out work, see Mrs. Barnardo and James Marchant, *Memoirs of the Late Dr. Barnardo* (London, 1907), 190, 194, 201–2.

34. John R. Gillis, *For Better, for Worse: British Marriages, 1600 to the Present* (New York: Oxford University Press, 1985), 246; Children's Home and Orphanage, *Annual Report for 1895–96* (London, 1896), 8.

35. For the treatment of English children sent to Canada, see Joy Parr, *Labouring Children: British Immigrant Apprentices to Canada, 1869–1924* (London: Croom Helm, 1980).

36. Children's Home and Orphanage, *Annual Report for 1879–80* (London, 1880), 7; *Annual Report for 1886–87* (London, 1887), 6; *Annual Report for 1895–96* (London, 1896), 13. By Dec. 1920 what was then known as the National Children's Home and Orphanage had arranged for the care and education of 15,048 children. Of this number just 262 (1.74 percent) "had been found in every way available for adoption" (Public Record Office, HO45/11540/354040, Litten to Sharpe, Dec. 21, 1920).

37. *Our Waifs and Strays*, Aug. 1886, 2; Harriet Ward, "The Charitable Relationship: Parents, Children and the Waifs and Strays Society" (Ph.D. diss., University of Bristol, 1990), 304–5.

38. John Stroud, *Thirteen Penny Stamps: The Story of the Church of England Children's Society (Waifs and Strays) from 1881 to the 1970s* (London: Hodder and Stoughton, 1971), 29–30, 54; R. M. Wrong, "Some Voluntary Organizations for the Welfare of Children," in *Voluntary Social Services*, ed. A. F. C. Bourdillon (London, 1945), 36–37. At various times Barnardo seems to have viewed the CEWSS as a philanthropic upstart whose financial support had been gained through "crooked methods," chief among them denigrating the doctor's work (*Our Waifs and Strays*, June 1895, 94–95).

39. Select Committee on Infant Life Protection/Safety of Nurse Children, PP, 1896, X, QQ. 860, 865; Stroud, *Thirteen Penny Stamps*, 67.

40. Report of the Departmental Committee [on] the Maintenance and Education of Children under the Charge of . . . Boards of Guardians, PP, 1896, XLIII, QQ. 12,956, 12,960.

41. Children's Society Archives, London: Executive Committee Minute Book 7, Aug. 19, 1901.

42. *Our Waifs and Strays*, Aug. 1891, 1.

43. Ward, "Charitable Relationship," 295–96.

44. *Christian Million*, Jan. 20, Feb. 17, 1887.

45. *Our Waifs and Strays*, Aug. 1891, 13; Feb. 1887, 8.

46. *Bazaar, Exchange, and Mart*, May 13, 25, June 17, 1898. The *Exchange and Mart* first appeared in 1868 as a weekly newspaper "established to provide a medium between the seller and buyer, and at a very cheap rate to enable anyone who wishes to dispose of

any article, either by exchange or by sale, to do so to the very best advantage" (May 13, 1868).

47. But on at least one occasion the mother of a child boarded out by the Waifs and Strays Society used the *Bazaar, Exchange, and Mart* to find adoptive parents. This mother, a widow "unable owing to a reverse of fortune to bring up the Child in a way befitting [her] station," soon located a Mr. A. B. Watson, owner of an engineering firm in Hull (Children's Society Archives, "Correspondence between Bruce Millar & Company, Solicitors, and A. B. Watson re adoption of a little girl," 1898–99, accession 89.53).

48. E. de M. Rudolf assured a local government board committee, "I have known instances repeatedly where foster-parents have come forward and offered to adopt children who have been placed with them, and have volunteered to forgo all payments as long as the children are allowed to remain entirely as their own" (Report of the Departmental Committee [on] the Maintenance and Education of Children Under the Charge of . . . Boards of Guardians, PP, 1896, XLIII, QQ. 12,870, 12,891).

49. "Edith B.," born in Aug. 1885, Children's Society Archives, case file 715. For similar examples of local women smoothing the path for adopting parents, see case files 243 and 318.

50. "Alice N.," born in Aug. 1894, Children's Society Archives, case file 8,762.

51. "Lilian W.," born in Apr. 1896, Children's Society Archives, case file 15,499.

52. "Hubert B.," born in 1878, Children's Society Archives, case file 674.

53. See the draft agreement in case file 8,762.

54. "Kathleen H.," born in Apr. 1896, Children's Society Archives, case file 15,438.

55. Michael Anderson, *Family Structure in Nineteenth Century Lancashire* (Cambridge: Cambridge University Press, 1971), 148–49; Michael Young and Peter Willmott, *Family and Kinship in East London* (Glencoe, Ill.: Free Press, 1957), 21–22.

56. Rachel Fuchs, *Abandoned Children: Foundlings and Child Welfare in Nineteenth-Century France* (Albany: State University of New York Press, 1984), 30–31; Anna Davin, *Growing up Poor: Home, School, and Street in London, 1870–1914* (London: Rivers Oram Press, 1996), 40.

57. Montague Williams, *Later Leaves* (London, 1891), 257–59.

58. Lady [Florence] Bell, *At the Works: A Study of a Manufacturing Town* (London, 1907), 116, 192–93.

59. Jerry White, *The Worst Street in North London: Campbell Bunk, Islington, between the Wars* (London: Routledge and Kegan Paul, 1986), 137–38.

60. Ellen Ross, *Love and Toil: Motherhood in Outcast London, 1870–1918* (New York: Oxford University Press, 1993), 134; Elizabeth Roberts, *An Oral History of Working-Class Women, 1890–1940* (Oxford: B. Blackwell, 1984), 103; Women's Co-operative Guild, *Maternity: Letters from Working-Women* (1915; New York: Garland, 1980), 60–61. District nurse Margaret Loane complained that "children are far too lightly handed over to childless [working-class] persons offering to adopt them" (*An Englishman's Castle* [London, 1909], 105).

61. George Eliot, *Silas Marner* (1861; New York, 1906), 238–39. The adoption of Tattycoram likewise appears ill conceived in Dickens's *Little Dorrit* (1857). See also the adoption of a foundling by the crusty wife of a Shadwell chimney sweep in "Mrs. Simon's Baby," chap. 4 of Henry W. Nevinson's *Neighbours of Ours* (New York, 1895).

62. There was in fact one predominantly anglophone nation still more wary of legalized adoption: the Republic of Ireland did not grant legal recognition until 1952, and

even then clamped religious restrictions on the adoption process (John A. Murphy, *Ireland in the Twentieth Century* [Dublin: Gill and Macmillan, 1989], 136).

63. [Mary Grey Lundie], *America As I Found It* (New York, 1852), 93–96.

64. Michael Grossberg, *Governing the Hearth: Law and the Family in Nineteenth-Century America* (Chapel Hill: University of North Carolina Press, 1985), 278.

65. *New York Times Magazine,* October 13, 1915, p. 9. Wealthy childless couples in the United States did on occasion insist that children's charities administer the Simon-Binet intelligence test to prospective adoptees, along with the more routine tuberculosis test, but well into the twentieth century American social workers remained skeptical of adoption, particularly for illegitimate children. See E. Wayne Carp, *Family Matters: Secrecy and Disclosure in the History of Adoption* (Cambridge, Mass.: Harvard University Press, 1998).

66. Howard Carrington, "Adoption By Advertisement," *The Survey* 35 (Dec. 11, 1915): 285–86.

67. John Stevenson, *British Society, 1914–45* (London: A. Lane, 1984), 94, 210.

68. Eighty-second Annual Report of the Registrar General, PP, 1920, XI: xxxiv–xxxv; Lettice Fisher, "The Unmarried Mother and Her Child," *Contemporary Review* 156 (Oct. 1939): 485–86; *Times* (London), Apr. 19, 1915; Mary J. H. Skrine, "The Little Black Lamb," *Spectator* 119 (Aug. 11, 1917): 137. The newly patriotic Women's Social and Political Union was the first major feminist group to advocate adoption as a remedy for the "war babies" problem (*Times* [London], May 6, 1915).

69. See, for example, the *Times's* front pages for Aug.–Nov. 1916. Since the minimum charge for a small "personal" advertisement was then five shillings, those seeking to adopt children most likely enjoyed a degree of financial comfort.

70. "The Epidemic of Adoption," *Spectator* 119 (July 28, 1917): 79; British Agencies for Adoption and Fostering, London, typescript "History of the [Lancashire and Cheshire Child] Adoption Council," [1977].

71. Public Record Office, HO45/11540/354040, Hartley to the home secretary, Dec. 6, 1917. Hartley also advocated "free divorce" and argued that where divorced parents could not amicably share child-care duties, the state might award custody of their children to childless couples (Catherine Gasquoine Hartley, *The Truth about Woman* [London, 1913], 358).

72. Norman Croom-Johnson, "The Adoption of Children," *Englishwoman* 116 (Aug. 1918): 53–54.

73. Parliamentary Debates, 5th ser., 182 (Apr. 3, 1925), 1708–9.

A Historical Comparison of Catholic and Jewish Adoption Practices in Chicago, 1833–1933

Paula F. Pfeffer

As the nation's population diversified in the nineteenth century, benevolent work in the United States began to develop along sectarian lines. This fact led to the common assumption that Roman Catholics and Jews differed both from one another and from the dominant Protestant group in the handling of their social welfare needs. In studying the way that Chicago's Catholics and Jews coped with the problem of adoption, however, the similarities in their responses are more striking than the differences. Both religious groups suffered from being considered despised outsiders, and as immigrants, they went through similar experiences in their acculturation to American society. They can thus be compared in terms of their treatment of newer immigrants of their religious group, their attitudes regarding welfare in general and adoption in particular, their fund-raising methods, their connections with government, and the relationships prevailing among their professional and volunteer agency personnel.[1] Like all sectarian social welfare providers, both Catholic and Jewish adoption workers have primarily been concerned with how to retain their distinctive religious identities and those of their agencies while integrating into mainstream American society.

Prior to the passage of the Illinois Adoption Act of 1867, the state did not recognize a legal theory of child adoption. Before then, privately sponsored orphan homes, many of them affiliated with religious institutions, took in the increasing numbers of homeless children created by a burgeoning population and a series of cholera epidemics. One of the early ways of solving the problem of homeless children was binding them out by indenture as apprentices or servants for a specified period, without their consent. This practice became even more widespread after the revised statutes of Illinois defined the laws governing apprentices in 1845. Indenture remained the favorite means of providing for the custody and instruction of orphaned or otherwise destitute children until about 1875.[2]

The recurrence of cholera epidemics, however, encouraged some families to seek children to take the place of lost loved ones. Without legal adoption procedures, a kind of guardianship developed. Distinct from indenture because it did not include service but instead provided for inspection of the receiving home, guardianship lasted until the child came of age. The rules of both indenture and guardianship dictated that the natural parents must never be told the whereabouts of their child, and the wishes of the child were not considered. Privately sponsored orphan homes, many of them affiliated with Protestant religious institutions, also took in increasing numbers of homeless children. Only a small percentage of these children were adoptable; most waifs were half orphans, destitute as a result of desertion or illness of the family breadwinner.

Illinois first recognized a legal theory of child adoption with the passage of the Adoption Act of 1867. Formulated to provide greater safeguards for homeless children, the act borrowed liberally from other states' legislation and set forth the principles of the theory of adoption, proposed a procedure, and placed it under the jurisdiction of the court. While claiming to place primary importance on the welfare of the child, the court alone determined the reputability of the adopting parents. Furthermore, to qualify as a resident of the state, the petitioner needed only temporary residence in Illinois, a provision that had the unforeseen consequence of encouraging some prospective parents to enter the state solely for the purpose of adopting a child.

In 1854 Reverend Charles Loring Brace of the New York Children's Aid Society began an experiment, sending "orphan trains" of homeless, dependent, or delinquent children from the streets of New York City to Illinois and other rural Midwestern locations. Brace did not attempt to support the youngsters' natural families, which would have enabled the children to remain at home. Instead, he preferred breaking up poor biological families to "save" the children. Brace also did not investigate the receiving homes either before or after placement. Rather, he assumed that farm homes and fresh air were better for children than overcrowded cities, even though the children had to labor in exchange for room and board. Nevertheless, Brace was an early promoter of placing out as opposed to institutional care for dependent children. The Catholic Church, however, became alarmed: although the majority of these children were Catholic, they were being sent to Protestant homes, where the Church fathers thought they would be proselytized since, as one observer noted, "Every Country district affords evidence of the successful work of the proselytizer, who, through the placing out system, has defrauded a Catholic child of its heritage of faith."[3]

Still, in the nineteenth and early twentieth centuries, there were many more adoptable children than families willing to adopt them. Because of the emphasis on keeping the biological family intact and the stigma attached to it, adoption was seldom seen as a remedy.[4] Consequently, alleviating the problem of unwelcome babies often depended upon the services of commercial "baby farmers," who took children in for a fee and promised to place them for adoption, a promise that was seldom fulfilled.[5] The combination of unscrupulous profiteers and the placing of their children into Protestant homes upset the Catholic and Jewish communities. As late as 1903 Catholics were still complaining about the Protestant "thirst for Catholic souls."[6]

Both Catholics and Jews found the attitude with which the dominant Protestant group dispensed charity to be cold, unfeeling, and discriminatory. The greatest concern of Catholics and Jews, however, was fear of the assimilation of their unfortunate children into the mainstream group "under the guardianship of various charitable and philanthropic associations, representing in greater part Protestant denominations." The placing of Catholic children in Protestant homes, explained one observer, became "an abuse that grew to such proportions that the Church authorities were finally compelled to adopt measures to safeguard the interests of the Catholic children."[7] Indeed, the perceived abuses caused both Catholics and Jews to take action to care for their own homeless children.

When Chicago became a town in 1833, its estimated population of 350 included nearly 150 Catholics, mostly French. A large influx of Catholics, primarily Irish and German, came in 1836 to build the Illinois and Michigan Canal. Their arrival resulted in the diversification of the Catholic population. In 1844 Chicago was established as a diocese, with William J. Quarter as its first bishop. In 1846, at the request of Bishop Quarter, Mercy Sisters from Pittsburgh arrived to teach and to operate an orphanage and a hospital. Spurred by the bishop, in 1847 Mother Agatha wrote to the Propagation of the Faith in France to request money for education of poor girls "and a building to take care of orphans." The bishop supported her efforts, stating the need for a Catholic orphanage "because of the hundreds of children who were orphaned and bound out to Protestants each year."[8] On the heels of a second major Catholic immigration to the city in 1848 and 1849, following the Irish potato famine and German revolutions, serious cholera epidemics hit the city in 1849 and 1854, creating still more orphans.

Following this second wave of immigration, lay male Catholic activists founded the Chicago conference of the St. Vincent de Paul Society in 1857, and it quickly became the principal means by which parishes helped their poor and dependent. Not all parishes had St. Vincent de Paul Societies, however, and the Chicago Fire of 1871 wiped out Church property valued at about a million dollars. The fire was followed by a depression in the late 1870s, the Great Railroad Strike of 1877, and the arrival of massive numbers of newcomers from southern and eastern Europe in the last quarter of the nineteenth century. Thus, the task of rebuilding institutions destroyed by the fire was made more daunting by the country's economic problems and the inordinate demands that the steady influx of new immigrants made on the Church's resources.[9]

In 1880 the Chicago diocese was elevated to an archdiocese and received its first archbishop, Patrick A. Feehan. Archbishop Feehan furthered the Church's previous policy of supporting the immigrants' aspirations to retain their own customs and heritage and celebrate mass in their own language, in their own churches, with priests of their own national origin. Feehan's tolerance of ethnicity, while appreciated by the various national groups, made it difficult for the diocese to bring the groups together and may even have contributed to animosity among the Irish, German, and Polish clergy. Nevertheless, his successor, Archbishop James Edward Quigley, followed the same policies.[10]

In contrast, Archbishop George Mundelein, who succeeded Quigley in 1917, believed that national parishes isolated their parishioners from American culture and from other Catholics. He consequently decided to restrict the number of national parishes built in the future and centralized power in his office by bringing diocesan finances under his personal supervision.[11] But ethnic loyalties prevented centralization efforts from being as complete as Mundelein envisioned. Institutions run and supported by Poles and Bohemians and other eastern European Catholics resisted Mundelein's control, believing that it favored the larger Irish institutions. As a result, the ethnic institutions "resisted cooperation in diocesan fund-raising and opposed diocesan supervision."[12]

The Catholic response to the adoption issue must be seen against this background as well as in light of the Catholic conviction that religion is something more than an external value to children but rather is an obligation basic to their nature. Committed to the basic principle that Catholic children placed for adoption could have their total needs met only in Catholic adoptive homes, in 1881 Catholics established a home for foundlings and pregnant, unmarried women and their infants, St. Vincent's Infant Asylum.[13] Four Daughters of Charity came from Emmitsburg, Maryland, to run the home on the city's Near North Side, housing forty babies, some unwed mothers, and some indigent married mothers. The anonymity of the mother was protected while efforts were made to place her child. The first infant was placed for adoption in January 1882. As the numbers of infants and mothers increased, Sister Walburga Gehring, the founder, appealed for additional facilities. In 1887 the sisters purchased property and erected an institution that was incorporated in 1888 under Illinois law as St. Vincent's Orphan Asylum. The new asylum could care for 250 children.[14]

Following the Parliament of Religions at the Columbian Exposition of 1893, many lay Catholics, women as well as men, became convinced of the necessity to enter the field of social action and founded a number of organizations for that purpose. Thus, in addition to the St. Vincent de Paul Society, which opened a central office in 1910, and the Visitation and Aid Society, a voluntary group of laypersons formed to administer to the poor and sick in public and private county institutions, the Catholic Women's League was founded in 1893 to help with child care centers.[15]

In contrast to the Catholics, Chicago had only a few isolated Jewish traders and peddlers prior to 1838, when the first permanent Jewish settlers arrived. The first major influx of Jews occurred in the 1850s and 1860s, following the German revolutions of 1848 and 1849. Primarily merchants and traders, these immigrants for the most part followed traditional religious practices, but, identifying with non-Jewish Germans, they quickly adapted to American society, and most shed their Orthodox customs for Reform Judaism, which fit better into American work ways.[16]

A second major influx of Jewish immigrants as well as Catholics arrived from eastern Europe beginning in the 1870s. Pushed out by persecution and anti-Semitism, these Jews came expecting freedom and streets paved with gold. From poor backgrounds, unlike their middle-class German predecessors, the new immigrants' ideas and behavior were governed by the culture from which they came: the Orthodox communal culture of the shtetl, or small Jewish town in which they had lived in Europe. Such an outlook inevitably clashed with the individualistic competitive values of American society that the German Jews strove to emulate. Fearing the newcomers as an embarrassment to their hard-won acceptance, the German Jews, several of whom had become wealthy financiers by the turn of the century, ridiculed the strange appearance of their eastern European brethren, with their long beards, black hats, and frock coats, as well as their devotion to ancient religious rituals and customs.[17] Germans efforts to Americanize their eastern European coreligionists mirrored those of Irish Catholics, whose efforts at Americanization of Catholic ethnics, especially Italians and Poles, were based on fears that lack of acculturation would promote anti-Catholic nativism.[18]

Like their Catholic counterparts, the new Jewish immigrants suffered from all the afflictions engendered by poverty: crowded, unsanitary living and working conditions; disease; and family breakdown. Based on the biblical admonition to care for those less fortunate, the German Jews established the United Hebrew Relief Association in 1859 to provide needy Jews with coal, food, and clothing. Nevertheless, concerned with efficiency and inculcation of habits of work and thrift, like their Protestant models, the German Jewish philanthropists also distinguished between the "deserving" and "undeserving" poor. The association's successor, the United Hebrew Charities, supported a handful of local institutions with a focus on family services.[19] In 1900 the Associated Jewish Charities came into being. While the United Hebrew Charities remained active as a subsidiary agency with a specific concern for family needs, the Associated Jewish Charities sought to replace competition in the collection of funds and duplication in their distribution with a standardized method of obtaining revenue.[20]

The values of efficiency and investigation practiced by the Germans seemed foreign to the eastern Europeans, who resented the way the Germans dispensed charity, referring to them as "Reform Jews, who give us bread which poisons our souls." The Germans' attitude, in addition to the nonobservance of Jewish traditions in their institutions, made eastern European Jews decide to take over care of their own needy as soon as possible.[21] Rather than working within budgets, they wanted unplanned giving to help the indigent whenever assistance was needed. Jews, however, also suffered from the Great Fire of 1871, which destroyed German Jewish businesses and community buildings as well as the German Jewish hospital.[22] A second fire in 1874 destroyed eastern European Jewish homes and synagogues, making even more acute the need to help that group's dependent cases.[23]

As the eastern European Jews also began to suffer from competition for funds, their leaders began to agitate for the federation of all Orthodox charities into one efficient organization, a movement that resulted in the founding of the Federated Orthodox Jewish Charities in 1911.[24] But the existence of two separate federations supervising local Jewish philanthropy tended toward the same kind of duplication the federations had been designed to combat. Thus, leaders soon began promoting the idea of a merger of the two groups. Orthodox leaders feared that union would compromise their rigid religious standards, but driven by economic necessity and reassured by the provision that "matters concerning religious laws, practices, ceremonies and Hebrew education" would be determined by the board of each affiliated organization, the federations agreed to amalgamation in 1922.[25]

As would be expected, both Catholic and Jewish women's groups were most directly concerned with mothers and dependent children. Despite the Church's insistence on domesticity as their proper vocation, Catholic laywomen began creating agencies for mothers and infants in the early twentieth century. But the expanding voluntarism of laywomen created tension with women religious, who found some of their ministries being duplicated or overtaken. This struggle for control of their charities, which pit laywomen against women religious and each of them against the clergy, accompanied the Church's effort to rationalize its philanthropy.[26]

A group predominantly comprised of Irish schoolteachers founded the St. Margaret's Relief Society in 1911 to maintain a home for young unmarried mothers and their babies. Resurrectionist Father Andrew Spetz, concerned that there was no facility for unwed pregnant Polish girls, found a home for the St. Margaret Society, and the St. Margaret Home and Maternity Hospital opened in 1911. Franciscan sisters operated the institution, and the doctors volunteered their services. St. Margaret's permitted girls to remain for three to six months after delivery so they could find employment and work out a day-care plan that could save them from having to give up their babies. The St. Margaret Society also became involved in pressuring for legislation to require the licensing of maternity and lying-in hospitals so young women would not be pressured into surrendering their infants to unscrupulous individuals.[27]

With the exception of isolated cases, the sources do not mention illegitimacy as a problem for Jews in Chicago before the 1920s. In 1934, the height of the Great Depression, ten children of unmarried parents were recommended for placement.[28] Although illegitimacy was not a major issue, many orphaned children resulted from the poverty, desertion, and disease prevalent among the newcomers.[29] Some of these children were unadoptable because they were merely half orphans—their fathers, the main breadwinners, had become overwhelmed with responsibility and deserted the family. Other children needed temporary shelter when their fathers became incapacitated as a result of disease or accident. In the days before unemployment insurance, poor mothers left alone could not afford to keep all their children at home.[30]

Because legal adoption does not exist in Jewish law, Reformed German Jewish women were more concerned than were the Orthodox with the plight of poor mothers and dependent children. Many Ultraorthodox still, to this day, do not believe in adoption. The caring for a dependent child who does not share a biological relationship with one's family, however, is very much a part of Jewish tradition. Ironically, there are fewer objections to Jews adopting non-Jewish children because the risk of incestuous marriages in the next generation does not then arise, and the possibility of incest is the greatest objection to adoption.[31]

Because Chicago did not have a Jewish orphan home, the city's homeless Jewish children were being sent either to Cleveland or to city asylums. By the 1890s there was a growing awareness of the disadvantages of this arrangement: the Cleveland asylum was becoming increasingly crowded, and Jewish parents and guardians objected to the placement of their children in non-Jewish city institutions. Consequently, after the dedication of the Jewish Home for the Aged in 1893, socially active, reform-minded German Jewish women organized to provide care for Jewish orphans and half orphans by building an orphanage in Chicago. The women maintained that they were adhering "to the holiest and most admirable traditions" of their ancestors: "Not only from motives of policy, but from feeling of the purest sympathy and commiseration for the innocent children left to drift helplessly and unaided upon the vast and troubled sea of life, do we unite our efforts, . . . towards the spiritual and physical uplifting of these unfortunate ones."[32]

The proposed orphanage, however, became caught up in the debate that had been raging within the larger social welfare community over whether institutional care or home care was best for dependent children, a debate that had been ongoing since the time of Charles Loring Brace. At the 1909 White House Conference on the Care of Dependent Children, President Theodore Roosevelt came down on the side of home placement. Roosevelt's speech legitimized the anti-institutional forces that had been gathering momentum for decades. Placing children in families rather than orphanages was less costly for the public, which was one reason for the desirability of home placement.[33] Opponents of orphanages also argued that children in them led monotonous, repetitive lives that robbed them of initiative and creativity.

Anti-institutionalism was given an additional boost when most states passed mothers' pension laws, led by Illinois in 1911. A Progressive measure, mothers' pensions were designed to obviate the need for poor women to go out to work, thereby enabling them to keep their families together by staying home and raising their children. The payments, however, were never sufficient to achieve the desired end.[34] Ironically, as historian Kenneth Cmiel has pointed out, although the number of dependent children in Illinois receiving aid from mothers' pensions continuously rose, the number of children in institutions did not decline.[35]

In 1884 Eliza Frank established and endowed the Society for the Education of Jewish Orphans, a group that placed orphans and half orphans in private homes.[36] Nevertheless, on receipt of a twenty-five thousand dollar gift from an Iowa man who made his bequest contingent on the community raising an equal amount, a small orphan home was opened in 1894. Five years later, a larger Chicago Home for Jewish Orphans was dedicated, adjoining the Home for the Aged.[37] When still larger quarters were needed, the directors approached Julius Rosenwald, the head of Sears, Roebuck, and Company and a generous philanthropist, for a contribution. To their surprise, he refused, maintaining that an institution was an unscientific solution to the orphan problem. Influenced by studies that blamed the high death rate of institution-alized infants on lack of mother's milk and love, Rosenwald believed in home placement: orphan children should be provided with suitable homes under careful supervision. Consequently, he offered to fund the type of boarding-out plan being supported by the new, professionally trained social workers and sociologists as well as by Frank. The directors of the Chicago Home for Jewish Orphans, however, rejected Rosenwald's offer and proceeded with their original building plans, a decision that caused a breach in the organization, with some directors resigning. But proponents of the orphan home were convinced that institutional care was a practical necessity under conditions existing at the time and projected for the future.[38]

Acting on his beliefs despite the rebuff, in 1907 Rosenwald and a few others founded the Jewish Home Finding Society of Chicago (JHFS) to enable fit mothers to keep their children at home rather than in orphan asylums.[39] With a staff devoted to social casework and without a building to support, the JHFS held itself in readiness to care for any dependent Jewish child in the Chicago area "who has no fit mother or willing relative to care for it."[40] The JHFS became the primary Jewish agency responsible for adoption. Each application received careful consideration. The board members inspected prospective foster homes after thoroughly investigating the "standing of the applicant, socially, financially and morally." If the home was deemed satisfactory after unannounced inspections, the child was placed there on probation for six months and then was eligible for adoption into that home.[41]

Finding sufficient homes, however, became a problem. Although the JHFS sought to place children with Jewish families, 27 percent of the 242 homes used for foster or adoptive children in 1924 were not Jewish. The JHFS society was so committed to placement in families that board members believed placement in any family was of greater value than a religious upbringing in an institution. Sixty children were placed for adoption between the JHFS's organization in 1907 and 1912, fourteen of them in 1911–12.[42] In contrast, Catholics supported institutional settings where they could be assured of the children's religious training to a far greater extent than did Jews or Protestants. Yet some early critics opposed the policy, with one prelate arguing, "It is in families that God intended that children should live."[43]

Both Catholic and Jewish welfare organizations found themselves influenced by the growing professionalization of social work. Heavy reliance on volunteers had become a problem because of their undependability.[44] By the turn of the century, developing social work methods and an increasing emphasis on professional training provided compelling reasons to replace volunteer help with trained personnel. Development of the case method technique constituted the most important contribution professional social workers made to the social welfare field. The casework method endeavored to help individuals adjust to their environment by attempting to treat each family or individual as a unique problem and discover the data pertinent and significant to that particular family's history.[45] In addition, by affirming natural family ties, the 1909 White House Conference on Children helped to convince professional child care workers that unwed mothers should not, except in extreme cases, surrender their babies for adoption. Thus, professional caseworkers seldom considered adoption in cases of illegitimacy even though they lacked any scientific studies of the question.[46]

Promotion of child welfare enjoyed the support of the Progressive movement, which saw adoption as a solution to the social problems of illegitimacy and institutional infant mortality. But because adoption workers contented themselves with providing homes for homeless children and children for childless couples rather than trying to promote social reform, some Progressives did not believe the adoption issue merited much attention. The problem of ten thousand homeless babies born annually and the relatively few childless couples who wanted children but were unable to have them seemed miniscule compared to the problem of millions of children who lacked sufficient housing and adequate nutrition or who were forced to work at an early age to support their indigent families. Adoption advocates, however, reasoned differently, and hoped to popularize the practice and make it more respectable.[47]

Beginning in the 1910s, paid adoption workers began to change their policy of suiting the child to the home to one based on the theory that the most important requirement for a good adoption was a home that met the needs of the adopted child. Intent on gaining greater legitimacy and recognition by emphasizing credentials and standards, in 1923 professional social workers in the Chicago area arranged to have the Council of Social Agencies appoint a special committee to study adoption procedures and report its findings to the Cook County courts. The committee found that applicants refused a baby by accredited agencies because of moral unfitness had no difficulty in securing a child from an unaccredited agency if, as frequently happened, the courts did not check petitions.[48]

Professionals then began acting to eliminate lax adoption practices. In contrast to the early days, when children had been placed without court sanction strictly on the written consent of one or both parents, professional social workers formulated a set of standards for child placement in adoptive homes based on the findings of their study. Their quest for higher standards culminated in the legislature's passage of the revised Adoption Act of 1925, which provided for investigation of both the biological and the adoptive parents and a six-month period after placement before adoption could be finalized. It also provided for the court appointment of a guardian *ad litem* to consent to the adoption of an illegitimate child, even when the natural mother gave her consent, a provision that remains in effect to this day.[49]

Professionals and volunteers divided over paternity issues. Paid social workers believed that alleged fathers' family background should be known before making permanent disposition of infants, thereby forcing fathers to support their children. Reflecting social class differences, although they acknowledged the danger of false accusations and blackmail, paid social workers did not wish to see the culpable sons of elite families get off scot-free.[50] Professionals believed that charitable societies and private individuals should not be asked to assume the financial burden of raising children on behalf of strangers without first ascertaining if friends and relatives could provide for the children.[51] Conversely, volunteers, who most often came from the upper class, favored complete secrecy regarding the baby's antecedents.

As an accompaniment to professionalization, many adoption agencies developed a series of social and mental examinations and utilized scrutinizing personal questions and interviews. This increasing rigidity, becoming evident as early as the 1920s, made it more difficult for "common" people to adopt and often induced couples to seek other, nonagency practitioners. Prospective adoptive parents, tired of waiting to hear from or rejected by agencies, began to turn to maternity wards, cooperative doctors, and other independent sources for adoptable babies. These independent and black market adoptions became more common than agency adoptions among mothers looking for an uncomplicated way to surrender their babies, adoptive couples discouraged by agency strictness, and courts and legislatures that remained indifferent to existing adoption laws. Thus, a widespread traffic in babies developed that contributed to the popular concept that adoption was a disreputable and, as eugenicists and child care agents suggested, a risky business because of the fear that illegitimate babies "carried the iniquities of their fathers."[52]

Paradoxically, beginning in the 1920s, the practice acquired a tinge of glamour and respectability when the rich and famous began adopting babies, thereby creating the impression that only wealthy or prominent people adopted children. Where formerly most placed-out children had gone to working-class families, by the late 1920s families who adopted children came primarily from the business and professional classes. Although child care workers denied it and stressed that parents from all walks of life adopted children, by the 1930s it was generally believed that only wealthy couples could adopt agency babies.[53]

Chicago's Jewish and Catholic agencies were experiencing difficulties because of the professionalization of social work. Strained relations and problems of communication developed between paid and unpaid social workers. In Catholic institutions, as at least one commentator noted, "many of our religious communities have a distinct impression that lay workers fail to appreciate or sympathize with them," at the same time admitting that "religious communities irritate us when they appear to oppose our social work standards."[54]

As early as 1902 the president of the National Conference of Jewish Communal Service stated that mass migration had made volunteer administration of charity increasingly unworkable. In 1909 there were only seventy-three paid Jewish philanthropic workers in the nation, in part because of poor salaries and low status. The numbers increased over the years, and in 1924 the Graduate School of Jewish Social Work was opened in New York City. Although the school was unable to survive through the depression of the 1930s, its graduates staffed both Jewish and nonsectarian agencies with qualified personnel.[55] Catholics started the National Catholic School of Social Service in the early 1920s, but it ran into difficulty when the Catholic University of America decided to take it over: university officials did not approve of women on the campus or of educating women and priests in the same social work courses. After a long-running battle, Catholic University finally absorbed the School of Social Service after World War II.[56] In 1910, 350 lay persons, including many members of the St. Vincent de Paul Society, met at Catholic University in Washington, D.C., and established the National Conference of Catholic Charities. Concerned about the lack of coordination both among Catholic charity organizations and between Catholic and non-Catholic groups as well as about tensions between volunteers and professionals, the conference recommended that Catholic institutions adopt modern social work techniques. In 1912, when Chicago's Catholic population topped the million mark, locals formed the Chicago Committee of the National Conference of Catholic Charities.[57]

At a 1917 meeting called by the St. Vincent de Paul Society, and with the support of Archbishop Mundelein, the new Associated Catholic Charities was formed as the central fund-raising body for Chicago diocesan charities. A five dollar donation entitled one to a year's membership. As with Jews, the hope was that centralized fund-raising would alleviate the problem of wealthy donors being besieged by a myriad of charitable requests.[58] The archbishop appointed the board of directors, and the funds collected were turned over to him for distribution. Mundelein then established the Central Charity Bureau to verify requests and distribute the monies collected. Because there were not enough volunteers to assist all the needy and not all parishes had St. Vincent de Paul Conferences, the Central Charity Bureau began to hire full-time professional social workers. Though the St. Vincent de Paul Society hoped that the use of paid workers would not eliminate volunteers, the paid staff inevitably eclipsed the part-time volunteers, with the result that Catholic Charities too became a professionalized agency.[59]

Having taxed themselves to build large orphanages, both Catholics and Jews were reluctant to see them stand empty. Nevertheless, first Jews and later Catholics succumbed to the professional advocacy of home placement. Consequently, despite the organization's commitment to institutionalization, one of the first programs established by Catholic Charities was the Adoption Department, which provided services for unwed mothers and their infants who needed adoptive parents. Its primary purpose was to assure that children without parents were received into loving families that featured a husband and wife capable of being parents to a child not born to them. Although the Adoption Department expressed compassion for childless couples, concern for them took second place to children's welfare.[60]

St. Vincent's, which had been handling its own adoptions since 1881, was ambivalent about Catholic Charities. A month after St. Vincent's opened, the city of Chicago began utilizing it as the city's repository for abandoned babies, with the first foundling brought in by the police on September 9, 1881. In the beginning, St. Vincent's existed on charitable contributions and the nominal fees charged to mothers who could afford to pay something, but by 1896 it became imperative to find other sources of revenue. Because it became impossible for the sisters to care for so many foundlings without compensation, the Visitation and Aid Society lobbied the city fathers to have St. Vincent's declared the official foundling home for the city, a title it retained from the passage of the ordinance in 1897 until it closed its doors in 1971. The contract between St. Vincent's and the city provided that the institution would be paid no more than twelve thousand dollars a year as part of the costs of taking care of foundlings.[61] St. Vincent's receipt of city of Chicago funds helped set a precedent for Catholic-government cooperation.[62]

Jewish interest in government funding came later, with passage by the state legislature of the Manual Training and Industrial Schools Act in 1919. The Chicago Home for Jewish Orphans was incorporated as the Chicago Manual Training School for Jewish Boys and the Chicago Industrial Training School for Jewish Girls, and workshops were set up to secure funds from the juvenile court for children the court committed to the home.[63]

Despite receiving some government support, Catholic women's groups and their Jewish counterparts spent much of their time fund-raising. In addition to establishing auxiliaries, they gave teas, sponsored bake and rummage sales, and gave benefit fairs and balls. In addition, the women sewed clothing for the children. Adequate funding nevertheless remained a problem.[64]

Not only have mothers and children historically been seen as women's concerns, but the majority of adoption workers have been women. The organizations they founded to help the poor and care for orphans traditionally served a double function for women, providing the necessary service of ministering to society's dependents and providing women workers with a means of achieving emotional fulfillment, learning managerial skills, and acquiring status.[65] Thus, by viewing their philanthropic activities as religious duty, both Catholic and Jewish women came to use their participation in benevolent societies as a way of expanding their religiously prescribed roles.

Catholic welfare institutions were often founded by and depended on the unpaid labor of their nuns. German Jewish women, in contrast to those from eastern Europe, brought with them a tradition of more active participation in charitable work. Consequently, these women were instrumental in initiating most of their group's various relief agencies, only to find them later taken over by men. Such public activity contrasted not only with that of the more traditional eastern European Jewish women but also with that of Catholic laywomen, who were confined to the domestic sphere. Although having public lives was frowned on, these women supplied important support services through their ladies' auxiliaries.[66]

Because government at all levels supplied only a small percentage of the funding necessary to keep welfare institutions operating, paid workers came to believe that not only should social work be professionalized, so also should fund-raising. Federated fund-raising proved its efficacy during World War I. After the armistice, war chests were converted into community chests, later known as community funds. The Associated Catholic Charities began to experience competition from the Community Fund by 1924 and found itself under attack two years later when the fund claimed that most of the families it served were Catholic.[67] The Community Fund presented a problem for both Catholic and Jewish welfare agencies in another way: under the terms of the fund, each individual agency was supposed to submit its budget to the federation, but the Catholic and Jewish agencies had to submit their budgets to their parent organizations, which then decided how much each individual agency should get. The Jewish Federation compromised over the situation and then helped Catholic Charities do the same.[68]

The St. Vincent's Sisters, accustomed to being responsible for their own financing and goals, did not at first join Catholic Charities, a decision that conflicted with Cardinal Mundelein's plan to centralize diocesan fund-raising. Mundelein consequently built Misericordia Hospital and Home for Infants on the South Side of the city to serve unmarried mothers, their babies, and married women who could not afford to deliver elsewhere. A separate institution, Misericordia was owned by the diocese and staffed by Sisters of Mercy, who, unlike the Daughters of Charity, were headquartered in Chicago.[69] Mundelein defended his decision to maintain an additional institution when he requested funds at the 1919 annual meeting of Associated Catholic Charities by explaining that when the Commission consisting of a priest and a layman that he sent went to study Protestant and nonsectarian maternity institutions, they were told, "Thank God, the Catholics are at last going to do something; 25 to 30 percent of our work is among Catholics."[70]

When St. Vincent's opened in an enlarged facility in 1930, the Daughters of Charity entered into a closer working relationship with Catholic Charities, which assumed responsibility for the interest on their mortgage. Mundelein had incorporated the Catholic Home Bureau in 1921 to accept guardianship of children from the courts and place them in foster or adoptive homes. By 1933 the Catholic Home Bureau was referring couples who wished to adopt to St. Vincent's.[71] Although the sisters were unhappy about the loss of autonomy under the new association, their decision was forced by financial stringency during the depression.[72]

During the 1920s, the professionally dominated Chicago Council of Social Agencies attempted to coordinate the activities of charitable agencies in the area. Mundelein, elevated to cardinal in 1924, forbade Catholic charity organizations from joining the council because he was afraid they would lose their Catholic identity and become involved in public policy decisions on such issues as birth control and sterilization to which the Church was morally opposed.[73] For their part, professional social workers considered the St. Vincent de Paul Society's use of volunteers to be an outmoded method of handling charitable cases. During these years, the Chicago Catholic Charities barely participated in the National Conference of Catholic Charities because the local group was not comfortable with the larger organization's emphasis on professionalization of social work.[74]

But both Catholic and Jewish child care agencies found themselves forced to change in reaction to the Great Depression. When it became clear that the relief task was too monumental for private philanthropy and even for the states, the bulk of the burden of welfare work was transferred from private agencies to the federal government under Franklin Roosevelt's New Deal. Jewish Charities lost between 40 and 50 percent of its annual income from subscribers between 1929 and 1932 and, in an economy and efficiency move, began proceeding toward amalgamating three of its child care agencies (the Chicago Home for Jewish Orphans, the Marx Nathan Orphan Home, and the JHFS) into what became one all-inclusive institution, the Jewish Children's Bureau, in 1937.[75]

As early as 1928 Catholic Charities began to be concerned about the county being in arrears for several months. Yet, perceiving any outside oversight as a threat to its autonomy, Cardinal Mundelein and Catholic Charities failed to show interest when the city of Chicago first began contemplating a community chest. Although Mundelein resisted joining United Charities in the 1920s, during the 1930s his organization became overwhelmed by the magnitude of providing for the needy in the Depression and daunted by the task of mounting an independent fund drive. Mundelein realized that he had no choice, and Catholic Charities agreed to cooperate with the Community Fund of Metropolitan Chicago in 1933. A year later, Catholic Charities decided to become a participant in the fund.[76] Although the fund indirectly attempted to supervise the organizations of the Catholic Charities by approving agencies and their budgets and although the relationship was not always a happy one, Catholic Charities could not afford to give up the financial support that the fund provided.

While the Catholic Home Bureau had previously worked with the JHFS and other Chicago child care agencies, joining the Community Fund marked the beginning of closer cooperation with Jewish Charities. With the decision of Chicago Catholic Charities to end their "costly aloofness" and heed the advice of the National Catholic Charities to actively participate in nonsectarian social welfare organizations, the two groups of immigrant outsiders began to work together.[77] But because of the centralizing tendencies and emphasis on professionalism of the businessmen who ran the Community Fund, the central office of the Catholic Charities became more important, and the role played by volunteer laypersons diminished still further. For adoption agencies, that meant the use of casework by professionals to determine the compatibility of the adoptive child and the receiving home. Consequently, like their Jewish and secular counterparts, Catholic social welfare institutions became increasingly staffed by professional social workers.[78] Also, albeit reluctantly, with professionalization, Catholics began to weaken their commitment to institutionalization and incorporate more and more home placements for their dependent children.

Thus, from the time of their arrival in Chicago through the years of the Great Depression, Catholics and Jews had surprisingly similar responses to the arrival of massive numbers of new immigrants to their communities, developed similar attitudes about benevolence in general and adoption in particular, moved toward deinstitutionalization of children and professionalization of welfare workers and fund-raising, and became dependent on government financial support. The primary difference between the welfare institutions of the two religions lay in the fact that although Jews were guided by the biblical admonition to aid the poor and dependent, their welfare institutions in America were originally based on Protestant models, which even Orthodox Jewish institutions came to follow. Catholic agencies, conversely, had historically been staffed by sisters who embodied elements of both the volunteer and the professional. Although they worked without pay like secular volunteers, like salaried workers the sisters adhered to strict schedules, often working many more hours than even the most dedicated professionals.[79] The work ethic of these selfless sisters enabled Catholic agencies to be slower to professionalize and to remain committed longer to the institutionalization of their homeless children than their Jewish counterparts.

Although adoption has never been a major concern of the community at large, it does illuminate the broader issue of sectarian social welfare. That, in turn, involves the way immigrants acculturated to America, the way newcomers and older established residents negotiated their differences and unified to provide for the needy child, the way religious welfare agencies eventually recognized the need for accommodation to other religious and secular organizations, the way religious agencies recognized the need for government funding to better serve their constituencies, and the way these agencies began to phase out their religiously inspired volunteer staff to accept the more secular, professional approach of their paid colleagues. Professionalization occurred despite the conflict it engendered between the professionals and the volunteers within the welfare agencies.

Professionalization proved to have major consequences for Catholics in particular. Rather than Catholic Charities, Catholics in need today would most likely find assistance from public agencies and be helped by Catholic professionals working in public welfare departments. Yet the evidence suggests that the impersonal bureaucracy of government welfare has turned many Catholics away from both their former liberal financial contributions and from volunteering their services to charitable causes at the same rates as Jewish or Protestant Americans. In a turnaround from attitudes earlier in the century, a survey of Catholic, Jewish, and Protestant welfare agencies conducted in the 1960s found Catholics to be the least concerned "that government intrusion would follow government money." Historian Mary Oates has pointed out that one reason for this development is the difficulty that lay Catholics see in reaching the top leadership positions in Catholic welfare organizations, which are still dominated by clerics.[80]

Thus, although they continued to maintain their commitment to separate and sectarian welfare loosely linked with American welfare at large, over time both Catholics and Jews succeeded in gaining acceptance from the dominant community. In the process, Catholic and Jewish welfare organizations became more and more alike, a situation that becomes obvious through observation of their adoption practices.

NOTES

I wish to thank Professor June Sochen, Northeastern Illinois University; Sister Ann Harrington, B.V.M.; and Sister Mary Alma Sullivan, B.V.M., Loyola University Chicago, who read earlier drafts of this work. They are not, however, responsible for any errors of fact or interpretation.

1. The following definitions are used in this work: Social welfare volunteer: an individual who contributes his or her services, without financial remuneration, to the organization, administration, or operation of formally organized services under the auspices of public or voluntary agencies (Violet M. Sieder, "Volunteers," in *Encyclopedia of Social Work*, 16th ed. [New York: National Association of Social Workers, 1971], 1525). Social work professional: one who has exclusive possession of a systematic body of knowledge, a monopoly of skills obtained from higher education and training, and who participates in a subculture whose members share a group identity and common values (Walter I. Trattner, *From Poor Law to Welfare State: A History of Social Welfare in America* [New York: Free Press, 1974], 193).

2. This paragraph and the next two are based on Elinor Nims, *The Illinois Adoption Law and Its Administration* (Chicago: University of Chicago Press, 1928), 9; Robert H. Bremner, *From the Depths: The Discovery of Poverty in the United States* (New York: New York University Press, 1956), 47; Timothy A. Hacsi, *Second Home: Orphan Asylums and Poor Families in America* (Cambridge: Harvard University Press, 1997), 113–20. For information on indenture and placing out, see Timothy A. Hacsi, "From Indenture to Family Foster Care: A Brief History of Child Placing," *Child Welfare* 74 (Jan.–Feb. 1995): 162–80.

3. Marilyn Irvin Holt, *The Orphan Trains: Placing out in America* (Lincoln: University of Nebraska Press, 1992), 41–45, 83. See also Jeanne F. Cook, "A History of Placing Out: The Orphan Trains," *Child Welfare* 74 (Jan.–Feb. 1995): 181–97; Viviana A. Zelizer, *Pricing the Priceless Child: The Changing Social Value of Children* (New York: Basic Books, 1985), 172; Trattner, *From Poor Law to Welfare State*, 117–20; M. B. O' Sullivan, "Phases of Charitable Work among Children; The Committee of Priests and the Charitable Bureau," *Donahoe's Magazine* 47 (July 1903): 26.

4. E. Wayne Carp, *Family Matters: Secrecy and Disclosure in the History of Adoption* (Cambridge: Harvard University Press, 1998), 17.

5. Zelizer, *Pricing the Priceless Child*, 171–74.

6. O'Sullivan, "Phases," 25.

7. Ibid., 30; Holt, *Orphan Trains*, 91, 106, 135–36, 181.

8. Quoted in Roger J. Coughlin and Cathryn A. Riplinger, *The Story of Charitable*

118   Adoption in America

Care in the Archdiocese of Chicago, 1844–1959 (Chicago: Catholic Charities of Chicago, 1981, 1983), 60–61.

9. Ibid., 52–120.

10. Ibid., 120, 197.

11. According to his biographer, "Ethnicity posed the greatest challenge to Mundelein's financial and personnel policies" (Edward R. Kantowicz, *Corporation Sole: Cardinal Mundelein and Chicago Catholicism* [Notre Dame, Ind.: University of Notre Dame Press, 1983], 65, 73, 81; Dorothy M. Brown and Elizabeth McKeown, *The Poor Belong to Us: Catholic Charities and American Welfare* [Cambridge: Harvard University Press, 1997], 58).

12. Brown and McKeown, *Poor Belong to Us,* 58.

13. *New Catholic Encyclopedia* (New York: McGraw Hill, 1961), 138; Rev. Msgr. Harry C. Koenig, S.T.D., ed., *Caritas Christi Urget Nos: A History of the Offices, Agencies, and Institutions of the Archdiocese of Chicago* (Chicago: Catholic Bishop of Chicago, 1981), 2:986.

14. History of St. Vincent's Infant Hospital, Nov. 21, 1963, Daughters of Charity Archives, Evansville, Ind.; Maurice Lamm Blatt, M.D., ScD, "St. Vincent's Infant and Maternity Hospital: Its Past and Future," *Illinois Medical Journal* 60 (Jan. 1931): 1–8. While James J. Kenneally does not specifically mention Chicago in this connection, the policy of secret records applied to Chicago as well as other large cities. See Kenneally, *The History of American Catholic Women* (New York: Crossroad, 1990), 70.

15. See information in Daughters of Charity Archives, Evansville, Indiana. See also Coughlin and Riplinger, *Story,* 177–78. The Visitation and Aid Society disbanded before 1911. In 1911 the league established the Catholic Women's League Protectorate to save young women coming to Chicago from being lured into sweatshops or prostitution.

16. Mitchell Alan Horwich, *Conflict and Child Care Policy in the Chicago Jewish Community, 1893–1942: The Early Years of the Jewish Children's Bureau of Chicago* (Chicago: Jewish Children's Bureau, 1977), 15–16. See also information in Jewish Federation of Metropolitan Chicago Collection, Norman and Helen Asher Library, Spertus College of Judaica, Chicago (hereafter cited as JFMC). The view given here is the traditional one. Hasia Diner, however, has argued "that the differences between the two waves of Jewish immigrants were less pronounced than previously assumed and that the concept of immigration waves oversimplifies the history of Jewish migration and adjustment" (*A Time for Gathering: The Second Migration* [Baltimore: Johns Hopkins University Press, 1992], 2).

17. See United Hebrew Relief Association Minute Book, 1865–89, Oct. 5, 1865, Oct. 25, 1868, folder 1, JFMC, for derogatory comments about Polish Jews. See also Horwich, *Conflict and Child Care Policy,* 16–17.

18. Gerald Sorin, "Mutual Contempt, Mutual Benefit: The Strained Encounter between German and Eastern European Jews in America, 1880–1920," *American Jewish History* 81 (autumn 1993): 46.

19. United Hebrew Relief Association Minute Book, 1865–89, folder 1, JFMC.

20. See information in JFMC. See also Horwich, *Conflict and Child Care Policy,* 17–18; Hyman L. Meites, *History of the Jews of Chicago* (1924; rpt. Chicago: Chicago Jewish Historical Society and Wellington Publishing, 1990), 580, 592–93. The success of the Chicago Associated Jewish Charities led to the creation of similar movements in other cities.

21. Philip B. Bregstone, *Chicago and Its Jews: A Cultural History* (Chicago: privately published, 1933), 102.

22. United Hebrew Relief Association Minute Book, 1865–89, Apr. 20, 1873, folder #1, JFMC.

23. Horwich, *Conflict and Child Care Policy,* 19–20.

24. Bernard Horwich was the most prominent eastern European leader. The eastern European Jewish community opened its own Marx Nathan Jewish Orphan Asylum in 1906. The name was changed to Marks Nathan Jewish Orphan Home and, in 1939, to Marks Nathan Hall (Marks Nathan Hall Records, folder #348, JFMC).

25. Julius Rosenwald played an important role in the founding and maintenance of both the more liberal Associated Jewish Charities and the Federated Orthodox Jewish Charities and was unanimously chosen to head the new Jewish Charities of Chicago (Associated Jewish Charities of Chicago Minutes, Oct. 19, 1922, folder 12, folder 4, JFMC; Jewish Charities of Chicago Minutes, Dec. 28, 1922, JFMC; Meites, *History,* 586–90).

26. Paula M. Kane, *Separatism and Subculture: Boston Catholicism, 1900–1920* (Chapel Hill: University of North Carolina Press, 1994), 204. See also Kenneally, *History,* 43–44.

27. In 1918, after receiving money from Associated Catholic Charities, St. Margaret's was able to care for 151 primarily young immigrant girls and 105 babies. The 1917 legislation they helped pass stated, "No child from such maternity or lying-in hospital shall be placed in a family, home or be legally adopted until such home shall have been investigated and approved by the State Board of Administration" (Coughlin and Riplinger, *Story,* 179–80).

28. Jewish Children's Welfare Society Statement of Income and Expense for Year Ended Dec. 31, 1934, range 7 side B shelf 12, Jewish Children's Bureau Papers, Chicago Jewish Archives, Spertus College of Judaica (hereafter cited as JCB).

29. "Plan for Central Jewish Child Caring Agency in Greater New York," study begun by Samuel Goldsmith, 1931, folder 184, JFMC; Child Welfare Study, "Care of Dependent and Neglected Children in Chicago Area," 1937, folder 188, JFMC.

30. E. Wayne Carp, "Orphanages versus Adoption: The Triumph of Biological Kinship, 1800–1923," in *With Us Always: A History of Private Charity and Public Welfare,* ed. Donald T. Critchlow and Charles H. Parker (Lanham, Mass.: Rowman and Littlefield, 1998), 125.

31. In the event of adoption of a non-Jewish child, the child must be formally converted to Judaism.

32. "Constitution and By-Laws of the Chicago Home for Jewish Orphans," pamphlet, [ca. 1898], JFMC.

33. Carp, "Orphanages versus Adoption," 124–25. On mothers' pensions, see Joanne L. Goodwin, *Gender and the Politics of Welfare Reform: Mothers' Pensions in Chicago, 1911–1929* (Chicago: University of Chicago Press, 1997).

34. Carp, "Orphanages versus Adoption," 125.

35. Kenneth Cmiel, *A Home of Another Kind: One Chicago Orphanage and the Tangle of Child Welfare* (Chicago: University of Chicago Press, 1995), 95.

36. Henry Frank to Joseph Frank, May 10, 1884, folder 184, JFMC.

37. Abram Slimmer of Waverly, Iowa, was the benefactor (folder 3, JFMC; Meites, *History,* 183–84).

38. Meites, *History,* 215–16, 608–10.

39. The other founders were Minnie F. Low, Judge Julian B. Mack, Adolph Kurz, Emma B. Mandl, and L. M. Stumer. Jennie Mandel (later Mrs. Adolph Kurz) was the first superintendent (Meites, *History,* 209).

40. Superintendent TRB to H. L. Meites, Nov. 28, 1923, box 1, folder 1, JCB.

41. Report of the Superintendent to the President and Directors of the JHFS of Chicago, ca. 1911–12, JCB; Report of the Board of Directors of the JHFS of Chicago, prepared by Dr. Emil G. Hirsch, box 1, folder 2, JCB.

42. Horwich, *Conflict and Child Care Policy,* 26–27; Report of the Superintendent to the President and Directors of the JHFS of Chicago, ca. 1911–12, box 1, folder 2, JCB. In 1935 they had fifty-nine inquiries and applications for adoption, thirty from Chicago and twenty-nine from out of town; they placed two children in Chicago (Annual Report of the JHFS for 1936, by Jacob Kepecs, Jewish Children's Welfare Society Statement of Income and Expense for Year Ended December 31, 1934, range 7 side b shelf 12, JCB).

43. Quoted in Mary J. Oates, *The Catholic Philanthropic Tradition in America* (Bloomington: Indiana University Press, 1995), 73. In New York City the Sisters of Charity placed out children from the Foundling Hospital with Catholic families (Holt, *Orphan Trains,* 135–37).

44. Dorothy G. Becker, "Exit Lady Bountiful; The Volunteer and the Professional Social Worker," *Social Service Review* 38 (Mar. 1964): 64; Susan Tiffin, *In Whose Best Interest? Child Welfare Reform in the Progressive Era* (Westport, Conn.: Greenwood Press, 1982), 258.

45. Bremner, *From the Depths,* 55–56; Trattner, *From Poor Law to Welfare State,* 213. The casework method was created by Mary E. Richmond, director of the Russell Sage Foundation's Charity Organization Department.

46. My evidence, along with that of E. Wayne Carp and Peter Romanofsky, differs from Regina Kunzel's claim that professional social workers favored separation of the unwed mother from her child. See Carp, "Professional Social Workers, Adoption, and the Problem of Illegitimacy, 1915–1945," *Journal of Policy History* 6, no. 3 (1994): 162–84; Romanofsky, "The Early History of Adoption Practices," (Ph.D. diss., University of Missouri at Columbia, 1969), 130–33; Paula F. Pfeffer, "Homeless Children, Childless Homes," *Chicago History* 16 (spring 1987): 51–65; Regina G. Kunzel, "The Professionalization of Benevolence," *Journal of Social History* 22 (fall 1988): 21–43. Ironically, in recent years, professionals have been accused of pressuring unwed mothers to keep their babies.

47. Romanofsky, "Early History," 188, 112–16. Carp, *Family Matters,* disagrees with this point of view.

48. Information found in Illinois Children's Home and Aid Society Papers, University of Illinois at Chicago (hereafter cited as ICHAS). See also Paula F. Pfeffer, "The Transition from Voluntarism to Professionalism in Social Welfare Agencies," paper presented at the Duquesne History Forum, Pittsburgh, Oct. 1983; Pfeffer, "Homeless Children," 51–65.

49. [Isabel] Devine, "Care of Dependent and Neglected Children in the Chicago Area," Dec. 1934–Nov. 1936, folder 188, JFMC; Nims, *Illinois Adoption Law,* 75–76, 30.

50. Superintendent (Clarence V. Williams) to Hastings H. Hart, Mar. 18, 1924; Anna Ren Gross to Russell Sage Foundation, Mar. 3, 1924; Francis T. Longcope to Mr. Williams, Apr. 25, 1924; H. H. Hart to Mrs. Alfred H. Gross, Mar. 8, 1924, all in ICHAS.

51. The cost of bringing up and educating a child from birth to the age of self-

support amounted to the expenditure of somewhere between two thousand and three thousand dollars at 1924 dollar value (H. H. Hart to Mrs. Alfred H. Gross, Mar. 8, 1924, ICHAS).

52. Romanofsky, "Early History," 152–56, 161; Holt, *Orphan Trains,* 128.

53. Pfeffer, "Homeless Children," 51–65; Romanofsky, "Early History," 175–76. Those who adopted babies through the private, nonsectarian Cradle Society of Evanston, Illinois, included New York Mayors Jimmie Walker and Fiorello LaGuardia and entertainers Al Jolson and Ruby Keeler, George Burns and Gracie Allen, and Bob Hope (Cradle Papers, Evanston Historical Society, Evanston).

54. Brown and McKeown, *Poor Belong to Us,* 103.

55. Miriam R. Ephraim, "Introduction: The Meaning of the Conference for the American Jewish Community," in *Trends and Issues in Jewish Social Welfare in the United States,* ed. Robert Morris and Michael Freund (Philadelphia: Jewish Publication Society of America, 1966), xxv–xxvi, 286.

56. Brown and McKeown, *Poor Belong to Us,* 71–72, 82–84.

57. Ephraim, "Introduction," xxvi; *First National Conference of Catholic Charities, Proceedings,* (Washington, D.C.: Catholic University of America, 1910), 9–11, 54; Coughlin and Riplinger, *Story,* 184–85. For an analysis of the problems prior to the first National Conference of Catholic Charities, see William J. Kirby, "Problems in Charity," *Catholic World* 91 (Sept. 1910): 790–800.

58. Kantowicz, *Corporation Sole,* 137.

59. The Polish Clergy Association objected to the organization of diocesan charitable organizations that destroyed the parochial organizations and sodalities of charity. They charged Archbishop Mundelein with being insensitive to the poverty of the immigrants in establishing the Associated Catholic Charities and never fully accepted Catholic Charities as their primary charitable institution (Coughlin and Riplinger, *Story,* 205–6, 207, 210–11, 215). For an analysis of tensions between professional social workers and volunteers in Catholic charitable agencies, see John O'Grady, "Lay Participation in Catholic Charity," *Catholic Charities Review* 9 (Dec. 1925): 378–84.

60. Koenig, ed., *Caritas Christi,* 2:835.

61. Minutes, City Council Regular Meeting, July 12, 1897, 618, 554; Social Service Directory, Chicago, 1926, 170, both found in Municipal Reference Library of Chicago, Chicago Public Library; Father Roger J. Coughlin, interview by author, July 30, 1993.

62. In 1883 the Cook County courts began sending juvenile delinquents to St. Mary's Training School near Des Plaines, Illinois, and providing a subsidy for their upkeep (Kantowicz, *Corporation Sole,* 130). Largely because of Mundelein's support of the New Deal, Catholic Charities won a unique status, becoming an agency of the Welfare Fund of Cook County, the only private agency permitted to dispense public funds (Gene D. L. Jones, "The Chicago Catholic Charities, the Great Depression, and Public Monies," *Illinois Historical Journal* 83 [spring 1990]: 18–19; Kantowicz, *Corporation Sole,* 146).

63. Elizabeth Frary, Anne V. Culligan, and Isabel M. Devine, "Report of Study of the Chicago Home for Jewish Orphans," typescript, Papers of the Jewish Federation of Metropolitan Chicago, Chicago Jewish Archives, Spertus College of Judaica, file 17, Chicago Home for Jewish Orphans Studies (1921–36). Historical information adapted from Nathan Berman, "A Study of the Development of the Care of the Dependent and Neglected Jewish Children in the Chicago Area," (MA, School of Social Service Administration, University of Chicago, 1933).

64. See, for example, information found in Daughters of Charity Archives. See also Oates, *Catholic Philanthropic Tradition*, 98–99.

65. Jane Addams was among the first to make this observation (*Twenty Years at Hull-House, with Autobiographical Notes* [New York: Macmillan, 1966], chap. 6, "The Subjective Necessity for Social Settlements").

66. Sorin, "Mutual Contempt," 51; Mary J. Oates, "The Female Factor in Nineteenth-Century Catholic Philanthropy," paper presented at the Conference of the Southern Association of Women Historians, University of North Carolina, June 8, 1991; Richard Mark Chapman, "'To Do These Mitzvahs': Jewish Philanthropy and Social Service in Minneapolis, 1900–1950" (Ph.D. diss., University of Minnesota, 1993), 31, 39. Chapman's comments apply equally well to Chicago. Catholic institutions, however, unlike those of other religions, were able to draw on the lifetime commitment of their priests and nuns, who were willing to live at a subsistence level to provide for their unfortunate brethren.

67. Coughlin and Riplinger, *Story*, 212–13.

68. Trattner, *From Poor Law to Welfare State*, 223.

69. The Daughters of Charity originally came from France. The Sisters of Charity of Emmitsburg, Maryland, incurred the displeasure of Bishop Kenrick of St. Louis when, on their own, they decided to unite with the Daughters of Charity in France (Kenneally, *History*, 50).

70. Quoted in Coughlin and Riplinger, *Story*, 217. Misericordia discontinued its hospital function in 1951, although it continued to offer residential care for unwed mothers and their infants, changing its name to Misericordia Home. Thus, both St. Vincent and Misericordia were giving residential care to unwed mothers and their children. In 1954, however, Misericordia changed its function, becoming an institution for profoundly retarded infants and small children (Koenig, ed., *Caritas Christi*, 2: 906–7, 835–36).

71. Coughlin and Riplinger, *Story*, 218; 203; Koenig, ed., *Caritas Christi*, 2:906–7, 835–36.

72. Sister Margaret Flynn, D.C., to author, Dec. 10, 1993; notes from Sister Anthony Prugger, MSW, ACSW, Dec. 10, 1993, in possession of author. During construction, the children were temporarily moved to the order's summer house in Park Ridge, Illinois.

73. Jones, "Chicago Catholic Charities," 18.

74. Coughlin and Riplinger, *Story*, 213–14. For discussion of the value of professionalization, see also 74. Rev. C. Hubert LeBlond, "Diocesan Charities of Cleveland," *Catholic Charities, Proceedings*, 1920, 85, 88; Marie Rohn, "From the Point of View of Public Agencies," and Marilla Greene, "From the Point of View of Non-Sectarian Agencies," ibid, 1933, 204–7.

75. Samuel A. Goldsmith to Charles I. Herron, June 7, 1932, folder 348, JFMC. The Chicago Home for Jewish Orphans was re-formed and merged with the Orthodox Marx Nathan Orphan Home in 1953 (folder 348, JFMC).

76. Kantowicz claims that Mundelein's refusal to cooperate is one reason a community chest did not develop earlier in Chicago (*Corporation Sole*, 134). Mundelein's "experience in the federation allowed him to position his diocesan charities agencies to act as a conduit for state funds from the Illinois Emergency Relief Commission and to remain an agent of the state under the New Deal's FERA program" (Brown and McKeown, *Poor Belong to Us*, 59).

77. *Catholic Charities, Proceedings,* 1920, 85; *Proceedings,* 1933, 207.

78. Koenig, ed., *Caritas Christi,* 2:813–18; Coughlin and Riplinger, *Story,* 226–27, 233, 246. For debate over professionalization and volunteer workers' fear of losing their jobs, see also Robert Biggs, "The Trained Worker," *Catholic Charities, Proceedings,* 1912, pt. 2, 104–12.

79. Kenneally calls the sisters "the force holding the Church together" (*History,* 58). The official history of the institutions of the Archdiocese of Chicago, published in 1981, paid homage to the women religious, estimating that based on a forty-hour week, it would take two and one-third lay employees to replace one nun who worked unlimited hours as a house parent in a children's institution (Koenig, ed., *Caritas Christi,* 2:818). The decline in numbers of women religious since the late 1960s, however, would irreparably change the historic foundation of Catholic social welfare, making it still more professionalized and more impersonal in its methods of operation.

80. Brown and McKeown, *Poor Belong to Us,* 194–95; Oates, *Catholic Philanthropic Tradition,* 131, 142, 166–68.

Rescue a Child and Save the Nation

The Social Construction of Adoption in the
Delineator, 1907–1911

Julie Berebitsky

Every morning, George Wilder, president of Butterick Publishing Company, noticed the ragged and dirty children who milled around outside his building. Where did these children live? Who were their parents? What was to become of them? How could he help? Wilder's concern sparked the creation of the Child-Rescue Campaign in the *Delineator,* the country's third-largest women's magazine, with close to a million subscribers. The campaign hoped to match up the nation's childless homes and homeless children and end the practice of caring for dependent children in institutions. Although Wilder wanted to help, he also feared that American homes would not open their doors to poor, homeless waifs. He was wrong. Hundreds of readers wrote in to adopt the first two children profiled. The series was an immediate and extended success, placing more than two thousand children in adoptive homes over the course of its three-year run from late 1907 to early 1911.[1]

The story of the Child-Rescue Campaign is, however, more than a simple tale of a powerful man trying to help those less fortunate. The campaign marked the first time adoption was discussed in an ongoing public and popular forum; it gave a voice to the experience, demystified it, made it visible. The *Delineator* presented adoption as part of a woman's civic duty and as a form of rescue. Because the campaign was so popular and reached such a large audience, these representations influenced both the way the public understood adoption and the way women experienced adoptive motherhood. The series ultimately played an important role in popularizing adoption and promoting an expanded definition of motherhood.

The *Delineator*'s female readers responded enthusiastically to the series, but the magazine also sought to gain the respect and acclaim of national reformers and wanted to take a leading role in the larger Progressive-era child-saving movement. In its attempt to satisfy both its readers and the reformers, the *De-*

lineator found itself struggling to balance the interests of two very different constituencies. Although readers fully supported getting children out of institutions and into homes, they responded to the campaign in an intensely personal way that focused on helping individual children, especially those profiled. Many readers wanted the series to emphasize their needs and concerns as adoptive mothers or prospective adoptive mothers. For this group of women, adoption was not just a solution to a social problem but also the answer to their loneliness and maternal longings. Reformers, however, saw adoption as a fairly insignificant part of the solution to the problem of child dependency and believed the campaign should move beyond finding homes for individual children. As the magazine increased its role in the national child-saving movement, a tension—even a conflict—developed between the interests of the women readers who looked at the *Delineator* as a type of adoption agency and the desires of the editors to further expand the magazine's role in national reform efforts. In the end, the *Delineator* sacrificed the interests of these women for the allure of national influence.

Historians who have looked at the *Delineator*'s Child-Rescue Campaign have focused on the role it played in child-welfare reform and specifically its involvement in organizing the famous 1909 White House Conference on the Care of Dependent Children.[2] Furthermore, scholars examining the growing acceptance of adoption in the late nineteenth and early twentieth century have focused on large-scale cultural factors such as changes in the value of children and in philosophies regarding child welfare and the modernization and expansion of the legal system.[3] As important as these social changes were, individuals also played an important role in the growing popularity of adoption. This essay focuses on one important episode in the history of adoption when three distinct groups, each with its own interests and concerns, came together and presented to the public a new understanding of adoption. The Child-Rescue Campaign illuminates the realities of publishing a women's magazine in a climate of fierce competition, the difficulty of a for-profit venture taking a leading role in reform, the changing definition of motherhood, and the power of a mass-circulation magazine to popularize, legitimate, and shape the culture's understanding of a new social phenomenon.

The Campaign Begins

In October 1907, the *Delineator* published "The Child without a Home," which told of the twenty-five thousand poor, primarily immigrant children who lived without a mother's love in institutions throughout New York. Although the article sympathetically portrayed the plight of dependent, immigrant children, it also underscored the potential threat they posed to society. The series officially began the next month in an issue that contained the article, "The Home without a Child," which urged the nation's women, especially childless married women, to adopt homeless children. This issue also contained the first installment of the Child-Rescue Campaign. Theodore Dreiser had taken over the editorship of the *Delineator* in June 1907. Dreiser was a novelist, but his first book, *Sister Carrie* (1901), failed to rouse the public and riled many critics who thought it was "immoral." Discouraged, he turned to editing and the social status and financial stability it provided. Dreiser explained to the magazine's readers that each month the campaign would feature the photos and life stories of dependent children who were available to any interested reader who wanted to take them out of an institution and into her home. Although the initial issue stated that the children could be taken by the placing-out system (what we refer to today as foster care), indenture, or adoption, readers showed an overwhelming willingness to adopt the children legally, and the subsequent children profiled were offered for adoption. The series was an immediate success. "The Child without a Home" article received more responses than any other story in that issue, and well over three hundred readers wrote in requesting the first two children profiled.[4]

The series soon generated interest beyond the magazine's readership. The January and February 1908 issues contained letters of support from a number of public officials, especially from the mayors of large cities with child-dependency problems, and from prominent child welfare reformers, including Homer Folks, Hastings H. Hart, and Thomas Mulry. The letters from the reformers, however, although generally positive, noted that only a small number of children in institutions were suitable for adoption since many had at least one living parent and others were too old to be likely candidates. The editors of *Charities and The Commons*, the leading social work periodical of the time, were less enthusiastic. They noted that profiling children for adoption was a good way of stirring up public interest in child welfare issues. But they also wondered if the campaign itself was "a particularly necessary or particularly useful thing to do." Despite the *Delineator's* portrayal of thousands of children languishing in orphanages waiting to be rescued, the editors of *Charities and The Commons* believed child-placing agencies had never "met with any great difficulty in securing plenty of applications" for children who were eligible for adoption. They urged the *Delineator* to move beyond profiling individual children and begin educating readers on broader issues.[5]

Appealing to a Mother's Instinct, a Citizen's Duty

The campaign had struck an especially responsive chord with the *Delineator's* readers. At the time, the publication of women's magazines was an especially competitive business. To attract and hold subscribers, editors tried to develop a close, familial relationship with their readers, urging them to write letters relating their opinions, advice, and experiences, which were then published. The Child-Rescue Campaign generated a tremendous amount of reader response, fully 20 percent of all the correspondence the editorial department received. The first letters the *Delineator* published expressed an intense longing for children felt by childless women and women whose children had died who all hoped to adopt the children to "fill the vacancy in [their] home[s] and still the ache in [their] heart[s]." The *Delineator* had urged women to adopt by appealing to their sense of patriotic and civic duty in addition to their motherly instinct. Yet these letters suggest women responded on a personal level; they needed the children as much as the children needed them.[6]

Nonetheless, adoption at the turn of the century was uncommon enough and fears about bad heredity prevalent enough that many women needed assurance, encouragement, and a place to voice their fears before they could comfortably adopt a child. Writing to the *Delineator* allowed women to partake in—or at least feel as if they were partaking in—the culture's discourse on motherhood, family life, and child welfare. The *Delineator* mediated and directed this discourse through its choice of what letters to print. However, the success of the campaign—its acceptance by its women readers—still depended on women finding the *Delineator's* arguments in favor of adoption compelling and the magazine's definitions of motherhood and family agreeable.

Over the course of the Child-Rescue Campaign, the *Delineator* contained a number of articles that extolled the virtues of motherhood. These articles most often were first-person accounts written by famous women such as Julia Ward Howe, author of the "Battle Hymn of the Republic." These women asserted that motherhood was their highest achievement, a "holy task" and a "privilege." Articles suggested that mother love was higher and purer than marital love and that only through the self-sacrifice and devotion of motherhood could a woman reach her full potential or explore the "depths and heights" of her "nature." All agreed that a child's "touch" was "absolutely necessary" for women's "highest development." The series also articulated a definition of motherhood based on a woman's capacity to love and nurture a child, not on blood ties. In letters and short stories telling of their personal experiences, adoptive mothers argued against those who said that the only real mothers were women who had experienced the travails of pregnancy and birth. One adoptive mother asserted that "from the hour that [our adopted daughter] came into our possession she has seemed really *our very own*. [Her] shrill piping cry at early dawn filled me with a wonder that could not have been greater had I brought forth the little one with anguish."[7]

Women who adopted had a "mother consciousness"; women who abandoned their infants and children to the mercy of the city lacked such a consciousness. The fact that a woman might give up her child to an institution did not necessarily mean she lacked a maternal instinct: women who acknowledged they could no longer care for their children and consciously surrendered them for their best interest were portrayed as heroes, having made the supreme maternal sacrifice. By portraying adoptive mothers as women whose greatest wish was motherhood and who believed "there is no life for a woman without children," the series sought to elevate the value of motherhood. Adoptive mothers were mothers by choice. Their active quest for children could be positively contrasted with the "indifferent acquiescence" and "passive acceptance of a state commended by society" that the *Delineator* believed described many birth mothers' attitude toward motherhood.[8]

The *Delineator* also emphasized the importance of environment to a child's ultimate development, thereby helping women overcome any lingering fears about taking a child with a questionable background. The Child-Rescue Campaign coincided with a strong eugenics movement that warned of the evils of the hereditary taint. The *Delineator* countered by offering the opinions of both adoptive mothers and reformers such as Jacob Riis who maintained that they had witnessed firsthand that "heredity is much, but environment is more." The *Delineator* maintained that "an atmosphere of mother-love" could overcome any child's "evil heredity" and result in "manly and womanly, honorable citizens." At the same time, the editors raised the alarming specter of a society terrorized by these same children if they were not rescued from the streets. As mothers, women had the future of society in their hands: women had a duty. They would determine whether these children grew up to be worthy and useful citizens or to fill the jails and almshouses.[9]

Many people believed that middle-class women were already derelict in their duty. The Child-Rescue Campaign coincided with a drastic decline in the birthrate among white, middle-class women. Meanwhile, the "new" immigrants from eastern and southern Europe were reproducing at double the rate of native-born Americans. While eugenicists, sociologists, and psychologists studied and lamented, Theodore Roosevelt succinctly summed up what many feared: America's "superior stock" was committing "race suicide." To ensure the stability of the nation and the future of democracy, Roosevelt and others urged "old stock" American women to do their "duty" and procreate. If native-born, middle-class women were not going to have more children, the *Delineator* believed, they could at least raise the masses of dependent, largely immigrant children into solid U.S. citizens.[10] Again and again, the *Delineator* appealed to women's sense of their civic duty, a duty that they could fulfill best through their role as mother.[11] Again and again, the *Delineator* painted the stark contrast between a child raised with a mother's love and one raised without: "upright men and women" or a "burden on the commonwealth," vagabonds, paupers, and criminals or honest, cleanly citizens, a "potential addition to the productive capacity ... of the nation" or to the "destructive forces of the community."[12] In looking back on the first year of the series, Wilder summed up its progress: "we found for [the profiled children] good influences upon whom no one can tell what other influences might have come and through them on down the ages to the end of earthly things good shall be where evil might have been."[13]

The *Delineator*'s editors emphatically and unquestionably trusted that placing these children with Christian, native-born, middle-class mothers was the way to save society and improve the citizenry. This belief mirrored the ideology behind the larger movement to Americanize new immigrants and suggested a fear of ethnic difference.[14] In 1918 James West, who had been one of the leading forces behind the Child-Rescue Campaign and was now chief executive of the Boy Scouts of America, wrote to Dreiser regarding one of the young boys profiled in the series. The boy, John, was now fourteen. His adoptive mother had written to West because her son had accidentally lost his Scout medal, and she hoped that West could replace it. The mother, aware of West's role in the series, took two pages to update him on the boy's progress in school and in the Scouts and mentioned the child's German ancestry. West was so pleased with this "definite evidence" of the success of the campaign that he sent a copy of the mother's letter to Dreiser.

In his cover letter, West mentioned the child's success and the joy he brought to his adoptive mother, but he especially focused on the redemptive quality of adoption. As he told Dreiser, in addition to the boy's progress in school, "there is the dramatic feature that the boy is of German parentage but in spite of this fact, is developing into a fine patriotic loyal American citizen." West's focus on the child's ethnicity could be understood within the context of the anti-German hysteria that had swept the nation at the outbreak of World War I. It also reflected his (and the *Delineator*'s) understanding of adoption as social conservation and a means to protect and save society.[15]

Adoption as Rescue

The *Delineator* also chose a narrative formula for the children's profiles that encouraged adoption and in many ways shaped the way adoptive parents experienced the adoption process. The profiles seemed to contain only the details of a child's background. But, in fact, the *Delineator* constructed the stories to generate enough sympathy that the magazine's middle-class readers would be motivated to adopt the children yet strove to do so without offending readers' sensibilities or straining their understanding of children as innocents. To this end, the *Delineator*'s profiles used the literary convention of the rescue, an extremely common plot device in popular fiction at the time.

The rescue of a child appeared regularly in domestic novels of the nineteenth and early twentieth centuries. The rescue plot gave readers the thrills of a tragedy with the comfort of a happy ending. A rescue changed the destiny of the rescued and made a hero of the rescuer, embodying the American ideal of individual action. It also involved risk: would the rescuer be rewarded for her fateful intervention or would she ultimately regret it? In rescue fiction, the rescuer never repented her action because saved children always grew up to be responsible, moral adults and often made exceptional contributions to society. The rescued always paid back the rescuer. In addition, these stories reflected two basic beliefs: humane, caring action was rewarded, and a child could overcome initial adversity and rise to success through hard work and personal integrity.[16] The rescue plot was the perfect structure for the profiles, allowing the *Delineator* to present the children's histories in an exciting yet sympathetic way that demanded the readers' action and promised an ultimate reward. The pathetic tales of children who languished in institutions, abandoned by unfeeling parents or orphaned through a tragic accident, generated instant interest. Familiarity with the rescue convention provided readers with a clear blueprint for action: the stories described children in desperate circumstances—all that was left was for the *Delineator*'s readers to step in and rescue the children from their imminent fate. Most importantly, the formula provided a sense of security in the outcome: the rescued children would grow up to be ideal citizens, as in fiction. The rescue narrative also focused attention on the new relationship between the vulnerable child and the protective adoptive parent, effectively erasing the birth parent(s) from view. Many prospective adopters feared that a birth parent would return to claim the child. However, the *Delineator*'s profiles made it clear that these children were free from that threat: a tragic death, a heroic surrender, or a cowardly abandonment had paved the way for their rescue.

By constructing the children's stories as tragedies in which they were guiltless victims deserving of rescue by women who possessed both a strong mother's consciousness and a sense of national duty, the *Delineator* deflected attention away from any disturbing aspects of a child's background. Had the profiles been too realistic, too gritty, a child could have seemed too great a risk. Baby Marion, who was profiled in the third issue of the series, is a case in point. Marion was illegitimate and had been abandoned. The *Delineator* reported that "a well-dressed, attractive [white] woman" had stopped at the home of an African-American family on the pretext of finding someone to do housework. While pretending to examine the home's "cleanliness," the woman managed, unobserved, to leave the baby, who was wrapped in paper, on a table. After the woman left, the family found the "emaciated" two-week-old, and when the child became severely ill a few days later, they turned her over to the authorities.

In fact, the case records of the Board of Children's Guardians in Washington, D.C., who had custody of Marion told a slightly different story. Marion's mother had stopped at an African-American family's home but had done so on the pretext of using the outhouse, not finding a housekeeper. The case record also makes no mention of Marion's mother's appearance. Most importantly, the *Delineator* failed to mention that when found, Marion was "covered with sores."

The image of a child covered with sores might have awakened readers' sympathy, but it also might have made them shrink back in fear. The children's stories may not have represented their subjects' actual experiences, but the tales no doubt promoted adoption by moving the discourse away from troubling details. A number of people showed interest in Marion, including a "well-to-do" childless couple and a Maryland couple who adopted her as a companion for their only child.[17]

A New Definition of Motherhood

Fears aside, the primary motivation for the majority of women who adopted was the genuine desire to mother, to give care and love to a child—an understandable desire given the culture's glorification of mothers and valuation of women primarily as mothers. At the same time, however, their experience of adoption was shaped by the *Delineator*'s portrayal of adoption as rescue, as women's duty. To understand adoption at this point in history, it is crucial to examine women's individual experiences within the context of the prevailing narratives about adoption at that time.

The Child-Rescue Campaign made adoption publicly visible in a way it had never been before. This exposure made it easier for women to adopt for a number of reasons: it eased their fears about the mysteries of adoption; it provided them with the practical information necessary to find a child with whom to ease their maternal longings; it supported their desire to adopt by giving them a reason—civic duty—for taking a child into their home; it made adoption seem less alien, both to them and to nosy neighbors or prying relatives; and it provided adoptive mothers or prospective adoptive mothers with a virtual community of other women like themselves.

But in naming and describing the experience, the *Delineator* also began to define it, to give it a specific form that necessarily influenced the way adoptive mothers came to conceptualize their experiences. The *Delineator* gave women a context within which to understand their experiences and explain them to others. Hence, a desire to mother was not incompatible with a duty to rescue. In letters to the *Delineator,* women described their experiences in ways that reflected both the values of the series and their intensely personal feelings. As one adoptive mother stated, Ralph was "a beautiful child, with so much temperament and character that no one else had succeeded in handling him until I got him. . . . He was a waif, and has it in him to make a fine man, but could easily become a poor one under the wrong circumstances. . . . I never really lived until Ralph came to be my little boy." At a time when adoption was not yet completely accepted, the construction of adoption as rescue ultimately might have helped women who wanted to adopt but previously had not done so because they feared the sting of disapproving eyes. The complete social acceptance of "sentimental adoptions"—that is, taking a child solely to create a family—was still a few years away. These narratives allowed adoptive mothers to present their experiences in such a way that the decision to adopt could not be challenged: they were fulfilling their civic duty and expressing their sincere desire for a child and genuine mother's love.[18]

Abandoning Readers, Embracing Reformers

The *Delineator*'s role in the national child-saving movement reflected the larger realities of publishing in the early 1900s and especially the personalities of those in charge of the magazine. According to his biographers, Dreiser understood the pathos and pain of the poor as simply a reflection of the laws of nature. He was also driven by the desire to overcome the poverty of his birth and achieve respectability. It is possible that along with his fatalistic beliefs, Dreiser possessed a sincere sympathy for and desire to help the weak. But even if Dreiser had doubts about the ultimate efficacy of the campaign, editing a powerful women's magazine with national influence gave him the status he craved.[19]

Publisher George Wilder had his own set of beliefs and concerns. Wilder wore two hats: he wanted to help humanity, but he also wanted a successful magazine. Wilder's humanitarian impulse leaned toward helping individuals who en masse would create a better society rather than toward working for large-scale reforms: he believed that changing individuals would change society, an outlook more in tune with nineteenth-century approaches to reform than twentieth-century ideas. His idea to match up childless homes and homeless children reflected this philosophy. Wilder took an active hand in overseeing the magazine and wholeheartedly believed in the Child-Rescue Campaign. In October 1908 he wrote to Dreiser, telling him to "push, Push, PUSH" the child rescue work "harder this year than ever." Wilder's confidence in the goodness of the campaign was so great that, as he told Dreiser, "Gabriel, keeping the book up yonder, may possibly have used the tears of joy shed by these children & their new found mothers to wipe away some of your sins & even mine recorded on his pages."[20]

While Wilder dreamed of heaven, Dreiser looked for ways to meet the criticisms of child welfare reformers and to expand the series' impact. From the beginning, the series had advocated home-placing over institutional care for dependent children in addition to the more immediate goal of matching children with mothers. It was, however, becoming more and more difficult to balance the personal side of the campaign with the national reform work geared toward abolishing institutional care. Wilder seemed unable to decide which was more important. His letter to Dreiser continued, "Confound these approvals of our work by Presidents and Secretaries of Home Finding Societies. Give me one letter from a woman's heart to whom the Joys of Motherhood have come through this campaign. Of course, I want the approval of these officials. I don't mean just what I have said. But . . . one letter telling the joy brought to some woman's heart through a little child will get more results than one hundred approvals."[21] Wilder's reform impulse, his personal belief in the power of changing individuals, and his responsibilities as a businessman were in conflict. Wilder was keenly aware that readers found personal, emotional appeals more compelling than dry, factual admonitions from experts, but he also wanted the prestige and rewards of leading a major reform.

The *Delineator* needed to keep its subscription numbers high to justify its position in the reform community. Keeping readers happy meant keeping the monthly profiles of children and addressing women's concerns as adoptive mothers. Reformers, however, wanted the magazine to abandon the profiles and focus on informational issue-oriented child welfare stories. As James West explained to reformers, he used the stories and photos "because it guarantee[d] a direct personal interest" even though he knew "that in most cases it would be a comparatively easy matter to find good homes for the particular children . . . we have presented."[22]

The *Delineator* stated that its profiles were not meant to focus on specific children but rather to represent the types of children available. Yet there is no evidence to suggest that readers saw the children as mere types. Indeed, female readers responded to the children as individuals. For example, the story of a five-year-old, "little Daisy," whose mother had died and whose father could no longer support her, moved more than six hundred readers to write in to adopt this child "bright as the blossom whose name she bears."[23]

The *Delineator*'s desire to lead the battle "for the best interests of the child," thereby gaining national influence, respect, and probably more subscribers, caused the magazine to neglect—even abuse—readers' interests. The constant parade of adoptable children misled readers: there was not an overabundance of children eagerly waiting to be adopted. In fact, there was already something of a shortage of children available for adoption. As reformers of the time knew and as historians have shown again and again, the overwhelming number of children in institutions were there only temporarily and could not be adopted because one or both of their parents were still alive.[24]

The *Delineator* did acknowledge, even repeatedly, that there were more homes available than children, but the magazine did so in a way that obscured the truth. In April 1910, for example, the *Delineator* published a letter from "an unusually earnest woman" who had not been able to get a child. "Last fall I wrote you in regard to taking a little girl. The [child-placing agent] corresponded with me and was satisfied enough by her investigation, but she has been unable to get me a little girl. Now I would like to ask where are all the homeless children that *The Delineator* sends out an appeal for from month to month? What need is there of wasting so much space in your magazine, if it is such hard work to find a child when the home is waiting?" The *Delineator* responded by blaming the shortage on the policies of institutions, eager to continue receiving their "drafts upon the public treasury," that refused to release the hundreds of children "imprisoned" within their "cold, dreary" walls. According to the *Delineator*, the problem was institutional greed rather than the children's personal status.[25] Consequently, the *Delineator* could admonish its readers to work even harder in their efforts to save the children and abolish institutions.

To "guarantee interest," the *Delineator* had structured the Child-Rescue Campaign around finding individual mothers for individual children, but this emphasis conflicted with the realities of the magazine's larger reform goal. In discussing the end of institutional care, the *Delineator* never emphasized that most children needed temporary foster care, not permanent adoptive homes. And every indication suggests that the *Delineator*'s readers wanted children to raise as their own forever. The published letters from readers refer to issues of specific concern to adoptive parents and describe relationships based on a biological model of parenthood. One reader wrote that her adopted son "believes we are his real parents," while another stated that her family loved their adopted son "as if he were bone of our bone and flesh of our flesh."[26] These letters reflect fears that a birth parent would return to disrupt the new families, not pleasure at helping a parent in temporary distress by caring for a child.

There had been a movement to care for dependent children in homes rather than in institutions as early as the 1890s, well before the *Delineator* began its Child-Rescue Campaign. When James West joined the campaign sometime in 1908, the stage was set for the magazine to take a leading role in child welfare work and the home-placing movement. West was a friend of President Theodore Roosevelt. West and Dreiser met with the president in October 1908, a meeting that resulted in the 1909 White House Conference. At the conference, child welfare advocates and President Roosevelt wholeheartedly adopted the policy of home care. The war was won and, by all accounts, the *Delineator* had played a vital role. The victory, however, left the magazine with an extremely popular campaign but no cause. In a period of fierce competition among women's magazines, the *Delineator* naturally hesitated to abandon such a popular series, especially since the White House conference had generated so much positive press. Every indication showed that the profiles continued to touch the hearts of countless women. And interest in children justified the *Delineator*'s role in the national reform movement. Yet if there was no problem, readers would not tolerate the waste of so much space or the call for them to expend so much energy.[27]

After the White House conference, the *Delineator*'s monthly series began to stress the need for mothers' pensions, a significant shift in focus. Now the emphasis was not solely on how to save the dependent child from a life of degradation but also on how to ward off dependency. This change reflected the larger movement among reformers from a "save the child" philosophy that had prevailed in the nineteenth century to a "save the family" perspective in the twentieth. Whereas nineteenth-century reformers had quickly removed children from the corrupting influence of their immoral and/or poor families, reformers now believed both that poor families needed the civilizing influence of their children to keep them from falling further from grace and that nothing could replace a birth mother's love.[28]

In his report to Congress on the conference, Roosevelt urged that the "widowed or deserted mother, if a good woman . . . should ordinarily be helped in such fashion as will enable her to bring up her children herself in their natural home." The *Delineator* seized on this challenge and urged readers to support the new cause. Possibly realizing that this new focus challenged the basic premise of the Child-Rescue Campaign, the *Delineator* assured readers that this effort would "make none the less important the need of homes for the care of homeless children." This, of course, was blatantly untrue: the establishment of mothers' pensions that would help widowed and deserted mothers to keep their children would further reduce the number of adoptable children.[29]

In addition, the ideology behind mothers' pensions—the importance of the "natural" family, the primacy of blood ties, and the irreplaceability of a birth mother's love—was at odds with the campaign's efforts to destigmatize adoption and expand the definition of *mother* to includes ties of care as well as blood. I am not suggesting that the *Delineator's* proadoption readers opposed mothers' pensions. Rather, the magazine's attempt to be all things to all people represented a potential clash of interests and often resulted in articles with misleading, contradictory, or inconsistent information. One wonders if the many women who saw the Child-Rescue Campaign as a friend in their quests to find children and an ally in their efforts to create families saw the conflict between their desires and the *Delineator's* growing emphasis on mothers' pensions. One wonders if the focus on blood ties caused a sense of betrayal in the adoptive mothers who seemed so grateful to have their concerns voiced, their experiences named.

The Child-Rescue Campaign ended abruptly and without explanation in February 1911, shortly after Dreiser left as the *Delineator's* editor. Although West showed that the campaign still generated a huge amount of reader response, the new editors decided against continuing the series, and West soon left to work for the Boy Scouts of America. The series reappeared once in January 1912, but the reform angle was gone. Instead, the *Delineator* urged readers to adopt as a Christmas gift to themselves. In August 1912, under the direction of a reform-minded journalist, William Hard, the *Delineator* launched a campaign for mothers' pensions. Whereas the Child-Rescue Campaign had called on women to open their mothers' hearts wide enough to take in children not of their flesh, the new campaign urged women to spread their mother love by working to help other mothers keep their children. Women who took in dependent children were no longer cheered as the possessors of a strong mother consciousness; now they were the strangers who received the children torn from poor mothers.[30]

Conclusion

The Child-Rescue Campaign began as a solution to a distinct problem as identified and understood by one man. Wilder's construction of the problem reflected his (and much of the larger society's) fears about immigration, race suicide, and the social threat posed by uncontrolled, undisciplined, un-American youth. Implicit in his solution of matching up childless homes and homeless children was the belief that native-born, middle-class homes were superior not only to institutions but also to the children's natural families, at the very least in the social terms of providing the children with future opportunities and American values. It is nothing new to state that adoption always includes a judgment about who is a better parent for a child and that this assessment necessarily reflects the culture's beliefs at that moment in time about what qualities make a good parent. What is fascinating about the Child-Rescue Campaign, however, is that this judgment shifted as the series moved away from Wilder's attempts to match poor, dependent children with more prosperous and stable homes and toward embracing reformers' efforts to keep birth mothers and children together. This shift highlights the social construction of motherhood and speaks to the question, "Who at any given time determines who and what a mother is?"

When fear was the primary motivation behind the campaign, the *Delineator* portrayed adoptive mothers as society's key to salvation and best hope for the future. Although the Child-Rescue Campaign presented adoptive mothers positively throughout the series, over time the discourse shifted in favor of birth mothers. In July 1908 the *Delineator* acknowledged that separating a birth mother from her child was sad. But the magazine also believed that a birth mother, "however low her lot has fallen, surrenders her baby willingly, feeling, with the remnant of mother-love that lives within her, that her child must have a better chance in life than that which has come to her."[31] As the *Delineator*'s craving for more national influence grew and the staff's involvement with child-saving reformers who now favored keeping families together increased, the editors' understanding of the problem—and hence their solution to it—changed. By October 1909 the *Delineator* stated that surrendering a child was a "frightful sacrifice" and that providing a child with another home was only "the best we can do."[32] What once was a heroic sacrifice was now horrific.

If this shift compromised the interests of women who wanted to adopt, the series was nonetheless instrumental in popularizing and destigmatizing adoption, whether or not doing was the magazine's intent. Adoptions had been on the increase since 1851, when Massachusetts passed the country's first adoption law and other states soon followed. But despite its growing popularity, adoption was still not publicly or candidly discussed. Although articles on adoption had previously appeared in popular magazines on a few occasions, the Child-Rescue Campaign was the first time the spotlight focused on adoption for an extended period of time. In addition to allowing women to work out some of their fears about adoption and address some of the issues adoptive parents faced, the series also served a practical purpose by showing interested parties where and how to adopt children. The campaign's overwhelming success showed that women were ready to adopt and believed that adoption created a real family in which children were treated not as workers but as family members and mothers felt the same love and devotion as if they had given birth.

NOTES

1. Wilder told this story about the inspiration behind the Child-Rescue Campaign in a 1909 newspaper interview (*Delineator* Scrapbook, box 421, Papers of Theodore Dreiser, Special Collections, Van Pelt–Dietrich Library, University of Pennsylvania).

It is difficult to determine the exact number of children who found adoptive homes as a direct result of the *Delineator*'s campaign. The magazine claimed a direct link between the campaign and the adoption of at least two thousand children; however, it is possible that the campaign inspired even more people to adopt (Dreiser papers, folder 6585).

The *Delineator* began in 1873 as a ladies' fashion magazine promoting Butterick dress patterns. By 1907 it had expanded to include articles on homemaking and occasionally featured stories on social issues. By 1912 the mail circulation had almost reached the one million mark (Frank L. Mott, *A History of American Magazines, 1865–1885* [Cambridge: Harvard University Press, 1938], 3:481–90).

2. Peter Romanofsky, "The Early History of Adoption Practices, 1870–1930" (Ph.D. diss., University of Missouri at Columbia, 1969); Harold A. Jambor, "Theodore Dreiser, the *Delineator* Magazine, and Dependent Children: A Background Note on the Calling of the 1909 White House Conference," *Social Service Review* 32 (1958): 33–40; Elvena Bage Tillman, "The Rights of Childhood: The National Child Welfare Movement, 1890–1919" (Ph.D. diss. University of Wisconsin, 1968); LeRoy Ashby, *Saving the Waifs* (Philadelphia: Temple University Press, 1984), 53–55.

3. Viviana A. Zelizer, *Pricing the Priceless Child: The Changing Social Value of Children* (New York: Basic Books, 1985), 169–207; Michael Grossberg, *Governing the Hearth: Law and the Family in Nineteenth-Century America* (Chapel Hill: University of North Carolina Press, 1985), 268–85; Jamil S. Zainaldin, "The Origins of Modern Legal Adoption: Child Exchange in Boston, 1851–1893" (Ph.D. diss., University of Chicago, 1976).

4. Mabel Potter Daggett, "The Child without a Home," *Delineator* 70 (Oct. 1907): 505–10; Lydia Kingsmill Commander, "The Home without a Child," *Delineator* 70 (Nov. 1907): 720–23, 830; *Delineator* 71 (Mar. 1908): 337, 425.

138   Adoption in America

5. *Delineator* 71 (Jan. 1908): 100–103; *Charities and the Commons* 19 (Feb. 22, 1908): 1612–13.

6. Mary Ellen Waller, "Popular Women's Magazines, 1890–1917" (Ph.D. diss., Columbia University, 1987), 47–48; Dreiser papers, folder 1465, *Delineator* correspondence, Dec. 24, 1910; *Delineator* 71 (Feb. 1908): 253–54.

7. See for example, Julia Ward Howe, "The Joys of Motherhood," *Delineator* 71 (May 1908): 806; Julia Ward Howe "What My Children Mean to Me," *Delineator* 74 (Sept. 1909): 212; *Delineator* 72 (Aug. 1908): 263; *Delineator* 74 (Aug. 1909): 134.

8. *Delineator* 71 (Mar. 1908): 425; *Delineator* 74 (Dec. 1909): 566; Helen Christine Bennett, "The Gift of Life," *Delineator* 72 (Aug. 1908): 263; *Delineator* 73 (Feb. 1909): 249.

9. *Delineator* 74 (Aug. 1909): 134; *Delineator* 70 (Nov. 1907): 719; *Delineator* 72 (July 1908): 113; Jacob Riis, "God's Children, Give Them a Chance: A Comparison of the Influence of Heredity and Environment," *Delineator* 71 (May 1908): 809; Lucy Huffaker, "Waifs Who Have Become Famous," *Delineator* 71 (June 1908): 1005.

10. Elaine Tyler May, *Barren in the Promised Land* (New York: Basic Books, 1995), chap. 2; *Delineator* 70 (Nov. 1907): 719.

11. Linda Kerber has argued that since the American Revolution, women's citizenship has been connected to their role as mothers (*Women of the Republic* [New York: W. W. Norton, 1986]).

12. *Delineator* 72 (Oct. 1908): 576, 578; *Delineator* 73 (May 1909): 696.

13. George Wilder to Dreiser, ca. Oct. 1908, Dreiser papers, folder 882.

14. *Delineator* (Apr. 1908): 611; John Higham, *Strangers in the Land: Patterns of American Nativism, 1860–1925* (New Brunswick, N.J.: Rutgers University Press, 1955).

15. Dreiser papers, folder 6585, James West correspondence, Apr. 27, 1918. John had been abandoned by his birth parents at the age of eleven months. He was four years old when the *Delineator* profiled him in the Jan. 1908 issue. He was adopted by a couple whose only son had died. His adoptive mother's ancestors had arrived on the Mayflower.

16. Diana Reep, *The Rescue and Romance: Popular Novels before World War I* (Bowling Green, Ohio: Bowling Green State University Press, 1982).

17. *Delineator* 71 (Jan. 1908): 98; Board of Children's Guardians (BCG), Children's History, 2130; BCG Agent Letters, 1908, 10, both in Records of the District of Columbia, record group 351, National Archives, Washington, D.C.; *Delineator* (Apr. 1908): 608.

18. *Delineator* 74 (Aug. 1909): 134; *Delineator* 73 (Jan. 1909): 103. For a discussion of the move toward sentimental adoptions, see Zelizer, *Pricing the Priceless Child,* 169–207.

19. Richard Lingeman, *Theodore Dreiser: An American Journey, 1908–1945* (New York: G. P. Putnam's Sons, 1990).

20. Wilder to Dreiser, ca. Oct. 1908, Dreiser papers, folder 882 (Butterick correspondence).

21. Ibid.

22. Dreiser papers, folder 1465, Dec. 24, 1910.

23. *Delineator* 73 (Feb. 1909): 250; *Delineator* 73 (June 1909).

24. LeRoy Ashby, *Endangered Children: Dependency, Neglect, and Abuse in American History* (New York: Twayne, 1997), 32, 232–33; Julie Berebitsky, "'To Raise as Your Own': The Growth of Legal Adoption in Washington," *Washington History* 6 (spring–summer

1994): 4–26; Jamil S. Zainaldin and Peter L. Tyor, "Asylum and Society: An Approach to Industrial Change," *Journal of Social History* 13 (fall 1979): 31–32.

25. *Delineator* 76 (Apr. 1910): 323.

26. *Delineator* 74 (Aug. 1909): 134; *Delineator* 76 (Dec. 1910): 515.

27. For a thorough discussion of the role of the *Delineator* and Dreiser in the 1909 White House Conference on the Care of Dependent Children, see Harold A. Jambor, "Theodore Dreiser, the *Delineator* Magazine, and Dependent Children: A Background Note on the Calling of the 1909 White House Conference," *Social Service Review* 32 (1958): 33–40.

28. Susan Tiffin, *In Whose Best Interest? Child Welfare Reform in the Progressive Era* (Westport, Conn.: Greenwood Press, 1982). For the *Delineator*'s growing focus on mothers' pensions, see the Oct. 1909, Dec. 1909, and Aug. 1910 issues.

29. *Delineator* 76 (Aug. 1910): 128; Zelizer, *Pricing the Priceless Child*, 200.

30. Theda Skocpol, *Protecting Soldiers and Mothers: The Political Origins of Social Policy in the United States* (Cambridge: Belknap Press of Harvard University Press, 1992), 432–42.

31. *Delineator* 72 (July 1908): 114.

32. *Delineator* 74 (Oct. 1908): 311.

A Nation's Need for Adoption and Competing Realities

The Washington Children's Home Society, 1895–1915

Patricia S. Hart

American society has had a vested role in adoption from the time it became an established method of saving children at the turn of the century. Although many of the specific issues surrounding adoption have changed since then, we still look to adoption to provide solutions for some of the nation's most heartrending conditions, from child neglect, abuse, and abandonment to fulfilling the yearnings of infertile couples.[1]

Perceived as a problem solver for more than a century, adoption has always been a politically charged subject that can never be experienced by participants in complete isolation from social expectations, both positive and negative.[2] Now, as the history of adoption and its role in society is being written, evidence from case records shows that participant experience is invaluable in balancing historical analysis based primarily on what contemporary reformers and others had to say about adoption. Case histories show that participants sought to fulfill their own desires through adoption and did not always act in accord with social expectations. Furthermore, often overdrawn social theory about nineteenth-century class relations and nationhood might also be profitably tested against evidence provided by case histories. The subjective experience of participants, which is essentially ignored by much postmodern theory as irrelevant, contests broad and inclusive theories about social intent with evidence to the contrary.

Postmodern approaches that might seem applicable to understanding adoption history are often of limited utility. The social theory of Michel Foucault, published in his *The History of Sexuality,* vol. 1, *An Introduction,* potentially bears on the question of how and why dependent children were joined to middle-class families beginning in the nineteenth century. Foucault contends

140

that by the end of the nineteenth century, the middle class had thoroughly embraced sexuality for itself and intensified its significance, manifesting its self-
preoccupation through endless discussion about procreation of healthy, productive, middle-class bodies ready to inherit the privileges of a healthy,
expansive, vigorous body politic. Foucault posits that over the course of the late
nineteenth century, as heavy industry increasingly demanded labor that could
be supplied only by bodies of laboring men, sexuality was extended from the
"hegemonic center" to include the lower-class populations. At that point, the
sexual comportment of the poor became a subject of surveillance, pedagogy,
and medical specialization.[3]

At the end of the nineteenth century, when adoption started to take shape
as part of modern child welfare reform, Protestant reformers did indeed in-
tend to mold illegitimate, dependent, or abused children to useful citizenship
by way of adoption into Christian middle-class families. However, to follow
Foucault and make the reforming the poor and nation building the sole focus
of the history of adoption obscures the varied, competing experiences of
adoption participants. Qualitative and quantitative analyses of adoption case
histories can help establish different ways of understanding adoption within
culture. The historical evidence on which this essay is based comes from a
larger study of 289 case records, every tenth record from the first twenty years
at the Washington Children's Home Society (WCHS). The WCHS, founded in
Seattle in 1895 as a private organization affiliated with the National Children's
Home Society (NCHS), was committed to finding permanent adoptive homes
for legally relinquished children.[4] As evidence from the case records shows,
adoption experience defies easy generalizations about class, family, and the expectations of society as a whole.

Adoption in the Nineteenth Century

The sentimental family ideal, including a nurturing approach to children, had
become the predominant white middle-class American model in the 1830s and
1840s. The belief that children depended on the tender quality of their nurturing families influenced judges to consider the best interest of the child when
deciding custody and to increase maternal preference in child-custody cases. As
the century progressed, the "best interest of the child" doctrine helped set legal
precedence for biological bonds of parenthood (not just paternity) to be severed when the interests of the child were ill served, although entrenched resis-
tance to doing so persisted. The first adoption law, passed in Massachusetts in
1851, made adoption a statutory procedure executable in state probate courts.
Home placements, some leading to adoptions, were being made by charitable
institutions even before 1851, and by serving as a model for most other states,
the Massachusetts law legitimized and facilitated the practice. Early home

placements, however, did not usually lead to formal adoption. Beginning in the latter half of the nineteenth century, the New York Children's Aid Society, under the direction of Charles Loring Brace, placed tens of thousands of children from the urban East into mostly rural Midwestern families from orphan trains, yet few of these home placements led to legal adoption, which required legal relinquishment. Martin Van Buren Van Arsdale of Illinois, a Protestant minister, and his later followers were critical of home placements that did not lead to adoptions and of institutions where children who had no family languished, often for years. In founding the NCHS, Van Arsdale hoped to find every homeless child a permanent Christian home.[5]

By the turn of the century, "best interest of the child" policies were increasingly reflected in the state's participation in deciding when children needed protection. The resulting Progressive Era legislation helped adoption gain a foothold as a component of social welfare policy by tying adoption to child protection, although severance of blood ties did not become the preferred method of dealing with child dependency.[6] Progressive Era values defined parental worthiness and children's fitness for adoption, shaping and pervading adoption practice and affecting all those in its orbit (the adopted child, the biological parents, and the adoptive family) until the child was an adult. Under the direction of mostly Protestant ministers in private, independent but federated NCHS societies, adoption practice during this period tended to suppress a child's recollection of or connections to his or her past, until the child was grown, and to reinforce paths to Christian salvation and U.S. citizenship.

Adoption as a method of child saving came into first flower during a period of Progressive reform when the poor, particularly immigrants, were undergoing intense scrutiny. The constitution of the family was considered a bellwether of how the nation would be able to cope with industrialization, an immense wave of immigration, expansion, and westward migration. As historians LeRoy Ashby and Stephanie Coontz contend, the nineteenth-century "discovery" of the child actually represented a distinct historical moment when the social agendas of reformers brought children temporarily into political focus. Middle-class children were the subject of a sustained, loving gaze, while poor children came and went from view, according to political winds. Yet by all accounts, late-nineteenth- and early-twentieth-century reformers were particularly focused on incorporating children in a nationalistic project founded on useful citizenship. The preferred method of incorporation was the family.[7]

By the end of the first decade of the twentieth century, Theodore Roosevelt had proclaimed the American family the highest achievement of civilization for its allegedly unique capacity to mold citizens. Both the future of the nation and the future of the species seemed to balance on the ability of native-born white women to raise children with middle-class standards of self-sufficiency, moral uprightness, and Protestant sobriety. As the potential represented by the child became a national emblem, childhood as an idealized state became distanced from the gritty realities of social and economic conditions affecting a great number of people, including immigrants and anyone not white. In context of the greatest wave of immigration the nation had ever known and the appalling conditions in which many immigrants lived in large U.S. cities, it is perhaps not surprising that a nation already vested in the project of perpetuating middle-class American values might seize on the hope that the nation could be spared the impact of immigration and industrialization if children could be severed from corrupting influences—including, in cases of abandonment, abuse, or neglect, their parents—and absorbed quickly into the social body. So while the nation was intensely concerned about the descent of the species and its collective welfare and turned this concern into pressure for the "right sort" to procreate and socially reproduce native, white, middle-class values, it extended its communitarian project to the children of the poor.[8]

A Home for Every Child, a Child for Every Home

Adoption supporter W. D. Wood, president of the WCHS in 1906, understood that the incorporation of homeless children into middle-class families was not a simple matter. When Wood said at the WCHS annual meeting that year, "The greatest event in modern times is the discovery of the child," he was strumming rhetorical chords already well rehearsed by Progressive Era reformers. But in his address, Wood was appealing in particular for a "discovery" of the homeless child because he believed that "even mother-love looks with small sympathy upon the homeless chick of another brood." Wood was pleading the same cause advanced by the Reverend Harrison D. Brown and Libby Beach Brown, husband and wife founders of the WCHS, who had been championing adoption of socially dependent children in Washington since 1896 and who themselves were carrying forward Van Arsdale's mission. Their common quest was to find every homeless child a Christian home.[9]

Wood played on cultural themes that had been shaping the practice of child saving for decades. For example, he placed the child within the "economy of God" as the "key to the Kingdom of Heaven on earth, the greatest factor, the greatest possibility, the greatest opportunity, in all of our human affairs." Wood echoed President Theodore Roosevelt by demanding a "square deal" for the homeless child. Wood also saw the child as an educator, an "Americanizer," and "key to the foreign family." Conversely, Wood pointed out that despite a middle-class American cultural climate that beatified childhood, the sentimental appeal on behalf of children often fell on deaf ears when the child in question was not a blood relative.[10]

Indeed, the adoption of homeless, neglected, or abused children by nonrelatives stirred up powerful fears fueled by eugenicists, nativists, medical experts, and even well-meaning reformers of the poor. Adoption supporters, like Wood, staunchly maintained that Christian faith and a family environment would prevail over heredity and adversity. Wood continued,

> Heredity has to do with the physical instrumentalities, but not with the soul. That comes direct from God to every child. It is always pure, always ready to co-operate with uplifting environment to control and subdue physical heredity. . . . We may therefore safely count that the pure soul, helped by a good environment of ten or fifteen years in the life of a child, beginning at a tender age, will, under normal physical and mental facilities, always triumph over heredity.[11]

Supporters such as Wood believed that adoption would provide a path for the personal salvation of the homeless child, for the "normalization" of the "unnatural" condition of childlessness, for the assimilation of dependent children living at the margins of society, and for exercise of the social gospel movement of the period, particularly in its faith that within every child lay a perfect soul, not a bad seed.

The WCHS was a young but exemplary representative of home-finding societies founded throughout the United States. Between 1896 and 1915, adoption became an established method of child saving in Washington state and across the nation, and cultural attitudes toward the practice began taking definite shape. Progressive Era child savers who championed adoption as a moral, humane, and efficient means of helping wholly dependent children also embraced a larger mission of saving the society from misfits and of molding citizens for the nation. The adage for the era, "It is better to save a child than retrain a criminal" tied adoption as a solution, through child saving generally, to the potential threat of deviance and delinquency. During this period, adoption advocates and courts joined forces to acquire new powers from state legislatures to legalize the dissolution of ties between biologically related individuals in cases of abuse, neglect, and abandonment and to legitimize families formed through adoption. What set NCHS adoption policy off from existing home placement practice, such as orphan trains or temporary foster placement, was that home-finding societies required legal relinquishment and formal, legal documentation of adoption after placement.[12]

Foucault's assertion that the poor only became visible to the middle class when needed for labor suggests, by extension, that the middle class became interested in homeless children only when it had a need for their labor or desire for them to complete childless families. But legal adoption was in fact a move away from the exploitation of children as laborers, a complaint adoption advocates made about home placements from orphan trains. Furthermore, adoption workers of this period did not "steal" the children of the poor to raise in middle-class families, another criticism aimed at orphan trains. On the contrary, removing children from their parents' care was offensive to most sensibilities and done only as a last resort. Poverty was generally considered a moral shortcoming on the part of adults but not a legitimate reason for relinquishment. Furthermore, at the WCHS and similar home-placement societies, the need for suitable homes for school-age children was nearly always greater than the supply.[13]

Although the Progressive Era is noted for its child-saving rhetoric, economic critiques, and muckraking, the national dialogue of opportunity and progress set the tone for adoption. It is perhaps not surprising that at the WCHS, Progressive critiques of the conditions that produced dependent children were relatively muted compared to the language of social mobility and "business sense," which was pervasive. H. D. Brown suspected that orphanage personnel were vested in keeping children institutionalized because it was their source of livelihood. Brown claimed that adoption saved the public the cost of caring for children in orphanages year after year. Although poverty or its specter was the condition most commonly associated with child relinquishment, the WCHS most often cited moral reasons—illegitimacy, abandonment, divorce, drinking—as the true causes of child dependency and relinquishment. That the moral transgressions were cited for relinquishment seems to confirm Foucault's allegation that when the poor became visible to the middle class in the form of needy children, the political form that attention took was the surveillance of sexual behavior, reproduction, and marriage relations.[14]

Yet, as historian Linda Gordon points out, the poor who come under the scrutiny of social welfare reformers learned to shape institutions to their own needs whenever they could.[15] The same holds true, to a degree, for participants in adoption—including relinquishing parents—according to information available from the records. Women relinquished to spare children abuse and provide them protection. Men and women relinquished when adoption seemed the only way for their children to have decent lives. Men relinquished so their children could receive consistent, caring female nurturing. Young women relinquished to avoid social sanctions against illegitimacy and hopeless poverty. Of course, the defeat embodied in the use of such strategies can scarcely describe the despair and diminished hopes experienced by those exhausted lives. Therefore, there are many limits to what a historian can justifiably call agency when parents voluntarily placed their children. For example, adoption workers encountered relinquishing parents in interviews or in court, where the legal basis of relinquishment could be established. In a process that required the relinquishing parents to acknowledge and confess to their misfortunes and shortcomings, complex situations tended to be reduced to moral transgressions. In addition, the terms of relinquishment starkly delineate the societal limits of the incorporation of the poor: children were considered redeemable; parents usually were not. In separating children from the conditions contributing to their misery, relinquishment masked the underlying causes of that misery in a cloak of morality.

With regard to the conditions leading to relinquishment, information from adoption records is revealing. Men, women, and children who lacked food, shelter, clothing, and other basic life requirements were a fixture of the booming West—not only of the urban East—with Washington State a typical example. In WCHS literature of the period, the society listed legitimate reasons to adopt, among them, "You protect society and the state by the transformation of a prospective vagrant and criminal into a noble [a code word for native-born and white] high-minded, helpful citizen."[16] Adoption was thus proposed as a solution to an already existing and increasing need for the care of wholly dependent children and as an inoculation against the creation of a permanent criminal or alien underclass.

Yet the relinquishing parents were usually neither criminal nor foreigners. The majority were not recent immigrants, although relinquishing parents claimed more than two dozen ethnic affiliations. Only a tiny percentage of the relinquishing parents could be called criminal by any contemporary legal definition of the term. However, the parents of children who were relinquished for adoption usually did exist at the impoverished margins of the Northwest economy, which grew at a phenomenal rate between 1895 and 1915. At nearly a quarter of a million people, the population of Seattle was six times larger in 1910 than it was in 1900. Railroads, homesteading, ranching and agriculture, coal mining, forestry, shipping, and commerce all contributed to the economic booms that attracted immigration from abroad and large migrations from the Midwest. The extractive and agricultural industries were notoriously vulnerable to busts, and the men who were fathers of relinquished children were generally employed at the lowest rung of these industries or were part of a floating pool of seasonally employed wage earners.[17]

Forty-seven percent of the women who relinquished their children were also working and not getting by. Failure to provide support for dependents for more than a year was grounds for divorce in Washington State, although few abandoned women with children would have sought divorce. The effects of a year or more without access to a male wage and without other resources left many women and children in deplorable condition. WCHS workers were not insensitive to the causes of destitution and fought for legislation to end various forms of sexual and labor exploitation. However, the effects of destitution were noted in the case histories in terms that carried pejorative connotations—words such as *filthy, dissipated, diseased, underdeveloped, lice-infested,* and *bad blood*—pointing to moral rather than economic or social failure. The general silence about the economic dimensions of relinquishment rather than of the moral and sexual transgressions of relinquishing parents is, however, implicitly acknowledged by case workers who emphasized the economic promise adoption held for children who were chosen for adoption into middle-class families.[18]

Turn-of-the-century poverty in Washington State differs from eastern urban tenement dwelling in being somewhat dispersed in the urban areas and existing in pockets around mining towns, railroads, and timber camps and on Indian reservations. Yet misery in Washington was just as deep and, if anything, was made more desperate by its isolation from sources of support or organized charity. The WCHS attempted to fill that void with its statewide adoption network. Poor white women of all ages, caught in insupportable situations and isolated physically, socially, and economically legally relinquished children, usually citing death of a spouse, nonsupport, divorce, or a combination of nonsupport and drunken abuse on the court forms. Relinquishment for adoption was a last resort of most women and men. Women had often exhausted every resource available to feed, clothe, shelter, and care for the needs of their children, many of whom suffered from chronic infections, lice, exposure, and malnutrition when they came into WCHS care. Washington's coal mining districts produced children destitute through oppressive poverty, parental illness, desertion, and industrial accidents. In 1909, a mother relinquished six little boys clothed through the winter in flour sacks at Roslyn. Her husband's parting act was to sell off the cookstove. No dishes or food were found in the house, and the bones of two of the children were softened by malnutrition. The mother stated that she wanted to keep the children together as long as she could. Such women had little or no reason to expect conditions to improve with time.[19]

Men whose wives died (women rarely deserted) voluntarily relinquished children when no adequate female caretaker could be found and the men did not feel able by themselves to care for the children. Recent immigrants from ethnic groups settled thinly in the area could find themselves with no relatives to help when a spouse died. "Father [has] no relatives or any one to help him in care of children," reads the file of two children relinquished by a Filipino working as a milkman whose Costa Rican wife had died. "Father has no relative to help him in the care of the children," reports the file of a child with three siblings relinquished by an Australian coal miner working in Roslyn. The letter of a recent Finnish immigrant was reprinted in the WCHS newsletter: "I am under heavy sorrow because I lost my wife by dying and left boy baby, and I have not any relation or other friend to nurse or take care of the child and I am wishing to get my baby to good hands to take care of him and I hereby beg you if you give me some information how I can get my boy into the institute." Forced relinquishment in motherless homes for reasons of neglect or abuse also brought children into WCHS care.[20]

Adoption existed within a range of child welfare arrangements, and poor families used relatives, friends, churches, orphanages, and other temporary boarding arrangements that accommodated more children in need than can ever be known. But when poverty combined with death or devastating illness of a supporting parent; the delinquency of a dependent child; or neglect, abuse, or alcoholism, relinquishment ceased to be a choice and was frequently mandated by the court.

Save a Child or Retrain a Criminal

Foucault writes that children were "sexualized" by adults who worried that, without intervention, children of the poor could "reproduce" degenerate traits, both physical and social, thus threatening the entire society and species. Undeniably, many child experts of the day considered children of the poor to be sexual beings and even sexual threats. In Judge Archibald W. Frater's Juvenile Court in Seattle, which handled most referrals to the WCHS after the first few years of the society's existence, diagnosticians were hired to ferret out confessions about masturbation and precocious sexual behavior. Scientific technologies were applied to the problem, with regimes of forced feeding and outdoor exercise and even surgical interventions such as circumcision, in the belief that they could prevent and cure "self abuse."[21]

Conversely, adoption advocates stridently and constantly refuted pseudoscientific polemics on hereditary determinism and eugenic solutions. One strategy the WCHS used to counter eugenic arguments was to displace them with appeals that spiritualized children and childhood or compared them to delicate grafted buds rather than bad seeds. Spiritualized children were perfect children, regardless of their origins. The grafted-bud model, however, carried with it an undertone of degeneracy and decay of the parent "stock," and this model could rationalize and legitimize a line drawn between reluctance to extend charity to poor adults while working unapologetically in favor of "saving" their children. Yet in practice, the WCHS sought out sources of support to enable children to remain in their homes when possible. The WCHS also developed an aid department to manage cases where permanent relinquishment was not appropriate. By 1915, it also found temporary foster homes for children whose families were in crisis.[22]

A connection exists between the spiritualized, sentimentalized, and idealized childhood of the late Victorian middle class and the idea that children, once severed from their biologic families, would be successfully reborn in better homes. The optimism of the social gospel mission saw a potential for redemption in the poor, neglected, or abused child. That optimism influenced attempts to reform and remake the real, physical child to redeem the ideal, spiritual child. WCHS workers often perceived children as malleable and their affections transferable (a graft on a tree). The result may have been a tendency to suppress the real, material, and temporal in favor of the potential and ideal.

Available WCHS accounts portray the matrons of the receiving homes and other employees as caring and affectionate but at the same time believing that it was their duty and in the best interest of the children to reform their bodies and habits.

Except for infants, children usually entered WCHS care after a series of deepening crises rather than after a single catastrophic event.[23] Their bodies frequently showed signs of chronic illness and malnutrition and even serious injury. When they arrived at the WCHS, children were quarantined, examined, and sometimes given operations for circumcision, adenoid removal, or tonsillectomy. Their temperaments were assessed, and their belongings, including their clothing, were replaced. When they had been cured of illnesses or social behavior that might "contaminate" the other children at the home, they were incorporated into the work, play, eating, and sleeping routines intended to bring children to health and happiness.[24]

Children entering the receiving home had of course recently experienced separations and losses. At relinquishment, children were separated from their parents. Excluding illegitimate babies, as many as 70 percent of the children were subsequently separated from siblings. The stories WCHS adoption workers told their supporters valorized the WCHS's role in child saving and minimized the anxiety and grief likely to have been suffered by children separated from familiar people and places. However, because children acquired adequate food, clothing, shelter, and some personal care in the receiving home, many became ambivalent about leaving it, simultaneously wanting an adoptive home and wishing to remain safe where they were. An older boy described the receiving home as "a good enough place to stay": "We all like Mrs. Meyers, and they cook good things and give us plenty, especially Sundays and Thanksgiving, but a fellow never knows what is coming to him. . . . I would like to try another home on a farm, for they have so many good apples, also horses and generally one dog. I wouldn't mind staying here if I knew I could stay, but they are always talking about our going to homes. . . . There are four [boys] here now, but perhaps some one will ask for us tomorrow. I won't be a cry baby anyway."[25] Many older children had their dreams of adoption repeatedly thwarted; others rejected adoption altogether and settled for arrangements offering maximum benefits and minimal oversight. As one older boy stated, "No one has come to see me to get me to go to a home, and I don't care: I'd as soon stay [at the receiving home] as not, I like it."[26]

Receiving-home matrons and caseworkers certainly were not blind to children's feelings. These administrators often pleaded for sensitivity and patience for children at placement, but the adults also tended to see children's suffering as temporary and liminal, remediable by caring people with the right motives: The child's past became a temporary illness to be cured. At worst, the receiving home was a site of separation, grief, and reform. At the same time, the receiving home, with its concerned maternal figures, was a place of comparative comfort, shared experience, occasional reunions, special celebrations, and material well-being.[27]

Most children arrived distressed by downward spiraling conditions, such as those caused by poverty, death of a parents, dislocation, deteriorating adult relationships, or serious neglect or physical abuse. Children who were illegitimate, who performed below grade for their age, and who swore, stole, and lied were still considered redeemable and adoptable. Physical disability did not necessarily rule out adoption, but some children were considered too badly damaged emotionally to make promising candidates for adoption, particularly when they were eight or older. The WCHS did not usually attempt to find homes for children over the age of fourteen. Children who were the products of incest and those who had syphilis were not considered adoptable.[28]

WCHS residences used over the years, including the large brick receiving home in the Seattle suburb of Ravenna, were intended as "wayside inns" for children on their way to adoptive homes, although the residences also served as places of trial and return for many children. While infants left the receiving home quickly and were adopted in about 65 percent of their placements, full orphans (6 percent of the total sample) were adopted at a rate of only 25 percent and sometimes languished at the receiving home for months. Some children grew up before they settled into a family, and a few children were placed more than a dozen times in a few years. As mediators of children's past and future, the WCHS expected change and adjustment from children, personal transformations that might even include religious conversion. The expectations were not unreasonable from the perspective of the WCHS, which sought middle-class Protestant homes for placement, homes that often pined for the cherubic, blond baby girls who were always in short supply. Relinquished children without middle-class morals, manners, and appearance were at a disadvantage in being selected for an adoptive home and were typically returned within the ninety-day trial period. Older children who did not have childish appeal settled for paid positions with room and board in homes needing an extra hand with younger children or with farming.[29]

Civic Duty versus Other Desires

The WCHS's mission, to fulfill "God's plan" by finding a home for every child and a child for every Christian home, was hailed from Protestant pulpits across Washington state, and hundreds of prospective parents sent in applications, but not necessarily for the children the WCHS actually had for placement. Homes were needed for school-age children, but prospective parents often wanted younger children, especially attractive babies, with few attachments to the past.[30]

What made potential adoptive families acceptable to the WCHS was a combination of successful breadwinning on the husband's part and full-time selfless motherhood on the wife's. (An adoptive mother's dependency on her husband's income was considered a virtue, while the economic dependency of a typical relinquishing mother was considered at best a tragedy and more commonly a failure.) Adoption was an idea that hit its stride with the maternalist ideology of the Progressive era, when mothering had extended its traditional biologic roles and endless child raising into the public arena as civic housekeeping. The motherhood message was strong, and adoption potentially opened a new avenue of civic motherhood. By taking a homeless child into her family, a woman could experience motherhood in a very public and civic sense.[31]

Civic motherhood, within the context of the political urging for the native-born, white middle class to reproduce itself, seems to point toward adoption as a "cure" for the reproductive and civic "failure" of infertile couples. But in fact, civics seems to have had little measurable effect on prospective parents' desire for children. Infertility—what in Foucauldian terms is the failure of the "Malthusian couple" to meet the demands of the body politic—seems to have had little to do with why families chose to adopt. The case records show that prospective parents demanded that their desires for love, companionship, family resemblance, and a specific age, sex, and temperament be taken into consideration at placement. They asked for children to enrich their marriages and add joy to their home lives, to replace children for whom they grieved or who had moved on, or to help when they were needed. Home-placement workers were vigilant in weeding out applicants who wanted children for free labor, who did not have sufficient regard for schooling, who were unwilling to legally adopt, or who did not treat children as part of their families. Nevertheless the nascent "home study," which ministers and members of local advisory committees were assigned to do, became a rubber stamp for church members wanting children, which may have accounted, in part, for the high rates at which children were returned to the receiving home after placement. As time passed, the WCHS attempted to be more particular about its family selection and more careful about a particular child's fit into a family. Even then, returns and replacements were routine.[32]

Surveillance of homes after placement to protect the children's best interests was intended to extend until they reached adulthood, and the WCHS claimed in 1911 that it visited all children on the "active" list between one and six times each year.[33] In fact, once children were adopted, home visits were sometimes years apart, although it is likely that many visits were made but not noted in adoption case files during the society's early years. There was a great difference in the adoption rates for infants and for the oldest children, with most of the infants adopted and most of the older children moving from place to place, home to home, in a pattern well known to today's foster care counselors. Many of these traveling children left the WCHS's orbit before finding permanent homes.

It is very difficult to document and therefore easy to overlook adoption's meaning for adoptive parents and children who learned to live with and love one another. The great happiness created by the movement of children into homes of adults who wanted them is indisputable and was expressed in dozens of letters to the WCHS newsletter, where adoptive parents shared their most intimate hopes and desires to love and be loved by their adoptive children. Infants, through rituals resembling birth ceremonies, were absorbed while they were still unconscious that prior relationships existed. One mother wrote, "He is the dearest baby and is so fat and sweet. We all love him, my husband being as foolish as I am over him. We got two nice blankets and tore them in two and the baby is wrapped up in half a blanket day and night . . . we are so afraid he might get a cold. . . . We lost our baby, and I know God intended this baby should fill its place. It seems like our own baby that we had talked and planned for so long."[34]

School-age children, for the most part, looked for ways to be included, to be loved and cared for, and to find ways to fit into their families. "Lucy is very anxious to work; I was canning fruit and she wanted to help, so I gave her some little jars and she canned them as nicely as I could have done," wrote one mother about her newly arrived daughter.[35]

A child wrote, "I will write you a few lines to let you know that I am well and like my home very much. I go to school every day. My report was excellent last month in everything except deportment, and I got very good in that. I go to church and Sunday school every Sunday. . . . I help mamma sweep the floors and I carry in wood and go up town." Another child reported that he had passed the fourth grade: "Papa gave me a Bible and I am proud of it. I have a garden and in it I have beans, peas, tomatoes, cabbage and turnips. I am going to be a Christian and a industrious boy."[36]

Even some very young children demonstrated a desire to keep in touch with the WCHS. There was an official policy of telling adopted children that they were adopted, and contact was encouraged and facilitated by the WCHS. In contrast, the WCHS kept secret the location of children from biologic relatives to protect the new bonds of the adoptive family and to create a space of forgetfulness for the children. The silence was intended to give a child a time and place to forget the hunger, hurt, neglect, fear, "bad habits," and immorality of birth parents. But as one mother admitted, it served just as well to shield adoptive parents from feelings of love or affection "lost" when an adopted child continued to recall those known in the past.[37]

Considering the lack of secrecy around the topic of adoption in adoptive homes, the age of children adopted, and the fact that many children had living family residing in the same state, it is not surprising that as adults, almost one quarter of the children in the sample contacted the WCHS with requests for documentation of their birth or queries about their birth relatives. The information was generally freely given until about the mid-1960s, when secrecy became policy. Until that time, the WCHS provided an institutional source of personal information that was useful to adults adopted as children.[38]

Competing Realities

Adoption entered public debate freighted with the social expectations of an anxious nation that molded the debate around idealized notions of motherhood, childhood, and middle-class family life. From past issues of the society's monthly newsletter, the *Washington Children's Home Finder,* and other sources, it is possible to piece together what adoption advocates have said about adoption. Adoption advocates drew on Protestant and Progressive Era values to fashion and empower the idea of adoption as a way to help wholly dependent children, to complete "God's plan" for "whole" families, to mold citizens, and to prevent the creation of a permanent criminal underclass.

However, the study of the socially constructed nature of adoption and its emerging role in child saving at the turn of the century should not be considered a complete history of adoption. For a fuller picture, individual case histories need to be examined to show how those who experienced adoption gave it meaning, forcing caseworkers to take into consideration the needs and desires of individuals immediately affected by it—birth parents, adopted children, and adoptive families. Evidence from case histories of children relinquished for adoption at the WCHS between its founding in 1895 and 1915 shows that participants in adoption did not necessarily act in concert with society's expectations. Of course, then, as now, the actors in adoption dealt with issues of difference, legitimacy, and identity, both within their adoptive families and in society, and were therefore shaped by the social climate. Participants' points of view were, of course, mediated by the caseworkers who recorded the information, but these accounts nevertheless provide a rich source of evidence offering important insight. Above all, the records show that adoption was differently experienced by those relinquishing, those adopted, and those adopting.

Foucault's broad explanation of how the middle class became preoccupied with its own social and sexual reproduction, extending those anxieties to the regulation of the poor only when they were needed to fuel industrialization, is really of limited use in explaining how adoption joined homeless and impoverished children to middle-class families. Bitter as relinquishment was, child savers and many relinquishing parents were guided by the faith that they were acting in the best interest of the child, not in the best interest of the middle class. Among other goals, adoption was intended to remedy exploitation of children for labor or, in the case of older children, at least to make their labors serve children's interests. Informed by Progressive values and prejudices, families were encouraged to adopt to avoid the formation of a permanent underclass, not to perpetuate one. Finally, the participants in adoption acted in ways that Foucault's seamless explanation rejects, subjectively and not merely as objects of political debate.

While acknowledging the importance of analyzing the emerging knowledge about adoption and the use of power in adoption practice, I am also concerned that participants in adoption do not merely become the objects of adoption debate but rather retain their material, historical, subjective experience as actors in their own lives.

During the two decades represented by this study of the WCHS, adoption came to be an acceptable, though not preferred, way of meeting the needs of dependent children when there was no hope of keeping them with their families. It could not, however, succeed, as its highly idealistic founders had hoped, in finding a home for every child and a child for every home. Instead, the WCHS and similar organizations guided by the purpose of finding homes for children and completing families found themselves locating permanent homes for many, building permanent child-care institutions of their own, and creating a child-saving movement that celebrated some types of knowledge while creating silences around others. Then, as now, the underlying causes and consequences of homelessness, neglect, and abuse found no single or simple solution in adoption. But then, as now, adoption did provide relief, support, affection, and interwoven histories—in short, kinship and community—to thousands of people. Unfairly, what adoption does so well remains shackled by what it cannot and never realistically could do—meet all the needs of a nation whose social policies continue to demonstrate its ambivalence about its poor and dependent members.

NOTES

1. As a measure of the public's continued concern about adoption and foster care, I counted seventy-four articles on those topics in the *New York Times* for 1998, including a three-part, front-page series.

2. For groundbreaking work on the impact of social values on adoptive families, see H. David Kirk, *Shared Fate: A Theory of Adoption and Mental Health* (London: Free Press, 1964). Kirk's *Adoptive Kinship: A Modern Institution in Need of Reform* (Toronto: Butterworths, 1981) reflects on, revises, and extends the concepts in *Shared Fate*. Katarina Wegar and others have pointed out that adoption in American society is a "creature of the public"—that is, it is shaped by social needs and expectations (Wegar, *Adoption, Identity, and Kinship: The Debate over Sealed Birth Records* [New Haven: Yale University Press, 1997], 6–8, 40–41, 47). See also Judith S. Modell, *Kinship with Strangers: Adoption and Interpretations of Kinship in American Culture* (Berkeley: University of California Press, 1994), 2–3, 19–21, 226. E. Wayne Carp's *Family Matters: Secrecy and Disclosure in*

the History of Adoption (Cambridge: Harvard University Press, 1998), which focuses on the development of secrecy in adoption, is also the most complete history of adoption in the United States.

3. Michel Foucault, *The History of Sexuality*, vol. 1, *An Introduction* (New York: Vintage Books, 1980), 104–5.

4. Patricia Hart, "A Home for Every Child, a Child for Every Home: Relinquishment and Adoption at the Washington Children's Home Society, 1896–1915" (Ph.D. diss., Washington State University, 1997). To protect the privacy of individuals, the case numbers have been coded, and the coded list is available through the WCHS, according to society policy.

5. Michael Grossberg, *Governing the Hearth: Law and the Family in Nineteenth-Century America* (Chapel Hill: University of North Carolina Press, 1985), 237–59. Grossberg contends that a republican family model replaced a hierarchical, patriarchal model after the American Revolution. Authority for raising children was transferred to women, and children were seen more as potential citizens, less as male possessions. By extension, rights residing in biologic parents generally were diluted, creating the possibility for surrogate parents to acquire custody. For a succinct history of adoption in the United States, see the Introduction to this volume.

6. Historians disagree about the acceptability of adoption to child savers and later to professional social workers. For example, whether an unmarried woman should raise her child was an issue under intense dispute during the Progressive era. Regina G. Kunzel has stated that evangelical amateur child savers such as those running the Florence Crittenton homes favored unwed mothers keeping their babies because they hoped the baby would help regenerate the mother. She argues that professional social workers increasingly favored adoption because they subscribed to the "best interest of the child" doctrine (*Fallen Women, Problem Girls: Unmarried Mothers and the Professionalization of Social Work, 1890–1945* [New Haven: Yale University Press, 1993], 127–29). Disputing Kunzel, E. Wayne Carp contends that lack of laws or regulation governing adoption made it easy for unmarried mothers to abandon their babies to amateur philanthropic organizations during the nineteenth century. He argues that early-twentieth-century professional social workers very reluctantly separated unwed mother and child and generally opposed adoption ("Professional Social Workers, Adoption, and the Problem of Illegitimacy, 1915–1945," *Journal of Policy History* 6, no. 3 [1994]: 161–83). I contend that the matter was anything but settled even among evangelical Protestant adoption advocates. Some ministers working with Children's Home Society agencies believed that the mother had a moral responsibility to stay with the child through the first year, and others thought that she should breast-feed her baby only for a few weeks or months. The WCHS argued that a woman's wage was insufficient to support a child at board. Regarding child savers' ambivalence about separation of unwed mother and her child, see Linda Gordon, *Heroes of Their Own Lives: The Politics and History of Family Violence, Boston 1880–1960* (New York: Viking, 1988), 101–3.

7. LeRoy Ashby, *Endangered Children: Dependency, Neglect, and Abuse in American History* (New York: Twayne, 1997), 2; Stephanie Coontz, *The Way We Never Were: American Families and the Nostalgia Trap* (New York: Basic Books, 1992), 10–11.

8. "The Greatest Act in the Administration of President Roosevelt," *Washington Children's Home Finder* (hereafter cited as *WCHF*) 12 (Feb. 1909): 3; "Conference on the Care of Dependent Children," *WCHF* 12 (Feb. 1909): 3–4; "Echoes from the Children's

Conference at Washington, D.C.," *WCHF* 12 (Mar. 1909): 3–5. Roosevelt supported suffrage for women but advocated a deeply gendered role division between the sexes in society: Motherhood came before all else for women, in his view. Roosevelt relentlessly attacked the use of birth control of any sort by white women (quoted in Linda Gordon, *Woman's Body, Woman's Right: A Social History of Birth Control in America* [New York: Grossman, 1976], 136). See also Theodore Roosevelt, "Women's Rights; and the Duties of Both Men and Women," *Outlook* 100 (1912): 262–66; "Mr. Roosevelt's Views on Race Suicide," *Ladies' Home Journal*, Feb. 1906, 21; and "Race Decadence," *Outlook* 97 (Apr. 8, 1911): 763–69. See also "A Premium on Race Suicide," *Outlook* 105 (Sept. 20, 1911): 163–64; "The Greatest American Problem," *Delineator* 70 (June 1907): 966–67. See also Elaine Tyler May, *Barren in the Promised Land: Childless Americans and the Pursuit of Happiness* (New York: Basic Books, 1995), 78–93; Ethel Wadsworth Cartland, "Childless Americans," *Outlook* 105 (Nov. 15, 1913): 585–87.

9. W. D. Wood, "The Homeless Child," address delivered at the WCHS annual meeting, June 24, 1906, reprinted in *WCHF* 10 (July 1906): 4; H. D. Brown, "History of the Washington Children's Home Society," unpublished manuscript, [1930], Children's Home Society of Washington Archives, Seattle, Washington, chap. 3, [7–8]; Ashby, *Endangered Children*, 35–54; Marilyn Irvin Holt, *The Orphan Trains: Placing out in America* (Lincoln: University of Nebraska Press, 1992).

10. Wood, "Homeless Child," 4, 7, 8.

11. Ibid., 8.

12. Hart, "A Home for Every Child," 4–6.

13. Brown, "History," chap. 11, [34–35]; "Annual Report," *WCHF* 14 (June 1910), 6; "Child Welfare Crisis," *WCHF* 18 (Jan.–Feb. 1915): 3; "Comparative Statistics," *WCHF* 10 (Aug. 1906): 6–8. In 1906, 224 of the 874 dependent children in the state came into the care of the WCHS, which already had 800 wards. Another 300 children, most of them reportedly Roman Catholic, were cared for by the House of Good Shepherd, Mt. Carmel Mission, the Brothers' School of Seattle, the Tacoma St. Joseph's Orphanage, and the Tacoma City Orphanage. The rest were cared for by the Baptist Missionary Children's Home of Burton; the Parkland Lutheran Children's Home; the Martha and Maria Orphan Asylum, Poulsbo; the King County Industrial School, Mercer Island; the Home of the Friendless and St. Joseph's Orphanage, Spokane; and the Woolsey Orphan Home, Tacoma.

14. "A Trinity of Reasons Why," included (1) because it is the best way; (2) because it is the least expensive, and (3) because it is efficient (*WCHF* supplement 12 [Feb. 1909]: 9). On different values placed on children in American history, see Viviana A. Zelizer, *Pricing the Priceless Child: The Changing Social Value of Children* (New York: Basic Books, 1985), esp. 169–207. See also "Emergency Fund," *WCHF* 13 (Sept. 1909): 3; "Average Cost per Child for Permanent Care," *WCHF* 19 (Feb. 1916): 3; and "Misconception," *WCHF* 10 (May 1907): 7.

The Reverend O. P. Christian, state superintendent of the Children's Home Finding and Aid Society of Idaho, saw Children's Home Society agencies in the West providing special services to children who lived in areas remote from church and school, kept "captive" in filthy, vermin-infected homes, where they were early taught to drink. Children's Home Societies reached into the rural areas through advisory boards ("The Child-Placing Method Peculiarly Adopted to Western Methods" [comments of Rev. Christian], *WCHF* 13 [June 1909]: 1). Ashby points out that mothers' pensions, which evolved into Aid to Dependent Children in the 1930s, were woefully inadequate to meet needs and were awarded on "vague 'moral fitness' issues" (*Endangered Children,* 112). For a discussion of maternalism, the family wage, and mothers' pensions, see Linda Gordon, *Pitied but Not Entitled: Single Mothers and the History of Welfare* (New York: Free Press, 1994), chap. 3.

15. Gordon, *Heroes.*

16. "Why You Should Take a Child to Bring Up," *WCHF* 15 (Oct. 1911): 10.

17. Gordon, *Pitied but Not Entitled,* 6. Causes of relinquishment stated in 289 cases break down as follows: illegitimacy, 33 percent; inability to care for child due to death of one parent, 19 percent; abandonment, 18 percent; unstated, 8 percent; death of both parents, 6 percent; divorce, 6 percent; neglect/abuse, 5 percent; placed with relative, 3 percent; destitution, 2 percent; parent mentally unable to care for child, less than 1 percent (Norbert MacDonald, *Distant Neighbors: A Comparative History of Seattle and Vancouver* [Lincoln: University of Nebraska Press, 1987], 58–60). In 1896, the year the WCHS began its work in Seattle, the city was at the bottom of a severe nationwide depression, with widespread unemployment in the building trades. Seattle was also affected by the national depression of 1908–9, when the value of construction dropped precipitously. The city's population nevertheless continued to increase dramatically (MacDonald, *Distant Neighbors,* 44–45, 58–63).

Seattle's economy diversified early, and only about 5 percent of the city's working male population was directly engaged in extractive, resource-based industries. However, 36.2 percent of birth fathers (45 of 124 men whose employment status was stated) were coal miners, general laborers, farm workers, loggers, railroad workers, or mill workers. Another 28.2 percent did not indicate employment status, but some of them certainly were unemployed workers in these occupations (MacDonald, *Distant Neighbors,* 75–76).

18. While 47 percent of women whose status was recorded for the years 1896–1915 stated that they worked for wages, census figures for Washington State in 1900 indicate that only 13 percent of all females at least ten years old were gainfully employed (U.S. Census, 1900, 2:88–89). Working women were overrepresented among relinquishing mothers because they were poor; however, the census also certainly undercounted working women. For an analysis of the undercount of working women in the census, see Christine E. Bose, "Devaluing Women's Work: The Undercount of Women's Employment in 1900 and 1980," in *Hidden Aspects of Women's Work,* ed. Christine Bose, Roslyn Feldberg, and Natalie Sokoloff (New York: Praeger, 1987), 95–115. Bose estimates an actual labor force participation of women in 1900 between 48.5 and 56.7 percent based on a formula measuring farm labor, factory outwork, and gainful employment at home.

Gordon, *Pitied but Not Entitled,* 6, 21–22. Divorce and drinking were the two commonly cited conditions blamed for child dependency, but divorce, unlike drink, was difficult to get. Divorce did not produce anywhere near the number of homeless children for which it was blamed. At the WCHS, divorce was cited in only 6 percent of the relinquishments.

19. "Children Clothed with Flour Sacks," *WCHF* 13 (Oct. 1909): 3.

20. WCHS case nos. 1508, 710; "Help for a Poor Father," *WCHF* 6 (June 1904): 4.

21. Foucault, *History of Sexuality,* 104–5; Archibald W. Frater and Lilburn Merrill, "Why Children Go Wrong: Court Methods, Mother's Pensions and Community

Dangers," and Lilburn Merrill, "Physical and Mental Conditions," both in *Annual Report of the Seattle Juvenile Court for 1913* (Seattle, 1914), 4–5, 30–43.

22. See, for example, in "Training is Everything," *WCHF* 6 (Jan. 1904): 4; Joel E. Field, "Heredity Does Not Always Tell," *WCHF* 9 (May 1906): 4; "Heredity and Environment," *WCHF* 10 (Nov. 1906): 5; "Dr. Bernardo's Opinion," *WCHF* 11 (Dec. 1907): 9; "An Important Question," *WCHF* 14 (Feb. 1911): 4; "Heredity and Environment," *WCHF* 11 (Nov. 1907): 11; "Heredity versus Environment," *WCHF* 18 (Mar.–Apr. 1915): 6; "Adopted Children," *WCHF* 6 (Apr. 1904): 1; "'Take This Child Away and Nurse It for Me, and I Will Give Thee Thy Wages,'" *WCHF* 6 (Apr. 1904): 2; "A Woman's Miracle," *WCHF* 6 (Apr. 1904): 3; "Everyday Children," *WCHF* 9 (Jan. 1906): 4; "Not Perfect Children," *WCHF* 9 (Mar. 1906): 6; and N.t., *WCHF* 14 (Mar. 1911): 8.

23. Children were brought to the receiving home at Seattle or Spokane in most cases. Children were temporarily lodged in private homes when the receiving home was full or when only temporary aid was needed. Infants were boarded in private homes instead of at the Spokane receiving home but were kept in the nursery at the Seattle receiving home ("The Annual Report of the State Superintendent," *WCHF* 12 [June 1908]: 4).

24. "Children of the Coal Mines," *WCHF* 14 (Dec. 1910): 6; "Black Diamond's Grit," *WCHF* 8 (Dec. 1910): 7; "Children Clothed with Flour Sacks," *WCHF* 13 (Oct. 1909): 3. The mining districts supplied the dependent children, and mine owners made regular donations of coal to the receiving home. See also "Forced to Harvest Sagebrush to Provide Themselves with Needed Fuel" (originally published in the *Yakima Herald*), *WCHF* 13 (Feb. 1910): 5; "Motherless and Fatherless," *WCHF* 9 (Sept. 1905): 6; "In a Better Home," *WCHF* 12 (July 1908): 4–5; N.t., *WCHF* 14 (Mar. 1911): 8; "Taxpayers' Travelers," *WCHF* 16 (Feb. 1913): 5.

25. "Soliloquy of a Big Boy," *WCHF* 12 (Jan. 1909): 8–9.

26. "Seattle Receiving Home, through the Eyes of a Boy," *WCHF* 17 (Sept. 1913): 7.

27. "Christmas at the Home," *WCHF* 13 (Jan. 1910): 5–6; "Christmas Babies," *WCHF* 7 (Jan. 1905): 1; "Fourth of July," *WCHF* 14 (July 1910): 8; "Glorious Fourth," *WCHF* (July–Aug. 1911): 5.

28. Venereal disease was on the steady rise in the years under study here, so testing for infection was not an idle gesture. The WCHS advocated registering every case in the state and treating the infection like an epidemic of smallpox, as infection was so widespread ("The Sixteenth Annual Report of the Washington Children's Home Society," *WCHF* 16 [June 1912]: 9; "The Nineteenth Annual Report of the Washington Children's Home Society," *WCHF* 19 [Sept. 1915]: 5). Venereal disease also contributed to a drop in fertility during these years (see May, *Barren*, 62–63).

29. "Nineteenth Annual Report," 5.

30. "To Applicants for Children," *WCHF* 12 (Feb. 1909): 8.

31. Robert Griswold, *Fatherhood in America: A History* (New York: Basic Books, 1993), 69. See also E. Anthony Rotundo, *American Manhood: Transformations in Masculinity from the Revolution to the Modern Era* (New York: Basic Books, 1993), esp. chaps. 9, 10. Julie Berebitsky cites articles in popular magazines that portray women as on the "verge of insanity" over their childlessness ("Redefining 'Real' Motherhood: The Experience of Adoptive Mothers, 1880–1940" [paper presented at the Tenth Berkshire Conference on the History of Women, Chapel Hill, June 9, 1996], 6). Berebitsky's study of unpublished sources shows "adoptive mothers to be women who just wanted children, who

just wanted to be mothers . . . their motivation was not a burning desire to do their patriotic duty by rescuing a child" (14). See WCHS case nos. 1009, 1012, 2012, 1113, 1315. See also "Wanted—A Home," *WCHF* 11 (Oct. 1907): 11; Jean K. Baird, "In Search of a Mother" (reprinted from the *Wisconsin Children's Home Finder*), *WCHF* 12 (Nov. 1908): 5–6.

32. WCHS case nos. 1414, 1807, 206, 1011, 1206, 2811, 1013, 1212, 210, 409, 1911, 2114, 1514, 613, 1212, 112, 713, 2008, 1310, 599, 903, 703.

33. "Workers' Conference," *WCHF* 14 (Jan. 1911): 7. This article also claimed to have "documents" (presumably referring to adoption papers) made out for 90 percent of the children in WCHS care. WCHS case nos. 199, 107, 410, 1507, 1811, 1409, 509, 2109.

34. *WCHF* 6 (Feb. 1904): 4.

35. *WCHF* 7 (Aug. 1904): 3.

36. *WCHF* 6 (Feb. 1904): 3; 11 (Aug.–Sept. 1907): 11. For other letters from adoptive parents and children, see *WCHF* 12 (Aug. 1908): 7; 9 (July 1905): 6; 12 (Dec. 1908): 11; 6 (June 1904): 3–4; 5 (Dec. 1902): 4; 6 (May 1904): 3; 6 (Mar. 1904): 4; 7 (Dec. 1904): 4; 10 (Aug. 1906): 10–11; 11 (July 1907): 7; 7 (July 1904): 3; 13 (Feb. 1910): 9; 11 (May 1908): 10, 11; 7 (Sept. 1904): 3; 12 (July 1908): 10–11; 16 (Mar. 1913): 8; 12 (Jan. 1909): 11; 12 (Sept. 1908): 11; "The Baby and the Kodak," *WCHF* 10 (Oct. 1906): 7.

37. *WCHF* 11 (May 1908): 10–11.

38. E. Wayne Carp has identified three periods defining WCHS policy regarding the society's willingness to divulge identifying and nonidentifying information to adults. The first, from the society's founding to 1955, represents a period when such information was made available. The second period, lasting until about 1970, was a period of transition, when despite state confidentiality law, caseworkers still divulged such information on a discretionary basis. After 1970, the policy hardened, and identifying information was never given unless by court order. Eighty-one adults or their relatives or appointees contacted the society, or 28 percent of 289 cases, which does not take into account the deaths of children. This percentage closely coincides with the average calculated in Carp's study spanning nine decades ("The Sealed Adoption Records Controversy in Historical Perspective: The Case of the Children's Home Society of Washington, 1895–1988," *Journal of Sociology and Social Welfare* 19 [June 1992]: 27).

Adoption Agencies and the Search for the Ideal Family, 1918–1965

Brian Paul Gill

Introduction: The New Selectivity in Adoption Practice

Earlier essays in this volume have described the work of Charles Loring Brace's pioneering agency, the New York Children's Aid Society (CAS), which began placing children in substitute families in 1853, at almost exactly the same time that state legislatures began passing the first modern adoption laws. The CAS was the ancestor of the modern adoption agency. Few of the children placed by the CAS were legally adopted, and some were viewed primarily as inexpensive laborers, but many became full members of their new families, adopted in fact if not in law.[1] Nevertheless, although Brace's intentions may have been noble, his agency's efforts were perhaps too dependent on the goodwill of foster parents, and some children were placed in homes where they were neglected, abused, or exploited.[2] Around the turn of the century, a new generation of agencies sought to avoid such tragedies by establishing systematic screening processes for prospective foster/adoptive parents. These agencies aimed to select parents who would not abuse children, who had the material means to support children, and who would provide a minimal level of schooling and religious observance.[3] The standards were not rigorous, but they were adopted with the clear aim of preventing harm to children.

Meanwhile, a deep cultural shift in the valuation of children (ably chronicled by Viviana Zelizer)[4] was beginning to affect the characteristics of the children placed and would soon lead to another dramatic change in agency standards for adoptive parents. In the nineteenth century, most of the children who were placed out into substitute families were old enough to begin making an immediate contribution to the family economy. Beginning around World War I, however, children were increasingly desired for reasons more sentimental than economic, generally by adults who were otherwise childless. These prospective parents wanted children who would be as fully as possible their own, beginning in infancy. The demand for babies to adopt began climbing in the 1920s and exploded with the culture of domesticity after World War II.[5]

Excess demand for young children gave adoption agencies a new opportunity, beginning in the 1920s, to be selective in the choice of adoptive parents. Selectivity was consistent with the interests of agency workers, who hoped to raise their professional status by demonstrating particular expertise in the creation of adoptive families. Indeed, the professional expertise of the social worker in the adoption agency was the foundation of the worker's right to choose adoptive parents: "The only basis on which adoption agencies can . . . ask for community backing of their right to make ultimate decisions about the families with which children are placed is demonstrated competence," declared Ruth Brenner, a leading adoption worker, in 1951.[6]

To demonstrate competence, the agencies moved away from the turn-of-the-century emphasis on preventing harm to children, instead aiming higher: they began to claim a unique ability to create the "best" adoptive families. In 1951, explaining the market reality that permitted agency perfectionism, two agency workers described the caseworker's job as selecting "those couples who have the best potentials as parents, recognizing the ten to one ratio of supply and demand in applicants and babies for adoption."[7] A policy statement of the Children's Home Society of California announced the agency's responsibility for choosing "the best possible home" for each child.[8] The 1958 *Standards* of the Child Welfare League of America (CWLA) implored agencies to study enough applicants to guarantee "an optimum choice for each child."[9] Merely excluding applicants who would make bad parents was not enough. A paper presented at the 1960 National Conference of Social Welfare made clear the agencies' perfectionist ambitions, declaring that the "major concern in adoptive placements is not with psychopathology, rehabilitation, or financial need, but with contriving the best possible parent-child relationships by selecting parents from a rather large group of applicants. . . . The social agency has the responsibility of selecting the best qualified couples."[10] In sum, the adoption agencies came to believe that they had a responsibility to use their professional expertise not merely to screen out bad applicants but also to create only the "best" adoptive families.

The Normal as Normative

Agencies assumed that the "best" families were those who were most "normal."[11] A 1933 U.S. Children's Bureau pamphlet declared that all children should have "a chance to live in a normal family group"; a quarter-century later, the National Conference of Catholic Charities echoed that sentiment, stating that "the objective in adoption procedure is to provide a normal home life for a child."[12] Dorothy Hutchinson, an adoption worker whose 1943 volume, *In Quest of*

Foster Parents, was the most widely read professional text of the period, maintained that the "selection of foster homes has at best been based on the assumption that although there is no such thing as a perfect home there is such thing as a normal family." She added, "Normality is something that is hard to define, yet easy to feel and see. In it is assumed a wide range of behavior and attitude, not a narrowly fixed concept." Although Hutchinson typified the common agency position that normality was "the crux of the matter" in selecting applicants for parenthood, her assertion that it defined "a wide range of behavior and attitude" was misleading. Hutchinson and many other agency workers devoted considerable effort to defining normality narrowly.[13]

As this essay will demonstrate, between the 1920s and the 1960s, adoption agencies employed three principles in the service of creating the "best"—and most "normal"—adoptive families. First, agencies sought to create adoptive families that resembled biological families as closely as possible. Second, agencies excluded disabled children from adoption. Third, agencies took a new interest in the inner lives of prospective parents, aiming to choose only those who were psychologically ideal. In concert, these three principles involved the pursuit of an aesthetic ideal of the family, a pursuit that was perhaps the most ambitious program of social engineering (in its perfectionism, if not its scale) seen in twentieth-century America. Indeed, adoption agencies pursued the creation of aesthetically ideal families even when that goal was in tension with the interests of children waiting for adoption.

Simulating the Biological Family

The quest for normality that followed the new selectivity on the part of adoption agencies involved, first, a systematic effort to create adoptive families on the model of the biological family. During the Progressive era, by contrast, agencies had sought to place children in homes that met uniform and relatively objective standards of quality, regardless of whether the merged family looked like a "normal" biological family. The notion that adoptive families ought to be as much like biological families as possible was rapidly assimilated by adoption professionals after World War I and went largely unchallenged until the 1950s. As one agency director argued in 1939, when a child could not be cared for by his own parents, "the best substitute for his own home would be another family home resembling as closely as possible what his home would have been."[14] Nearly two decades later, the CWLA, the adoption agencies' umbrella professional organization, reaffirmed this view, arguing that the adoptive relationship ideally "approximates as nearly as possible the relationship between natural parent and child."[15]

The agencies' efforts to simulate the biological family went unexamined and unexplained. The presumption in favor of the biological model was so pervasive that an explanation was thought unnecessary. Although they were in the business of creating nonbiological families, adoption workers assumed that the biological family was the appropriate model for the adoptive family. The goodness of the biological family required no explanation because it was "natural," apparently ordained by God. When adoption workers talked about the challenges of "playing God,"[16] they assumed that their role in adoptive families resembled God's role in biological families. As anthropologist Judith Modell has pointed out, Americans have commonly viewed adoptive families in biological terms: "people in a culture in which parenthood is created by birth—a biological fact—understand a parenthood that is created by law—a contractual arrangement . . . by making the constructed relationship as much like the biological as possible."[17] Adoption agencies shared this cultural vision, and they had the power to enforce it.

Matching

In practice, the pursuit of the biological family model involved an attempt to match children's characteristics to those of the adoptive parents. Between World War I and the mid-1950s, adoption agencies sought to create families in which parents and child were physically, ethnically, racially, religiously, and intellectually alike. In 1910 one agency director provided the definitive statement of the more general matching philosophy that would prevail in later decades, declaring that "there are first-class, second-class and third-class children, and there are first-class, second-class and third-class homes."[18]

Florence Clothier, a psychiatrist at the New England Home for Little Wanderers and an influential 1940s adoption expert, justified matching by explaining, "As the child grows up and approaches maturity, it will be easier for him and for the adoptive parents if his appearance and constitutional type are not too foreign to that of the family of which he is a part." In Clothier's view, the benefits to adoptive parents and children resulting from similarity justified matching across a wide range of variables, including race ("The racial antecedents of the child and of the adoptive parents should be the same or as like as possible"), physical appearance ("Physical characteristics of the true mother and father should be borne in mind when adoptive parents are being considered for a child"), and personality ("the temperaments of the child's true parents should not be in complete contradiction to the temperaments of the adoptive parents"). Elsewhere, Clothier also advocated matching the intellectual capacities of parents and child. Even the national origins of the child's ancestors were relevant: Clothier suggested that although "there are no scientific data on the point, and though heredity may play but a slight role, there may be some validity to the lay concept that breeding or cultural tradition will show itself." She disapproved, for example, of the placement of a light-skinned, freckle-faced boy with olive-skinned Italian-American parents.[19]

By midcentury, matching of parents and child had become standard practice in adoption agencies nationwide. The three characteristics that received the most attention were intelligence, religion, and race. With regard to the first category, a 1922–23 U.S. Children's Bureau survey of ten adoption agencies in six states reported, "All the agencies placed Catholic children in Catholic homes, Jewish children in Jewish homes, and Protestant children in Protestant homes."[20] An infant's religion was defined by reference to the religious affiliation of her biological mother, and religious matching was sometimes enforced even against the wishes of the biological mother.[21] Matching by religion remained standard adoption agency practice through the mid-1950s.[22]

The CWLA's influential *Standards for Organizations Providing Foster Family Care* (1933) advocated matching by intelligence, prescribing, "Overplacement (placement of mentally dull or backward children with unusually intelligent and cultivated foster parents) as well as underplacement (placement of bright children in homes with little mental stimulus or cultural opportunity) should be avoided."[23] Confronted with a limited ability to measure the child's intelligence directly, agencies sometimes simply assumed that "it is more likely that a child of superior [biological] parents will be superior than will a child of dull parents," making it "common practice" to place the child of unusually intelligent biological parents with unusually intelligent adoptive parents, according to a CWLA survey conducted in the late 1950s.[24] At the other end of the scale, seventy-five of the agencies responding to the CWLA's inquiry reported "that they place children of less-than-average intelligence with parents who also have limited intelligence."[25]

Racial matching was the most firmly institutionalized form of matching. In 1944–45, a sample of ninety-one agency placements in California found not a single transracial placement.[26] A decade later, a 1956 CWLA survey reported unequivocally that "agencies are not placing Negro children in white homes or white children in Negro homes."[27] The power of the racial matching ethic is demonstrated by the fact that it trumped other forms of matching when conflicts occurred. For example, a Jewish adoption agency in New York occasionally acquired custody of the children of Jewish mothers and black fathers. Because it could not find many black Jewish adoptive families, it was faced with a choice between racial and religious matching. The agency chose racial matching, believing it had a "duty to place such children in good Negro Christian homes."[28]

Although religion, intelligence, and race were the most prominent of the matched characteristics, agencies hoped to match children and parents across a laundry list of other variables, as Clothier's comments suggested. In 1950, for example, the regulations of the California Department of Social Welfare declared not only that the "racial background of the adopting parents and the child should be similar" and that the "child shall be placed with adoptive parents whose religious faith is the same as his own or that of his parents" but also that the "personality, temperament, education, intelligence and cultural level, stature, and coloring of the adoptive parents shall be considered in relation to the personality, temperament, physical appearance, coloring, cultural background, and potential mental ability of the child."[29] In 1956 the CWLA surveyed the adoption practices of 270 agencies that accounted for about half of all agency adoptions nationwide. The survey found overwhelming support for matching on many variables. Large majorities of agencies reported that they considered it important to match by "religious background," "racial background," "temperamental needs," "educational background," "physical resemblance to child," "cultural background," "nationality background," and "level of intelligence and intellectual potential."[30] As the director of the Boston Children's Friend Society summed up in 1950, matching was "an endeavor to have the child as nearly as possible resemble the adoptive parents."[31]

Matching Policies and Child Welfare

Policies requiring racial and religious matching, which prevailed for most of the century, delayed or prevented the placement of many children. To be sure, the agencies tried to justify matching in terms of child welfare, arguing that dark-skinned children would be out of place in fair-skinned families and that Catholic children belonged in Catholic homes. To the extent that matching was intended simply to recognize the individual needs of individual children, such arguments made sense. But the agencies were obsessed with matching for its own sake. The notion that "third-class children" belong in "third-class homes" appealed to an aesthetic ideal of what a family should be, not to a concern for the best interests of the children. While agencies turned away prospective parents who were white Jews or Protestants, children who were Catholic or black often languished in institutions and boarding homes.[32] If placement in a permanent adoptive family was best for the child—the consensus view among social welfare professionals since the turn of the century—then the agencies' long-standing commitment to matching did not serve the interests of children.

The limited flexibility of the agencies' screening criteria in the face of dramatic differences in supply and demand likewise suggested that the primary agency goal was the creation of ideal families. Higher standards for the adoptive parents of healthy, white (non-Catholic) babies were made possible by the increasing demand for such children after 1920 and especially after 1940. It soon became clear, however, that many children in need of adoptive parents were not healthy, white infants and consequently were not in great demand. Many agencies, for example, had great difficulty finding enough homes for black children.[33] Despite the oversupply of black children in need of parents, however, black applicants for parenthood found it difficult to adopt through agencies. A CWLA-sponsored study of black adoptions through a major agency in Pittsburgh in the 1950s found that less than 20 percent of black applicants completed adoptions, compared to 40 percent of white applicants. The single most frequently cited reason for the rejection or withdrawal of black applicants was a failure to demonstrate infertility, a matter of dubious relationship to child welfare. The application process remained both extensive and intrusive: successful black applicants had to attend an average of 12.7 interviews before completing an adoption.[34] In the early 1960s, agencies in one major metropolitan area continued to reject a quarter of black applicants despite the backlog of black children available for adoption. Among these agencies, the proportion of black applicants who ultimately adopted was no higher than the proportion of white applicants who ultimately adopted, despite the dramatic difference in the availability of infants.[35]

While putting obstacles in the way of permanent placement of minority children, agencies were also showing little respect for the de facto parenting relationships that often arose between children and adults who accepted boarding money to care for children (known today as foster parents). Adoption agencies of the period usually refused to consider boarding parents for adoptive placements: parents who accepted money to care for a child were not considered good enough to become permanent adoptive parents and were not carefully matched on the same array of variables used to create adoptive families.[36] Indeed, a number of legal cases indicated the adoption agencies' willingness to remove a child from a stable relationship with a boarding family because the boarding parents failed to meet the idealized standards for adoptive parents.[37] To be sure, the agencies claimed to be acting in the children's interest: they wanted to place the children in "better" families. But their pursuit of the "best" sometimes blinded the agencies to the direct harm to the child that could result from disrupting an existing parenting relationship.

Excluding "Defective" Children

Adoption agencies were strongly influenced by hereditarian notions of child development. In early-twentieth-century America, the "nature versus nurture" debate was especially heated: an optimistic reform movement aimed at improving social environments coexisted uneasily with an intense public interest in eugenics. Many social workers resolved the tension between these two competing ideological views by concluding that although "normal" people could be affected by positive environmental influences, genetics determined the fate of "defectives."[38] This resolution had implications for professional adoption practice that would endure for half a century.

Not all of the children turned over to the agencies were matched to an approved set of adoptive parents. Before an infant became eligible for adoptive placement, the agency determined whether the child was adoptable. Not only would-be adopters but also would-be adoptees had to meet agency approval. The agencies regarded children with disabilities as "defective" and, according to eugenic theory, beyond help. Prospective adopters, by contrast, had proven themselves—by meeting agency screening standards—to be nondefective. In the view of the agencies, these prospective parents were therefore entitled to nondefective children. "Defective" children did not belong in ideally "normal" families and were therefore ineligible for adoptive placement.

From the end of World War I until the end of World War II, agency authorities spoke with one voice against the placement of children with disabilities.[39] In 1919 Edmond Butler, executive secretary of New York's Catholic Home Bureau, bluntly declared, "No child should be placed out who is suffering from any physical or mental defect."[40] Two years later, a major text by two prominent adoption workers asserted, "There will always be a certain number of children whose heredity is such that the agency will question whether they will prove sufficiently normal for family and community life."[41] One often-cited commentator likewise declared in 1934, "No placement for adoption should be permitted until a reasonable effort has been made to ascertain whether the child is suitable for adoption." Such an effort, he argued, should include investigation of various "hereditary diseases" and "the quality and social competence of the immediate relatives" as well as the child's own development and behavior. In addition, agencies should "have available the services of an adequately trained clinical psychologist, to ensure that feebleminded children shall not be adopted."[42] Similarly, Clothier argued in 1942 that some ailments should give adoption workers pause even if evidenced only in the child's biological parents: "Social workers should question carefully, but not arbitrarily rule out, the possibility of adoption of infants whose hereditary history is weighted with psychosis, feeblemindedness, epilepsy, addiction, criminality, or general emotional instability."[43] The 1949 regulations of the California Department of Social Welfare expected children available for adoption to be "suitable for adoption, from the standpoint of health, heredity, intelligence and personality."[44] Mental disabilities were the agencies' greatest concern: children with less than normal intelligence were most zealously targeted for exclusion from the adoption market as defectives.[45]

The agencies' standards for adoptability could exclude a large number of children. In 1946 the New York City welfare department referred 730 children to adoption agencies, but the agencies placed only 336 of the children, returning 276 to the department "as unsuitable for adoption."[46] The agencies' refusal to place disabled children belied any claim that their paramount concern was the welfare of the children. Although a few agency workers tried to argue that such children were better off in institutions than in adoptive homes, some conceded that the policy was designed not for the children but for the prospective parents. The agencies sought to provide their customers—adoptive parents—a flawless product. As Joseph Reid, executive director of the CWLA, noted in 1957, it had not been long since agencies "were convinced and attempted to convince the public that they could guarantee them a perfect child; that by coming to an agency, adoptive parents could be sure that the child was without physical, emotional or mental defect, that his heredity was sound and adopting a child was a far less risky procedure than having one normally."[47] If excluding disabled children did not serve the children's interests, it did serve the agencies' interest in creating families that met aesthetic standards. In the agencies' view, "normal" families did not have "defective" children.

Good Parenting as Psychology

Beginning in the late 1920s, the intensification of agency efforts to create "normal" families involved increased attention not only to the biological family model and to the characteristics of prospective adoptees but also to the psychological makeup of prospective parents. For the agencies, normality meant that applicants had to fit a psychological model defined in terms strongly reflecting the prevailing ideology of the family. As discussed subsequently, applicants were expected to be "normal" in age, in motivation to adopt, and in gender roles. Despite protestations to the contrary, the narrowness of Hutchinson's vision of normality is strikingly illustrated by her examples of the range of permissible eccentricity, which included a prospective mother "who smokes and serves a cocktail" and a would-be father "who cuts the grass on Sunday attired only in shorts." Although she was willing to accept these kinds of applicants as "families with individuality and color," Hutchinson frowned on true eccentricity, opposing placement "in families regarded [in their communities] as 'queer' or too far 'off center.'"[48]

Assessing the normality of the psychological makeup of applicants for adoption required a new attention to their private lives. One agency worker, for example, declared in 1930 that adoption agencies had a responsibility to "*know* the home—not being satisfied with the outer picture [it] presents, but striving to evaluate the complex inner life which we call personality."[49] By midcentury, the importance of the "complex inner life" of the applicants had become conventional wisdom. Strongly influenced by Freud's view of the significance of unconscious drives, adoption workers were fond of pointing out that a full understanding of personality required a look behind a client's public demeanor and stated motivations. As another agency worker argued in 1937, "Some of the deepest inner aspects of intimate family life will often only be glimpsed by the worker and frequently the foster parents themselves are neither articulate about themselves nor even conscious of what motivates their actions."[50]

Parental Motives

One point of entry into the unconscious emotional lives of applicants was an examination of their motivation to adopt. In 1938, for example, a Louisiana adoption worker declared that "the motive behind an adoption is more important by far that even the social and economic situation of the adoptive parents."[51] A few years later, Clothier argued that applicants' motives were often unconscious ones: "It is the responsibility of the skilled social worker to understand and to evaluate not only the superficial motives that the adoptive parents present, but also the deep, underlying needs that have driven them to attempt to work out their inner dissatisfactions through the adoption of a baby."[52] By 1946 the significance of motives was so widely accepted that Brenner, of New York's Free Synagogue Child Adoption Committee, could declare unequivocally, "The unconscious motivation for the adoption of a baby is by far the most important factor for its failure or success."[53]

The list of unacceptable motives for adoption was extensive. Summing up a number of unacceptable reasons for adoption, Abraham Simon, a longtime St. Louis adoption worker, implored agencies to ask, "Is the drive to adopt quite free of desperate attempts to still the pain of childlessness, or to abort mourning over the death of a loved child, or to counteract distress stemming from other traumatic or depriving life experiences, or to solve some other personal and social problems, as for example, 'keeping up with the Joneses' in children as well as ranch houses, fur coats and current year's model in automobiles?" For Simon's "ideal type adoptive applicant," all of these questions would be answered in the affirmative.[54]

Agencies generally assumed that the particular (and "normal") reason a couple would choose adoption as the method of acquiring a child was their inability to bear children biologically.[55] But following the views of Freudian theorists, agencies worried that unconscious fears might cause "psychogenic" infertility. Psychogenic infertility, the agencies believed, signaled deep emotional conflicts and implied that some of the couples who applied for adoption unconsciously rejected parenting. In the 1940s and 1950s, agencies commonly imposed a requirement of infertility as a prerequisite for adoption.[56] Increasingly, they demanded a medical investigation of infertility. In 1951 one professional source reported that "most agencies have ruled out couples where no organic reason for sterility can be found."[57]

Psychological Normality: Age Limits

In addition to exploring applicants' motives for adoption, agencies used various other indicators as signals of psychological health. In the 1940s, 1950s, and 1960s, agencies reduced maximum age limits for adoptive parents, so that applicants who were much beyond their mid-thirties had little chance of adopting a child through an agency.[58] Life expectancy was not the primary reason for excluding older applicants. In 1942 Clothier explained the relationship between the age of parents and their psychological capacity for parenting, describing applicants beyond forty as "elderly":

> Elderly couples who have waited years in the hope of having a child of their own, and who finally accept it as inevitable that they cannot, must be considered carefully before they are given a child. Their routine of a well-ordered life will be interrupted, and rigid personalities, traveling in deep grooves, cannot accept a rude upheaval with complacency.

And inflexibility was not the only psychological disadvantage of couples older than "normal" biological parents, in Clothier's view: "Elderly couples who have longed for many years for a baby may, when they receive one, cling to it as an infant. They may limit its capacity for development by an oversolicitous, overprotective attitude."[59]

Clothier was unusual in attempting to explain the age restriction as a signal of psychological characteristics relevant to parenting. More commonly, agency workers simply asserted that youthful parents were "normal," without explaining why normality mattered to the welfare of the child. The age restriction reflects the use of the biological family as a model for the adoptive families being created. For example, a 1941 U.S. Children's Bureau publication argued that the

> age of a foster parent has special significance in relation to the age of the child he is adopting. The parents of a young child are most often 20 to 30 years of age, and if a foster child is to have the normal place of an own child in the lives of his foster parents it would seem desirable that the foster parents should be of approximately the same age as the natural parents.[60]

Psychological Normality: Married Life and Gender Roles

Adoption professionals insisted that adoptive parents be married couples because marriage indicated normality, and normality was regarded as synonymous with psychological health. In 1939, surveying the field, one agency director confidently reported, "All are agreed that two foster-parents are highly desirable for each child, some organizations insisting upon both as a requisite of placing." He explained, "Normality in family life and training is the aim of placing in a family, and a home cannot be considered complete or able to give entirely normal experience where one parent is missing."[61] The CWLA's 1956 survey of adoption agency practice found that fewer than 10 of the approximately 250 responding agencies were willing to consider applications by single persons, regardless of whether they were widowed, divorced, or never married.[62]

Freudian psychology supported the agencies' refusal to consider unmarried applicants. As Clothier explained, "To attain what we regard as psychosexual maturity in our culture, the child needs close association with both a mother and a father during the early years of life. Normal Oedipus development cannot occur in an environment in which one parent figure is lacking." Clothier went on to explain that a "boy has need of a father figure whose personality, by the process of identification, he can strengthen his masculinity. He has need also of a mother figure to awaken and call up his love impulses and tenderness. His relationship to his mother will serve as a prototype of his future love relationships." In Clothier's view, a "girl, too, needs happy relationships with both a mother and a father, if she is to attain a feminine identification and, in adult life, a tender relationship with a man that is not overshadowed by fear and aggression." Indeed, she believed that girls without "wholesome father-daughter" interactions often ended up as unwed mothers. Clothier concluded by returning her focus to the single adoptive parent, arguing that the "unmarried adoptive parent is in danger of investing all her (it is usually a woman) emotional interest in the child and thus smothering its emotional growth. The role of adoptive parent is easier if there is a stable marriage as a background for the interplay of feelings."[63]

Armed with psychoanalytic wisdom, adoption agencies from the 1930s through the early 1960s sought out couples with ideal marital relationships. As one professional text put it in 1939, "Nothing is of more importance to an agency in selecting its foster homes than the marital status of foster parents." The authors of the text added, "The relations existing between a man and his wife furnish valuable clues to the nature of homes."[64] The 1958 CWLA *Standards for Adoption Service* divided "criteria of capacity for adoptive parenthood" into six categories, one of which was "quality of marital relationship."[65] Brenner believed that the marital relationship was "of vital importance to the success of the adoption."[66] Hutchinson likewise decreed that the "relationship between husband and wife has crucial significance for the child to be placed." "Normality," Hutchinson added, appealing to the watchword of the era, "is what the worker is looking for."[67]

Agencies sought out couples that fit the prevailing gender norms. In 1947, for example, one agency worker declared simply, "It is important that the man be an adequate father-image and the woman an adequate mother-image."[68] Hutchinson's 1943 book was more specific, asserting that a would-be adoptive mother "who is 'down on men'[,] has little respect for them[,] and must be entirely self-sufficient reflects a degree of independence which is unfavorable from the stand-point of her relationship with her husband, the possible child to be placed, or the agency with which she is to work." By contrast, she spoke favorably of an applicant who "sounds feminine and as though she enjoyed being so, considering her collection of recipes, her cooking, her interest in children, and her pleasure in family life." More generally, Hutchinson reinforced the view that "child care is, after all, in the main a woman's job."[69] The 1958 CWLA *Standards* concurred with this view, regarding "acceptance of sex roles" as a sign of "emotional maturity" in applicants for parenthood.[70] Finally, a 1963 text asked, "Who seems to be the aggressive one and who the passive one? Do they seem to fulfill their roles in terms of proper kinds of identity? Is the man a fairly masculine person? Is the woman a feminine person?"[71] Adoption workers between the 1940s and 1960s regarded conformity to accepted gender roles as an essential ingredient of psychological health.

Short of homosexuality and divorce, perhaps the gravest sin a mother could commit against gender norms during this period was to venture into the working world. Most adoption commentators did not flinch from taking their gendered view of the world to its logical conclusion: they expected adoptive mothers to stay at home. In Simon's view, for example, a major "role" that a wife should fulfill was "homemaker"; likewise, a husband should "fulfill his social role as breadwinner."[72] Similarly, a couple consisting of an engineer husband and a homemaker wife earned Hutchinson's praise: "Both Mr. G. and Mrs. G. accept their respective masculine and feminine roles. The division of labor between them is a normal one, and they both like being what they are—a man and a woman."[73] A comprehensive 1957 study of adoptions at sixty agencies scattered around the United States found that only two of the women approved (with their husbands) to adopt healthy white infants intended to work after receiving children.[74]

Conclusion: Family Values and Child Welfare

The agencies almost never attempted to explain why the most "normal" families were the best families. They systematically confused the descriptive and evaluative meanings of *normal*. Adoption agencies drew evaluative (normative) conclusions from descriptive facts—the typical middle-class family of the postwar years was viewed as normatively good by virtue of nothing more than its typicality. Because biological children resembled biological parents, agencies assumed that adopted children should resemble adoptive parents. Because most children were not disabled, agencies assumed that disabled children should not be adopted. Because most white, middle-class, married couples followed traditional gender patterns, agencies assumed that adoptive couples should follow traditional gender patterns.

Adoption agencies not only assumed that descriptively normal families were normatively best but also failed to appreciate the distinction between creating the "best" or "normal" families on the one hand and promoting positive child welfare outcomes on the other. Agencies' definition of the ideal family was an aesthetic one. This is not to say that they defined the "best" or "normal" families in terms that were exclusively related to physical appearance, although that was one component of the definition, and adopted children were expected to look like their adoptive parents. But the agencies' aesthetic vision also included psychological, social, and cultural components. The agencies' task was aesthetic in the broadest, Platonic sense: they sought to create families that most nearly approached an idealized Form (with a capital *F*) of the family. But aesthetically ideal families and positive outcomes for children are distinct ends. In pursuing ideally "normal" adoptive families, adoption agencies often made the welfare of the child a secondary consideration to their aesthetic vision.

In consequence, the interests of certain groups of children—notably disabled children, minority children, and children with strong psychological ties to nonadoptive foster parents—were systematically slighted by various agency practices aimed at the creation of the "best" or "normal" families. Although this kind of exclusivity—with regard to disabled children as well as minority applicants and boarding parents—made little sense if the agencies' goal was to find adoptive families for as many children as possible, it followed logically if the goal was to ensure that all adoptive families met a standard of aesthetic excellence. Placing a child with less than ideal parents would have implicated the agency in the creation of a less than ideal family.

During this period, the paramount value in agency practice was the ideally "normal" family. Midcentury adoption agencies had considerable success implementing their ideal. Applicants who did not fit the agencies' profile of ideal parents—such as career women, couples over forty, single applicants, and gays and lesbians, for example—were excluded without much difficulty. Children with disabilities (especially mental disabilities) were likewise excluded from family life, at least until the mid-1940s. And by preventing the creation of families of mixed race and families of mixed religion, agencies also ensured that adopted children would not end up with the "wrong" parents. A study of adoptive families undertaken in the late 1950s confirmed that agencies were remarkably successful in establishing uniform national standards. The study involved adoptions sampled from placements made by sixty agencies in nine varied communities around the United States and found that accepted couples were remarkably similar everywhere. According to the author's "composite portrait," the typical couple adopting through an agency was married, in their mid-thirties, childless, and infertile for a clear physical reason. Neither parent had been previously married. Both parents practiced the same religion and were active in their local church. Both were on friendly terms with their families, and both remembered happy childhoods. As mentioned earlier, only two of the adoptive mothers of healthy, white infants planned to work after adopting children. The couples "seemed psychologically well within the range of the normal."[75]

To be sure, this vision of the ideal family was not an original invention of the adoption agencies. Indeed, their obsession with normality suggests exactly the opposite: rather than constructing a new ideal of family, their goal was to reflect and reinforce an existing ideal. A narrow vision of the family, derived from psychoanalytic theory and strongly imbued with traditional gender roles, permeated the academy, the professions, and popular culture alike.[76] Adoption agencies were acolytes of a widely shared cult of normality. But if adoption agencies merely borrowed their image of the ideal family, they were unique in having the power to enforce such a vision. They actively shaped new families on the conventional model and actively sought to prevent the creation of families that would deviate from the model. Agencies created adoptive families in their image of an ideally "normal" family. In sum, adoption agencies at midcentury are perhaps best understood as guardians of a conventional (white, middle-class) definition of family against the threat that was implicit in the legal creation of unnatural kinship.

NOTES

1. See Michael Patrick, Evelyn Sheets, and Evelyn Trickel, *We Are a Part of History: The Story of the Orphan Trains* (Santa Fe, N.M.: Lightning Tree, 1990), 43; and letters from foster parents quoted in Charles Loring Brace, *The Dangerous Classes of New York, and Twenty Years' Work among Them* (New York: Wynkoop and Hallenbeck, 1872), 259.

2. See, for example, Hastings Hart's account of questionable placements by the CAS, "Placing out Children in the West," *Proceedings of the National Conference of Charities and Correction* 11 (1884): 143–50. Until the mid–twentieth century, the term *foster parents* had a more general use than it does today. It described not only temporary substitute parents (who are often paid a boarding fee for children under their care) but also adoptive parents. When the term appears in this chapter, it will be used in its more general sense to mean any kind of substitute parent unless otherwise indicated. I will describe temporary substitute parents as "boarding parents."

3. See, for example, Homer Folks, "Family Life for Dependent and Wayward Children: Part I—Dependent Children," in *The Care of Dependent, Neglected, and Wayward Children*, ed. Anna Garlin Spencer and Charles W. Birtwell (Baltimore: Johns Hopkins University Press, 1894), 69–80; Hastings H. Hart, *Preventive Treatment of Neglected Children* (New York: Charities Publication Committee, 1910); Edwin D. Solenberger, "Standards of Efficiency in Boarding-out Children," *Proceedings of the National Conference of Charities and Correction* 41 (1914): 178–83; William H. Slingerland, *Child-Placing in Families* (New York: Russell Sage Foundation, 1918). For a detailed discussion of the standards for parent selection during the Progressive era, see Brian P. Gill, "The Jurisprudence of Good Parenting: The Selection of Adoptive Parents, 1894–1964" (Ph.D., diss., University of California at Berkeley, 1997), chap. 3.

4. Viviana A. Zelizer, *Pricing the Priceless Child: The Changing Social Value of Children* (New York: Basic Books, 1985).

5. National statistics show a dramatic increase in the total number of adoptions from 1944 through the late 1960s. See Michael Schapiro, *A Study of Adoption Practice* (New York: CWLA, 1956), 1:109; Kathy S. Stolley, "Statistics on Adoption in the United States," *Future of Children* 3 (spring 1993): 30. Prior to 1944, national statistics are unavailable, but all of the anecdotal evidence suggests slower but steady growth. See also Elizabeth S. Cole and Kathryn S. Donley, "History, Values, and Placement Policy Issues in Adoption," in *The Psychology of Adoption,* ed. David M. Brodzinsky and Marshall D. Schechter (New York: Oxford University Press, 1990), 273–94; Zelizer, *Pricing the Priceless Child,* 195–200. Folks reported a surplus of applicants for healthy infants as early as 1894 ("Family Life," 76–77), but this was only a hint of things to come: nationwide recognition of an enduring surplus of prospective parents (for healthy, white children) occurred in the third and fourth decades of the twentieth century. See Sophie van Senden Theis and Constance Goodrich, *The Child in the Foster Home* (New York: New York School of Social Work, 1921), 40; Sophie van Senden Theis, *How Foster Children Turn Out* (New York: State Charities Aid Association, 1924), 60–61; Ida R. Parker, *"Fit and Proper"? A Study of Legal Adoptions in Massachusetts* (Boston: Church Home Society, 1927), 63; Grace Abbott, ed., *The Child and the State* (Chicago: University of Chicago Press, 1938), 2: 199–200; Eleanor G. Gallagher, *The Adopted Child* (New York: Reynal and Hitchcock, 1936), 10.

6. Ruth F. Brenner, *A Follow-up Study of Adoptive Families* (New York: Child Adoption Research Committee, 1951), 140–41. Agency workers had unbounded confidence in their professional authority to create families. Leaders in the field encouraged workers' professional confidence: as one well-known adoption worker argued in 1943, "A requisite for fulfilling the function of evaluation is the necessity for the worker to feel that she has a right to choose" (Dorothy Hutchinson, *In Quest of Foster Parents* [New York: Columbia University Press, 1943], 94).

7. Frieda M. Kuhlmann and Helen P. Robinson, "Rorschach Tests as a Diagnostic Tool in Adoption Studies," *Social Casework* 32 (1951): 15–22. My study resembles classic jurisprudence in that it takes the words of the actors seriously. Here, however, the actors are not courts and the words are not judicial opinions. Instead, the actors are adoption agencies and the words are the discourse of their professional literature. Most of the articles cited were written by professional adoption workers who were active in the field; other quotations have the authority of the CWLA or the U.S. Children's Bureau (both highly influential in adoption practice) behind them. Where possible, I have also attempted to show the connection between rhetoric and practice with survey data and other adoption statistics. Unfortunately, the cloud of secrecy surrounding midcentury adoption practice makes data on actual agency operation nearly impossible to find. E. Wayne Carp is as yet the only professional historian to be granted access to the records of even one adoption agency (see his *Family Matters: Secrecy and Disclosure in the History of Adoption* [Cambridge: Harvard University Press, 1998]).

8. Quoted in Winifred Cobbledick, "A Study of Adoption Agency Criteria in 'Matching' Children to Homes" (master's thesis, University of California, 1949), 74.

9. CWLA, *CWLA Standards for Adoption Service* (New York: CWLA, 1958), 34.

10. Donald Brieland, "The Selection of Adoptive Parents at Intake," *Casework Papers, National Conference on Social Welfare* 87 (1960): 86. For additional statements describing agency efforts to find the "best," see Florence Brown, "What Do We Seek in Adoptive Parents?" *Social Casework* 32 (1951): 156; California Department of Social

Welfare, *Manual of Adoption Policies and Procedures* (Sacramento: Department of Social Welfare, 1947–56), sec. 2420-00; Schapiro, *Study*, 1.

11. I thank Franklin Zimring for suggesting the phrase *The Normal as Normative*.

12. Blanche J. Paget, *The ABC of Foster-Family Care for Children*, vol. 216 (Washington, D.C.: U.S. Children's Bureau, 1933), 2–3; National Conference of Catholic Charities, *Adoption Practices in Catholic Agencies* (Washington, D.C.: National Conference of Catholic Charities, 1957), 43.

13. Hutchinson, *In Quest*, 91–92, 9–10, 52.

14. Robert E. Mills, "Principles Underlying the Placing of Children in Care outside Their Own Homes," in *The Placing of Children in Families* (Geneva: League of Nations Advisory Committee on Social Questions, 1939), 13.

15. Schapiro, *Study*, 130.

16. See, for example, Ruth F. Brenner, "The Selection of Adoptive Parents," *Child Welfare League of America Bulletin* 25 (Dec. 1946): 1; Leslie E. Luehrs, "The Worker's Role in Adoption," in CWLA, *Adoption Practice* (New York: CWLA, 1941), 5, 7.

17. Judith S. Modell, *Kinship with Strangers: Adoption and Interpretations of Kinship in American Culture* (Berkeley: University of California Press, 1994), 2.

18. Hart, *Preventive Treatment*, 236.

19. Florence Clothier, "Placing the Child for Adoption," *Mental Hygiene* 26 (1942): 268, 269; Florence Clothier, "Some Aspects of the Problem of Adoption," *American Journal of Orthopsychiatry* 9 (1939): 610.

20. Katherine P. Hewins and L. Josephine Webster, *The Work of Child-Placing Agencies* (Washington, D.C.: U.S. Children's Bureau, 1927), 4.

21. See, for example, *Petitions of Goldman* (Mass. 1954), 121 N.E.2d 843, 844–45.

22. See, for example, Theis, *How Foster Children Turn Out*, 60; U.S. Children's Bureau, *Foster-Home Care for Dependent Children* (Washington, D.C.: U.S. Government Printing Office, 1924), 14; Esther McClain, *Child Placing in Ohio* (Columbus: Division of Charities, Department of Public Welfare, 1928), 8; White House Conference on Child Health and Protection, *Addresses and Abstracts of Committee Reports* (New York: Century, 1931), 330; CWLA, *Standards for Children's Organizations Providing Foster Family Care* (New York: CWLA, 1933), 18; California Department of Social Welfare, *Standards for Child Placing Agencies in California* (Sacramento: Department of Social Welfare, 1947), 8; Cobbledick, "Study," 46; California Department of Social Welfare, *Manual*, sec. 2470-00; David Fanshel, *A Study in Negro Adoption* (New York: CWLA, 1957), 13; CWLA, *CWLA Standards for Adoption Service*, 25–26.

23. CWLA, *Standards for Children's Organizations*, 18.

24. Schapiro, *Study*, 85. As one agency director put it, in matching the intelligence of infants with adoptive parents, "it is necessary to rely heavily on developmental tests and an estimate of the natural parents' intelligence and aptitudes" (Cobbledick, "Study," 49–50). For example, her agency placed the biological child of a nuclear physicist in the family of a college professor (Winifred Cobbledick Neff, interview by author, Apr. 24, 1996).

25. Schapiro, *Study*, 57.

26. California Adoption Survey Committee, *Report* (Sacramento: Department of Social Welfare, 1946), 38.

27. Schapiro, *Study*, 85.

28. Abraham G. Duker, "Jewish Attitudes toward Child Adoption," in Schapiro, *Study*, 144.

29. California Department of Social Welfare, *Manual*, sec. 2470-00, rev. Mar. 24, 1950.

30. Schapiro, *Study*, 84. For additional statements variously endorsing matching of adoptive parents and children by race, ethnicity, appearance, and personality, see California Department of Social Welfare, *Standards*, 8; Hazel S. Morrison, "Research Study in an Adoption Program," *Child Welfare* 29 (July 1950): 12; CWLA, *Adoption Practices, Procedures, and Problems* (New York: CWLA, 1952), 35. For example, "Tall adopting parents often have value for height, and consequently are considered for babies whose parents are tall. Short parents correspondingly may be chosen for children whose parents were shorter in stature. The same matching is done with body build and other physical characteristics" (Cobbledick, "Study," 57).

31. Morrison, "Research Study," 12.

32. Mary Ruth Colby, *Problems and Procedures in Adoption* (Washington, D.C.: U.S. Children's Bureau, 1941), 39; Cobbledick, "Study," 46; CWLA, *Adoption Practices*, 1–2; Fanshel, *Study*, 9; Rael Jean Isaac, "Children Who Need Adoption: A Radical View," *Atlantic* (Nov. 1963): 47; Rael Jean Isaac, *Adopting a Child Today* (New York: Harper and Row, 1965), 218; Howard Bluth, "Factors in the Decision to Adopt Independently," *Child Welfare* 46 (1967): 505–7. The proportion of Catholic dependent children housed in institutions was higher than average throughout the first two-thirds of the century (Martin Wolins and Irving Piliavin, *Institution or Foster Family: A Century of Debate* [New York: CWLA, 1964], 37). Although many prospective parents were willing to adopt across religious lines, the number of white applicants willing to adopt nonwhite babies before 1965 is unclear. Nevertheless, the increasing number of Asian babies adopted by white families after the Korean War and the success of the experimental Indian Child Adoption project (beginning in 1958) suggest that applicants were often more willing to cross racial lines than were agencies. See Ruth-Arlene W. Howe, "Adoption Practice, Issues, and Laws 1958–83," *Family Law Quarterly* 17 (1983): 182; Arnold L. Lyslo, "Background Information on the Indian Adoption Project, 1958 through 1967," in *Far from the Reservation: The Transracial Adoption of American Indian Children*, ed. David Fanshel (Metuchen, N.J.: Scarecrow, 1972), 43; Richard Steinman, "How Important Is 'Likeness' in Adoption?" *Child Welfare* 32 (Oct. 1953): 9.

33. CWLA, *Adoption Practices*, 1–2; Fanshel, *Study*, 9.

34. Fanshel, *Study*, 10–13, 62–72, 49. The total number of applicants from which these proportions are derived excluded those who were initially rejected for "categorical" reasons, such as religion, age, and residence. The rates of official rejection among blacks and whites were comparable, while the rate of black withdrawal was substantially higher than that of white withdrawal. This is deceptive, however, because a withdrawal often occurs in advance of a likely rejection. The fact that failure to demonstrate infertility was the leading factor in both rejections and withdrawals of black applicants (as discussed later in this essay) confirms that the line between rejections and withdrawals is highly permeable. The mean number of interviews for white applicants completing an adoption was also high, at 11.6 (Fanshel, *Study*, 50).

35. Trudy Bradley, *An Exploration of Case Workers' Perceptions of Adoptive Applicants* (New York: CWLA, 1966), 61. Of applicants who completed a first interview, half of blacks and half of whites were ultimately accepted for adoption. Another CWLA study in Chicago found that even in agencies actively attempting to recruit black applicants, social workers often placed considerable hurdles in the way of black would-be parents (Isaac, *Adopting a Child*, 125–26, citing Rita Dukette and Thelma G. Thompson, *Adoptive Resources for Negro Children* [New York: CWLA, 1959]).

36. See CWLA, *Adoption Practices*, 29–30, 31. As one commentator reported in 1957, "A widely held view in the field is that it is poor policy to convert a home which was established as a foster home for a child into an adoptive placement" (Fanshel, *Study*, 76).

37. See, for example, *The Dougherty Adoption Case* (1948), 358 Pa. 620, 58 A.2d 77; *Lewis v. Louisville and Jefferson County Children's Home* (1949), 309 Ky. 655, 218 S.W.2d 683; *Adoption of Shields* (1958), 4 Wis. 2d 219, 89 N.W.2d 827; *Ex parte Frantum* (1957), 214 Md. 100, 133 A.2d 408; *In re Amorello* (1956), 229 La. 304, 85 So. 2d 883.

38. Roy Lubove, *The Professional Altruist: The Emergence of Social Work as a Career, 1880–1930* (Cambridge: Harvard University Press, 1965), 71–72. I thank Franklin Zimring for pointing out that both views were consistent with the Progressive hope that social planning would change the world.

39. In addition to the examples that follow, see Carp, *Family Matters*, 32.

40. Edmond J. Butler, "Standards of Child Placing and Supervision," in *Standards of Child Welfare: A Report of the Children's Bureau Conferences*, ed. William L. Chenery and Ella A. Merritt (1919; rpt. New York: Arno Press, 1974), 354. Butler repeated the statement in 1924 (Butler, "The Essentials of Placement in Free Family Homes," in U.S. Children's Bureau, *Foster-Home Care*, 37).

41. Theis and Goodrich, *The Child*, 26.

42. R. L. Jenkins, "Adoption Practices and the Physician," *Journal of the American Medical Association* 103 (1934): 405. The CWLA subsequently reprinted this article as a pamphlet.

43. Clothier, "Placing," 260–61. See also Julia Ann Bishop, "The Child's Part in Adoption Placement," in CWLA, *Adoption Practice*, 16: "By adoptability, beyond legal release for adoption, is meant, a reasonably clear heredity, essentially sound physical equipment, normal mentality and an emotional capacity for an adoptive relationship."

44. California Department of Social Welfare, *Manual*, sec. 2330-00, rev. Jan. 28, 1949.

45. See, for example, Ora Pendleton, "New Aims in Adoptions," *Annals of the American Academy of Political and Social Science* 151 (1930): 158; White House Conference on Child Health and Protection, *Dependent and Neglected Children* (New York: D. Appleton-Century, 1933), 265–66; Abbott, ed., *Child*, 2:166; Cobbledick, "Study," 22.

46. New York City Committee on Adoptions, *Adoption in New York City* (New York: Welfare Council of New York City, 1948), 19. The report does not say what happened to the remaining 118 children; presumably, they were still under the care of the adoption agencies, waiting for adoption.

47. Joseph H. Reid, "Principles, Values, and Assumptions Underlying Adoption Practice," *Social Work* 2 (Jan. 1957): 25.

48. Hutchinson, *In Quest*, 88.

49. Pendleton, "New Aims," 157–58. She added, "We must be more concerned with their inner than their outer world" (159).

50. Sophie van Senden Theis, *Social Aspects of Child Adoption* (New York: CWLA, 1937), 7.

51. Susan Gillean, "The Responsibility of Private Child Welfare Agencies for Adoptions," *Child Welfare League of America Bulletin* 17 (June 1938): 1.

52. Clothier, "Placing," 265.

53. Brenner, "Selection," 3. See also Jenkins, "Adoption Practices," 403; Clothier, "Some Aspects," 610; Constance Rathbun, "The Adoptive Foster Parent," *Child Welfare*

League of America Bulletin 23 (Nov. 1944): 5; California Department of Social Welfare, *Standards,* 2; John Bowlby, *Maternal Care and Mental Health* (Geneva: World Health Organization, 1951), rpt. in I. Evelyn Smith, ed., *Readings in Adoption* (New York: Philosophical Library, 1963), 439; Brenner, *Follow-up Study,* 134; Brown, "What Do We Seek?" 156; Viola W. Bernard, "Application of Psychoanalytic Concepts to Adoption Agency Practice," in *Psychoanalysis and Social Work,* ed. Marcel Heiman (n.p.: International Universities Press, 1953), rpt. in Smith, ed., *Readings,* 419; Ruth Medway Davis and Polly Bouck, "Crucial Importance of Adoption Home Study," *Child Welfare* 34 (Mar. 1955): 21; California Department of Social Welfare, *Manual,* sec. 2330. A 1956 CWLA survey found that "it is generally accepted that one of the most important factors in determining suitability of applicants for adoptive parenthood is the determination of their motives in applying for a child. It is also generally agreed that applicants may or may not be aware of their true motives in asking for a child" (Schapiro, *Study,* 78).

54. Abraham J. Simon, "Evaluation of Adoptive Parents," in Schapiro, *Study,* 160–62, 163.

55. See, for example, Charlotte Towle, "The Evaluation of Homes in Preparation for Child Placements," *Mental Hygiene* 11 (1927): 463; Jenkins, "Adoption Practices," 404; Colby, *Problems and Procedures,* 34–35; Elizabeth Harral, "The Foster Parent and the Agency in the Adoption Process," *Proceedings of the National Conference of Social Work* 68 (1941): 417; Robert P. Knight, "Some Problems Involved in Selecting and Rearing Adopted Children," *Bulletin of the Menninger Clinic* 5 (1941): 66; Simon, "Evaluation," 160–62; Helen Fradkin, *The Adoption Home Study* (Trenton, N.J.: Bureau of Children's Services, 1963), 10.

56. See, for example, Brenner, "Selection," 3; CWLA, *Adoption Practices,* 33; Cobbledick, "Study," 29; Kuhlmann and Robinson, "Rorschach Tests," 16; Abraham J. Simon, "Social Agency Adoption: A Psycho-Sociological Study in Prediction" (Ph.D. diss., Washington University, 1953), 117–18; California Department of Social Welfare, *Adoptions in California: Manual of Policies and Procedures* (Sacramento: Department of Social Welfare, 1956–66), 56; Schapiro, *Study,* 75. One investigator found that an agency trying to recruit more black applicants (because a large number of black children were unadopted) continued to require infertility, even though the requirement dramatically reduced the number of blacks who could be approved as adoptive parents (Fanshel, *Study,* 62–64).

57. Kuhlmann and Robinson, "Rorschach Tests," 16. Similarly, Simon suggested that ideal adoptive applicants would have an identified organic cause ("Social Agency Adoption," 117–18). Other adoption workers suggested that failure to find a physical cause should not automatically end in rejection. See CWLA, *Adoption Practices,* 34; Bernard, "Application," 421. A 1953 study of the practice of a Pittsburgh adoption agency found that failure (or refusal) to demonstrate infertility was the single most common psychological reason for rejection (Fanshel, *Study,* 71–72).

58. See, for example, CWLA, *Adoption Practices,* 36, on the 1948 CWLA conference, which reported that the "majority of agencies indicated that applicants beyond the age of 40 are not usually considered for a child under 2 years of age." A preconference workshop in advance of the 1951 CWLA adoption conference challenged the notion that children were worse off with adoptive parents who were unnaturally older than biological parents would be. But this was a lonely dissent: at the conference itself, sixty-nine of seventy-nine agencies responding said they would not place infants in homes where

parents were over forty (CWLA, *Adoption Practices*, 3–34). See also National Conference of Catholic Charities, *Adoption Practices*, 46; Brown, "What Do We Seek?" 159.

59. Clothier, "Placing," 266–67.

60. Colby, *Problems and Procedures*, 34–35.

61. Mills, "Principles," 24.

62. Schapiro, *Study*, 75. Not surprisingly, a 1957 survey of Catholic adoption agencies found similar results: 97 percent of Catholic agencies required applicants to be married couples (National Conference of Catholic Charities, *Adoption Practices*, 100). As early as 1941, a U.S. Children's Bureau study of adoption reported, "It has been generally accepted that an adoptive family should be a normal family composed of a father and a mother" (Colby, *Problems and Procedures*, 15).

63. Clothier, "Placing," 267.

64. Edith M. H. Baylor and Elio D. Monachesi, *The Rehabilitation of Children: The Theory and Practice of Child Placement* (New York: Harper and Brothers, 1939), 323.

65. CWLA, *CWLA Standards for Adoption Service*, 38–39.

66. Brenner, "Selection," 3.

67. Hutchinson, *In Quest*, 71.

68. Ruth Michaels, "Casework Considerations in Rejecting the Adoption Application," *Journal of Social Casework* 28 (1947): 371.

69. Hutchinson, *In Quest*, 12–13, 46.

70. CWLA, *CWLA Standards for Adoption Service*, 38–39.

71. Fradkin, *Adoption Home Study*, 16.

72. Simon, "Evaluation," 160–62. For a similar view, see Fradkin, *Adoption Home Study*, 128–229.

73. Hutchinson, *In Quest*, 62.

74. Henry Maas, "The Successful Adoptive Parent Applicant," *Social Work* 5 (1960): 14–20.

75. Ibid., 15, 16–17, 19.

76. See Arlene S. Skolnick, *Embattled Paradise: The American Family in an Age of Uncertainty* (New York: Basic Books, 1991); Barbara Ehrenreich and Deirdre English, *For Her Own Good: 150 Years of the Experts' Advice to Women* (Garden City, N.Y.: Anchor Press/Doubleday, 1978). As Judith Modell has observed in *Kinship*, creating a family that is not bound by blood is, in a culture in which family is defined by blood, is a heroic act. Lacking the essential blood relationship, the adoptive family is both threatened by and a threat to the conventional ideal of family. Modell explains that the absence of a biological connection undermines the legitimacy of the adoptive family and simultaneously suggests an alternate vision of family that denies the significance of blood. Her anthropological study of adoption demonstrates that American culture understands adoptive parenting as a reflection of biological parenting. This understanding of adoption, fundamentally conservative, reinforces the legitimacy of the adoptive family and reduces the threat to the conventional family model. My historical study of the parent-selection practices used by adoption agencies over the course of the century complements Modell's interpretation: I chronicle the enforcement of the conservative cultural view of adoption.

When in Doubt, Count

World War II as a Watershed in the History of Adoption

E. Wayne Carp and Anna Leon-Guerrero

The title of this essay was inspired by English historian G. Kitson Clark, who advised anyone venturing a generalization, "do not guess, try to count, and if you cannot count, admit you are guessing."[1] Clark's advice has been almost impossible to follow in writing the history of adoption. In addition to historians' difficulty in gaining access to adoption agencies' confidential case records, in 1975 the federal government's National Center for Social Statistics ceased collecting data on adoptions.[2] As a result, there are no historical longitudinal statistical studies of adoption triad members—birth parents, adoptees, and adoptive parents—or of adoption agencies' policies. Instead, we have snapshot studies, frozen in time, of triad members. But even the best of these, like Benson Jaffee and David Fanshel's *How They Fared in Adoption: A Follow-up Study*, omit birth parents.[3] By sampling one out of every ten case records of the Children's Home Society of Washington (CHSW) from 1895 to 1973, this essay hopes to fill this gap in our knowledge of adoption agencies' constituencies and practices, with preliminary findings that can be tested by future historical studies of adoption agencies.[4]

Another goal of this essay is to use statistical data to test the thesis that World War II marked a third watershed in the history of adoption, following the Massachusetts Adoption Act of 1851 and the beginnings of adoption reform and the sentimentalization of adoption during the Progressive era.[5] Historians have documented how World War II was a transforming event in the nation's economy, political system, and foreign policy; in Americans' social values and expectations; and in the U.S. global role.[6] Other historians, however, see important continuities before and after the war and claim that the idea of World War II as a watershed is exaggerated or oversimplified.[7] For example, the war had little direct impact on many communities, the distribution of wealth and power remained unchanged, domestic policy remained substantially the same, and important social changes often did not occur until a decade or more after the war. These historians maintain that if significant changes did occur during World War II—new roles for women, civil rights activism, integration of the suburbs, increase in the size of the national government, and growth of the military-industrial complex—the war might have accelerated or reinforced these long-term changes but did not produce them.[8] However, in the history of adoption, our data reveal that in many respects, World War II brought dramatic changes in the lives of the CHSW's constituents and in the CHSW's policies.

Method

The CHSW adoption case records are extremely rich both in qualitative and quantitative information relating to the history of adoption. In this essay, we use the CHSW's case records, supplemented by CHSW staff minutes and annual reports, to provide a quantitative social profile of the agency's constituency and how it changed over time. Where possible, we use the records of the Child Welfare League of America and the U.S. Children's Bureau and social work journals to place the CHSW data in a comparative framework for representative purposes. Our empirical basis was the 21,500 CHSW case records, which we then subjected to systematic random sampling, reading one of every ten records. The resulting database of 2,150 adoption files was then transferred into Statistical Package for the Social Sciences 8.0 format. We analyzed these data to detect trends regarding what kinds of people relinquished children (birth parents' marital status, age, occupation, education, and motivation), what sort of children were placed in the CHSW (sex, race, legitimacy status, length of stay, age at placement, and age at adoption) and why, and what types of families adopted children (adoptive parents' marital status, age, occupation, motivation for adopting, and child preference). The analysis presented here is descriptive in nature, consisting primarily of frequency summaries, valid percentages, or calculation of means for selected variables. Table summaries are presented in either five- or ten-year collapsed time intervals.[9]

Historical Background of the CHSW

The CHSW is a private, statewide, voluntary, nonprofit organization founded in 1895 by a Methodist minister, Harrison D. Brown, and his wife, Libbie Beach Brown, the former superintendent of a Lincoln, Nebraska, orphanage, the Home for the Friendless. The CHSW's mission was to seek out homeless, neglected, or destitute children and place them in families for adoption. Throughout the twentieth century, as the demand for child welfare services increased, the society slowly added staff members, expanded geographically, and began to develop other adoption-related services. In the late 1960s the CHSW

The Children's Home Society of Washington corporate headquarters and North-west Region Administrative offices in Seattle in 1909 being rebuilt after a fire destroyed its rented receiving room.

averaged 421 adoptions a year, approximately 25 percent of all adoptions in the state of Washington. By 1970, just before it ended the practice of placing children in adoptive homes, the society operated six branches throughout the state and administered programs that included homes for unmarried mothers, foster care for children prior to adoption, institutional or group care for older children, and, of course, adoption. During the first seventy-eight years of its existence, the CHSW oversaw more than 94,000 adoptions.[10]

Birth Parents

Before World War II, the age, education, occupation, and marital status of the birth parents who relinquished children for adoption are pretty much a mystery to historians.[11] Poorly kept records during the early twentieth century, the social stigma surrounding illegitimacy, and the inability of researchers to access adoption case records have drawn a veil over the social characteristics of this category of adoption agency clients. If there is a stereotype regarding birth mothers, it is one of poor, uneducated, working-class, unwed, very young women. Though not as full as one might desire, the CHSW records provide enough data to draw a more concise and significantly different portrait.

From 1895 to 1973, the average age of birth mothers who relinquished children to the CHSW was 23. Table 1 also clearly shows that except for the decade of the Great Depression, the age of CHSW birth mothers steadily declined. Before World War II, birth mothers were certainly not teenagers. For the first forty-five years of the CHSW's existence, birth mothers' unadjusted average age remained fairly constant, at 25.7 years.[12] In the following three decades, however, birth mothers' unadjusted average ages declined sharply, to 22, as the nation's unwed pregnancy rate rapidly increased. As table 1 shows, the fundamental break with the past came with World War II: between 1940 and 1944, the average age of birth mothers declined from the Depression decade age of 27 to 21.4, a level not seen again until the sexual revolution of the late 1960s.

Throughout the CHSW's existence, birth fathers were older than birth mothers. Whereas birth mothers' average age was 23, that of birth fathers was 27. Like birth mothers, birth fathers' average age declined continuously from the Depression to the 1970s. Similarly, World War II represented a watershed, with birth fathers' average ages declining from 33 to 27, almost a 25 percent drop during the period.

As table 2 reveals, from the 1920s, when CHSW officials began collecting such information, until 1973, an average of 52 percent of the mothers who relinquished children for adoption had less than a high school education. Not surprisingly, as states increasingly enacted mandatory school-attendance laws, the percentage of CHSW birth mothers who had less than a high school education declined steadily. Before 1920, birth mothers' low attendance at high school was not terribly at odds with the rest of the nation's adolescents because only two states, Idaho and Ohio, unconditionally required full-time attendance until age fifteen, leaving two-thirds of America's youth without any secondary education. But while high school enrollment in the nation doubled during the 1920s, with 47 percent of all youth between ages 14 and 17 attending school, 89 percent of CHSW birth mothers during that time did not have any high school education.[13] Birth mothers' educational attainment increased throughout much of the period under study, with the number of mothers who were high school graduates tripling during the 1930s and nearly doubling again during the 1940s. New Deal and wartime expenditures on education accounted for much of this increase.[14] The educational attainment of CHSW birth mothers increased spectacularly during the 1950s and 1960s, when the proportion of college-educated women relinquishing children to the CHSW grew more than fivefold from its 1940s level of 6 percent.

CHSW birth fathers were better educated than birth mothers, with an average of only 37 percent having less than a high school education between 1920 and 1973. Before World War II, when a significant proportion of American males were foreign born and factory work was common, a high school education was not a prerequisite for employment. The 1940s constituted a watershed

TABLE 1. Average Age of CHSW Birth Parents, 1900–1973

	1900–1904	1905–1909	1910–14	1915–19	1920–24	1925–29	1930–34	1935–39	1940–44	1945–49	1950–54	1955–59	1960–64	1965–69	1970–73	Overall
Birth mother																
age	29	27	25	26	23	24	26	28	21	25	23	23	22	21	19	23
Total	1	18	61	43	44	52	95	85	43	80	91	158	206	233	157	1,367
Birth father																
age	—	30	31	38	28	30	33	33	27	28	26	27	25	23	22	27
Total	—	18	59	44	37	43	98	88	37	73	74	141	195	224	150	1,281

TABLE 2.   Educational Attainment of CHSW Birth Parents, 1920–73 (in percentages)

	1920–29	1930–39	1940–49	1950–59	1960–69	1970–73	Overall
Birth mother							
Less than high school	89	79	63	52	38	51	52
High school graduate	6	18	32	33	31	26	28
Some college or higher	6	4	6	15	32	23	20
Total	36	144	89	227	429	160	1,085
Birth father							
Less than high school	—	70	45	36	27	31	37
High school graduate	—	23	41	39	41	38	38
Some college or higher	—	8	15	25	32	31	26
Total	—	118	69	175	372	141	875

Note: Due to rounding, percentage totals do not always add up to 100 percent.

in birth fathers' education with almost a 100 percent increase in the number of birth fathers who had a high school diploma and some college education. The G.I. Bill of 1944 allowed millions of former servicemen to attend college after the war, and high educational attainment became increasingly necessary for employment: as a result, the percentage of birth fathers with some college education again steeply increased to nearly 25 percent during the 1950s.[15]

Between 1900 and 1973, women's participation in the workforce was severely limited by age, marital status, class, race, gender, and sexual discrimination. Thus, it is not surprising that, as table 3 shows, only 1 percent of CHSW birth mothers worked at professional jobs, with another 4 percent working in the traditionally female occupation of nursing and 2 percent holding skilled-labor positions. Almost 30 percent of birth mothers labored in domestic service and unskilled jobs, and 20 percent held clerical jobs. However, 43 percent of birth mothers were not in the workforce: 20 percent attended high school, 10 percent were in college, and 13 percent were homemakers.

Before World War II, CHSW birth mothers' employment patterns differed considerably from those of the nation as a whole. William H. Chafe has documented a sharp prewar shift in women's employment from jobs as domestics, farm laborers, unskilled factory operatives, and teachers to white-collar and clerical positions, which by 1940 engaged 45 percent of female workers. In addition, the percentage of women workers engaged in the professions rose from 11.9 to 14.2. Still, as Chafe notes, "In 1940, the percentage of women at work was almost exactly what it had been in 1910."[16] In contrast, between 1900 and 1939, CHSW birth mothers remained in domestic service (51 percent) and unskilled jobs (8.5 percent) to a much greater extent, with only 10 percent in clerical positions. Similarly, birth mothers were vastly underrepresented as professionals in the workforce, averaging only 1.3 percent before the war, while birth mothers employed as nurses averaged only 3.7 percent. And whereas in 1900,

TABLE 3. Occupations of CHSW Birth Mothers, 1905–73 (in percentages)

	1905–1909	1910–14	1915–19	1920–24	1925–29	1930–34	1935–39	1940–44	1945–49	1950–54	1955–59	1960–64	1965–69	1970–73	Overall
Professional or self-employed	0	3 (1)	0	0	2 (1)	0	2 (1)	0	2 (1)	3 (2)	1 (1)	2 (4)	2 (5)	1 (1)	1 (17)
Nursing	10 (1)	0	8 (2)	3 (1)	2 (1)	0	0	0	2 (1)	11 (8)	7 (10)	6 (11)	4 (10)	4 (6)	4 (51)
Skilled laborer	0	3 (1)	0	0	2 (1)	3 (2)	0	3 (1)	2 (1)	4 (3)	1 (2)	2 (3)	2 (4)	2 (3)	2 (21)
Domestic service	70 (7)	70 (23)	50 (12)	40 (14)	32 (15)	34 (23)	43 (24)	48 (15)	49 (30)	28 (20)	21 (29)	15 (27)	8 (18)	11 (16)	24 (273)
Unskilled laborer	10 (1)	9 (3)	4 (1)		8 (4)	7 (5)	18 (10)	0	7 (4)	3 (2)	7 (10)	2 (4)	3 (6)	1 (2)	5 (52)
Clerical	0	9 (3)	21 (5)	11 (4)	11 (5)	12 (8)	18 (10)	10 (3)	15 (9)	11 (8)	26 (37)	20 (36)	32 (72)	17 (24)	20 (224)
High school student	0	0	0	29 (10)	9 (4)	6 (4)	7 (4)	23 (7)	13 (8)	21 (15)	17 (24)	23 (43)	22 (50)	43 (62)	20 (231)
College student	0	0	4 (1)	3 (1)	2 (1)	0	0	0	2 (1)	7 (5)	4 (6)	16 (29)	20 (45)	13 (19)	10 (108)
Homemaker	10 (1)	6 (2)	13 (3)	14 (5)	32 (15)	37 (25)	12 (7)	13 (4)	10 (6)	11 (8)	14 (20)	14 (25)	7 (16)	8 (11)	13 (148)
Military	0	0	0	0	0	0	0	3 (1)	0	0	1 (2)	1 (2)	0	1 (1)	1 (6)
Total	10	33	24	35	47	67	56	31	61	71	141	184	226	145	1,131

Note: Figures in parentheses refer to the number of cases. Due to rounding, percentage totals do not always add up to 100 percent.

90 percent of CHSW birth mothers were in the workforce, by 1939, the percentage had shrunk to 67 percent.

The war years did not constitute a revolution, temporary or otherwise, in occupational status for CHSW birth mothers. Major changes in birth mothers' employment patterns had occurred five years earlier. Table 3 reveals the sharp decline in the percentage of homemakers relinquishing children between 1930–34, when the rate was 37 percent, and 1935–39, when it dropped to 12 percent, where it remained during the war years. As homemakers entered the job market between 1935 and 1939, significant increases occurred in the percentage of CHSW birth mothers employed in domestic service (25 percent), unskilled labor (100 percent), and clerical work (50 percent). During the war, the employment patterns of CHSW birth mothers differed substantially from those of other women. Contrary to the wartime experiences of married women, who by the end of the war constituted twice the percentage of birth mothers (24 percent) and a majority of all working women,[17] CHSW birth mothers saw a noticeable decrease in the percentage employed in clerical work (55 percent) and more than a threefold increase in the percentage enrolled in high school.

Despite birth mothers' increased postwar education, a significantly higher percentage of them still worked outside the home than did the female population in general. Whereas the war years represented a turning point in the history of women's employment in terms of the jump in absolute numbers, CHSW birth mothers reversed that pattern. By the 1970s, when women accounted for 43 percent of the labor market,[18] 64 percent of CHSW birth mothers remained out of the paid workforce either as high school or college students or as homemakers (see table 3). Like birth mothers, few birth fathers between 1900 and 1973 held professional jobs (6 percent). Table 4 reveals that a large majority of birth fathers were unskilled or farm laborers or were in military service (35 and 15 percent, respectively). Twelve percent of birth fathers were foremen/skilled laborers, and 4 percent were salesmen. The war years constituted a watershed in CHSW birth fathers' occupations. During the Great Depression, 7 percent of birth fathers were unemployed, but during the war, that percentage declined to a mere 2 percent. Similarly, the unadjusted average percentage of birth fathers who were unskilled or farm laborers decreased by more than 65 percent during the war (see table 4). Many of these men undoubtedly entered the armed forces: not surprisingly, the number of birth fathers in the military jumped from 2 percent during the Depression decade to 36 percent during the war years (table 4). Significantly, after the war, a much higher percentage of birth fathers remained in the armed services than had been the case before the conflict.

The marital status of CHSW birth parents varied over time. According to table 5, between 1895 and 1973, 62 percent of CHSW birth mothers identified

TABLE 4. Occupations of CHSW Birth Fathers, 1895–1973 (in percentages)

	1905–1909	1910–14	1915–19	1920–24	1925–29	1930–34	1935–39	1940–44	1945–49	1950–54	1955–59	1960–64	1965–69	1970–73	Overall
Professional	20 (3)	6 (3)	5 (2)	3 (1)	8 (4)	0	4 (3)	3 (1)	5 (3)	5 (4)	10 (14)	5 (9)	7 (14)	4 (5)	6 (66)
Unskilled or farm laborer	53 (8)	45 (22)	43 (17)	53 (19)	57 (28)	54 (47)	56 (42)	19 (7)	32 (21)	38 (28)	35 (49)	30 (52)	22 (44)	16 (21)	35 (405)
Military	0	4 (2)	10 (4)	6 (2)	4 (2)	3 (3)	1 (1)	36 (13)	39 (25)	34 (25)	23 (32)	16 (27)	10 (21)	16 (21)	15 (178)
Foreman or skilled laborer	0	14 (7)	20 (8)	19 (7)	4 (2)	8 (7)	7 (6)	17 (6)	8 (5)	8 (6)	9 (13)	15 (26)	14 (31)	14 (18)	12 (142)
Salesman	0	2 (1)	0	3 (1)	8 (4)	11 (10)	5 (4)	6 (2)	3 (2)	3 (2)	5 (7)	2 (4)	6 (13)	2 (2)	4 (52)
Proprietor or owner	0	2 (1)	3 (1)	3 (1)	4 (2)	2 (2)	0	3 (1)	0	1 (1)	1 (2)	0	1 (2)	0	1 (13)
Clerical	20 (3)	0	3 (1)	3 (1)	0	5 (4)	4 (3)	0	1 (1)	0	1 (1)	1 (1)	1 (2)	2 (2)	2 (21)
Service	7 (1)	10 (5)	8 (3)	3 (1)	0	3 (3)	5 (5)	3 (1)	3 (2)	0	1 (1)	2 (2)	1 (1)	2 (2)	2 (25)
Farmer or rancher	0	16 (8)	12 (5)	6 (2)	4 (2)	1 (1)	3 (2)	6 (2)	3 (2)	0	0	0	1 (1)	0	2 (25)
Civil service	0	0	0	0	0	1 (1)	1 (1)	0	1 (1)	1 (1)	2 (3)	2 (3)	2 (4)	1 (1)	1 (15)
Unemployed	0	0	0	0	0	7 (6)	8 (6)	23 (1)	2 (1)	0	3 (4)	2 (4)	4 (7)	6 (8)	3 (37)
College student	0	0	0	3 (1)	6 (3)	0	3 (2)	3 (1)	2 (1)	5 (4)	4 (6)	18 (31)	17 (35)	17 (22)	9 (106)
High school student	0	0	0	0	4 (2)	3 (3)	0	3 (1)	2 (1)	4 (3)	6 (9)	8 (14)	13 (27)	20 (26)	7 (86)
Total	15	49	40	36	49	87	75	36	65	74	142	173	202	128	1,171

Note: Figures in parentheses refer to the number of cases. Due to rounding, percentage totals do not always add up to 100 percent.

themselves as unmarried. Married couples averaged 13 percent of birth parents, and separated and divorced couples averaged 8 percent and 7 percent, respectively. As unemployment skyrocketed during the Depression, families found themselves unable to support their children, and the number of married couples relinquishing children jumped from 17 percent during 1930–34 to 25 percent during the next five-year period (see table 5).

The Depression years and World War II were turning points in birth parents' marital status. In the decade before the war, 9 percent of all birth parents who relinquished children to the CHSW were widows who could not support their children despite the existence of mothers' pensions, and another 14 percent were widowers who could not find female caregivers for their children. Thus, nearly one in four relinquishing parents had suffered the death of a spouse. During and after World War II, high employment and unprecedented prosperity coupled with the Social Security Act's Aid to Dependent Children program to sharply reduce the percentages of widows and widowers placing their children with the CHSW. By the 1970s, widows constituted just 1 percent of relinquishing parents, and no widowers placed children with the CHSW.

Similar radical trends occurred among the single parents who relinquished children to the CHSW. Before World War II, single parents averaged 41 percent of all CHSW birth parents. During the war, single parents increased to 65 percent of those relinquishing children, reflecting the significant increase in out-of-wedlock pregnancies nationwide from 88,000 in 1938 to 103,000 in 1940 to 129,000 in 1945.[19] The number of illegitimate births continued to climb rapidly, reaching 201,000 in 1958 and 245,000 in 1962.[20] By the 1970s, single parents constituted 85 percent of all CHSW birth parents.

Birth parents relinquished children or had them removed by the courts for various reasons. Table 6 reveals that between 1895 and 1973, the most frequent reason for surrendering a child to the CHSW was out-of-wedlock birth, which accounted for more than half of all children relinquished. Family breakup (parental divorce or separation) and poverty were distant runners-up at around 10 percent. Three other categories deserve comment. Although social workers freely used the terms *insane* and *feebleminded*, especially during the Progressive Era, only 2 percent of CHSW birth mothers were so labeled during the period under study. The number of CHSW women who said that they were rape or incest victims was also very small, at 1 percent. Finally, 2 percent of CHSW clients claimed not to want their children.[21] Among the specific reasons given for not wanting their children, the most common were that the parents were too old, the parents did not want the responsibility, and spousal infidelity.[22]

Table 6 also reveals that the Second World War constituted a watershed in the reasons for relinquishing their children to the CHSW. In the decade before the war, 22 percent of birth parents relinquished their children because they had been born out of wedlock, but 55 percent relinquished children for reasons

TABLE 5. Marital Status of CHSW Birth Parents, 1895–1973 (in percentages)

	1895–99	1900–1904	1905–1909	1910–14	1915–19	1920–24	1925–29	1930–34	1935–39	1940–44	1945–49	1950–54	1955–59	1960–64	1965–69	1970–73	Overall
Single	29	27	42	52	42	57	46	42	36	65	55	61	64	67	79	85	62
	(4)	(7)	(16)	(44)	(25)	(29)	(27)	(37)	(33)	(35)	(46)	(61)	(104)	(145)	(191)	(138)	(942)
Married	29	23	12	10	7	10	14	17	25	13	18	15	14	14	9	8	13
	(4)	(6)	(5)	(8)	(4)	(5)	(8)	(15)	(23)	(7)	(15)	(15)	(22)	(30)	(21)	(13)	(201)
Separated	1	19	11	6	3	6	15	9	12	11	7	14	8	10	5	2	8
	(1)	(5)	(4)	(5)	(2)	(3)	(9)	(8)	(11)	(6)	(6)	(14)	(13)	(22)	(12)	(3)	(124)
Divorced	0	0	3	6	5	6	5	1	11	7	10	8	13	9	7	5	7
			(1)	(5)	(3)	(3)	(3)	(1)	(10)	(4)	(8)	(8)	(21)	(20)	(17)	(8)	(112)
Widowed	21	12	11	4	15	10	14	14	4	0	5	2	1	1	1	1	4
	(3)	(3)	(4)	(3)	(9)	(5)	(8)	(12)	(4)		(4)	(2)	(1)	(1)	(1)	(1)	(61)
Widower	14	19	21	23	27	12	7	17	12	4	5	0	1	0	0	0	6
	(2)	(5)	(8)	(19)	(16)	(6)	(4)	(15)	(11)	(2)	(4)		(1)				(93)
Total	14	26	38	84	59	51	59	88	92	54	83	100	162	218	242	163	1,533

Note: Figures in parentheses refer to the number of cases. Due to rounding, percentage totals do not always add up to 100 percent.

TABLE 6. Causes of Children's Relinquishment, 1895–1973 (in percentages)

	1895–99	1900–1909	1910–19	1920–29	1930–39	1940–49	1950–59	1960–69	1970–73	Overall
Illegitimacy	28 (5)	21 (17)	34 (67)	31 (47)	22 (56)	48 (80)	62 (182)	75 (348)	89 (149)	53 (951)
Family breakup	0	4 (3)	29 (56)	26 (40)	19 (47)	11 (19)	4 (12)	3 (16)	1 (2)	11 (195)
Poverty	33 (6)	18 (14)	6 (11)	5 (8)	13 (33)	6 (10)	14 (40)	12 (59)	3 (5)	10 (186)
Neglect	0	9 (7)	4 (8)	1 (1)	2 (6)	2 (4)	2 (6)	0	0	2 (32)
Abandoned	22 (4)	20 (16)	13 (25)	11 (17)	7 (18)	4 (6)	3 (8)	1 (2)	0	5 (96)
Orphaned	17 (3)	10 (8)	5 (10)	7 (10)	2 (5)	1 (1)	1 (4)	0	0	2 (41)
Illness	0	8 (6)	2 (3)	3 (4)	6 (14)	2 (4)	1 (3)	1 (1)	0	2 (35)
Insane	0	3 (2)	3 (6)	5 (7)	2 (6)	2 (4)	1 (4)	1 (4)	0	2 (33)
Unfit parent(s)	0	6 (5)	4 (8)	8 (12)	11 (28)	5 (8)	1 (4)	1 (4)	0	4 (69)
Unwanted	0	3 (2)	0	1 (1)	1 (1)	2 (4)	1 (2)	3 (15)	3 (5)	2 (30)
Temporary boarding	0	0	0	0	10 (24)	15 (25)	4 (12)	1 (1)	0	4 (62)
Behavior problem	0	0	1 (1)	1 (2)	3 (8)	1 (2)	4 (12)	6 (26)	4 (7)	3 (58)
Mother raped/incest	0	0	0	3 (4)	2 (6)	1 (1)	1 (4)	0 (6)	0	1 (21)
Total	18	80	195	153	252	168	293	482	168	1,809

Note: Figures in parenthesis refer to the number of cases. Due to rounding, percentage totals do not add up to 100 percent.

that could have been mitigated by social intervention—family breakup, poverty, temporary boarding, abandonment, illness, parental refusal to accept responsibility, or behavior problems. After World War II, out-of-wedlock births soon eclipsed all other reasons for the relinquishment of children. The largest increase occurred during the 1940s, when the percentage more than doubled; by the 1970s, out-of-wedlock births accounted for 89 percent of all children surrendered to the CHSW. Aid to Dependent Children had created a safety net for families, mitigating the importance of the various factors that had been responsible for more than half of the CHSW's children before World War II. By the 1970s, children were relinquished because of a family breakup in only 1 percent of cases and for reasons of poverty in only 3 percent. No children were relinquished because of parental abandonment, neglect, or unfitness, and no children were temporarily boarded. However, after World War II, the percentage of children placed in the CHSW for behavior problems increased. During the 1960s, the proportion of "problem" children climbed to 6 percent, and by the 1970s behavioral difficulties represented the second most frequent reason that birth parents relinquished their children.

Adopted Children

As table 7 shows, between 1895 and 1973, 54 percent of children admitted to the CHSW were boys, with a low of 49 percent during the 1930s and a high of 63 percent during the 1940s. More specifically, during 1935–39, only 43 percent of children admitted were male, while during 1940–44, that number reached 63 percent, the highest percentage ever for a five-year period. Traditional gender roles may provide one explanation for the fact that girls were a majority only during the Depression: parents placed daughters in the CHSW to protect them from neglect and malnutrition while encouraging boys to fend for themselves or to enter the workplace to help support the family.[23]

As table 8 illustrates, most children (98 percent) admitted to the CHSW during the CHSW's first four decades were classified as white. This is not surprising, especially because Blacks constituted only a tiny fraction of Washington State's population before World War II.[24] However, the war years represented a turning point in opening up America's child welfare system to the "unadoptable" child. After the war, African Americans were the first to be affected by this liberalization. Although social services for black children came slowly, African-American militancy against continuing wartime segregation and discrimination, a sharp increase in the number of nonwhite out-of-wedlock births, and federal and state action and court rulings in favor of equal rights resulted in the nation's adoption agencies placing increasing numbers of black children.[25] In 1949, Lois Wildy, director of casework at the Illinois Children's Home and Aid Society, proudly informed her colleagues that placements of

TABLE 7. Male Children Admitted to CHSW, 1895–1973 (in percentages)

	1895–99	1900–1904	1905–1909	1910–14	1915–19	1920–24	1925–29	1930–34	1935–39	1940–44	1945–49	1950–54	1955–59	1960–64	1965–69	1970–73	Overall
Male children	58	47	59	58	52	66	51	54	43	63	62	60	59	50	56	40	54
Total	23	34	91	120	88	76	84	143	118	71	100	116	181	237	259	169	1,910

TABLE 8   Race of Children Admitted to CHSW, 1895–1973 (in percentages)

	1900–1909	1910–19	1920–29	1930–39	1940–49	1950–59	1960–69	1970–73	Overall
White	98	98	98	97	97	89	89	91	93
	(103)	(205)	(157)	(251)	(165)	(254)	(423)	(150)	(1,708)
Black	1	2	1	2	1	6	4	6	3
	(1)	(2)	(1)	(4)	(1)	(16)	(21)	(10)	(56)
Native	1	1	0	1	1	3	2	1	2
American	(1)	(1)		(4)	(2)	(8)	(11)	(1)	(28)
Asian	0	1	1	0	1	3	4	2	2
		(1)	(2)		(2)	(8)	(18)	(4)	(35)
Total	105	209	160	259	170	286	473	165	1,827

Note: Figures in parentheses refer to the number of cases.

black children had averaged twenty-five a year since 1944.[26] Over the next decade, many agencies found themselves with more black children than could be placed locally and consequently began intense mass media publicity campaigns and programs specially designed to recruit African-American adoptive parents.[27]

The CHSW was one of these agencies. During the 1940s, Washington's Black population quadrupled.[28] In the mid-1950s, under the leadership of director Spencer Crookes, the CHSW initiated the Minority Home Finding Committee to recruit Black adoptive parents. The CHSW made special efforts to publicize the availability of Black children by placing announcements in local newspapers; in its house organ, the *Home Finder;* and on television. In addition, the committee distributed pamphlets in libraries and churches and asked Black parents who had already adopted children to refer other prospective parents. In 1957 the CHSW produced *Your Very Own,* a recruiting film about an African-American couple that adopted a baby. The film was lent to groups interested in adopting minority children, such as Black groups in the Council of Seattle Women's Clubs.[29] These efforts paid off: between 1949 and 1959, the CHSW placed about thirty-five Black children (6 percent of all placements).[30]

Table 9 demonstrates that from 1895 to 1973, the average age of children admitted to the CHSW was 31 months, much higher than the popular stereotype that equates adoption with babies. Much of this older-child adoption occurred before World War II. From 1895 to 1939, the children placed in the CHSW averaged 53 months of age, a number that declined to 17 months from 1940 through the 1970s. During the Depression decade, the average age of admitted children was 59 months, but during the following ten years, the average age declined to 27 months, a drop of more than 50 percent. Driving children's ages downward were a steep increase in the number of illegitimate births and the youthfulness of mothers, both of which were initially a product of the social

During the early 1950s, the Children's Home Society was a pioneer in placing African-American babies.

instability of World War II.[31] In the 1950s, the average dropped by another 50 percent, to 19 months, and during the 1970s it reached a low of 4 months.[32]

Even before the surge in illegitimacy began in the 1940s, social workers as well as the general public commonly believed that most children relinquished for adoption were born out of wedlock. But this was untrue for the CHSW as well as for other adoption agencies. As table 10 shows, for the first four decades of the CHSW's existence, the percentage of children admitted to the CHSW who were born in wedlock ranged from a high of 71 percent to a low of 55 percent, with an average of 62 percent. As discussed earlier, most of these children came to the CHSW because of their parents' breakup, poverty, death, illness, neglect, or abandonment. Again, World War II marked a major shift in the character of the CHSW's clientele. The percentage of legitimate CHSW children plunged to 39 percent during the war[33] and continued its steep descent to 18 percent in the 1950s and 10 percent in the 1960s. The Aid to Dependent Children program, wartime prosperity, and the pronatalism of the baby boom era undoubtedly contributed to the ability and desire of single mothers and married couples to avoid separation from their children.[34]

The length of time children remained in the CHSW before being placed in adoptive homes also declined throughout the twentieth century. Table 11 illustrates that the average child's stay at the CHSW was three months, a fairly short time, especially considering that some children spent as long as six years in the nation's orphanages.[35] Before the 1940s, adoption workers sought to create perfect families by matching children and parents with similar physical and mental characteristics.[36] This strategy resulted in considerable delay in placing children for adoption, ranging anywhere from 4 months to 2 years or longer. Social workers justified observing children for lengthy periods of time in a number of ways. Maud Morlock, a U.S. Children's Bureau official and an expert on adoption, noted that the bureau recommended an observation period of four to six months. She stressed the need "to give the mother an opportunity to make her decision when she is in a more normal emotional state" and to give the agency time to know the mother. Morlock also noted the need to observe the infant's physical health, looking for congenital defects, which mandated institutionalization rather than adoption, and evidence of dangerous hereditary traits, a concern that reflected the lingering fears aroused by the spurious Progressive-era eugenics movement. Infants were also subjected to IQ tests to ascertain their mental abilities.[37]

The length of time between acceptance by the CHSW and placement in an adoptive home almost doubled from four months in the 1920s to seven

TABLE 9. Average Age of Children Admitted to CHSW, 1895–1973 (in months)

	1895–99	1900–1909	1910–19	1920–29	1930–39	1940–49	1950–59	1960–69	1970–73	Overall
Age	57	53	54	48	59	27	19	13	4	31
Total	21	112	191	149	239	161	289	480	162	1,804

TABLE 10. Legitimate Births of Children Admitted to CHSW, 1895–1973 (in percentages)

	1895–99	1900–1909	1910–19	1920–29	1930–39	1940–49	1950–59	1960–69	1970–73	Overall
Legitimate births	71	63	59	55	63	37	18	10	4	32
Total	21	67	181	139	231	150	275	467	162	1,693

TABLE 11. Length of Stay of Children in CHSW, 1895–1973 (in months)

	1895–99	1900–1909	1910–19	1920–29	1930–39	1940–49	1950–59	1960–69	1970–73	Overall
Stay	8	4	6	4	6	7	4	2	1	3
Total	15	78	92	58	42	101	232	431	153	1,202

months in the 1940s. The increase in time at the CHSW alarmed officials, who realized that its practice was at odds with the national trend toward what social workers labeled early placement. As early as 1940, a few professional adoption workers, convinced by psychologists and psychiatrists of the crucial importance of the infant-mother relationship, questioned delaying the placement of babies for six months or longer and cautiously began placing children in adoptive homes at four or five months or even earlier.[38] Studies by Anna Freud and Dorothy Burlingham showed separation's devastating psychological effects on English children removed from their parents during World War II, thereby encouraging other adoption workers to make early placements.[39] The Catholic Home Bureau in New York City, for example, reported that the percentage of babies placed early (after an average of merely thirty-eight days) almost doubled, to 19 percent, between 1945 and 1949.[40] Adoption workers were much reassured in their practice of early placements by the 1951 publication of British psychiatrist John Bowlby's *Maternal Care and Mental Health*. Citing a mass of clinical evidence, Bowlby demonstrated the adverse effects of "maternal deprivation" (the lack of a mother's care) on the development of infants' character and mental health. He recommended strongly that "the baby should be adopted as early in his life as possible," specifying that "the first two months should become the rule."[41] By 1955, the Los Angeles County Bureau of Adoptions, one of the largest agencies in the United States, reported its success in placing infants directly from the hospital.[42]

Responding to changing national trends in social work, the CHSW moved quickly in the 1950s to conform to the new practice of early placement. CHSW officials cut the length of time babies remained in its care by 50 percent from 7 to 4 months. A 1957 CHSW report revealed that 65 percent of the infants placed for adoption were with their adoptive families reaching the age of three months of age and 20 percent joined their families at less than one month.[43]

Even three to four months seemed excessive to CHSW adoption workers. By 1959, the CHSW, working through its Casework Study Planning Committee, sought to determine "how we can achieve placement at one month or before of our healthy Caucasian infants" and to identify the causes for delays in the placement of these babies. A comprehensive committee report on placements between June and September 1959 sheds much light on contemporary attitudes and the agency's policies and practices. The report found that the 128 children placed by the agency during this four-month period fell into two well-defined groups: 59 healthy Caucasian infants without legal fathers for whom early placement was arranged, and 69 children for whom early placement was not feasible. CHSW adoption workers deemed 20 percent of the 69 children not eligible for early placement because of medical problems. Another 20 percent could not be placed because their fathers had not legally given permission to adopt. Time was needed to trace birth fathers and secure their relinquishment or to take the legal steps required if the fathers' whereabouts were unknown. Forty-five percent of the children in the CHSW's care were not placed because they were African American or of mixed race (Filipino, Native American, Chinese, Japanese), evidence of the difficulties in placing minority children despite the CHSW's outreach program. Seven percent of the agency's children could not be placed because they were older than twelve months, revealing post–World War II adoptive parents' decided preference for newborns. Finally, 3 percent of the children not placed early were described as having slow psychological development; 3 percent had a questionable social history, which meant that their mothers were mentally ill and their fathers unknown; and one unfortunate child was not placed early because of his "unusual physical appearance."[44] During the 1970s a child's average length of stay at the CHSW dropped still further, to 1 month.

The CHSW's ostensible purpose was to place children in adoptive homes; between 1895 and 1973 the steady rise in adoptions, from 27 percent to 90 percent, suggests that the agency succeeded (see table 12). But overall, only 65

TABLE 12.   Final Outcome of Children Admitted to CHSW, 1895–1973 (in percentages)

	1895–99	1900–1909	1910–19	1920–29	1930–39	1940–49	1950–59	1960–69	1970–73	Overall
Adopted	27	37	54	74	33	67	73	73	90	65
	(6)	(46)	(110)	(101)	(83)	(110)	(245)	(470)	(161)	(1,332)
Returned to CHSW	9	2	3	3	2	0	1	1	0	1
numerous times	(2)	(2)	(7)	(4)	(4)		(3)	(1)		(23)
Placed with family,	5	0	7	3	4	1	1	0	1	2
not adopted	(1)		(14)	(4)	(11)	(2)	(1)		(1)	(34)
Contract	18	13	0	0	0	0	0	0	0	1
	(4)	(16)								(20)
Death	9	17	3	4	3	1	1	1	1	3
	(2)	(21)	(6)	(6)	(7)	(1)	(3)	(5)	(1)	(52)
Placed with relatives	0	1	4	2	3	2	0	1	0	1
		(1)	(8)	(2)	(8)	(3)		(1)		(23)
Returned to parents	14	10	7	3	40	24	7	4	2	11
	(3)	(12)	(15)	(4)	(100)	(40)	(25)	(25)	(4)	(228)
Institutionalized	5	2	3	4	6	2	2	1	0	2
	(1)	(3)	(6)	(5)	(14)	(4)	(5)	(7)		(45)
Returned to juvenile/superior court	0	0	0	2	5	1	2	1	2	2
				(2)	(13)	(2)	(8)	(9)	(4)	(38)
Mother kept child	0	0	0	0	1	0	10	19	5	8
					(1)		(35)	(121)	(8)	(165)
Outcome missing	14	19	19	7	4	1	3	1	0	5
	(3)	(24)	(39)	(9)	(11)	(2)	(10)	(4)		(102)
Total	22	125	205	137	252	164	335	643	179	2,062

Note: Figures in parentheses refer to the number of cases. Due to rounding, percentage totals do not always add up to 100 percent.

percent of the CHSW's charges are known to have been adopted. This surprisingly low percentage results in part from a lack of data caused by poor record keeping, especially before 1920: as table 12 reveals, outcomes were missing from 17 percent of cases. Just as important in explaining the relatively low percentage of CHSW adoptions were the pre–World War II alternatives to adoption and the strength of both cultural factors and social work ideals.

Before World War II, adoption was a stigmatized institution and faced an uphill battle for acceptance among Americans, who generally valued blood over adoptive kinship. America's cultural bias against adoptive kinship was reinforced by the general belief that the progeny of out-of-wedlock mothers carried such genetic defects as "feeblemindedness" or were criminally inclined.[45] Initially, CHSW authorities addressed such cultural attitudes by "selling" adoption. In the early years, for example, officials permitted adoptive families to return children if not completely happy with them, and 9 percent did so during the CHSW's first five years of existence. Similarly, during these early years, CHSW officials did not insist that families adopt the child, with the result that 5 percent of children were placed in families but not adopted. Likewise, couples could choose between indenturing children by contract and adoption, and between 1895 and 1909, 15.5 percent of families opted for indenture. (After 1910 the demand for children rose and the number of would-be adoptive parents outnumbered the children available, and CHSW officials ceased permitting indenture.) During the first fifteen years of the CHSW's existence, mortality rates were high: sickly infants, overcrowding, and a lack of medical attention resulted in the death of 13 percent of the CHSW's children before they could be adopted.

Moreover, professional adoption workers believed in the importance of blood kinship and adhered to a social work ideal mandating that children not be removed from home for reasons of poverty. Consequently, social workers preferred to return children to their parents if possible.[46] Before World War II, CHSW adoption workers returned 15 percent of the agency's children to their parents, while another 2 percent were placed with other birth relatives. Not surprisingly, the Great Depression (40 percent) and the war years (24 percent) saw the largest percentages of children returned to parents who had placed them in the CHSW for temporary boarding care.

Between the 1930s and 1940s, the percentage of CHSW children adopted grew dramatically. Various prewar factors that had accounted for the relatively low percentage of adoptees became attenuated or disappeared completely. In particular, Americans' belief that adoption was a second-rate kinship system weakened. Although adoption would still carry with it a stigma (as it does today), the Holocaust and Hitler's eugenics program made any claim based on the superiority of blood and genes unacceptable. In the place of heredity, Americans embraced the power of the environment and parental love—nurture was believed to be more powerful than nature. In an era of pronatalism, optimism, and prosperity, the stigma of adoption waned as tens of thousands of couples looked favorably on adoption as a solution to childlessness. Consequently, CHSW officials no longer had to "sell" adoption to a skeptical public. In addition, after World War II, professional adoption workers embraced various strands of psychoanalytic theory that labeled unmarried mothers mentally unstable and, for the first time, vigorously advocated the separation of mother and child. As a result of popular demand and encouragement from social workers, adoption became the first choice for all concerned.[47] Between 1950 and 1973, the CHSW witnessed a decline in the percentage of children institutionalized, placed in foster care, or dying while with the agency. However, one postwar phenomenon bucked this trend toward adoption: 11 percent of the unmarried mothers who came to the CHSW's maternity home intending to relinquish their babies chose to keep them. This development would eventually reduce drastically the number of healthy, white infants available for adoption.

Adoptive Parents

The occupations and educational level of adoptive parents, by which for the time period covered in this essay usually means adoptive fathers, differed significantly from those of birth parents. Whereas the vast majority of birth mothers in the workforce labored as domestics and in unskilled jobs, table 13 shows that 81 percent of adoptive fathers worked at such high-prestige jobs as professional or manager (32 percent), foreman/skilled craftsman (17 percent), salesman (9 percent), farmer or rancher (9 percent), business proprietor (7 percent), and government civil servant (7 percent). Only 11 percent of adoptive fathers were unskilled laborers, and hardly any were enrolled in high school or in college.[48]

World War II did not constitute a watershed in the occupational structure of adoptive parents. Nevertheless, between 1900 and 1973 several incremental and broad trends can be identified. As Washington state became increasingly urban, the percentage of adoptive parents who were farmers or ranchers decreased from 32 percent in 1900–1909 to 4 percent in the 1970s. Similarly, the percentage of adoptive parents who worked in unskilled jobs declined steadily from 21 percent in 1900–1909 to 10 percent in the 1970s. The percentage of adoptive parents who were self-employed or salaried professionals increased from 9 percent in 1900–1909 to 42 percent in the 1970s. Indicative of the massive growth in government services after World War II, adoptive fathers were well represented in civil service jobs, growing from none in 1900 to 11 percent in the 1970s. Over the course of the twentieth century, the CHSW increasingly chose adoptive parents from higher-prestige occupations.

Adoptive parents' overall median income level was in the $6,000 to $8,999 range (see table 14). These figures have limited significance because inflation

TABLE 13.   Occupation of Adoptive Father, 1895–1973 (in percentages)

	1895–99	1900–1909	1910–1919	1920–29	1930–39	1940–49	1950–59	1960–69	1970–73	Overall
Professional	14	9	24	19	22	28	34	37	42	32
	(1)	(3)	(23)	(16)	(11)	(30)	(72)	(146)	(58)	(360)
Foreman or skilled laborer	14	18	12	21	18	21	15	16	19	17
	(1)	(6)	(11)	(18)	(9)	(22)	(31)	(62)	(26)	(186)
Salesman	27	3	5	14	14	9	8	8	9	9
	(2)	(1)	(5)	(12)	(7)	(9)	(18)	(30)	(13)	(97)
Farmer or rancher	14	32	28	13	8	11	6	3	4	9
	(1)	(11)	(26)	(11)	(4)	(12)	(12)	(13)	(5)	(95)
Proprietor or owner	14	3	14	10	14	8	9	5	5	7
	(1)	(1)	(13)	(8)	(7)	(8)	(20)	(19)	(7)	(84)
Civil service	14	0	2	2	6	7	6	8	11	7
	(1)		(2)	(2)	(3)	(8)	(14)	(31)	(15)	(76)
Unskilled or farm laborer	0	27	9	16	8	10	13	11	4	11
		(9)	(8)	(13)	(4)	(11)	(30)	(42)	(6)	(123)
Clerical	0	3	5	2	6	1	1	1	1	1
		(1)	(5)	(2)	(3)	(1)	(3)	(1)	(1)	(17)
Service[a]	0	0	0	1	0	0	1	1	0	0
				(1)			(1)	(1)		(3)
Military	0	3	1	0	2	4	6	12	4	7
		(1)	(1)		(1)	(4)	(13)	(47)	(6)	(73)
High school student	0	3	0	0	0	0	0	0	0	0
		(1)								(1)
College student	0	0	0	0	0	1	0	1	0	0
						(1)		(2)		(4)
Total	7	34	94	84	49	106	214	394	137	1,119

Note: Figures in parentheses refer to the number of cases. Due to rounding, percentage totals do not always add up to 100 percent.
 [a] Gardener, porter, bartender, cab driver.

and labor productivity changed the purchasing value of money throughout the twentieth century. In addition, the CHSW application form did not ask prospective adoptive parents to place a dollar amount on their income until the 1920s, and the data for the 1930s are statistically invalid. Still, before World War II, when the median income for American families was $1,160, the incomes of the CHSW's adoptive parents ranged from $9,000 to more than $21,000. These figures support the contemporary perception that adoption was only for socially prominent, wealthy individuals.[49] In addition, between 1895 and 1973, 80 percent of the CHSW's adoptive parents owned homes, a phenomenon that added to the perception of wealth (see table 15). The public's exaggerated idea of adoptive parents' wealthy status was reinforced by the prominence the media gave to the adoption of babies by World War I hero Eddie Rickenbacker, Hollywood stars George Burns and Gracie Allen, and popular New York Mayor Fiorello LaGuardia. By the mid-1930s, social workers were actively denying the

During the 1950s baby boom, tens of thousands of childless couples adopted children and moved to the suburbs.

relationship and assuring the public that millionaire status was not necessary to adopt a child.[50]

During the 1940s, the CHSW's tendency to place children with wealthy adoptive parents changed significantly, as 23 percent of the agency's adoptive parents fell below the 1947 median income of $3,157 for white Americans.[51] Still, 77 percent were above the median income, though only a small percentage of those, 8 percent, could be classed as wealthy. The trend toward choosing middle-class families as adoptive parents continued. In 1950s, when the median income of white American families was $4,605, 60 percent of the children placed by the CHSW went to families earning between $3,000 and $5,999, and only 35 percent of adoptive couples were significantly above the median income, while 5 percent could be classified as wealthy. Similarly in the 1960s, when the median income of white American families rose to $6,858, 18 percent of the CHSW's adopters were below the median level, 44 were at or slightly above the median level, and 38 percent were significantly above the median level. Over its history, instead of favoring the rich, the CHSW increasing placed a majority of the children with middle-class adoptive parents with incomes below or slightly above the median of white, American families.

These pre–World War II well-educated, middle-class, prospective adoptive parents had a decided preference for adopting girls. In 1907, for example, the

TABLE 14.   Income of CHSW Adoptive Parents, 1920–73 (in percentages)

	1920–29	1930–39	1940–49	1950–59	1960–69	1970–73	Overall
$1,000–2,999	0	0	23	2	0	0	3
			(19)	(4)			(23)
$3,000–5,999	0	100	60	60	18	1	29
		(1)	(50)	(144)	(74)	(1)	(270)
$6,000–8,999	0	0	8	26	44	19	30
			(7)	(62)	(181)	(29)	(279)
$9,000–11,999	4	0	6	9	25	35	20
	(1)		(5)	(21)	(102)	(55)	(184)
$12,000–14,999	8	0	1	2	8	26	9
	(2)		(1)	(6)	(35)	(41)	(85)
$15,000–17,999	36	0	1	1	2	10	4
	(9)		(1)	(1)	(10)	(16)	(37)
$18,000–20,999	44	0	0	1	2	4	3
	(11)			(1)	(10)	(7)	(29)
$21,000 and higher	8	0	1	1	1	4	1
	(2)		(1)	(1)	(3)	(6)	(13)
Total	(25)	1	84	240	415	155	920

Note: Figures in parentheses refer to the number of cases. Due to rounding, percentage totals do not always add up to 100 percent.

TABLE 15.   Home Ownership of CHSW Adoptive Parents, 1895–1973 (in percentages)

	1895–99	1900–1909	1910–19	1920–29	1930–39	1940–49	1950–59	1960–69	1970–73	Overall
Own	67	81	68	72	64	75	82	81	96	80
	(4)	(29)	(61)	(33)	(27)	(59)	(174)	(315)	(132)	(834)
Rent	33	19	32	28	36	25	18	19	4	20
	(2)	(7)	(29)	(13)	(15)	(20)	(38)	(73)	(6)	(203)
Total	6	36	90	46	42	79	212	388	138	1,037

Note: Figures in parentheses refer to the number of cases.

Delineator's popular campaign to promote adoption noted that there were twice as many requests for girls as for boys and that every would-be adoptive parent wanted "a two-year old, blue-eyed, golden haired little girl with curls."[52] The reasons that researchers have proposed for the preference for girls include the belief that they were easier to raise than boys, the ultimate decision-making power of adoptive mothers who wanted girls for companionship, and a cultural revolution in adoption practices that stressed sentimental over economic motivations in taking children into the home.[53] Table 23 demonstrates that during the 1930s, 59 percent of the CHSW's prospective adoptive parents desired girls.[54] However, as table 16 shows, between 1940 and 1944, 44 percent of applicants desired boys, and only 22 percent preferred girls (the rest indicated no preference). And overall, throughout the CHSW's history, adoptive parents preferred girls by only a small margin over boys (38 to 30 percent).[55]

More significant and largely overlooked is the number of prospective adoptive parents who were willing to accept children of either sex: throughout the CHSW's history, 31 percent of applicants fell into this category. World War II again represents a watershed. Before World War II, only 14 percent of applicants indicated that they would accept a child of either sex. After the war, that number more than doubled, to 35 percent. This newfound flexibility was a consequence of postwar pronatalism, which made adoption immensely popular, exacerbated the demand for adoptable infants, and created a shortage of babies.

It is a truism in adoption history that when placing a child, agencies overwhelmingly favored childless couples. The CHSW's practice before World War II supports this perception, with 93 percent of children placed with childless families. However, a longer view of CHSW adoption practices modifies this finding. As table 17 reveals, over the CHSW's entire history, childless couples constituted only 75 percent of recipients, while a surprising 11 percent of adoptive parents already had one or two biological children and another 14 percent had one or two adopted children. The 1940s marked the beginning of a significant trend away from placing children with childless couples, as CHSW officials increasingly favored those who already had biological children. An even more dramatic change in the CHSW's placement policy was the favorable assessment of adoptive parents. Before World War II, the CHSW rarely placed children with parents who already had one adopted child and never placed children with a family that had adopted two children. As late as 1944, the CHSW's official policy was not to accept applications from prospective parents who already had adopted two or more children.[56] These CHSW policies opposed both popular and social work prejudices, which favored the ideal of the two-child family and condemned singletons as "generally maladjusted, self-centered, and self-willed, attention seeking and dependent on others, temperamental and anxious, generally unhappy and unlikable."[57] As one doctor put it during the 1920s, "if you have an only child, you should either drown him or adopt

TABLE 16. Gender Preference of Adoptive Parents, 1895–1973 (in percentages)

	1895–99	1900–1904	1905–1909	1910–14	1915–19	1920–24	1925–29	1930–34	1935–39	1940–44	1945–49	1950–54	1955–59	1960–64	1965–69	1970–73	Overall
Girl	44 (4)	20 (2)	58 (15)	53 (28)	49 (18)	44 (17)	13 (2)	50 (10)	67 (16)	22 (5)	35 (19)	30 (21)	29 (33)	43 (53)	36 (60)	35 (41)	38 (344)
Boy	44 (4)	50 (5)	27 (7)	38 (20)	41 (15)	41 (16)	56 (9)	35 (7)	21 (5)	43 (10)	22 (12)	26 (18)	29 (33)	21 (26)	33 (55)	24 (28)	30 (270)
Either	0	30 (3)	15 (4)	8 (4)	11 (4)	13 (5)	13 (2)	15 (3)	13 (3)	35 (8)	43 (23)	44 (30)	41 (47)	35 (43)	30 (50)	42 (50)	31 (279)
Twins	11 (1)	0	0	2 (1)	0	3 (1)	19 (3)	0	0	0	0	0	2 (2)	1 (1)	1 (1)	0	1 (10)
Total	9	10	26	53	37	39	16	20	24	23	54	69	115	123	166	119	903

Note: Figures in parentheses refer to the number of cases. Due to rounding, percentage totals do not always add up to 100 percent.

TABLE 17. Number of Other Children in CHSW Adoptive Parents' Homes before Adoption, 1895–1973 (in percentages)

	1895–99	1900–1909	1910–19	1920–29	1930–39	1940–49	1950–59	1960–69	1970–73	Overall
Childless	96 (23)	96 (121)	89 (187)	89 (144)	95 (250)	83 (142)	71 (244)	63 (407)	47 (84)	75 (1,602)
One child	0	3 (4)	8 (16)	6 (10)	3 (7)	7 (12)	7 (24)	8 (49)	14 (25)	7 (147)
Two or more children	4 (1)	1 (1)	2 (4)	4 (6)	1 (1)	0	2 (5)	6 (42)	14 (25)	4 (85)
One adopted child	0	0	1 (2)	1 (1)	1 (4)	10 (17)	19 (67)	20 (127)	21 (37)	12 (255)
Two adopted children	0	0	0	0	0	0	1 (4)	3 (23)	4 (8)	2 (35)
Total	24	126	209	161	262	171	344	648	179	2,124

Note: Figures in parentheses refer to the number of cases.

another."[58] In this respect, World War II again constituted a watershed. During the 1940s, the percentage of children placed with families that already had one adopted child soared tenfold, and the percentage almost doubled again during the 1950s. In the same decade, CHSW adoption workers began placing children with families that had already adopted two children, a practice that quadrupled by the 1970s. Again, the CHSW's practice contradicted contemporary social science advice, which by the 1970s had begun to show the advantages of being an only child and to dispel the popular belief that singletons were inherently disadvantaged.[59]

The ages of adoptive parents' previous children also shed light on the CHSW's child-placement policy. According to table 18, before World War II, the children already in adoptive homes were older: 19 percent were four years old or less, 40 percent were between five and ten years old, and 41 percent were older than ten. This policy changed dramatically in the 1940s, when adoption workers placed 84 percent of the children with families with younger children. However, this number dropped steadily from this peak, and the CHSW subsequently again placed children in homes with older children.

We are fortunate that in 1910, the CHSW revised its application form and began to ask would-be adopters to provide their reasons for hoping to adopt. Their motivations varied and changed over time, but for the most part, sentimental rather than instrumental reasons dominate. The CHSW's applicants did not want to adopt children for work or chores or even to provide heirs. As table 19 reveals, before World War II, only .33 percent of prospective adoptive parents indicated work purposes as their reason for adopting, and only 1 percent claimed they wanted to adopt for inheritance purposes. At the same time, 82 percent of prospective adopters sought children for sentimental reasons, including a desire for companionship, a desire to start a family, a willingness to adopt (in contrast to indenture), a love of children, and a wish to act altruistically.

TABLE 18.   Age of Other Children in CHSW Adoptive Parents' Homes, 1900–1973 (in percentages)

	1900–1909	1910–19	1920–29	1930–39	1940–49	1950–59	1960–69	1970–73	Overall
Infant (under 4 years of age)	0	22	27	27	84	78	73	70	66
		(4)	(12)	(3)	(21)	(69)	(127)	(48)	(284)
5–10 years of age	0	50	64	46	16	17	20	26	26
		(9)	(28)	(5)	(4)	(15)	(35)	(18)	(114)
Over 10 years	100	28	9	27	0	5	6	4	8
	(4)	(5)	(4)	(3)		(4)	(11)	(3)	(34)
Total	4	18	44	11	25	88	173	69	432

Note: Figures in parentheses refer to the number of cases. Due to rounding, percentage totals do not always add up to 100 percent.

But by another important index, age preferences, adoption's cultural transformation from instrumentalism to sentimentalism seems to have been much more incremental than Vivian A. Zelizer claims.[60] Every modern historical study on adoption assumes that pre–World War II adoptive parents desired infants, but a majority of the CHSW's applicants sought older children. In fact, table 20 shows that before 1930, only 19 percent of would-be adoptive parents preferred infants, and 41 percent sought children between one and three years of age. Most revealing, before the war roughly 50 percent of prospective adopters preferred children over age three, and 15 percent requested children over age five. These numbers strongly suggest a definite preference for older children, for reasons that included fear of newborns' vulnerability to sudden death, concern about the genetic makeup of prospective adopted children (feeblemindedness), and apprehension about the difficulty of caring for an infant. Additional evidence for adoptive parents' preference for older children can also be found in the records of other adoption agencies. Adoption expert Sophie van Senden Theis undertook a pioneering study in 1922. Examining 910 children placed in adoptive homes by the State Charities Aid Association of New

TABLE 19. CHSW Adoptive Parents' Motivations for Adoption, 1910–1973 (in percentages)

	1910–19	1920–29	1930–39	1940–49	1950–59	1960–69	1970–73	Overall
Chores	0	1 (1)	0	0	0	0	0	0 (1)
Inheritance	2 (1)	1 (1)	0	0	0	0	0	0 (2)
Companionship for self	22 (13)	47 (50)	5 (2)	1 (1)	1 (2)	0	0	7 (68)
Desire for family	36 (21)	12 (13)	36 (16)	6 (5)	1 (2)	1 (4)	1 (1)	6 (62)
Adoption	12 (7)	14 (15)	9 (4)	0	0	0	0	3 (26)
Love of children	14 (8)	12 (13)	11 (5)	2 (2)	0	0	0	3 (28)
Altruism	5 (3)	2 (2)	11 (5)	1 (1)	1 (1)	2 (6)	5 (6)	2 (24)
Physically unable to have children	0	4 (4)	7 (3)	84 (76)	97 (191)	93 (326)	93 (123)	74 (723)
Companionship for sibling	7 (4)	5 (5)	14 (6)	6 (5)	1 (2)	4 (13)	2 (2)	4 (37)
Replacement for death of child	3 (2)	2 (2)	7 (3)	1 (1)	0	0	1 (1)	1 (9)
Total	59	106	44	91	198	349	133	980

Note: Figures in parentheses refer to the number of cases. Due to rounding, percentage totals do not always add up to 100 percent.

York (SCAA), she found that only 12.4 percent of the children were under one year old, and 29.7 percent were under three. Thus, slightly more than 70 percent of the children placed by the SCAA were over three.[61] Similarly, a study of 852 children adopted in Massachusetts between 1922 and 1925 revealed that only 19 percent were under the age of one.[62]

The turning point in the CHSW's adoptive parents' preferences and, by extension, the complete sentimentalization of adoption occurred not in the first quarter of the twentieth century but in the 1940s and 1950s. Table 20 demonstrates that the percentage of adoptive parents who preferred newborns more than doubled between the 1930s and 1940s and reached 70 percent during the 1950s. By the 1970s, 98 percent of prospective adopted parents requested newborns. At the other end of the spectrum, would-be adoptive parents' desire for children five years of age or older vanished after the Great Depression. The sentimentalization of adoption during the 1940s was the result of numerous factors, including the low depression birthrate, wartime prosperity, and the baby boom pronatalism that put a premium on family and home life.[63]

World War II was also a watershed in adoptive parents' motivations to adopt a child, but the war itself had little to do with changing their attitudes. Instead, medical discoveries between the 1920s and 1940s concerning infertility and its treatment radically transformed the nature of both prospective adoptive par-

TABLE 20.   CHSW Adoptive Parents' Age Preferences for Children, 1900–1973 (in percentages)

	1900–1909	1910–19	1920–29	1930–39	1940–49	1950–59	1960–69	1970–73	Overall
Newborn	0	5	20	21	48	70	85	98	55
		(2)	(12)	(6)	(23)	(70)	(56)	(63)	(232)
1–6 months	16	42	19	28	19	19	2	0	16
	(3)	(16)	(11)	(8)	(9)	(18)	(1)		(66)
7–11 months	0	0	3	0	2	0	0	0	1
			(2)		(1)				(3)
12–18 months	21	16	24	7	13	6	9	0	10
	(4)	(6)	(14)	(2)	(6)	(6)	(6)		(44)
2 years	16	11	7	21	10	5	3	2	7
	(3)	(4)	(4)	(6)	(5)	(5)	(2)	(1)	(30)
3 years	5	18	12	10	2	0	0	0	4
	(1)	(7)	(7)	(3)	(1)				(19)
4 years	11	3	3	3	6	1	2	0	3
	(2)	(1)	(2)	(1)	(3)	(1)	(1)		(11)
5 or more years	32	5	12	10	0	0	0	0	4
	(6)	(2)	(7)	(3)					(18)
Total	19	38	59	29	48	100	66	64	423

Note: Figures in parentheses refer to the number of cases. Due to rounding, percentage totals do not always add up to 100 percent.

ents' motivations and the CHSW's policy toward choosing adopters. Before World War II, medical experts were unable to identify conclusively the causes of infertility. Consequently, only 2.5 percent of adoptive parents gave involuntary childlessness as a reason for adopting (see table 19). During the same period of time, however, scientists were making great strides in understanding women's reproductive endocrinology—estrogen was discovered, nonsurgical methods were devised for determining whether the fallopian tubes were open, details of ovarian function were explicated, and hormones were synthesized. In addition, mass-market magazines propagated the false idea that adoption enhanced the chances of pregnancy for involuntarily childless couples. Popular magazines, books, and films widely disseminated both news of scientific advances and false notions about the effects of adoption on conception, probably resulting in the dramatic increase between the 1930s and 1940s in the number of adoptive parents who gave physical inability to conceive as their reason for adopting a child. But as private infertility practices and infertility clinics for indigent patients sprang up in urban areas, childless couples had easy access to numerous diagnostic tests and complex treatments to overcome their infertility. And when these treatments failed, as was frequently the case, childless couples came in droves to the CHSW. From the Depression decade when a mere 4 percent of would-be adoptive parents stated they were unable to conceive, 84 percent in the decade of World War II made the same claim.[64] In the late 1940s, buffeted by the pronatalism of the baby boom, the CHSW reinforced this change in adoptive parents' motivations by insisting that medical proof of infertility was the sine qua non for receiving a child.

Conclusion

In many ways, World War II was a watershed in the lives of adoption triad members and, to a lesser degree, in the CHSW's adoption policies. Shifts in the demographic composition of the CHSW's clientele, new ideas in social work, wartime necessity, pronatalism, and prosperity were mostly responsible for these profound changes. As a result, the age at which birth parents relinquished their children declined radically, and birth parents became better educated and employed in higher-prestige occupations. Birth parents' marital status also underwent major changes during the war years, shifting from married couples who relinquished children for adoption for a multitude of preventable reasons such as poverty and family breakup to single mothers who relinquished their children so that they could escape the stigma of illegitimacy and start life anew. World War II also marked a watershed in children's ages of adoption, which steeply declined from an average of 4.5 years to 1.5 years. Moreover, World War II constituted a watershed in adoptive parents' gender preferences: desperately wanting children, many more postwar adoptive parents indicated that they would accept either a boy or a girl. Adoptive parents' preferences also changed from older children to newborns, thereby marking the complete sentimentalization of adoption. This essay, while relying almost exclusively on the CHSW's adoption case records, attempts to make its findings representative by incorporating all past studies relevant to the topics investigated. All of these studies support the essay's thesis that World War II constituted a watershed in the history of adoption. Still, this essay marks only the beginning; it is hoped it will spur adoption agencies to open their records to researchers to test and expand upon these conclusions.

NOTES

E. Wayne Carp gathered the quantitative data and researched and wrote the essay. Anna Leon-Guerrero provided invaluable technical assistance on the data analysis and presentation. Carp would like to acknowledge gratefully the many helpful suggestions and comments from Mark K. Jensen, Barbara Melosh, Susan L. Porter, and Paula Shields. He would also like to thank Sharon Osborne, Executive Director of the Children's Home Society of Washington (CHSW), for permission to use the CHSW's case records and Cheryl Murfin Bond, the CHSW's communications director, for her cooperation in securing illustrations for the essay.

1. G. Kitson Clark, *The Making of Victorian England* (Cambridge: Harvard University Press, 1962), 14.

2. A short history of this development can be found in National Committee for Adoption, *Factbook: United States Data, Issues, Regulations, and Resources* (Washington, D.C.: National Committee for Adoption, 1989), 56–58.

3. Benson Jaffee and David Fanshel, *How They Fared in Adoption: A Follow-up Study* (New York: Columbia University Press, 1970). See also Mary Ruth Colby, *Problems and Procedures in Adoption* (Washington D.C.: U.S. Government Printing Office, 1941); Alice M. Leahy, "Some Characteristics of Adoptive Parents," *American Journal of Sociology* 38 (Jan. 1933): 548–63.

4. The CHSW's original name was the Washington Children's Home Society. In 1959, the society's name was changed to make clear to the public that the child welfare institution was neither run nor supported by the state (Stephanie Cline and Dana Blue, *A Century of Turning Hope into Reality: A 100-Year Retrospect of Children's Home Society in Washington State* [Seattle: Children's Home Society of Washington, 1996], 58. To avoid confusion, the CHSW's current name will be used throughout this essay.

5. E. Wayne Carp, *Family Matters: Secrecy and Disclosure in the History of Adoption* (Cambridge: Harvard University Press, 1998), 11–12; E. Wayne Carp, "The Sentimentalization of Adoption: When, Why, How?" paper presented at the American Historical Association, San Francisco, Jan. 6, 2002. We are using the term *watershed* as a historical metaphor representing a dramatic division between two areas of time. See Marcus Cunliffe, "American Watersheds," *American Quarterly* 13 (winter 1961): 481.

6. Robert G. Spinney, *World War II in Nashville: Transformation of the Homefront* (Knoxville: University of Tennessee Press, 1998); William Chafe, *The American Woman: Her Changing Social, Economic, and Political Roles, 1920–1970* (New York: Oxford Uni-

versity Press, 1972); Richard Polenberg, *War and Society: The United States, 1941–1945* (Philadelphia: Lippincott, 1972); Richard M. Dalfiume, *Desegregation of the U.S. Armed Forces: Fighting on Two Fronts, 1939–1953* (Columbia: University of Missouri Press, 1969); Gerald D. Nash, *The American West Transformed: The Impact of the Second World War* (Bloomington: Indiana University Press, 1985).

7. Allan M. Winkler, *Home Front U.S.A.: America during World War II* (Arlington Heights, Ill.: H. Davidson, 1986); John Morton Blum, *V Was for Victory: Politics and American Culture during World War II* (New York: Harcourt Brace Jovanovich, 1976); Alan Clive, *State of War: Michigan in World War II* (Ann Arbor: University of Michigan Press, 1979).

8. For a balanced view, see John W. Jeffries, *Wartime America: The World War II Home Front* (Chicago: Ivan R. Dee, 1996), esp. chap. 1. For the most part, historians have failed to address the issue of the effects of World War II on social welfare policies. See, for example, Walter I. Trattner, *From Poor Law to Welfare State: A History of Social Welfare in America*, 5th ed. (New York: Free Press, 1994). One exception is June Axinn and Herman Levin, *Social Welfare: A History of the American Response to Need* (New York: Harper and Row, 1975), which views World War II as a period of dramatic change in the area of employment, income, and increased social and educational opportunity.

9. Exceptions include the intervals for 1895–99 and 1970–75.

10. Cline and Blue, *Century*.

11. See for example, Rickie Solinger, *Wake up Little Susie: Single Pregnancy and Race before Roe v. Wade* (New York: Routledge, 1992); Regina G. Kunzel, *Fallen Women, Problem Girls: Unmarried Mothers and the Professionalization of Social Work, 1890–1945* (New Haven: Yale University Press, 1993).

12. Birth mothers' age of 25.7 calculated by averaging table 1 categories "Birth mother Age 1900–1904" through "Birth mother Age 1940–44."

13. Edward A. Krug, *The Shaping of the American High School* (Madison: University of Wisconsin Press, 1972), 2:7, 42.

14. Michael L. Kurtz, *The Challenging of America, 1920–1945* (Arlington Heights, Ill.: Forum Press, 1986), 121–22.

15. Harvey Green, *The Uncertainty of Everyday Life, 1915–1945* (New York: Harper-Collins, 1992), 153.

16. William H. Chafe, *The Paradox of Change: American Women in the Twentieth Century* (New York: Oxford University Press, 1991), 68, 121.

17. Ibid., 130. Chafe notes that the female labor force had increased by more than six million, raising the total number of women in the labor force to twenty million (*Paradox*, 133).

18. Paula J. Dubeck and Kathryn Borman, eds., *Women and Work: A Handbook* (New York: Garland, 1996), table 1, p. 4.

19. The Child Welfare League of America noted a growing problem: how were agencies to deal with the adoption of children born out of wedlock to married women whose husbands were overseas? See *Child Welfare League of America Bulletin* 23 (Nov. 1944): 9, 15 (hereafter cited as *CWLA Bulletin*).

20. William M. Tuttle Jr., *"Daddy's Gone to War": The Second World War in the Lives of American Children* (New York: Oxford University Press, 1993), 28; Carp, *Family Matters*, 28. These are official government estimates. Tuttle suggests that the numbers were

probably much higher given the stigma surrounding having a child out of wedlock in the 1940s (Tuttle, *"Daddy's,"* 28).

21. See for example, Children's Home Society of Washington Case Records 10142, 14152, 14412, 15382, Children's Home Society of Washington, Records Department, Seattle (hereafter cited as CHSW CR).

22. For examples of parents who claimed to be too old to care for children, see CHSW CRs 14672, 18232, 20643; for parents not wanting responsibility, see CHSW CRs 8832, 10512, 17922; for unfaithful spouses, see CHSW CRs 13662, 16442, 17342, 20242, 20752.

23. Glenn H. Elder Jr., *Children of the Great Depression: Social Change in Life Experience* (Chicago: University of Chicago Press, 1974), 80.

24. Carp, *Family Matters,* 31–33. In 1940, Washington had only 7,424 Blacks out of a total population of 1.7 million (Robert E. Ficken and Charles P. LeWarne, *Washington: A Centennial History* [Seattle: University of Washington Press, 1988], 130, 155).

25. Andrew Billingsly and Jeanne M. Giovannoni, *Children of the Storm: Black Children and American Child Welfare* (New York: Harcourt, Brace, Jovanovich, 1972), 27–38, 72–73; Harvard Sitkoff, *A New Deal for Blacks: The Emergence of Civil Rights as a National Issue,* rev. ed. (New York: Hill and Wang, 1993), 11–18; Neil A. Wynn, "The Impact of the Second World War on the American Negro," *Journal of Contemporary History* 6 (May 1971): 42–54.

26. Lois Wildy, "Reader's Forum," *Child Welfare* 28 (Jan. 1949): 10–11.

27. For a brief description of twenty of the programs and projects, see Annie Lee Sandusky et al., *Families for Black Children: The Search for Adoptive Parents,* vol. 2, *Programs and Projects* (Washington, D.C.: U.S. Government Printing Office, 1972). See also Joyce A. Ladner, *Mixed Families: Adopting across Racial Boundaries* (New York: Anchor Press, 1977), 68–69; Patricia Collmeyer, "From 'Operation Brown Baby' to 'Opportunity': The Placement of Children of Color at the Boys and Girls Aid Society of Oregon," *Child Welfare* 74 (Jan.–Feb. 1995): 242–63.

28. Ficken and LeWarne, *Washington,* 155.

29. Minutes of Supervisors' Meeting, "Report of the Minority Home Finding Committee," Nov. 11, 1958; Minutes of Supervisors' Meeting, "Negro Home Finding Project and Booklet," Dec. 10, 1957, typescript, both in Children's Home Society of Washington, Records Department, Seattle (hereafter cited as CHSW Recs.); Cline and Blue, *Century,* 58–59.

30. The figure thirty-five is derived from Cline and Blue, *Century,* 59, which notes that from 1955 to 1965 the CHSW placed children in homes at a rate of one a day. They also note that the CHSW was minimally involved in intercountry adoptions, averaging only one a year.

31. Carp, *Family Matters,* 28, 110–11.

32. The Catholic Bureau of New York City noted a similar pattern of decline. In 1945, most children referred for adoption were over two years of age, but in 1949 most were under six months (Weltha M. Kelley, "The Placement of Young Infants for Adoption," *Child Welfare* 28 [July 1949]: 14).

33. The 39 percent for the war years 1940–44 differs from table 10's figure of 37 percent for the decade 1940–49 because it is the average of the years 1940–44 (39 percent) and 1945–49 (35 percent).

34. Colby, *Problems and Procedures,* 10; Blum, *V Was for Victory,* chap. 3; Landon Y.

Jones, *Great Expectations: America and the Baby Boom Generation* (New York: Coward, McCann, and Geoghegan, 1980), chap. 2.

35. Kenneth Cmiel, *A Home of Another Kind: One Chicago Orphanage and the Tangle of Child Welfare* (Chicago: University of Chicago Press, 1995), 22; Judith A. Dulberger, "Refuge or Repressor: The Role of the Orphan Asylum in the Lives of Poor Children and Their Families in Late-Nineteenth Century America" (Ph.D. diss., Carnegie Mellon University, 1988), 162; Nurith Zmora, *Orphanages Reconsidered: Child Care Institutions in Progressive Era Baltimore* (Philadelphia: Temple University Press, 1994), 53.

36. See Brian Paul Gill's essay in this volume.

37. Maud Morlock to Majorie C. Anderson, July 12, 1944, Children's Bureau Records, record group 102, central file 1941–44, file 7-3-3-4, box 169, National Archives, Washington, D.C. (hereafter cited as CBR), p. 1. Morlock was summarizing the opinions of several experts in the field, including Sophie van Senden Theis of the New York State Charities Aid Society, Ora Pendleton of the Children's Bureau of Philadelphia, and Cheny Jones of the New England Home for Little Wanderers.

38. Sophie van Senden Theis, "Some Aspects of Good Adoptive Practices," *CWLA Bulletin* 19 (Nov. 1940): 2–3; Lucie K. Browning, "The Placement of the Child Needing Adoption: Recent Changes in Practice," *CWLA Bulletin* 23 (Sept. 1944): 5–6, 13–14. The impact of psychological and psychiatric experts is ironic because these authorities claimed that unwed mothers were neurotic at best and psychotic at worst and advocated separating unwed birth mothers from their babies for the sake of the infants' mental health. Thus, after creating the problem, they proposed a solution. See Carp, *Family Matters*, 114–16.

39. Anna Freud and Dorothy T. Burlingham, *Infants without Families* (New York: International Universities Press, 1944). See also *The Writings of Anna Freud*, vol. 3 (New York: International Universities Press, 1973).

40. Kelley, "Placement," 14, 15. See also Mary Elizabeth Fairweather, "Early Placement in Adoption," *Child Welfare* 31 (Mar. 1952): 3–8.

41. John Bowlby, *Maternal Care and Mental Health* (Geneva: World Health Organization, 1951), 15–51, 101–8. See also Bowlby, *A Secure Base: Parent-Child Attachment and Healthy Human Development* (New York: Basic Books, 1988), chap. 2. For Bowlby's "deep influence on agencies," see the statement by CWLA President Joseph H. Reid, "Principles, Values, and Assumptions Underlying Adoption Practice," in *Readings in Adoption*, ed. I. Evelyn Smith (New York: Philosophical Library, 1963), 33.

42. Elizabeth I. Lynch and Alice E. Mertz, "Adoptive Placement of Infants Directly from the Hospital," *Social Casework* 36 (Dec. 1955): 450–57. The infants were placed when between seven and twenty months old.

43. Report, Children's Home Society of Washington to Community Chests and United Funds, Aug. 1957, typescript, 2. CHSW, Records Department, Seattle.

44. "Minutes of Casework Study Meeting," Nov. 11, 1959, CHSW Recs.; "Findings of the Children Placed by Children's Home Society," June–Sept. 1959, 2, CHSW Recs. Medical problems included premature birth, severe eczema, a hernia operation, considerable difficulty in feeding, a heart murmur, a major physical handicap, or a history of serious ailments, such as cystic fibrosis or epilepsy. The Casework Study Planning Committee also identified some of the factors responsible for delaying successfully placed infants more than one month: legal delays, minor health problems, insufficient number of adoptive homes immediately available, and staff overwork.

45. Carp, *Family Matters,* 17–18; E. Wayne Carp, "Professional Social Workers, Adoption, and the Problem of Illegitimacy, 1915–1945," *Journal of Policy History* 6, no. 3 (1994): 169–73.

46. Carp, *Family Matters,* 16–17.

47. Ibid., 27–29, 113–21.

48. Other studies confirm these findings. See, for example, Leahy, "Some Characteristics," 560–61; Jaffee and Fanshel, *How They Fared,* 51.

49. U.S. Census Bureau, *Historical Statistics of the United States, Colonial Times to 1970,* bicentennial ed., pt. 1 (Washington, D.C.: U.S. Government Printing Office, 1975), 297. The huge disparity between CHSW adoptive parents' incomes and the median income of Americans probably was not typical. But the finding that prewar adoptive parents were wealthier than average Americans is accurate. As Children's Bureau researcher Mary Ruth Colby demonstrated in her study of 1,221 adopted children, the median income of their adoptive parents was almost twice the median for U.S. families (*Problems and Procedures,* 40).

50. Peter Romanofsky, "The Early History of Adoption Practices, 1870–1930" (Ph.D. diss., University of Missouri at Columbia, 1960), 175–77.

51. Median incomes calculated from U.S. Census Bureau, *Historical Statistics,* 297.

52. Mabel P. Daggett, "The Child without a Home," *Delineator* 70 (Oct. 1907): 510.

53. Colby, *Problems and Procedures,* 6; Viviana A. Zelizer, *Pricing the Priceless Child: The Changing Social Value of Children* (New York: Basic Books, 1985), 194; Leahy, "Some Characteristics," 557.

54. The 59 percent is calculated from averaging the two 1930s columns and rounding upward.

55. Colby, *Problems and Procedures,* 6; Zelizer, *Pricing the Priceless Child,* 193–94.

56. "A Statement of Adoption Polices. Approved by the Board of Trustees," Feb. 1944, 1, CHSW Recs.

57. V. D. Thompson, "Family Size: Implicit Policies and Assumed Psychological Outcomes," *Journal of Social Issues* 30 (1974): 93–124; Bill McKibben, *Maybe One: A Personal and Environmental Argument for Single-Child Families* (New York: Simon and Schuster 1998), 18–27.

58. "Some Misplaced Children," *Survey* 56 (Apr. 15, 1926): 84.

59. Toni Falbo, "Only Children: A Review," in *The Single-Child Family,* ed. Toni Falbo (New York: Guilford Press, 1981), 1–24; Judith Blake, "The Only Child in America: Prejudice versus Performance," in *Family Relations: A Reader,* ed. Norval D. Glenn and Marion Tolbert Coleman (Chicago: Dorsey Press, 1988), 406–19; McKibben, *Maybe One,* 28–62.

60. Zelizer, *Pricing the Priceless Child,* chap. 6.

61. Sophie van Senden Theis, *How Foster Children Turn Out* (New York: State Charities Association, 1924), 13. Remarkably, nearly 40 percent were adopted between the ages of ten and sixteen (Theis, *How Foster Children Turn Out,* 14).

62. Ida R. Parker, *"Fit and Proper"? A Study of Legal Adoptions in Massachusetts* (Boston: Church Home Society, 1927), 12–13.

63. Carp, *Family Matters,* 28–29. For an elaboration of the sentimentalization of adoption thesis, see E. Wayne Carp, "The Sentimentalization of Adoption: When, Why and How"; paper presented at the American Historical Association, San Francisco, Jan. 6, 2002.

64. Margaret Marsh and Wanda Ronner, *The Empty Cradle: Infertility in America from Colonial Times to the Present* (Baltimore: Johns Hopkins University Press, 1996), chap. 5. In their otherwise excellent study, Marsh and Ronner incorrectly state that "according to a study of couples who had adopted children between 1931 and 1940, approximately 85 percent adopted because of infertility" (169). However, Jaffee and Fanshel's study, which Marsh and Ronner cite in support of this claim, clearly shows that only 35 percent of couples attributed their desire to adopt to infertility (*How They Fared*, 62, 63). Although higher than the percentage of prospective adoptive couples in this study, Jaffee and Fanshel's data are more in accord with this study's findings than Marsh and Ronner's data are.

Adoption Stories
Autobiographical Narrative and the Politics of Identity

Barbara Melosh

Adoption is Other in a culture and kinship system organized by biological re-production. This essay examines autobiographical narratives of adopted persons, birth mothers, and adoptive parents as uneasy negotiations of identity.[1] Memoirs of adoption by adoptive parents first appeared in the 1930s, but adoption autobiography was not established as a recognizable subgenre until the 1970s, when first adopted persons and then women who had relinquished children for adoption published their stories as testimony of their critique of adoption practices. Some of these accounts have been written by the founders of and activists in the adoption rights movement; virtually all acknowledge its influence. At the same time, the increasing number of such accounts and their broader audience suggest their wider cultural resonance. Even as the number of adoptions has fallen sharply since 1970,[2] adoption stories have claimed a heightened public visibility.

Autobiographical construction of self is social and historical. These narratives illuminate the experience and cultural meaning of adoption, even as their explorations of anomalous families illuminate, by contrast, contemporary discourses of motherhood, family, and cultural identity more generally. I read these narratives as memoirs that write the self in negotiation with wider cultural positions or discourses on adoption. After World War II, adoption became more common and more widely accepted than it had been before. For the first time, a broad white middle-class consensus proclaimed adoption the "best solution" to the "problem" of pregnancy out of wedlock. Regina Kunzel has traced the shift of white middle-class response from the evangelical reform of the early twentieth century, which saw the pregnant woman as a sinner in need of moral redemption, to the expert professional consensus of the 1930s and 1940s, which viewed out-of-wedlock pregnancy as the "symptom" of neurosis: their clients were not fallen women but problem girls. After World War II, rising rates of premarital pregnancy among white teenagers further tempered white middle-class zeal for condemning the sinner. At the same time, the pronatalism of the 1940s and 1950s generated new public discussion and sympathy for the plight of infertile couples. In this context, adoption became widely accepted as an alternative route to family formation. The boundaries of adoptive families widened, too, as some agencies began to place African-American and American Indian children with white adopters.[3]

"Expert" narratives of adoption both reflected and codified these conditions. Professional literature—primarily that of social work but also that of psychology and psychiatry—advocated adoption as the "best solution" to the "problem" of out-of-wedlock pregnancy, at least for white women. In this narrative, adoption served all three parties in the relationship. The unwed mother might recover from the stigma of pregnancy out of wedlock, gaining a second chance for marriage and respectable motherhood. The child surrendered for adoption would benefit from the improved life chances afforded by growing up in a two-parent family. And the adoptive parents could recoup the losses of infertility by forming families through adoption (though not all adoptive parents were infertile or childless, most "stranger adoption" was motivated by infertility, and the discussion tends to focus on this kind of adoption, which constitutes on average about half of all adoptions).

During the period 1945–1965, adoption practice became more uniform than it had been before or would be after. Though adoption was and remains controlled at the state level and therefore operates under varying legal codes, most adoptions were mediated by public or private agencies under the control of social workers. Courts widely accepted social workers' legitimacy as experts qualified to counsel relinquishing parents, to assess adoptive homes, and to defend the best interests of the children.[4] Confidential adoption became standard practice—that is, birth and adoptive parents generally did not meet, birth parents had no contact with their children after they were relinquished, and most states used sealed records that concealed the identity of birth parents and substituted the names of adoptive parents on the birth certificate of adopted persons.[5] This practice powerfully symbolizes the cultural status of adoption as substitute family: the amended birth certificate rewrites the actual circumstances of the adoptive family in a document that makes their relationship indistinguishable from blood kinship, at least in the public record. Concern for matching—placing children with adoptive parents who were similar in appearance, temperament, and intelligence—also attests to the interest in effacing the difference of adoption, of making the adoptive family indistinguishable from the biological family. As anthropologist Judith Modell has observed, this embrace of adoption embodied a telling contradiction.[6] On one hand, in the United States adoption is the full legal equivalent of biological kinship: adoptive children are represented "as if begotten," an equivalence expressed through physical similarities in matching families. On the other hand, the biological family remains the standard of kinship: the mark of the acceptance of adoption is the cultural denial of its difference from biological relatedness.

Still, the social kinship of adoption enjoyed remarkably widespread support in the two decades following World War II. Experts and the lay public participated in a broad proadoption consensus whose tenets might be summarized as follows: as the full equivalent of biological family, adoptive families were permanent. What law had ordained was not subject to disruption or renegotiation, except under the same extraordinary circumstances that might call for the disruption of families joined by blood. Adoptive families were singular and exclusive: adoption permanently severed the bonds of blood kinship, replacing them with the legal ties of adoption. Favorable views of adoption rested on assumptions that nurture figured more prominently than nature in shaping human development. Expert and popular opinion alike approved relinquishment, portraying it as a difficult but loving and responsible response to pregnancy out of wedlock. Both experts and lay persons affirmed the power of love to heal the wounds of adoption—the disappointments of infertility, the pain of relinquishment for mother and child, even the damage of deprivation or abuse.

By 1970, that broad consensus began to crumble. Further liberalization of sexual attitudes, improved birth-control technology, and legal abortion made the "best solution" seem anachronistic. Women could terminate unwelcome pregnancies or raise children born out of wedlock without automatically forfeiting middle-class prospects of respectability. The political ferment of the 1960s challenged the consensus around adoption in other ways. At home and abroad, nationalist movements produced sharp critiques of interracial and transnational adoptions. In 1972, the National Association of Black Social Workers declared its opposition to white adoption of black children, a position that reversed a growing trend toward such adoptive families in the 1950s and 1960s.[7] Activists defending tribal autonomy forced the termination of the American Indian Project, a national effort, jointly sponsored by the Child Welfare League and the Bureau of Indian Affairs, that sought to place Native American children with white adopters between 1958 and 1967.[8] As American leftists responded to nationalist movements in the Third World, some castigated international adoption as a form of imperialism. Around the world, in places that had become well-known sources of adoptive children, governments reassessed their participation in the international movement of children, and many moved to restrict out-of-country adoption. In scientific and popular discourses, environmentalism gradually yielded to a pervasive biological determinism that renewed old fears of the risks of adoption.

Adopted persons themselves contested the narrative of the "best solution," and women who had relinquished children for adoption soon followed. The sunny optimism of the "best solution," they argued, denied the trauma of adoption's rupture of biological kinship. Adopted persons protested the idea that legal identity could erase blood kinship. In a growing search movement, they fought cultural and legal prohibitions to establish ties with biological kin. Women who had relinquished children for adoption began to speak out. Rejecting the shield of silence provided by confidential adoption, they challenged the postwar consensus. In an autobiographical act of renaming and self-construction, they claimed the new identity of "birthmother," a neologism that repudiated the fundamental doctrine of adoption, that blood ties could be permanently severed by law. By the early 1970s, this growing critique of adoption had begun to take on the organization and self-consciousness of a social movement, later named the adoption rights movement.[9]

Adoption stories offer evidence of dramatically changing views of the institution while suggesting the ways that autobiographical narrative operates to shape, circulate, and reframe ideas about adoption. Most adoptive parents' accounts validate the postwar consensus in stories that celebrate alternative family formation. By contrast, many memoirs of adopted persons and birth mothers challenge the tenets of the postwar consensus by reclaiming the blood ties supposedly erased by adoption. All signify the difference of adoption in one way or another: these stories are notable because they explore kinship that violates the cultural expectations attached to biological family. And, in one way or another, all register the stigma attached to that difference: they are negotiations of what sociologist Erving Goffman called "spoiled identity."[10] These accounts illustrate fractures in the cultural ideology that proclaims adoption the equivalent of biological kin by exploring the ways in which adoption figures as difference, absence, and stigma, Other and inferior to blood kinship. Accounts by adoptive parents (usually mothers) struggle with the losses of infertility, the formation of a substitute identity of parenting not based in biology, and, often, the search for a child. Autobiographies by adopted persons deal with the absence and loss of the birth mother and the gaps and silences of adoption secrecy: most of these are narratives of a psychic and actual search for the birth mother. Birth mothers' memoirs offer poignant testaments to the experience of spoiled identity. Their stories are efforts to overcome the stigma of the "bad mother" and to find and reclaim children they relinquished for adoption. Adoption life writing is a genre heavily dominated by women. Most of these accounts are written by women—adoptive mothers, adopted persons, and birth mothers. Motherhood still figures more prominently in women's social and cultural identities than fatherhood does in men's, perhaps explaining the overrepresentation of female authors in adopters' accounts. Strikingly, adoptees' searches are dominated by the search for the birth mother, with birth fathers assuming greatly attenuated roles. Most accounts of adopted persons in search are written by women, reflecting women's predominance among searchers.[11] So far, birth fathers have remained silent in this literature, which includes no full-length account of a man's experience of relinquishment. Most likely, birth mothers rather than birth fathers are telling stories of relinquishment and regret because the unwed mother's "moral career" is more dramatically disrupted by out-of-wedlock pregnancy. Her transgression is more visible to others and to herself through the embodied experiences of pregnancy and childbirth. And motherhood still carries more cultural weight than does fatherhood: *mother love,* signifying an enduring and unconditional nurture, is a phrase without a male-gendered equivalent.

Stories of adoptive parents are negotiations of identity that proclaim the equivalence of biological and adoptive kinship. They are also quest narratives, tales of obstacles overcome on unconventional roads to parenthood. Accounts written since 1975 detail long searches for children, serving as advice manuals to other potential adoptive parents and as critiques of the restrictions of contemporary adoption practice. In the stock plot of these narratives, a heterosexual couple decides to have a child, encounters unexpected obstacles, pursues medical treatment for infertility, and then turns to adoption. Then, the couple encounters more obstacles—the scrutiny of social workers, the scarcity of children available for adoption, the maze of adoption law. The tale ends with joyful scenes of parenthood claimed through adoption and with affirmations of the bonds and satisfactions of adoptive kinship. That point of closure implicitly endorses the logic of the "as if begotten" family: once the family is formed, the difference of adoptive kinship disappears.

Most narratives recount the loss and stigma of infertility. One author, a Sunday school teacher, described the pain of attending a Mother's Day program: "I felt like a miserable, ragged beggar cowering on the fringes of a king's feast. The hollowness expanded until it swallowed me up in grief."[12] The rigors of medical treatment for infertility offer further mortification. As one author wryly recalls, "In the past ten years they'd stretched, blown, pushed, pulled and manipulated: tested, analyzed, psychiatrised and harangued me: they'd had half my quota of teeth and all my appendix: they made me take copper, iron, calcium, yeast, phosphorus, vitamins A to E and all the auxiliaries, herbal brews, and things better concealed under formulae."[13] In one recurring theme, authors describe another ritual mortification of infertility: accustomed to exercising control of their lives, they now find themselves humbled by recalcitrant biology.

As they turn to adoption, these writers face further tests and trials. Unlike biological parents, whose decision to have children is a private matter, adopters cannot become parents until they pass through the public scrutiny of agencies, relinquishing mothers, and the courts. Would-be adoptive parents must not only choose adoption but themselves be chosen. As prospective adopters compile financial statements, medical reports, marriage records, recommendations, and other documents required in agency adoption, they note the galling contrast between what comes naturally and adoptive kinship. As Io Arnolfi writes, "an adopted babe depends on one's worthiness to have him. It's the profoundest difference there is between natural and adoptive parents."[14] When Marjorie Winters and her husband sought to adopt in the early 1950s, she writes, they spent four years going from agency to agency: "We became humble petitioners, prostrate enough, we hoped, to satisfy the power-lust of some of the social workers we had to woo."[15] Judith Dahl and her lesbian partner first tried to adopt from a social work agency, which accepted them despite some uneasiness about assisting lesbian adopters. But after months of no progress, Dahl flatly concluded, "The system is created to prevent adoption from taking place." After unsuccessful attempts at artificial insemination, Dahl and her partner began to pursue independent adoption. Such prospective parents face another kind of trial. As Dahl describes it, "When you deal openly with the birth mother, you lay yourself wide open. And if you lose, you lose twice. You lose your child, and the relationship with the birth mother is broken in the midst of a shattered dream."[16]

These accounts are, in part, protests against policies that many view as unduly discouraging and difficult. At the same time, these stories function symbolically as performances of parenthood. The rigors of adoption become themselves a kind of qualification for parenthood, a heroic demonstration of commitment and will that is contrasted implicitly with biological parents' effortless surrender to nature. A telling defensiveness inflects this claim, testament to the powerful ideology of "natural" parenting and the stigma of adoption. Adoptive parents seem compelled to present themselves as better than average, more than the equals of biological parents. The process of evaluation in itself creates these pressures, exacerbated by adopters' awareness that prospective adopters greatly outnumber children available for adoption. The "good enough" parent, many fear, will not be good enough to prevail in the rigors of the selection process.

These accounts typically end with a celebration of adoptive parenthood. The writers dramatize a moment that serves to confirm their parenthood to themselves and others—when their baby is first placed in their arms, when an older child begins to call them mother and father, when the court finalizes an adoption, when they proclaim themselves real parents. For Terry Treseder, for example, that moment comes when a stranger on an airplane watches her with her sleeping infant and asks, "'Did you go natural?' Natural? Must be some birth method. I was about to explain that Michael was adopted, but changed my mind. Smiling brightly, I exclaimed, 'It was the most natural thing in the world.'"[17] Treseder here refuses to name adoption as difference, instead silently revising the meaning of natural childbirth to embrace adoptive parenthood.

Writing in the 1980s and 1990s, some authors directly confront and refute assumptions about adoptive kinship as second-best, an inferior substitute for blood kinship. In ironic testament to the power of blood ties, though, these writers often do so by claiming adoption as itself natural. Elizabeth Bartholet opens her memoir with a harrowing account of the fiscal, physical, and emotional costs of nine years of infertility treatment. In retrospective, she views this quest for pregnancy not as a natural drive for parenthood but as evidence of a socially constructed ideal of biological kinship that renders adoption "the last resort." Yet she ends by invoking nature even as she criticizes a society driven by a "biologic bias": "There may be some inborn need to procreate, but there are also inborn needs to nurture. Why does organized society seem to want to encourage its members to obsess over the former at the expense of the latter?"[18] In *With Child: One Couple's Journey to Their Adopted Children*, Susan T. Viguers also claims adoption as natural parenthood: she inverts readers' expectations of the phrase "with child" (usually a reference to a parturient woman) by following with a subtitle that indicates her story is about a couple's experience of adoptive parenthood.[19] A 1989 manual on open adoption is titled *Adoption without Fear*, echoing Grantley Dick-Read's influential *Childbirth without Fear*, a 1944 book advocating natural childbirth.[20]

If these adoption stories serve in part to naturalize adoption and affirm adoptive kinship, some recent counternarratives reveal the fracturing of the consensus that once supported adoption. One example is adoption stories that write beyond the ending of family formation, where difference is supposed to disappear into the equivalence of the "as if begotten" adoptive family. Several memoirs deal with parenting children in nonmatching families, where the difference of adoption is visible to observers: these adopters and their children are confronted by outsiders' questions and comments, and the children deal with racial prejudice or outright attacks.[21] Douglas Bates's *Gift Children: A Story of Race, Family, and Adoption in a Divided America* (1993) tells the story of his interracial family. He and his wife adopted two African-American daughters in 1970, motivated in part by their commitment to the civil rights movement and its vision of integration. Twenty years later, he contemplates this decision from the standpoint of a father whose daughters are in crisis and whose interracial commitments many people now see as suspect: "Maybe, I grimly reasoned, it had been a terrible mistake." But in the end, Bates affirms the credo of adoption: "Eventually I would discover that love is the only thing that's real, that my children were special gifts, and that I'd do it all again."[22] A few exceptional authors venture onto the ground of the ultimate taboo, suggesting that love is not enough to redeem the losses of adoption. In *Beyond the Babylift: The Story of an Adoption*, Pamela Purdy confesses her struggle to confront her feelings of "anger, embarrassment, hostility" over a troubled mixed-race older child and her isolation in the face of sentimental platitudes of people who praise her for her altruism. She prays, "Lord, help me to love him. . . . I know you do, even if I can't."[23] Ann Kimble Loux's *The Limits of Hope* (1997) inverts the narrative of obstacles overcome. Her daunting story depicts a marriage and family nearly destroyed by the overwhelming problems of two daughters, adopted at ages three and four. Loux's biological children, she tells us, posed the usual challenges; by contrast, her adoptive daughters plunged the family into years of struggle with intractable behavioral and learning problems, delinquency, drug abuse, and prostitution. Her daughters, Loux believes, were irretrievably damaged by the devastating effects of early deprivation and abuse. Love is not enough, Loux concludes, flatly rejecting the confident environmentalism of the postwar consensus.[24]

Another vivid counternarrative emerges in widely publicized cases of contested adoption. These cases undermine a fundamental part of the postwar adoption consensus in their visible and painful demonstrations of the vulnerability of one of its primary tenets, that adoptive families are permanent and exclusive. In memoirs of such conflicts, all written by women, the authors contend for the name of mother, claiming it either as irrevocable blood tie, or as a status that must be earned by the investments of nurture. In *Losing Jessica*, Robby DeBoer argues the case she and her husband lost in court; after a protracted and widely publicized conflict, these prospective adopters were ordered to return two-and-a-half-year-old Jessica to her birth father.[25] Copy on the dust jacket frames the book as "the story of a mother's unequivocal love for her child, the strongest, most compelling, and most unbreakable human bond of all." Nurture, not blood, makes one a mother, DeBoer claims. Nearly identical rhetoric of motherhood (also contending against the claims of biological fatherhood) is marshaled to promote Mary Beth Whitehead's *A Mother's Story*, "the moving story of a mother's love for her baby daughter, the agony of their separation, and her courageous fight for her baby's return."[26] This memoir recounts the "Baby M case," Whitehead's battle to reinstate her parental rights to a daughter she conceived and bore in a surrogacy agreement.

In the title of her account, *An Adoption Story*, Marguerite Ryan invokes the genre of adoption narrative, but her story of contested adoption violates the genre's usual conventions of closure. Angelina Rodriguez, Christopher's birth mother, had relinquished her parental rights and arranged to place her son for adoption with the Ryans. She sought to revoke that decision twelve weeks later, before the Ryans had finalized their adoption. (Under the law in California, where the relinquishment was executed, birth parents have six months to revoke their consent.) The Ryans fought a series of court battles, losing every decision. They were ultimately ordered to return the child to Angelina. They never did. When the narrative ends, he is six years old, and the Ryans have negotiated an uneasy relationship with Angelina, who visits her son regularly but allows the Ryans to retain custody and, in effect, to act as guardians.[27]

Adoption Story is the adoptive mother's brief for the claims of nurture over those of nature. Despite the legal determination that Angelina is Christopher's mother, this narrative operates to complicate and undermine her claim and to promote Marguerite's. Forthrightly rejecting even the appearance of neutrality, Marguerite Ryan explains to three-year-old Christopher, "I'm your real mother. Angelina's your birth mother." Marguerite acknowledges Angelina's devotion to Christopher and recognizes her plight as an uneducated and impoverished Salvadoran immigrant. Nonetheless, Marguerite repeatedly defends her claim to be the "real mother" through portrayals of Angelina's maternal incompetence. The book tells of one incident, for example, when Christopher is hurt on the playground; Angelina freezes in panic, while Marguerite acts quickly and decisively to stop his bleeding and calm him. In an awkward moment at a day care party attended by both women, another participant admires Christopher and asks, "Which is the mother? Is it you?" Angelina replies yes and then adds, "'Well . . . she is the mother, too. We are both the mother.'" But authorship gives Marguerite the last word. Near the end of the memoir, she asks skeptically, "Can a child have two mothers?" She is not convinced, conceding only that "Maybe the day will come when I can let others know I value her, give her public affirmation: 'This is Angelina, Christopher's other mother.'"[28]

Contested adoptions operate on the terrain of law, where only one woman can be named mother. By contrast, accounts of adopted persons reclaim the birth family. Most of these memoirs are search narratives, stories of the adopted person's quest for knowledge of the past and reunion with the birth mother. They operate within a genre established by four influential books, foundational texts of the adoption rights movement. Jean Paton's *Orphan Voyage,* published to little public notice in 1968, interspersed the author's story of searching for biological relatives with interviews with other adopted adults and advocacy for reform of traditional confidential adoption; instead, Paton argued, adopted persons had the right to information about their pasts and access to biological families.[29] In 1973, Florence Fisher published *The Search for Anna Fisher,* reviewed in both *Library Journal* and the *New York Times Book Review.*[30] Describing her long effort to discover the identity of the woman who gave birth to her and relinquished her for adoption, Fisher ended her narrative with a call to action. She founded the Adoptees' Liberty Movement Association (ALMA) to publicize the cause of adopted persons seeking their biological parents, to assist in the search process, and to press for changes in the laws that sealed adoption records and thus impeded searches. Soon thereafter, Betty Jean Lifton, a well-known playwright and writer and the wife of a nationally known psychiatrist, published *Twice Born* (1975). This memoir and Lifton's subsequent advocacy for adoption reform brought wider visibility to Paton's and Fisher's claims.[31]

Between 1972 and 1978, the widely circulated and influential research of Annette Baran, Arthur D. Sorosky, and Reuben Pannor brought the cachet of expert credentials to the growing critique of adoption secrecy. In *The Adoption*

Triangle (1978), these authors took up the cause of adoption activists by advocating the opening of adoption records and an end to confidential adoption.[32] Surveying birth parents (mostly mothers) and adopted persons, the authors applied the language of disability to adoption: adopted persons were "handicapped" because they were "severed" from their biological origins; to greater or lesser degree, their lives were shaped by the syndrome of "genealogical bewilderment."[33] This research affirmed the experiences of a growing number of adopted persons who sought knowledge of their origins and connection with birth relatives.

Search narratives are expressions and vehicles of the adoption rights movement. Members of adoptee organizations produce and circulate shorter accounts of search in newsletters and oral narratives within local and national chapters. In turn, these narratives serve to recruit new participants to the movement. Many authors of published memoirs explain that they decided to search after hearing the stories of other adoptees on radio or television, and then drew inspiration and learned strategies from organized search groups or their publications.[34] In addition, search has captured the imagination of a larger public. Stories of search and reunion have become subjects of advice columnists such as Ann Landers and staples of radio and television talk shows.

As a result, there is a certain rehearsed quality to many of the published narratives, a formulaic recitation of the shared assumptions and expectations of the search movement. Writers typically begin by explaining their motivations for searching. Writing against the adoption consensus, with its assumption that the adoptive family completely replaces birth kinship, the authors describe separation from blood kin as deprivation and often as stigma. In *Mother, Can You Hear Me?* Elizabeth Cooper Allen writes, "I was never without a feeling of loss and a sense of being different from others. There was some essential void in my connection with the natural order of origin—or birth. I was a foundling, a changeling."[35] Katrina Maxtone-Graham describes adoption as "amputation from history" in her autobiography, *An Adopted Woman*.[36] This language echoes the view of genealogical bewilderment advanced by some adoption rights activists, a sense of rupture from biological and historical origins. Doris McMillon also searches in hopes of relieving the "deadly emptiness" of a spirit scarred by her abusive, mentally ill adoptive mother.[37]

Most narratives also argue that the motivation to search is natural and intrinsic, specifically refuting the notion that search is a symptom of unhappy adoptive families. This argument has been widely circulated by the search movement to counter the stigma sometimes still attached to search. Notably, some memoirs exhibit a telling overcorrection here. Even in narratives that portray markedly painful relationships with adopted parents, authors seem constrained to argue that this is not the reason for the search. Allen, for example, describes her adoptive mother as "strong, controlling, and unbending . . . harsh."

She waited until both parents died before beginning a search for birth parents, and after her reunion with her birth mother, she proclaims that the experience has yielded "a new appreciation for the many very positive things my parents were able to give me."[38] Amy Dean's adoptive mother drank heavily, and when Dean was two and a half years old she was placed in foster care; two years later, her adoptive parents divorced, and her adoptive father got custody of her. Nonetheless, she reassures her father that her search isn't motivated by a longing for another mother: "It's not so much the *person* I want to find as the *answers* to my questions. I want to find my roots."[39] Similarly, Maxtone-Graham avers, "I was learning more and more . . . how little my search had to do . . . with my adoptive parents. My unhappiness as a child had not been their doing, I was beginning to realize, but the simple fact of adoption."[40]

In some accounts, writers recall adoption as shaming or stigma. For Jean Paton, writing in 1968, that stigma is the stain of illegitimacy. Adoptees' accounts, like those of adopters and birth mothers, often represent stigma as written on the body—as a silent and hidden defect (like infertility) or as a stigma (like stretch marks) threatening to mark the bearer and betray hidden secrets. Paton uses metaphors of physical deformity as she asserts that "no adoption can attain the potentiality of family life. I do not like this; it makes an illegitimate birth like a clubfoot or a harelip. But it is true."[41] Frances Lear's account recalls the old stigma of the adopted child as the bad seed, bearer of unknown defects. She recalls her tremendous relief on giving birth to healthy daughters: "The miracle was their existence, that I would actually give birth to a child, that I was capable of normal everything—conception, pregnancy, delivery—that the unknown genetic tracks that preceded me and that I had traveled would not, suddenly, in the body of my issue, lead to unimaginable diseases and traits and congenital poisons."[42] In *Mixed Blessing*, McMillon writes of the feelings of unworthiness engendered by her erratic and angry adoptive mother, who constantly warns of the influence of the "bad blood" inherited from McMillon's "whore" of a biological mother.[43]

For others, the stigma is relinquishment. Jean Downie felt second-best when she learned of her adoption at age fourteen, inferior to children born to their parents and uncomfortably obligated to her adoptive parents.[44] Tim Green describes the anxious striving of his childhood and adult life as an effect of adoption; rejected by his birth mother, he feared that his adoptive parents too would find him unacceptable unless he earned their love.[45] Robert Andersen, a psychiatrist, believes that his pervasive sense of inferiority is rooted in the realities of adoption, a theme conveyed in his title, *Second Choice: Growing up Adopted*.[46]

Search narratives then characteristically explain the quest to find birth relatives. Here the narratives borrow in part from the conventions of detective stories, as searchers try to piece together the missing pieces of a lost past, to bring hidden knowledge to light. Like detective stories, they build suspense through plot lines of deepening mystification with red herrings, unreliable witnesses, and obstructions to the investigation. But as stories of adoption, they also share some of the elements of adopters' narratives of their quest for parenthood. Like infertile people, adopters express frustration over their struggle to achieve a connection that belongs effortlessly to those in biological families. And, again as in adopters' narratives, search narratives often trace a process that begins with conventional methods and expands to unusual or transgressive methods. Most adopters eventually attempt unconventional or medically unsanctioned treatments of infertility: examples recounted in these memoirs include herbal treatments, acupuncture, headstands or handstands after intercourse, psychic healing, visualization, channeling. Searchers begin by trying to get official records through social work agencies and courts and pursue leads through sources such as newspapers, telephone books, and public records. If those methods fail, they hire private investigators, consult mediums and psychics, and use insider contacts or direct action to gain access to sequestered records. (These authors are united in their critique of sealed adoption records, a position that again reflects the politics of the search movement.) In all but one account (Andersen's), the search leads the author to birth relatives.[47]

The scene of reunion provides the climax to most search narratives. Such scenes invariably dramatize the physical encounter of birth mother and adoptee. In a restaging of the mother's intense scrutiny of her newborn infant, the reunited mother and child exchange searching gazes, looking eagerly for the physical resemblance that represents and confirms biological kinship.[48] Downie finds a birth aunt who shows Downie photographs and exclaims over her resemblance to a grandmother and half-sister.[49] Green encounters the "mirror image of myself": his birth mother is even wearing a leather trench coat like his. Recalling the emotion of reunion, Green portrays it as a reversal of the disembodiment that many adoptees describe: the moment of meeting is one of transformation into the body, "to see oneself incarnate."[50] Allen is disappointed at her first sight of Almeda, her birth mother: "I looked at the small body in the heavy winter clothes and could feel no connection." Later, she discerns a faint physical resemblance between herself and her mother as she looks at old photographs. She notes with satisfaction, "It was then that I knew that I truly was Almeda's daughter."[51] Dean scrutinizes photographs of herself and her birth mother, trying to find some similarity. Writing in epistolary form, she addresses her birth mother: "I look now at the pictures of you and me together. I glance back and forth, from me to you and you to me, but I can't discern any resemblance. This disappoints me. I think I had expectations, prior to seeing you, that we would look just like each other, or at least share some visible similarities."[52]

In the denouement, often relatively attenuated, the narrator describes outcomes that follow the initial reunion. For some, the search yields an ideal affinity with a welcoming mother. Maxtone-Graham, for example, feels an immediate rapport with her birth mother that the author attributes to their genetic relationship: "If I made an allusion, or cracked a joke, or uttered an abbreviated opinion, I never had to wonder, 'Will she get it?' As with people one has known all one's life, there was no need to make explanations."[53] More commonly, newly reunited relatives struggle to negotiate a relationship that does not fit available categories. Dean writes that her relationship with her birth mother "has a built-in closeness because of our mother-daughter connection and our blood bond, but also has a limited emotional 'comfort zone' to handle such closeness because we've never connected as mother and daughter. In reality, we're strangers."[54] McMillon finds both her birth parents but not the love and intimacy she had sought: "The problem was, I now had two new parents—strangers."[55]

Two exceptional narratives by adopted persons depart from the highly conventional structure that usually governs this genre. In both, the author is the object of the search, not the searcher. James Stingley's birth mother finds him, contacts him by letter, and initiates a meeting. His first encounter with her is jarringly at odds with others, rendered in the transgressive language of the sexual gaze: "She seemed in her mid-forties, but even by Los Angeles standards, she was stunning. Her cheekbones were high and wide, her chin dimpled. Her eyes were electric blue. Her lips were supple and sensuous. Her hair was fiery red, styled dramatically. . . . Her body, what I could see of it, was no less spectacular."[56] The aftermath—a volatile incestuous relationship—is no less unconventional. In Sarah Saffian's *Ithaka*, the author is thrown into confusion when her birth parents suddenly contact her.[57] Though Saffian had been thinking of searching for them, she finds herself ambivalent, self-protective, and wary. It is three years later when she finally feels ready to meet her birth family in person.

Most of these narratives affirm the search movement's credo that reunion heals the losses of the past. For some adopted persons, the search provides an extended kinship network. In some narratives, shared rituals affirm the widened boundaries of family, as in weddings attended by both birth and adoptive relatives. In virtually every account, photographs serve as a vital medium of reunion. Typically, searchers take photographs and have others take photographs of themselves with birth relatives. Reunited families tell their histories by reviewing family albums and videos and write new relatives into the story through photographs. In memoirs that include photographs, these visual images serve also as public performances of family.

For still others, the process of discovery is itself healing, as in Maxtone-Graham's reflections on finding her birth mother after many years of searching: "I . . . had been at last an instrument of my own fate. . . . I had had the power of action. And thus it was that I had become a real human being."[58] Allen describes the reunion as rebirth: "I was giving birth to Almeda within myself, and I was giving birth to myself as a more complete Elizabeth."[59] Most authors describe their search as a success even when they do not find what they had expected or hoped for. McMillon realizes that her search is really a quest to heal the losses of her childhood, scarred by an abusive adoptive mother: "Louise [her adoptive mother] was the vital factor in my life. . . . Josefine? Josefine was a total stranger, conjured up for comfort like an imaginary playmate, and I felt fear and anticipation at the meeting in Germany but no sense of homecoming, of family. Only the knowledge of finally finishing old business." With reunion, McMillon relinquishes the fantasy of "the perfect mother-image. . . . It was asking for an intimacy that few people ever reach, and the fact of the blood tie meant nothing at all." For her, wholeness comes not with reunion but as she becomes a mother herself. She recognizes a new tie with her stepdaughters—"My *real* daughters. *I* was their real mother, now, the mother who would raise them from this point on." And the last line celebrates her impending maternity of a child by birth: "I was pregnant. The real test of my growing up was just ahead."[60]

In the exceptional accounts with unhappy endings, search or reunion fail to overcome the losses of adoption—indeed, even deepen the adopted person's feelings of betrayal, rejection, and emptiness. Stingley's story ends with a sense of bitter betrayal at the hands of both adoptive and birth mothers: "If I believed anything now, it was that I had been a pawn between two women, each seeking her own satisfaction, each finally seeing me only as a disturbing reminder neither could wash her hands of." For him, reconciliation comes not in reunion but when he fathers a son: "It is because of him that I have come closer and closer to being the whole man that I have needed so desperately to become."[61] Andersen's unsuccessful search offers no relief from his feelings of rejection and inferiority, for he uncovers evidence that he was sold in a black-market adoption and comes to suspect that his mother was a prostitute.

Most narratives of birth mothers sharply criticize adoption practices. These accounts serve as rhetorical performances that challenge and rewrite the postwar narrative through public disclosure of hidden pasts. These women, prime beneficiaries of the secrecy of confidential adoption, break that silence to narrate their own adoption decisions. Challenging the tenets of the "best solution," many argue that relinquishment inflicted lasting wounds, unresolved grief, and intense longing for the child who was surrendered. Rebecca Harsin, for example, writes, "a birth-mother gives the most precious of gifts—her child—and society expects her to forget and go on with her life as though nothing had happened. That's just not the way it works."[62] With her title, *Waiting to Forget: A Mother Opens the Door to Her Secret Past,* Margaret Moorman simultaneously dramatizes the impossibility of forgetting, rejects secrecy, and claims the identity of mother.[63] These authors powerfully challenge the "best solution" by breaking the silence that was supposed to serve them; they name themselves publicly in defiance of the stigma of unwed motherhood.

However, as they repudiate one spoiled identity they confront another that is potentially as damaging. As Carol Schaefer writes, "We [she and her child's father] could not speak the unspeakable even to one another, that we had given our own baby to total strangers and abandoned him to an unknown destiny."[64] For these women, relinquishment, not unwed motherhood, is the stigma that is enduring and deeply felt. The authors express guilt and intense regret over this decision; refuting the postwar narrative of relinquishment as a recoupable loss, they portray it instead as an open wound. And, at the same time, they are addressing audiences in a context radically revised by changing sexual mores: in 1970, 80 percent of children born out of wedlock were relinquished for adoption; by 1983, fewer than 4 percent of unwed mothers made that decision.[65]

These narrators are women caught between two stories, neither of which is adequate to explain their experience. They violated the postwar narrative with their unresolved grief and sustained longing for relinquished children. Ironically, their stories of the shame of illicit pregnancy have been rendered anachronistic, and in a social milieu far more skeptical of adoption, they are stigmatized as mothers who gave away their children. These narratives, then, are also exculpatory: they attempt to evoke the intense stigma once attached to out-of-wedlock pregnancy to explain the decision to relinquish.

Birth mothers' stories vividly recall the shame of pregnancy out of wedlock in the 1950s and 1960s. Spending part of her pregnancy in a home for unwed mothers, Harsin recalled shopping with another resident of the home amid the stares of other shoppers, who she felt viewed the young women "as if we both had horrible disfigurements. I had never before been looked at as though I were something distasteful."[66] Many narratives offer examples of efforts to disguise or conceal pregnancy, whether by rigorous control of weight gain, use of confining girdles, or sequestration. Jean Thompson's *The House of Tomorrow* described her maternity home stay, around 1960, with its regimen of weekly weighing and strict dietary regulation. Residents were counseled to aim for a total weight gain of fifteen pounds. Consistent with contemporary medical prescriptions for small weight gains during pregnancy, the restriction was nonetheless enforced through discipline and punishment that would have exceeded anything a pregnant woman might experience in private life. If one of the "girls" exceeded the allowable limit for that week, she lost her "privileges," the daily and weekly passes that regulated inmates' excursions out of the home.[67]

For Schaefer, the physical changes of pregnancy figure as stigmata. She recalls how the women in the maternity home were preoccupied with stretch marks: "We were all concerned whenever a little line would appear. To hide the fact that we were damaged goods, we could lie that we had broken our hymens riding a bike when we were nine years old, but we were terrified that stretch marks would brand us forever as unwed mothers."[68] Moorman also recounts her dismay when her doctor tells her the stretch marks on her breasts will remain after she gives birth: "I hadn't realized there would be visible scars. I had been told, again and again, that I would give my baby up and *put all this behind me*. How could that happen if I, like Hester Prynne with her scarlet A, bore the sign of my disgrace forever?"[69]

The earliest of these narratives, Thompson's is the only one written within the postwar consensus of the "best solution." *House of Tomorrow*, published in 1966, recounts a pregnancy and relinquishment that took place about six years earlier. This narrative portrays the maternity home as discipline—a ritual banishment from society—but also as a source of solace and redemption. The "house of tomorrow" is a place to sequester oneself from the shame of unwed motherhood, to find ease in the camaraderie of other women in the same situation, and to regain respectability through the second chance of adoption. In conformity with the prewar narrative, Thompson depicts relinquishment as painful necessity and portrays her motherhood as a temporary stewardship: "He is someone else's son. . . . I'm not giving him away. He was never mine. I've just been responsible for him for a little while." Thompson's epilogue affirms the wisdom of her adoption decision. At the time of the writing, she is married, with "two children of my own." Speaking from the authority of her motherhood—this time legitimized by marriage—she both claims these children as "my own" and celebrates the selfless maternity of relinquishment: "I am reminded of the lesson I learned several years ago; your children are not your children—they dwell in the house of tomorrow."[70]

For others, relinquishment is a wound that will not heal. Relinquishment as well as pregnancy is experienced as a stigma expressed on and through the body. Schaefer uses vivid imagery of amputation and psychic dissociation: she is left with "half of myself," and in response, "I disconnected my feelings and was left with half a soul." After her marriage, Harsin tries to conceive for a year without becoming pregnant. She interprets her infertility as divine judgment: "I wasn't fit to be a mother. God didn't want me to have any more babies."[71] Schaefer worries that her son might somehow bear the stigmata of her transgressive pregnancy and relinquishment: "I still had doubts about my fitness to be a mother. Would my 'sin' hurt my second child somehow?"[72] Louise Jurgens believes that the emotional damage of relinquishment is written on birth mothers' bodies. Narrating her own gynecological disease and hysterectomy, she opines that medical problems have their sources "in the emotional paths of our lives." She believes that birth mothers suffer more disability than others, and she attributes this phenomenon to self-punishing emotions: "Fifty percent of the women who came to the meetings [of Concerned United Birthmothers] had created disease in their bodies."[73]

In these autobiographies, the body stands as testament to the real. Against the rhetoric of the "best solution," women's bodies proclaim their maternity and their unresolved loss. The memoirists repudiate relinquishment as empty legalism, instead claiming the identity of mother as inviolable, conferred by nature. In *Birthmark,* Lorraine Dusky muses on the anomaly of her situation as a mother without her child: "I read in a book by Margaret Drabble that the world is divided into two groups: those who have children and those who don't. . . . Me? Well, I can flit back and forth into either group. I fit in both, I fit in neither."[74] Schaefer repudiates the use of "birth mother," now widespread in expert and popular literature: "I hated the term . . . right away. It sounded like we were brood mares and implied that the relationship to our children ended at birth."[75] Jurgens describes the wrenching experience of seeing another woman named as her son's mother on his amended birth certificate: "Her relationship as his parent was one I could never have. I would never dare to pretend to be his parent. That was a privilege I could not have and a loss I would always mourn. But I had given birth to him. I had never stopped loving him. I was his mother, too."[76] Jurgens denies a claim to the status of parent, using this term unmarked by gender to refer to child raising, but affirms her identity as mother. And she claims the name of mother both as biological fact ("I had given birth to him") and as inalienable right sealed by maternal emotion ("I had never stopped loving him").

But to claim this identity, as these accounts do in active autobiographical acts of assertion, is often to disclaim their own agency in relinquishment. Most portray themselves as powerless victims of circumstance, pressured by parents and social workers. Jurgens titles her story "torn from the heart," a phrase that denies women's roles as legal executors of relinquishments and instead depicts adoption as coercion. Some activist birth mothers describe their children as "lost" to adoption, a word that obscures the adoption decision altogether and names no one as responsible for the loss.[77] This telling language testifies to the powerful stigma of relinquishment. The postwar adoption consensus portrayed relinquishment as an act of love, the mark of the "good" mother. With the faltering of that consensus, relinquishing mothers have no defense against the full cultural judgment brought to bear on the "bad" mother who rejects and abandons her child.

To explain the remarkable volition that they do exercise—in writing these accounts, in pursuing exhaustive searches for their children, and in some cases in speaking, writing, and organizing for the adoption rights movement—the authors invoke the power of nature as embodied in maternity. In retrospect, Dusky criticizes the professional ambitions that influenced her decision to relinquish her child: "I thought I could outsmart my gender by doing all the career things the right way, the way men did them."[78] But biology is destiny for Dusky: motherhood cannot be left behind. Birth fathers are largely absent from the adoption rights movement, Jurgens notes, and she opines that women predominate because "the birth mother's physical bond is so much stronger." When she finds her daughter, she presses the reluctant young woman to make contact with her birth father, explaining this as her "maternal urge" to reunite father and daughter.[79] Even when Sandra Musser's "found" daughter ends their relationship a month after their reunion, Musser continues to assert that "blood is thicker than water" and to claim the power of mother love. She writes to her daughter, "You were a part of me for nine months and share my flesh and blood—that makes you important to me . . . a mother's love is always stronger for her child than vice versa. . . . You can reject me, ignore me, or hate me—I will still continue to love you as one of my own."[80] Concerned United Birthparents, founded in Massachusetts in 1976, encompasses fathers as well as mothers in its gender-inclusive "birthparents," but its acronym of CUB and logo of a mother bear emphasize the claims of instinctual motherhood.

The narrative of natural motherhood as repudiation of the "best solution" has gained remarkable visibility and currency in the past two decades. Its broad influence is registered in an unusual memoir of a highly exceptional case, Michele Launders's *I Wish You Didn't Know My Name.* Launders's story is the Gothic inversion of the "best solution," for she is the birth mother of Lisa Steinberg, privately placed with Hedda Nussbaum and Joel Steinberg, at whose hands she died after prolonged abuse. And yet, even as it might seem to offer the ultimate cautionary tale about adoption, this memoir is framed in a way that complicates that reading. Coauthored by Penina Spiegel, the book opens with a brief note on their collaboration that reveals that Spiegel is an adoptive mother, and she dedicates the memoir "to birth mothers everywhere."[81]

In the very extensive media coverage of this case, adoption operated as a loaded signifier, invariably attached as a marker that set apart this family from others. How did it function for readers and viewers responding to this horrific story? In part I suspect it was a way of dealing with the class politics of the case: as white middle-class professionals, Nussbaum and Steinberg defied stereotypes of perpetrators of child abuse, and the case thus disrupted the usual assumptions that governed media presentation of domestic violence—that "we" do not do such things. Identified as adoptive parents, perhaps Nussbaum and Steinberg could be bracketed as not-really-parents, safely distanced from the implied audience (white and middle class) addressed by mass media. An underlying sense of the anomaly of adoption also operated, on some level, to reinforce the psychological portrait of Steinberg as monstrous, an unnatural fiend in an unnatural family. Notably, some readers and viewers indirectly confirmed this analysis when they repeatedly resisted the use of adoption as a marker. Pointing out that the placement had never been legalized, these respondents tried to exempt (legitimate) adoption from the stigma associated with Steinberg's shady dealings and his abusive parenting.

Adoption disorders our expectations of choice and chance in family life, and coverage of the case subliminally registered this unease. The contingency of adoption heightens the horror of Lisa's suffering and death. All children, in a sense, are hostages of the families into which they are born; Lisa, though, was not born to this couple but placed with them among thousands of others who might have claimed her as their own. Adoption also complicated the consideration of communal responsibility that ritually accompanies stories of child abuse. Without the guardianship of her natural parents, Lisa should have been shielded by state regulation of adoption. She was not, and her death thus underscored the gaps in accountability and the failed stewardship that are so often exposed in cases of child abuse.

As Launders confronts her daughter's horrifying fate, she reflects on the stunning betrayal of what is promised in the narrative of the "best solution." She explains her adoption decision in the language of selfless maternity approved by the postwar consensus: "I did it for Lisa. I had wanted her to have a good life, better than I could give her. I wanted her to have two parents, parents who were married."[82] The lawyer promised to place her daughter with married, Catholic adopters; instead, he gave Lisa to Steinberg and Nussbaum, unmarried and Jewish. Unbeknownst to Launders, her daughter was never legally adopted. Thus, good intentions go tragically awry, and Launders is the unknowing instrument of her daughter's doom. "This poor tortured child. I, her mother, had delivered her into the hands of her killers. I hoped that God had watched over her, because I certainly hadn't."[83]

Under the tremendous pressure of this history, Launders writes a memoir that is both confessional and covertly exculpatory. Launders portrays herself as a victim of circumstances, disgraced by sexual transgression. Her unfeeling boyfriend abandons her, she is "naive . . . alone and desperate."[84] These sentiments might have been lifted right from a birth mother narrative of a relinquishment executed in the 1950s or 1960s, and they are advanced as an explanation of Launders's course of action. Desperate to hide her pregnancy, she and her mother turn to a shady transaction with a lawyer who demands five hundred dollars in cash. But this does not ring true in a story of out-of-wedlock pregnancy in the 1980s. By then, large numbers of American women gave birth and raised children outside marriage, and the residual stigma of illegitimacy was flouted by favorable coverage of well-known stars who chose to rear children as single women. Newspapers, magazines, radio, and television widely covered the "epidemic" of infertility sweeping the United States and the energetic efforts of adults "desperate" to adopt. Launders could have turned to any one of dozens of licensed public and voluntary agencies in New York. She could have arranged independent adoption with prospective parents that she selected herself, with the mediation of a reputable lawyer or agency. The gaps and silences in Launders's narrative raise suspicions about the circumstances of this relinquishment, even as her use of birth mother stories attests to their currency and availability as models.

Launders's narrative also relies on readers' knowledge of the conventions of reunion stories; again, her story is a nightmare inversion. In many birth mother accounts, confidentiality is a burden that confines them in isolating secrecy; they reject secrecy and claim the freedom to tell their stories. Reunion provides the relief of learning that sons and daughters have fared well in their adoptive families. By contrast, Launders has her privacy stripped from her as she learns of her daughter's violent death in the spotlight of sensational publicity. On the public stage of the courtroom, she reclaims Lisa's body as her rightful mother.

Notably, though, even as this memoir recounts a case that exposed the worst possible outcome of adoption, the narrative ends by acknowledging both blood and adoptive kinship. Both a rabbi and a Catholic priest officiate at Lisa's funeral, arranged by Launders, in a gesture that honors Lisa's social identity (raised by Jews) even as it reclaims her birth identity (as a Catholic). The little girl's gravestone bears the name given to her by her adoptive parents, Lisa Steinberg. But Launders reclaims her motherhood in an inscription that lists Lisa's parents as and Michele Launders and Kevin.[85]

Launders's place in the events and her memoir both attest to the wide reach and success of birth mothers' critiques. In little more than a decade, women who relinquished children for adoption have claimed the identity of birth mother; moreover, others have recognized and validated it. When Lisa and her adoptive brother's substitute family failed so drastically, why did those around them turn automatically to the birth mothers who had relinquished these children? Reporters who found Launders heralded the discovery as the rightful restoration of Lisa to her true mother. Did they not also inflict unthinkable suffering on a woman who had tried to make a better life for her daughter than what she could offer? Equally remarkable is the professional support for reinstating kinship between Lisa's brother and his birth mother. Why assume that the little boy's best interest would be served by returning him to a mother who had decided earlier that she could not care for him? This is an exceptional, even singular, case, yet its complicated turns reveal much about the deep cultural ambivalence that surrounds adoption.

But in the face of a very widespread repudiation of the "best solution," it is worth noting the survival of this narrative in some subcultures. In memoirs published by religious presses, some birth mothers assert that relinquishment can still be a valid choice for women facing unwanted pregnancies at the end of the twentieth century. Their purpose is to encourage others to choose adoption rather than abortion or single motherhood. These stories are, in effect, counternarratives to the stories of birth mothers touched by the adoption rights movement.

Consider, for example, a 1991 memoir published by the Church of the Latter Day Saints. Coauthored by an adoptive mother, Terry Treseder, and a young woman pregnant out of wedlock, Terrilyn Ainscouth, *My Child, Your Child: A*

Childless Couple's Yearning and an Unwed Mother's Decision is told in alternating sections that converge as Ainscouth decides to relinquish her child for adoption and the church-run agency selects the Treseders as adopters. Church elders condemn premarital sex, but they offer Ainscouth a narrative of sin, repentance, and redemption that allows her to find dignity and belonging in the Church. A supportive older woman, for example, repudiates the stigma of illegitimacy: "Giving life to another human being was a miracle never to be confused with the act of transgression. It was not okay to break the law of chastity, but it was okay to give birth to a baby." The conclusion affirms adoption as second chance: Ainscouth makes peace with her decision, meets a loving man, marries and has "two beautiful children of my own." Treseder recalls joyfully the finalization of the adoption.[86]

This favorable view of adoption is shared by some contemporary Catholics and evangelical Protestants. Some write as antiabortion activists who are reaching out to unhappily pregnant women to persuade them not to abort: one of these women is Norma McCorvey, who was known as Jane Roe in the landmark case legalizing abortion. In *Won by Love*, she describes her repudiation of abortion and embrace of evangelical Christianity.[87] *To Keera with Love*, published by a Catholic press, is a firsthand account by a teenager who chooses adoption. The narrative both endorses and subtly amends the postwar "best solution": "I did what I felt was best for the life of my daughter," the narrator affirms. The selfless maternity of relinquishment is amplified in these post-1970 accounts, for in the era of legal abortion, Kayla has given her daughter two gifts: "The first gift was of life; the second was a chance for a balanced childhood between two parents."[88] For evangelical Protestants, adoption is the best solution because it saves babies from abortion and because it shores up the traditional family. Susan and Marvin Olasky address other evangelical activists in *More Than Kindness*, a book that exhorts conservatives to counter the stigma of adoption: otherwise, they warn, antiabortion activism will abet the growth of single-parent families. Adoption, in their view, is the superior alternative— the "loving and unselfish choice" that also supports "the conviction that the ideal family has two parents."[89] The authors advocate more services for women facing "crisis pregnancies," including expansion of an emerging network of small, Christian-run maternity homes that model Christian marriage. Ann Kiemel Anderson, a well-known evangelical author and lecturer, writes as an adoptive mother who has become an informal adoption broker sought out by readers and audience members who are inspired by her adoption stories.[90]

Bonnie Shullenberger speaks as a dissenter in her own religious community, an Episcopal minister who stands against the prochoice position of liberal Protestantism. She recounts her 1967 stay in a Salvation Army maternity home. Like many other birth mothers, she finds that she bears the psychic wounds of relinquishment for many years: "suppressed shame and grief combined to make a hidden sore that I had carried silently." But unlike others, Shullenberger does not conclude that adoption is a mistake, an unnatural separation of mother and child. Rather, she calls on Christians to oppose abortion and to offer healing and reconciliation to women wounded by relinquishment.[91]

Most birth mother memoirs are framed by the two prevailing frames for adoption since World War II: the narrative of the "best solution" and the revisions of the adoption rights movement. In two memoirs that refuse both frames, the authors instead use their experiences to expose and consider cultural constructions of motherhood, both biological and adoptive. Margaret Moorman and Jan L. Waldron criticize the "best solution," but they are also unpersuaded by the tenets of the adoption rights movement. Moorman effectively renders the sway of the "best solution" by including the seven-page autobiography she wrote in the 1960s, as part of the therapeutic process that social workers used to guide her relinquishment. In retrospect, she questions the social work assumptions and cultural expectations of that era. Like other birth mothers, she rejects the platitude that transgressive motherhood will be forgotten; as her title signals, she is still "waiting to forget," years later. But as she considers the contemporary critique of adoption, she also finds herself skeptical of the new narrative crafted by birth mothers. In her reflection on her decision to relinquish, Moorman refuses closure: she can neither embrace nor condemn this consequential act. Her search also ends without closure. She finds her son and contacts him by letter, but he does not want to meet her.

Waldron rejects the "willful romanticizing and reactionary rhetoric" of the "best solution," but she also rejects the celebration of natural motherhood in contemporary birth mother narratives. She arranges to meet her relinquished daughter (renamed Rebecca) in 1980, when the girl is just eleven years old. With the support of the girl's adoptive parents, Waldron seeks to forge a continuing relationship with her daughter. The moment of reunion signals the difficulties that are to follow. For Waldron, the meeting underscores their differences rather than their affinities: "I saw no signs of me in her. She did not have my nose, or eyes. Her skin was buttery brown. I was white. She seemed shier than I imagined a girl of mine to be. More withdrawn. Is a mother's daughter meant to seem so unrelated?" They proceed in fits and starts, with Waldron at first uncomfortable with Rebecca's ease in her house and her demands for gifts. Driven by guilt and obligation, Waldron tries to respond but finds herself awkward and lacking in mother love. Ten years later, they are estranged, separated by mutual recriminations and accusations. As the memoir ends, they are reunited in an uneasy truce. Nonetheless, Waldron closes with an emphasis on the anomaly of their relationship, "the unnaturalness of having a child who is not mine and, for her, having a mother who belongs to someone else." Their relation is forged not by blood but by language and will: "For more than half her life, the force and persistence of our communication have both liberated and bound Rebecca and me.

And that, finally, is why we are family."[92] What accounts for the extraordinary proliferation of adoption memoirs in recent years and for the wide circulation of these stories? Most persons, after all, are not adopted, adoptive parents, or birth parents: they are touched by adoption only at a remove, if at all. In part, these memoirs attest to the durable appeal of life writing, with its reflective view of the past, its search for the self, its place in the American project of self-construction. At the same time, these stories also offer a fresh angle on autobiographical narrative, a postmodern sensibility of unstable, fractured, shifting identities. Audiences may read these narratives against the grain—that is, readers may find pleasure in the same features of adoption that the authors experience as stigma. Separation from the past and rupture from genetic heritage are sources of pain for the authors of these memoirs, yet the same circumstances are celebrated in other parts of American culture. Many observers have noted the desire to escape from history and to begin anew as a recurring theme in American literature and history. Thus, what is rupture and loss for these authors may read as imaginative possibility for many of their readers.

The secrets and silences of adoption may exert their own appeal for some readers. Birth parents and adopted persons sometimes feel haunted by the missing part, the shadow families left behind by relinquishment, yet those raised in biological families may vicariously enjoy the idea of an alternative family. The "family romance," the child's fantasy that he or she is adopted, often noted in psychiatric literature, attests to the allure of an imagined family without the defects and imperfections of the families we know. Adoption secrecy lends suspense and intrigue to these stories. Search-and-reunion narratives in particular borrow from the conventions of detective stories, with their compelling narratives of guilty knowledge, betrayal, and the search for hidden truth.

And finally, perhaps these narratives have claimed a larger audience because they tap pervasive concerns and uncertainties about identity and family ties. They amplify the appeal of autobiographical narrative more generally, offering new perspective on ultimate questions of identity: "Who am I? Where do I belong?" Conflicts over adoption also create a space for discussion of moral questions and family ideologies that are often excluded from public debate. We sanction—indeed, we demand—careful oversight in the formation of adoptive families. Undertaken deliberately and under the scrutiny of the state, adoption allows intervention into matters usually shielded by considerations of privacy. Finally, adoption speaks to deeply felt hopes and anxieties about the possibilities and limits of pluralism. When we ask who belongs together, what makes a family, we are asking profound questions about the boundaries of tolerance, the limits of parental altruism, the obligations and expectations we attach to children. Adoption narratives are exceptional stories, but their differences may richly inform and illuminate ordinary lives.

NOTES

I am pleased to acknowledge E. Wayne Carp's helpful suggestions and Zofia Burr's insightful comments.

1. There is no comprehensive bibliographic aid to accounts on adoption, though Library of Congress subject headings now identify some of these. I think I have read most of the full-length accounts written by birth mothers, about three-quarters of those written by adopted persons, and perhaps a quarter of the accounts written by adoptive parents (by far the most prolific of the triad). I know of no full-length memoir by a birth father. For a collection of accounts from birth fathers, see Mary Martin Mason, *Out of the Shadows: Birthfather's Stories* (Edina, Minn.: O. J. Howard, 1995), which uses *birthfathers* broadly to include various experiences that separate men from children: several (but not all) of the essays are about fathers of children relinquished for adoption.

The best bibliography for these purposes is Susan G. Miles, *Adoption Literature for Children and Young Adults* (New York: Greenwood Press, 1986), which, despite its title, includes autobiographies and other material directed to adult audiences. I have found Miles quite comprehensive for the period before 1986—indeed, her bibliography includes books by small presses and vanity presses that are not even in the extensive collections of the Library of Congress. For more recent accounts, I rely on book reviews and the online catalog of the Library of Congress. *Birth mother* is now a Library of Congress subject heading. Miles lists fifty-one accounts by adoptive parents, eight by birth mothers, and twenty-three by adopted persons.

I have limited this discussion to full-length memoirs or autobiographies. Several published volumes include compilations of firsthand accounts. I do not consider those in detail here because of the additional interpretive issues introduced by procedures of editorial selection, interviewing and transcription, and selective compilation.

2. Although births out of wedlock increased after 1970, the number of "stranger" (nonstepparent) adoptions dropped steadily. In 1970 there were 89,000 adoptions; by 1975, there were 48,000. The federal government has not collected national statistics on adoption since 1975, but subsequent estimates suggest that this number has remained relatively constant. See Christine A. Bachrach, "Adoption Plans, Adopted Children, and Adoptive Mothers," *Journal of Marriage and the Family* 48 (May 1986): 243–53, esp. 245; and C. A. Bachrach, K. London, and P. Maza, "On the Path to Adoption: Adoption Seeking in the U.S.," *Journal of Marriage and the Family* 53 (Aug. 1991): 705–18.

3. For example, see Leontine R. Young, *Out of Wedlock: A Study of the Problems of the Unmarried Mother and Her Child* (New York: McGraw-Hill, 1954), 160–61. For discussion and critique of the treatment of pregnancy out of wedlock during this period, particularly of the racial politics that prescribed adoption for white women while largely ignoring black women altogether, see Rickie Solinger, *Wake up Little Susie: Single Pregnancy and Race before Roe v. Wade* (New York: Routledge, 1992). In *Fallen Women, Problem Girls: Unmarried Mothers and the Professionalization of Social Work, 1890–1945* (New Haven: Yale University Press, 1993), Regina Kunzel examines the emergence of expert views of pregnant women as neurotic. For a summary of the development of adoption as a formal institution with widespread popular support, see E. Wayne Carp, *Family Matters: Secrecy and Disclosure in the History of Adoption* (Cambridge: Harvard University Press, 1998), 1–35.

4. See Viviana A. Zelizer, *Pricing the Priceless Child: The Changing Social Value of*

Children (New York: Basic Books, 1985), 263 n.119. In 1941, she notes, only about a quarter of nonrelative adoptions were done by agencies. In 1971, nearly 80 percent took place under agency supervision.

5. For a fascinating account of the history of secrecy and disclosure in adoption and the emergence of confidential adoption, see Carp, *Family Matters*, 102–37.

6. Judith Modell, *Kinship with Strangers: Adoption and Interpretations of Kinship in American Culture* (Berkeley: University of California Press, 1994), 225–27.

7. For a discussion of the National Association of Black Social Workers' statement, see Mary Kathleen Benet, *The Politics of Adoption* (New York: Free Press, 1976), 140.

8. For a history and assessment of this project, see David Fanshel, *Far from the Reservation: The Transracial Adoption of American Indian Children* (Metuchen, N.J.: Scarecrow, 1972).

9. On the origins and development of the adoption rights movement, see Carp, *Family Matters*, 138–66.

10. Erving Goffman, *Stigma: Notes on the Management of Spoiled Identity* (Englewood Cliffs, N.J.: Prentice-Hall, 1963).

11. Judith S. Gediman and Linda P. Brown, *Birth Bond: Reunions between Birthparents and Adoptees—What Happens After* (Far Hills, N.J.: New Horizon Press, 1989), xxxi, 55. In her study of Canadian adopted persons in search, Karen March found that women outnumbered men by three to one, a distribution that she notes replicates that found by others studying search and reunion. March notes further that gender was the only distinguishing characteristic that separated searchers from nonsearchers (see *The Stranger Who Bore Me: Adoptee–Birth Mother Relationships* [Toronto: University of Toronto Press, 1995]). Katarina Wegar notes that most adoptees in search are white women in young adulthood (*Adoption, Identity, and Kinship: The Debate over Sealed Records* [New Haven: Yale University Press, 1997], 63–64).

12. Terry Treseder and Terrilyn Ainscouth, *My Child, Your Child: A Childless Couple's Yearning and an Unwed Mother's Decision* (Salt Lake City: Desert Book, 1991), 75.

13. Io Arnolfi, *We Adopted It* (London: Routledge and Kegan Paul, 1963), 36. This British account uses conventions common to those found in American memoirs of adoptive parents.

14. Ibid., 51–52.

15. Marjorie Winter, *For the Love of Martha* (New York: Julian Messner, 1956), 38.

16. Judith Dahl, *River of Promise: Two Women's Story of Love and Adoption* (San Diego: LauraMedia, 1989), 24, 63.

17. Treseder and Ainscouth, *My Child, Your Child*, 155.

18. Elizabeth Bartholet, *Family Bonds: Adoption and the Politics of Parenting* (Boston: Houghton Mifflin, 1993), 25, 231.

19. Susan T. Viguers, *With Child: One Couple's Journey to Their Adopted Children* (New York: Harcourt Brace Jovanovich, 1986).

20. James L. Gritter, ed., *Adoption without Fear* (San Antonio, Tex.: Corona, 1989).

21. See, for example, Ruth Piepenbrink, *Forever Family: Our Adventures in Adopting Older Children* (Huntington, Ind.: Our Sunday Visitor, 1981); Pamela Chatterton Purdy, *Beyond the Babylift: A Story of an Adoption* (Nashville: Abingdon Press, 1987); Sheri Register, *"Are Those Kids Yours?" American Families with Children Adopted from Other Countries* (New York: Free Press, 1991).

22. Douglas Bates, *Gift Children: A Story of Race, Family, and Adoption in a Divided America* (New York: Ticknor and Fields, 1993), 13.

23. Purdy, *Beyond the Babylift*, 31.

24. Ann Kimble Loux, *The Limits of Hope: An Adoptive Mother's Story* (Charlottesville: University of Virginia Press, 1997).

25. Robby DeBoer, *Losing Jessica* (New York: Doubleday, 1994).

26. Mary Beth Whitehead with Loretta Schwartz-Nobel, *A Mother's Story: The Truth about the Baby M Case* (New York: St. Martin's, 1989).

27. Marguerite Ryan, *An Adoption Story: A Son Is Given, the Gripping, True Story of Two Women's Dramatic Struggle for the Love of a Child* (New York: Rawson/Macmillan, 1989), 165.

28. Ibid., 165, 198, 183, 231.

29. Jean M. Paton, *Orphan Voyage* (New York: Vantage Press, 1968). This book did not receive any notice in book reviews. Paton worked in the early 1950s to find adopted adults and interview them on their views of adoption; the resulting book was *The Adopted Break Silence* (Philadelphia: Life History Study Center, 1954).

30. Florence Fisher, *The Search for Anna Fisher* (Boston: Arthur Fields, 1973).

31. Betty Jean Lifton, *Twice Born* (New York: McGraw-Hill, 1975).

32. Arthur D. Sorosky, Annette Baran, and Reuben Pannor, *The Adoption Triangle* (New York: Anchor/Doubleday, 1978). For an illuminating discussion and critique of this research, see Carp, *Family Matters*, 144–57.

33. Coined in 1965 by H. J. Sants, the term *genealogical bewilderment* was publicized and popularized by Sorosky, Baran, and Pannor's more widely circulated *Adoption Triangle*. See Sants, "Genealogical Bewilderment in Children with Substitute Parents," *Child Adoption* 47 (1965): 32–42.

34. Of course many organizations of adoptive parents and families also exist, and their newsletters and meetings are sites for the production and circulation of adopters' narratives. However, these organizations are more varied and specialized than organizations of adoptees in search. Many simply supply forums for the sharing of common experiences and sponsor alternative communities, such as organizations of mixed-race adoptive families. Others, like search groups, have activist orientations; for example, some groups are working to change laws on international adoption, or to sponsor a uniform adoption law to replace the various state laws that currently govern adoption. Still others are primarily directed toward prospective adopters, offering support and advice to people undertaking adoption.

35. Elizabeth Cooper Allen, *Mother, Can You Hear Me? The Extraordinary True Story of an Adopted Daughter's Reunion with Her Birth Mother after a Separation of Fifty Years* (New York: Dodd, Mead, 1983), 13.

36. Katrina Maxtone-Graham, *An Adopted Woman* (New York: Remi Books, 1983), 270.

37. Doris McMillon, *Mixed Blessing* (New York: St. Martin's, 1985), 127. McMillon's title refers both to the "mixed blessing" of her adoption and to her biracial identity as the birth daughter of a white woman and African-American man.

38. Amy E. Dean, *Letters to My Birthmother: An Adoptee's Diary of Her Search for Her Identity* (New York: Pharos Books/Scripps Howard, 1991), 42.

39. Allen, *Mother, Can You Hear Me?* 30, 179.

40. Maxtone-Graham, *Adopted Woman*, 91

244 Adoption in America

41. Paton, *Orphan Voyage,* 257.

42. Frances Lear, *The Second Seduction* (New York: Knopf, 1992), 110.

43. McMillon, *Mixed Blessing,* 12–13.

44. Jean Downie, *By Order of Adoption* (Plantation, Fla.: Distinctive Publishing, 1992), 3.

45. Tim Green, *A Man and His Mother: An Adopted Son's Search* (New York: Harper-Collins, 1997).

46. Robert Andersen, *Second Choice: Growing up Adopted* (Chesterfield, Mo.: Badger Hill Press, 1993).

47. Overall success rates of searches are impossible to estimate, since many are ongoing and in any case there is no way of counting everyone engaged in search. However, it seems safe to conclude that this rate of success greatly surpasses that experienced by searchers who are not writing memoirs. No doubt this reflects the pressure for closure in popular genres, which perhaps also explains why Andersen's account was published by a small press.

48. Marshall D. Schechter and Doris Bertocci note that adopted persons often express the desire to meet biological relatives who look like them, and the authors provide a psychological interpretation of the significance of physical resemblance (see "The Meaning of the Search" in *The Psychology of Adoption,* ed. David M. Brodzinsky and Marshall D. Schechter [New York: Oxford University Press, 1990], 81–83).

49. Downie, *By Order,* 49.

50. Green, *Man and His Mother,* 185, 186.

51. Allen, *Mother, Can You Hear Me?* 63–64, 102.

52. Dean, *Letters,* 107.

53. Maxtone-Graham, *Adopted Woman,* 278.

54. Dean, *Letters,* 94.

55. McMillon, *Mixed Blessing,* 246.

56. James Stingley, *Mother, Mother* (New York: St. Martin's, 1981), 8.

57. Sarah Saffian, *Ithaka: A Daughter's Memoir of Being Found* (New York: Basic/Perseus Books, 1998).

58. Maxtone-Graham, *Adopted Woman,* 267.

59. Allen, *Mother, Can You Hear Me?* 73.

60. McMillon, *Mixed Blessing,* 225, 247.

61. Stingley, *Mother, Mother,* 192, 219.

62. Rebecca Harsin, *Wanted: First Child. A Birth Mother's Story* (Santa Barbara, Calif.: Fithian Press, 1991), 106.

63. Margaret Moorman, *Waiting to Forget: A Mother Opens the Door to Her Secret Past* (New York: W. W. Norton, 1996).

64. Carol Schaefer, *The Other Mother: A Woman's Love for the Child She Gave up for Adoption* (New York: Soho Press, 1991), 110.

65. Anne B. Brodzinsky, "Surrendering an Infant for Adoption: The Birthmother Experience," in *Psychology,* ed. Brodzinsky and Schechter, 297.

66. Harsin, *Wanted,* 35.

67. Jean Thompson [pseud.], *The House of Tomorrow* (New York: Harper and Row, 1966), 45.

68. Schaefer, *Other Mother,* 38.

69. Moorman, *Waiting to Forget,* 68.

70. Thompson, *House,* 165, 178, 179.

71. Harsin, *Wanted,* 83.

72. Schaefer, *Other Mother,* 155.

73. Louise Jurgens, *Torn from the Heart: The Amazing True Story of a Birth Mother's Search for Her Lost Daughter* (Lower Lake, Calif.: Aslan, 1992), 70, 81.

74. Lorraine Dusky, *Birthmark* (New York: M. Evans, 1979), 15.

75. Schaefer, *Other Mother,* 181.

76. Jurgens, *Torn,* 220.

77. See Marsha Riben, *Shedding Light on the Dark Side of Adoption* (Detroit: Harlo, 1988), 9, 13. Elisa M. Barton proclaims herself a "lost" mother in her collection of electronic correspondence from relinquishing mothers, *Confessions of a Lost Mother* (Baltimore: Gateway Press, 1996).

78. Dusky, *Birthmark,* 9–10.

79. Jurgens, *Torn,* 80, 163.

80. Sandra Kay Musser, *What Kind of Love Is This? A Story of Adoption Reconciliation* (Oaklyn, N.J.: Jan Publications, 1982). Musser's first book, *I Would Have Searched Forever* (Plainfield, N.J.: Logos International, 1979), was an important early example of this genre of memoir. Musser is a prominent activist in the adoption rights movement. She has served a jail sentence for her unauthorized use of Social Security Administration records to assist searchers.

81. Michele Launders and Penina Spiegel, *I Wish You Didn't Know My Name: The Story of Michele Launders and Her Daughter Lisa* (New York: Arner, 1990). My only knowledge of this collaboration is derived from the comments in the text; I have not contacted Launders, Spiegel, or the publisher for more information about the circumstances of the book's writing.

82. Ibid., 7.

83. Ibid., 4.

84. Ibid., 42.

85. Trying to elude the spotlight throughout the case, Lisa's birth father refused to allow Launders to mark the grave with his full name. Ibid., 210.

86. Treseder and Ainscouth, *My Child, Your Child,* 62, 163, 170.

87. Norma McCorvey (with Gary Thomas), *Won by Love* (Nashville: Thomas Nelson, 1997).

88. Kayla M. Becker with Connie K. Heckert, *To Keera with Love: Abortion, Adoption, or Keeping the Baby: The Story of One Teen's Choice* (Kansas City, Mo.: Sheed and Ward, 1987), 117.

89. Susan Olasky and Marvin Olasky, *More Than Kindness: A Compassionate Approach to Crisis Childbearing* (Wheaton, Ill.: Crossway Books, 1990), 76.

90. Ann Kiemel Anderson, *And with the Gift Came Laughter* (Wheaton, Ill.: Tyndale House, 1987).

91. Bonnie Shullenberger, *A Time to Be Born* (Cambridge, Mass.: Cowley Publications, 1996), 63, 96–99, 102.

92. Jan L. Waldron, *Giving away Simone: A Memoir* (New York: Times/Random House, 1995), xvi, 115, 210–11.

Contributors

George K. Behlmer is professor of history at the University of Washington, where he teaches modern British, Irish, and European topics. He is the author of *Child Abuse and Moral Reform in England, 1870–1908* (1982) and of *Friends of the Family: The English Home and Its Guardians, 1850–1940* (1998) and coeditor of *Singular Continuities: Tradition, Nostalgia, and Identity in Modern British Culture* (2000). He is currently working on representations of the South Pacific's "cannibal isles."

Julie Berebitsky is assistant professor of history and director of the Women's Studies Program at the University of the South in Sewanee, Tennessee. She is the author of *Like Our Very Own: Adoption and the Changing Culture of Motherhood, 1851–1950* (2000).

E. Wayne Carp is chair and professor of history at Pacific Lutheran University. He is the author of *Family Matters: Secrecy and Disclosure in the History of Adoption* (1998), *To Starve the Army at Pleasure: Continental Army Administration and American Political Culture, 1775–1783* (1984), which won the National Historical Society Book Prize. He is also the author of *Bastard Nation and the Politics of Adoption Reform* (forthcoming, 2003), and of numerous articles on the history of adoption. He is currently writing a biography of Jean M. Paton, the mother of the adoption rights movement.

Brian Paul Gill is an analyst for the RAND corporation. A graduate of the University of California at Berkeley's doctoral program in jurisprudence and social policy, his dissertation is titled, "The Jurisprudence of Good Parenting: The Selection of Adoptive Parents, 1894–1964" (1997). In addition to a variety of projects in education policy, he is currently developing a new RAND research agenda in foster care and adoption.

Patricia S. Hart teaches American studies and journalism at the University of Idaho and is managing editor of *Frontiers: A Journal of Women's Studies at Washington State University*. She is the author of *A Home for Every Child: Child Relinquishment and Adoption at the Washington Children's Home Society, 1896–1915* (forthcoming, 2002).

Anna Leon-Guerrero, coauthor of *Social Statistics for a Diverse World* (1999) is associate professor of sociology at Pacific Lutheran University, where she teaches courses in statistics, social theory, and social problems.

Barbara Melosh is professor of English and history at George Mason University. She is the author of *Engendering Culture: Manhood and Womanhood in New Deal Public Art and Theater* (1991); *"The Physician's Hand": Work Culture and Conflict in American Nursing* (1982); and *Strangers and Kin: The American Way of Adoption* (2002). She is also the editor of *Gender and American History since 1890* (1993) and *American Nurses in Fiction* (1984).

Paula F. Pfeffer is associate professor of history at Loyola University Chicago. Her first book, *A. Philip Randolph: Pioneer of the Civil Rights Movement* (1990), received the 1991 Gustavus Myers Center for Human Rights Award. She is the author of "Homeless Children; Childless Homes," *Chicago History* (1987). Other more recent publications include "The Evolution of A. Philip Randolph and Bayard Rustin from Radicalism to Conservatism," in *Black Conservatism: Essays in Intellectual and Political History,* ed. Peter Eisenstadt (1999); "Eleanor Roosevelt and the National and World Woman's Parties," *Historian* (fall 1996); and "The Women Behind the Union: Halena Wilson, Rosina Tucker, and the Ladies Auxiliary to the Brotherhood of Sleeping Car Porters," *Labor History* (fall 1995).

Susan L. Porter is manager of research at the Society for the Preservation of New England Antiquities and a resident scholar in the women's studies program at Brandeis University Library. She is the author of "Victorian Values in the Marketplace: Single Women and Work in Boston, 1800–1850," *Social Science History* (spring 1993), and *Gendered Benevolence: Orphan Asylums in Antebellum America* (forthcoming), and is the editor of *Women of the Commonwealth: Work, Family, and Social Change in Nineteenth-Century Massachusetts* (1996).

Carol J. Singley is associate professor of English at Rutgers University, Camden. She is the author of *Edith Wharton: Matters of Mind and Spirit* (1995) and coeditor of two collections of essays, *Anxious Power: Reading, Writing, and Ambivalence in Narrative by Women* (1993) and *The Calvinist Roots of the Modern Era* (1997). She is also editor of the new Riverside edition of *The Age of Innocence* (2000) and *A Historical Guide to Edith Wharton* (forthcoming, 2002). She is currently writing a book on adoption narratives in American literature and culture.

Index

Adopted children: age of, 37–38, 40, 47–48n. 15, 49n. 29, 195–96, 298–99; and child-placement policies, 197–200, 203–8; gender distinctions, 40, 41, 48–49n. 26, 193; preference for infants, 40–41; and race, 193–95. *See also* Special-needs children

Adoptees: and adoption narratives, 221; search accounts by, 226

Adoptees' Liberty Movement Association (ALMA), 18, 226

Adoption: and abortion, 238–39; and African-American children, 14, 15, 164–66, 193–95, 220; black market, 10–11, 110–11, 231; and blood kinship, 180n. 76, 200, 220; Catholic theory of, 104, 109; and child abuse, 235–36; *Delineator* (magazine), effect on, 131–32; *Delineator* (magazine), views on, 136–37; demographic decline, 16, 32; and discourse on motherhood, 126–28, 151, 222; and federal government, 20; and feeblemindedness, 9, 167, 200, 209; and homosexuals, 20n. 9; and illegitimacy, 107, 190, 193, 196, 218–19; and incest, 107, 150, 230; and infertility, 13, 151, 210–11, 220; of infants, 40–41, 45; informal, 4, 28, 35–36, 102, 160; intercountry, 14, 17, 177n. 32 (*see also names of countries*); and "matching," 10, 161–65; meaning of, 53; and name changes, 4; and Native American children, 220; numbers of, 1, 13, 20n. 1, 175n. 5; and outcomes, 38–39; professionalization of, 109–10, 114, 115–16, 161; and psy-

choanalytic theory (Freud), 168–69, 171, 198, 215n. 38, 240 ; reasons for relinquishment of child, 190–93, 157n. 17, 283–84; redefinition of the "adoptable" child, 13–14; and role of women's groups, 113; and secrecy, 152–53; sentimentalization of, 27, 28, 37, 40, 132, 160–61, 208, 209–10; and special-needs children, 16, 20, 166–68; stigma of, 9, 20, 27, 64, 102–3, 135, 166–68, 200–201, 221, 223, 227, 228; transracial, 15–16, 220. *See also* Adoption, history of; Adoption, legal aspects of; Adoption agencies; Adoption autobiograpy; Adoption literature; Adoption records

Adoption, history of: and baby boom, 12–13; "baby farming," 83–84, 103; and Calvinism, 55–56, 58–61; in colonial Massachusetts, 3; during colonial era, 3; in Dutch New York, 3; effect of Great Depression, 114, 115; in England, 3, 6–7, 90–94; and eugenics movement, 9, 166–68, 212–13, 248; historiography, 27–29, 181–82; and indenture, 27–28, 40, 44, 45, 101–2, 200; nineteenth-century demographics, 4, 37–38; and orphan asylums, 3–4, 36–46, 85–93; and post–World War II demographic shift, 12–13; Progressive Era (1900–1917), 7, 142–43, 162, 238–39; in the Republic of Ireland, 99–100n. 62; watersheds in, 12, 13, 15, 28, 181, 190–93, 196, 208, 210, 211

Adoption, legal aspects of: "best interests of the child" standard, 5, 28, 43, 141,

249

Downie, Jean, 228, 229
Drabble, Margaret, 234
Dr. Barnardo Homes (England), 87–88
Dreiser, Theodore, 129, 132, 135; assumes
editorship of the *Delineator,* 126
Durril, Betsy, 33
Dusky, Lorraine, *Birthmark* (1979), 234,
234–35

East European Jewish immigrants, 105
Eliot, George, *Silas Marner,* 93
Embryo adoption, 2
Eugenics movement, 9, 128, 197; argu-
ments against, 148
Eugenics movement (German), 200

Fanshel, David, 217n. 64; *How They
Fared in Adoption: A Follow-up Study,*
181
Farrall, Mary, 64
Faulkner, William, *Light in August,* 57
Federal Emergency Relief Act (1933), 10
Federated Orthodox Jewish Charities,
106, 119n. 25
Feehan, Patrick A. (archbishop), 104
Fellows, Anstrice, 37, 48n. 26; on infant
adoption, 40–41; opposes orphan
asylums, 41, 43, 50n. 40
Fellows, Eunice, 37, 48n. 26; on infant
adoption, 40–41; opposes orphan
asylums, 41, 43, 50n. 40
Female Guardian Society, 62
Female Orphan Society of Norfolk,
Virginia (1804), 30
Fisher, Florence, 18; *The Search for Anna
Fisher,* 226
Folks, Homer, 126
Foucault, Michel, 10, 144, 148, 151, 158;
History of Sexuality, 140–41
Fovell, Hannah, 31–32, 33
Frank, Eliza, 108
Fraser, John, 38
Frater, Archibald W., 148
Free Synagogue Child Adoption Com-
mittee (New York), 169
Freud, Anna, 198
Frye, Sally Ann, 39

Gehring, Sister Walburga, 104
Gill, Brian Paul, methodological ap-
proach, 175n. 7
Goddard, Henry H., 9
Goffman, Erving, 221
Gordon, Linda, 145
Goschen, G. J., 85
Graduate School of Jewish Social Work
(New York City), 111
Gratz, Rebecca, 35
Great Depression (1929), 3, 10, 107, 116,
193, 200, 210; effect on adoption prac-
tices, 114, 115
Great Railroad Strike (1877), 103
Green, Tim, 228, 229
Grossberg, Michael, 19, 155n. 5

Hague Convention, 17
Hall, William Clarke, 84
Hard, William, 135
Harsin, Rebecca, 231, 232, 233
Hart, Ernest, 83
Hart, Hastings H., 126
Hawes, Benjamin, 38
Hawthorne, Nathaniel: "My Kinsman,
Major Molineux," 69; *The Scarlet Let-
ter,* 67
Hemenway, Henry B., invents amended
birth certificate, 8
Hitler, Adolf, and German eugenics, 200
Holocaust, the, 200
Home Finder, The, 195
Home for the Friendless (Nebraska), 182
Hope, Bob, 121n. 53
Horwich, Bernard, 119n. 24
Howard, Sheldon L., invents amended
birth certificate, 8
Howard M. Metzenbaum Multiethnic
Placement Act (1994), 16
*How They Fared in Adoption: A Follow-up
Study* (Jaffee and Fanshel), 181
Hutchinson, Dorothy, 168, 171, 172; *In
Quest of Foster Parents,* 161–62

Illegitimacy, 82–84; and adoption, 190,
193, 196, 218–19, 228
Illinois Adoption Act (1867), 101, 102